DAUGHTERS OF THE GREAT STAR

DAUGHTERS
of the GREAT STAR

Book 57 of the Hadra Archives,
as recorded by Tazmirrel of Nemanthi
under the guidance of Alyeeta the Witch

by Diana Rivers

Boston ♦ Lace Publications

Typeset and printed in the United States of America.

This is a paperback original from Lace Publications,
an imprint of Alyson Publications, Inc.,
40 Plympton St., Boston, Mass. 02118.
Distributed in England by GMP Publishers,
P.O. Box 247, London N17 9QR, England.

This book is printed on acid-free, recycled paper.

First edition, first printing: November 1992

5   4   3   2   1

ISBN 1-55583-314-4

DAUGHTERS OF THE GREAT STAR

Book 57 of the Hadra Archives,
as recorded by Tazmirrel of Nemanthi
under the guidance of Alyeeta the Witch

1

My birth name is Tazmirrel, Tazmirrel of Nemanthi, that being my natal village. I was named so for my mother's mother, whom I never knew, as she had died some years before I was born. In my family I have always been called Tazzia. Here among these women I am simply Tazzi.

I, Tazzi, am writing this down because Alyeeta told me to, because she said those who came later would want to know how it was at the beginning, how it all started. She said that it was important and must not be lost, that someone must record it. When I said, "Why not you, Alyeeta? Surely, you write better than any of us," she turned angry and told me no, that the Witches had their own story to tell, that it must be one of us speaking for ourselves. When I said, "How do I know our whole story? I can only tell that part that I have seen," she answered quickly, "That is enough. Others will tell theirs."

It was Alyeeta who supplied me with pen and paper, treasures hoarded from her former life that otherwise would never have come into my hands. And, of course, it was Alyeeta who taught me to read and write as she taught me so many other things in that short time. Such things are not usually taught to a dirt-child, the child of a dirt farm, least of all a girl. My only teacher before that had been Tolgath, the old Witch-healer of our village. She knew a few symbols such as were needed for her craft. Those she passed on to me, but she could not read a single word on the written page.

Poor Alyeeta, she did not have an easy time of it with me. I was full of protests and objections. It seemed too hard, I had started too old, it was not what I wanted to be learning. But she is stubborn, that one, not easily turned aside from her purpose, though I tried hard to warn her. Pushing and insisting, she forced me past my fears.

We are camped here for a while, waiting for the others. When they come, we will go north. This may be my only chance to set all this down. After that, the way our lives have been going, Goddess only knows when another chance will come.

Already I have written bits and pieces of this in what snatches of time I could find. Mostly, I have it written in my head. I can shut my eyes and see it all happening again. Sometimes at night, when I lie waiting for sleep, I summon up one scene or another. Sometimes I add that day's happenings to the tale. A year ago I could not have imagined such a story, not with me as part of it. If someone had tried to tell me, I would have laughed them away. A year ago I was the healer of my little village and thought to live there all my life, doing those same things I had always done.

Alyeeta said to go back to my very first memories of the powers, for that is the start of this story, so I will do my best here to recollect those times. Aside from my mother's love, which was a gift to me and no part of that other, my first memories are of speech with creatures. I cannot look back to a time when it was not there. I think I had it before I had speech with humans. Understand now, it is not like human language, this speech with creatures. It is not words strung together and spoken aloud. It is more like shared images, like feelings and signals, things sensed rather than said. I would sit waiting at the edge of the woods and creatures would gather: squirrels and rabbits, snakes and turtles and birds. Strange as it may seem, at first I did not know this to be a power or in any way special. I thought speech with creatures was common to all humans. When I learned others were deaf to it, I cried. It seemed so sad, like being deaf to the wind or blind to colors.

Gradually I began to understand that I was different, that others thought me the strange one, though I do not think they cried for me. Doors and windows would shut when I passed by. Children would call me names and turn away when I came to play. Some even tried to hurt me for my strangeness, push me down or throw stones. They soon learned that their intended harm returned to them. This, of course, did nothing to make them love me more. It only made them fearful and added to my strangeness in their eyes.

With all that, I think my first true companions were more likely goats and foxes than other children. I found them good company for my games.

They did not argue or tease. We never played a game that ended in a quarrel. This pleased me well enough, though I know it pained my poor mother. It grieved her much to see me set apart in this way. She loved me so and wanted others to love me as well. She blamed all my troubles on the passing of the Great Star, for that was the year of my birth. Then I could not understand her complaints. Now I know she was right — if indeed they can be called troubles. Mild and gentle as she was, I have seen her more than once shaking her fist up at the sky and muttering angrily, "You have stolen my daughter. If not for you, she would be like other children." Yet I think she loved me all the more for it.

Not so my father. He would seldom look at me directly. More likely he would give me some glowering sideways glance and mumble things that I now think were curses. He almost never spoke to me by name, but said to the ceiling or to the air around me or to my mother, "Tell that one that she left the barn door open," or, "Tell that one to go fetch the eggs," or whatever errand he wished to use me for. That was the one great grief of my childhood, that my father loathed me. There was nothing I could do to change that. Goddess knows I tried.

Had there been others like me in Nemanthi, we could have formed a bond with each other, made our own small circle of safety. As fate would have it, there was only one other girl-child in the village to be born "Under-the-Star" and we did not come together at that time. Though it feels as if Kara has always been there in my life, in truth she was not part of the beginning — but more of that later.

So what do I best remember of that time before Kara? The bull perhaps. Yes, walking out into the bull's pasture. I can still see him clearly — a huge, hairy, black beast in a field of bright, green grass. There were daisies there too, white daisies like stars in the green grass, and that black, four-legged hill of a creature looming against the blue sky. This was the same bull that had gored my father's leg the week before and tossed two of the village boys. Something drew me there as sure as the bee is drawn to flowers. My mother rushed out screaming when she saw where I was. I think some men came running with pitchforks, though in the end they stood watching and did no harm. The bull lowered his great, shaggy, horned head, blocking out the sun. Then he brought his nose down, down, down for me to rub with my small fist. Afterward he followed me while I amused us both by picking grass and flowers for him. He would likely have let me swing on his horns had I thought to do so.

9

My mother caught me up in her arms and crushed me to her when I came running in, some wilted daisies still clenched in my fist for her. I could feel her heart pounding. She did not scold me though. That was not her way. For myself I could not comprehend her fears. What could be more natural than to walk through the field with a bull at my heels? In fact, hard as it is to believe now, at that time I had no understanding of fear at all. It puzzled me, like a sickness that seemed to have no cure. When I tried to question my mother, she would look pained and confused and hug me to her. When I questioned others, they would turn away in anger. They, of course, thought me the one in need of curing. To them such fears were normal.

I was such an innocent at the time. Though it was all around me, I had as little comprehension of hate or anger as I did of fear. And in truth, what did I have to be afraid of then? I went into the sow's pen and sat leaning against her heaving side while her little ones scrambled back and forth across me. Birds would come to my hand at a call. When I was older, lured by their wild cries, I even went to meet with the Oolanth hill-cats that the villagers held in such dread, climbing up to their lairs in the rocky slopes beyond Nemanthi. That was later. By then I knew enough to keep silent. I told only Kara of it, no one else.

Before the hill-cats there was the wolf. Of all those encounters with animals, it was the wolf that most affected my young life and that in the end brought Kara to me. I was seven or eight at the time, no more I think. My mother had sent me to the cobbler's wife, carrying a basket heavy with eggs, bread, butter, and cheese. All this, I believe, was in trade for my father's new boots. A hungry old she-wolf, fierce-looking and with yellow eyes, came trotting right into the village. The other villagers fled screaming from the streets. In seconds, I was alone there with her. She came straight at me, tongue lolling and mouth agape as if she meant to eat me where I stood. When I spoke to her, she stopped and licked my hand. Seeing her so easily tamed, the villagers poured out of hiding. Now there was much loud, brave talk among them. Wanting to stone her, they shouted at me to take shelter. They were still afraid to come close enough to use their axes or their pitchforks, yet they had a great thirst for blood. Their fear, I think, had made them very angry.

Seeing they meant to kill her, I thrust my hand into her ruff and led her out of the village. We went into the deep forest where others did not like to go. There I sat on a rock, and while we talked, I fed her all I had been carrying: the dozen eggs, the two loaves of bread, a round of butter, and another one of cheese. That done, I told her never to return, that she could expect nothing but harm from humans.

My mother shook her head and looked at me strangely when I came back, but she said nothing of what had happened. With trembling hands she refilled the basket, though it must have been a great loss for us. Then, with the basket carried between us, we went together to the cobbler's house.

Now I must tell you, the coming of the wolf did nothing to soften the hearts of the villagers in my direction. One might think they would have felt some gratitude at being spared. After all, I had removed her without the loss of even one little lamb. Not so, not at all. Instead, they seemed angry that I had sheltered her life and so deprived them of their target. If anything, after that they shunned me even more. Still, they could not afford to be too openly hostile. By then I was already the apprentice healer, for Tolgath was growing too old and infirm to tend to it all. They might keep their distance and make small warding signs when they thought I could not see, but young as I was, they never knew when they might need my help to cure their calves or their babies. That, at least, kept them civil.

The sum of all this is that I had luck with creatures and little with humans. Though I was born into their hands and raised among them, still I grew up with all my village set against me. Do I sound bitter here? Believe me, I am. How could I not be? After all, I was only a child, and a loving one at that. I did not choose the time of my birth. And much, of course, has happened since to add to that bitterness. There came a time when I gathered it all, every slight and insult, gathered it to store like an abundant harvest, but that is a different part of this tale. Back then, I moved through it untouched. Looking back, what amazes me now is how little I cared then, how little any of it bothered me. I think I looked at others with a kind of wondering pity and grieved for them. Their hearts seemed clouded and troubled so much of the time. It was my poor mother who suffered then, not me.

So I had my mother, who cared for me above all else, and my little sister, Ghira, who followed after me whenever she could. Those two were all who loved me, but with the creatures, somehow that was enough. Not so! No, not true. There was one other whose love I could count on, whose love I could not have done without. Karaneeta, my Kara. But it is still so painful to speak of her. Yet how could there be any truth to this account if I left her out of it?

After the wolf, it was she, herself, who sought me out. I knew, of course, that the Potters had a daughter of near my age, white-skinned and red-haired like all their kind. Sometimes I would see her in the village streets, going about on her family's errands. Having so often been rebuffed by other children, I did not think to approach her. Besides, Potters are very private folk, not given to mixing much with others. They live separate from the villages they serve, mingling mostly with their own kind at markets and at fairs or traveling on the road, and marrying only other Potters so that they might remain true to type and different from the people they live among.

Her family's house and potting sheds lay across the bridge on the other side of the river and a short distance from the village. I had never had any cause to go there and knew little of them, save by gossip, and so was much surprised when she stopped me on the road one day. I was coming back from the village well with a full jug of water. She had been standing half concealed behind some bushes. I was even more surprised when she laid a hand on my arm and said in a hushed voice, almost a whisper, "I have been watching and waiting here for you. Set down your jug and come with me. We need to talk." This startled me, yet somehow I felt compelled to go with her. Also, I was in a rage of curiosity, so curious I did not even stop to think if she meant me good or ill. Nothing like this had ever happened to me in my life before.

As soon as we were out of sight, up that little path, she halted and turned to look me up and down as if in search of something. Where her eyes touched me it felt like the touch of fingers running up and down my body. My nerves tingled. At last she stopped at my face. Her large green eyes were staring straight into my soul. I began to shiver. No one, not even my mother, had ever dared to look directly into my eyes.

"Do you feel it too — the touch?" she asked urgently. I sensed her eagerness, but I could only nod. Words had left me. "You have the powers, too," she went on. "From all the talk, I thought you did. After the wolf came, I knew for sure. I watched you that day leading her away and thought, There is at least one other in this world who is like me. My father has forbidden me to speak to anyone of these things, but I cannot live with this silence any longer. It will kill me. I swear I will die soon if I can find no one to share this with."

I found myself nodding and nodding, saying stupidly, "Yes, I know. Yes, yes, I know. Yes..." There were tears running down my face. It was the first time ever that I cried for myself. Not until that moment had I

12

realized how hungry I was, how starved I had been all those years for human company, not company such as my mother or sister, much as I loved them, but someone with whom I could share my inner life, someone else who knew, who understood, and, above all, who was not afraid of me. I had not known I was starving, because I had never dreamt it could be different. In Kara's green eyes I saw doorways opening and my heart melted.

After that we became inseparable, testing and exploring our gifts, playing small games of power with each other: moving objects, drawing birds and animals to us, talking to each other without words — such glorious sharing after all those years of privation. I had never felt so happy or so free. How could any curse or insult touch my heart?

It was not so easy though. Neither of our families wanted us to see each other. In fact, I later found they had contrived all that time to keep us from meeting. Each considered the other dangerous for their daughter's reputation. Still, they could not beat us or compel us by force. As a healer I was free to go about the village on my own or search the woods and bogs for herbs. Kara was far more clever than I at stratagems and concealments and so found ways to meet with me in spite of her father's oft-voiced disapproval.

We spent as much time together as we could, often in little secret places by the river. It was in just such a place, in the second year of our friendship, that we made our great discovery. We had been swimming and were lying naked on the mossy bank, looking at each other's body. We were so different. Kara's red hair shone like bright metal against the green moss. Her body was even whiter where the sun had not touched it. Her hands and feet were broad, like all the Potter people's, and her body stocky. In contrast, I had the dark skin and dark hair of the Kourmairi, and was slim of body with thin hands and feet.

Was I the one, or was it Kara who moved first? Was she the one, running her hands down her own body and then down mine, Kara saying, "We look so different, so very different, yet we feel just the same." Suddenly we were touching each other all over, laughing and full of delight, wondering why, among all our other games, we had not found this one before. We began by tickling, then soon grew serious. It did not take long to discover that when we touched each other's body in certain places and in certain ways, currents of energy would course through us both, a joy so sharp it was almost like pain and yet not pain, for it left us with a great hunger for more. After that we played our new game whenever we could, growing more skilled at it, since we had the reading of each other's minds and bodies. Fortunately, Kara was no innocent like me. She knew instantly that we had fallen on something forbidden.

"Tell no one what we do here. It could be dangerous for us both."

"How can anything be dangerous that feels so beautiful? It is like a gift of the Goddess."

"So it may be, but believe me, Tazzia, others will not think so. They will think it evil and make our lives a misery." It was good she warned me, or I might have rushed home to tell my mother of this great new thing. I think it was the first real silence between us. It weighed on my heart, but I could not risk what I had found with Kara — Kara, who was my only friend. No, more than a friend: a sister. No, more than a sister: Kara, whose hands had opened a whole new world for me, whose fingers could take me to the stars.

★

In my tenth year, Old Tolgath died. I missed her. I missed her far more than I would have thought possible. After all, she had not been a kind or gentle teacher. Most of the time she had been sharp and impatient and as stingy with praise as if hoarding it for a long, cold winter. Many times she would have struck me if she could. But — and this finally was all that mattered — aside from Kara, she was the one person in the village who did not think me strange. That made her irreplaceable. For that, I could have forgiven her all the rest. There were times when I would even have hugged or kissed her if only she would have let me. She saw my powers as something to be trained, not to be hidden — a gift of sorts — though even Old Tolgath said to me once, "What are you? You are not a Witch. You are something else. Sometimes you frighten even me." That gave me something to think upon. Alyeeta said much the same thing to me years later.

Now I did not have even the comfort of Tolgath's advice. Perhaps from jealousy, perhaps not wanting to be done out of her work so soon, or perhaps because she thought me worth delaying for — not that she ever would have told me that — Tolgath had waited far too long to take an apprentice. I had come to her when I was in my seventh year. Now, a half-taught child, I was suddenly thrust into doing a woman's job. I grew up quickly after her death, hearing, seeing, and doing things most children are still sheltered from. I threw myself into the healing. Soon I grew better at it, not just more skilled, but better — even without Tolgath's help.

Rarely did I need her words or signs anymore, though sometimes I still used them. It seemed to lessen the fear of the villagers to see some familiar things being done. Familiar magic, however odd it might look, was still less frightening than unseen power, and it was that, it was the power that was showing itself in my healing. At times my hands throbbed with it and my head would ache. Often it seemed as if my fingertips had eyes and could tell at a touch where the trouble lay. Then, with no conscious thought, I could feel my way to the cure with ease.

Those next few years were busy ones for me. The healing work was fast spreading, for people were coming to me from other villages. I was helping my mother as well, sharing her work in the house and on the farm, wanting to lighten her load. Also, I was teaching my little sister what I knew so that she could assist me in my rounds, for she had good careful hands and a kind way. It was with some pride that I earned my keep for the house. I always hoped that, by my bringing home extra food and goods and sometimes even coins for my work, my father would come to see my worth. With the villagers, I think I had finally begun to gain some respect, or even some acceptance, as Tolgath had. Not so with my father. Nothing I did could touch his heart, and my brother, Kerris, mimicked him in every way he could. I must say for my father that he loved my mother much and had no wish to cause her pain. It was only for her sake, I think, that he made no open break with me.

When I was younger, it saddened me that my own father hated and feared me, or perhaps hated me because he feared me. I had so little knowledge of those feelings, but it grieved me to see the pain they cost him. Somehow I thought myself to be the cause and in my small way tried to make amends, always hoping it was a misunderstanding that could be cured, a door to be unlocked if only I could find the key. I would pick him a hat full of the first berries of summer or weave him a small circlet of leaves and flowers, my little peace offerings in this strange war I had not asked for. Hardly glancing at me, he would set aside my gifts with a grunt, to be disposed of later. Instead of being angry, I would feel sad and puzzled and try to think of some new stratagem.

All this ended the day of the trouble with the horse. At that time I must have been almost fourteen years of age. I was in the barnyard gathering eggs. My father and my brother, Kerris, were struggling to hitch a small mare to our wagon. She was nervous, being newly come into my father's hands in trade for some pigs. She kept tossing her head and stepping sideways to avoid the harness. My father was never a patient man. He

15

swore at her, and my brother so jerked her head about that she found herself suddenly backed into the wagon. Startled, she gave a snort of fear and reared up. When my father leapt forward to help my brother, she came down with her front hoof on his foot. With that he gave a shout of rage and pain. Terrified, she jerked free of my brother's grip and sprang away. In that instant I found myself between the horse and my father. He had picked up a heavy stick and had it raised over his head, ready to swing at her. I dropped the basket and threw up my hands to ward him back. "Please, Father, do not hit her. She is already afraid. I will gentle her for the wagon."

"Out of my way, Witch-child!" he snarled at me. He was beyond himself now with anger.

"Put down your stick! You only make her worse!" I shouted back at him, angry myself for once.

With a roar of rage, he swung his stick at me. Such was the force of the blow that when it rebounded and struck his forehead, it knocked him down. Suddenly he was lying flat on his back in the muddy yard with blood spurting from a gash across his forehead. He looked as if he had been struck dead. My brother ran toward the house. He was shouting for my mother to come quickly, that I had killed my father — I, who had never willingly harmed him in any way and had wanted only his love and his friendship. Too shocked to move, I stood rooted to the spot by the suddenness of it all. Before I could make myself take a step toward him, he had struggled to his feet. He was a fearful sight. Blood was streaming down his face and into his eyes. He wiped his hand across his face. With blood dripping from his fingers, he pointed them at me. "Witch-brood, you are no child of mine. Never come near me again." Then, with a cry, he staggered blindly into my mother's arms, and she led him to the house. My brother followed after them. At the doorway, he stopped to turn a hate-filled look at me. In the next instant the door slammed behind him, and I heard the latch fall.

Alone, head bowed, I stood where they had left me, staring at the bloody ground. My whole body began to shake. I could not stop. I shook as a sapling shakes in the storm winds. I felt it all, all of it, with no shielding and no protection. I felt the horse's terror, my brother's hate, my father's rage and pain, my mother's fear. This shaking went on and on till I seemed past all hope. I thought I would shake apart in pieces where I stood. Finally, I felt a soft nudge on my arm. There may have been others before that, but this was the first that reached through to me in that state. When I turned, the horse was standing by my elbow. I threw my arms around her neck. Suddenly freed to cry, I wept my heart out against her.

However much I feared for my father's life and wished to use my healing skills for him, I dared not go near the house. Instead, when the crying stopped, I climbed on the horse's back and guided her to the river. There I gave our secret call. Then I threw myself down on the riverbank. When Kara came, she gathered me into her arms and held me close while I sobbed out my story.

★

My father, of course, did not die. When I saw him next, he had a large lump on his head, but seemed otherwise undamaged. After that, we avoided each other as much as we could in that small house. Though I still grieved for him and for the absence of his love, I no longer tried to please him. Clearly, there was no hope of that. I merely left my earnings on the kitchen table where they could be seen. My brother also avoided me, but as we had not been friends for years, I found that no great loss. When we crossed paths, he would mutter, "Witch-brat," and spit off to the side, mumbling some warding words. It was my mother's looks that hurt me, looks that seemed so full of love and pity and, yes, even fear. Even my little sister, Ghira, was like a stranger with me for a while. They all seemed to have forgotten that I was not the one who had struck my father. That blow had been meant for me.

One good thing, however, came of that day. I had a horse, a horse for riding and for company as well. From then on my father would not touch her. He said she was "witched" and so no more use to him. Such a gentle little thing, she wanted to follow me everywhere like a dog. Her body was black with silver dapples, but all four of her legs were brown as marsh mud, and so, not knowing what else she had been called, I named her Marshlegs.

After that, I threw myself into learning to ride her as I had thrown myself into healing. My battered, aching spirit found some easing there. I would bind back my hair, fasten my skirt up out of the way, and be off across the fields or into the woods. No one taught me except maybe Marshlegs herself. By feel, I learned with my body, and of course we had good contact, mind to mind. After a time, it got so I could move with the horse as if we were one body and breathed one breath. On her back I would ride to all my healings or go deep into the forest, sometimes alone, but more often with Kara. Kara was just learning to play the flute at that time, and so my bitterest memories of my father are all mixed with the sweetness of Kara's flute music and the hunger of our loving. She even shaped some tunes just for me while we lay together in our secret places in the woods.

Before that final rupture with my father, I had been a happy child. Strange as it seems to me now, the hatred in my village had never really touched me until then. After that day, something in me altered. I never had that innocence again. I felt the meanness around me, paid heed to all those small things I would not have noticed before: the little signs made, the ugly words, the looks, the tone of voice. It was then that I started gathering and storing such things, hoarding them all somewhere in my heart. I saw each incident and marked it, remembering it all, every word, every look, recalling the face and the voice, sealing each person's nastiness in my mind. That was when the change in me began. And aside from the bitterness eating at me, there was also the waiting. Always, always, I found myself waiting for the next blow to fall.

Yet, strange to say, in some ways my life was better. For a girl, I had great freedom, more than any other in the village. I did as I pleased, answered to no one, and was seldom home. I had a horse to ride everywhere, something I know my brother envied me. He had only the old plow horse when it was not too tired or already in use.

That next blow took two years to fall and came from a very different and unexpected quarter. Kara and I continued to see each other and play our games of power and of pleasure. In time we grew careless. Her father came on us that way. Having gone to the river to dig clay in a new place, he found us lying on the bank, unclothed, with our hands on each other's body. Even now I can still see the look of fury and loathing on his face, I can still hear his howl of rage.

Had we been two ordinary girls and not two with powers, I truly think he would have killed me with his bare fists and beaten his daughter close to death. He knew better than that. He knew he could not even strike us. Yet I could see how much he wished to. Several times he clenched his fists and raised his arms only to drop them again. His face turned deep red, so red I feared he might die of rage right before our eyes. I had heard of such things happening. Several times he tried to speak. At last his words came out in a strangled whisper: "Cover your shame! Put on your clothes! You must never see each other again! Never! Do not speak of this to anyone, do you hear?! Not one word to anyone if you value your lives!"

Kara had warned me, but nothing she said could have prepared me for the depth of that anger. Nothing! It was like a madness that had suddenly come on him, all the worse for his having to restrain it. Kara went with her father and I went home, shaken and bewildered. I still could not see any great wrong in what we did.

Her father must have spoken to mine, for that night my father sent my brother and sister out of the house and called me into the kitchen. It was the first time in years he had spoken to me directly and by name. My mother was sitting in the corner. I could see she had been crying. As soon as I came in, before I even had a chance to sit, my father began, "Tazzia, you must never see this Potter girl again. Her father is most upset. He wants to make a good Potter match for her. It seems he thinks your company will taint her reputation and her chances." He went on and on in this way. I was relieved. I could tell Kara's father had not told him all, had told him very little, in fact.

I nodded and shook my head and said, "Yes, Father," or, "No, Father," at all the places I was meant to. While he spoke, I looked down at the floor. I did not want him to see into my face. No matter what I promised at that moment, I knew that if I could, if there was any way at all, I would see Kara again. I would see her many times, only now we would be far more careful. It was the first time in my life I was aware of telling an untruth and doing so with full intention.

We did continue to meet, of course, but now it was much harder. Kara was already a Potter's apprentice and would soon be a full Potter herself, so much of her time was taken. Also, her brothers were told to watch her carefully. Luckily, they had girls in another village whom they went to meet with when they could. We would come together late at night or early in the morning. But there was no innocence left in us. We were full of hunger, fierce need, and watchfulness.

So much seemed changed after that. The village that had been my whole world shrank suddenly. Like clothes that have grown too tight, it seemed small and confining. If I had grown up reading books and hearing stories, I might have thought to take Kara and go elsewhere. But where could we have gone and what could we have worked at to stay alive? What did I know but this small place where everything was familiar? I had never been farther than the market village of Koorish. Still, I felt restless and penned in, no longer belonging in Nemanthi and with no other place to be. One thing was clear, however: as long as Kara was there, then that is where I would stay, no matter what fell.

But Kara herself was different — strange and unsettled. Her clear green eyes were clouded with half-truths, though, of course, we could not really lie to each other, since we had mind-touch. She shifted back and forth and drove me near to madness with her changes. First she would say that we must not see each other anymore and that we must never touch in that way again. It was not right and proper, she would tell me. She would soon be a full Potter herself and must put aside childish things. Her family was looking for a husband for her. Then she would be a married woman with a family of her own and could not be my friend any more.

As she spoke, Kara's face would look hard and cold, as if cut from stone. I would go away from her, bleeding with grief. Just as I would be starting to make peace with the terrible pain of that, she would seek me out, making our secret signal. When we met, she would throw her arms around me and cling to me, crying and saying over and over, "Our kind can never marry. It is not what we are meant for. I will not leave you, Tazzia. No matter what they say, they cannot make me. You must promise me the same." Then we would fall into each other's body with all the hunger of grief and separation. But there was a wild look in her eyes that frightened me, and not much gentleness between us any more.

Later, I would catch glimpses of her with a young man, white of skin and with curly red hair. They would be laughing together, his arm around her waist. He could walk with her freely on the streets, while she and I had to signal each other in secret and meet in the woods like thieves. Something twisted in my heart, some feeling that was new and very ugly.

Within a month the betrothal was announced. But in the end it was not Kara or my father either who propelled me out of my natal village. It was Jortho, my brother's friend.

2

This Jortho was a large, ungainly youth with a perpetually morose expression. For some reason — I certainly gave him no encouragement in that direction — he took a fancy to me in the manner of men and women and began following me about. He was not easily discouraged and soon became a great nuisance. With my shadowed reputation, I had thought myself safe from that kind of attention. In truth, I had no interest in young men in that way, none at all. If I had, he certainly was not the one I would have chosen. There were several young men in the village, slim and dark and quick, who would have been far more to my liking. Still, he was my brother's friend. As there was already enough enmity between us, I tried, for my brother's sake, to be polite to this Jortho. At the same time, I had to make sure never to be alone in his presence and never to let him come up on me unawares.

This went on for some months. It would have been trying enough by itself, but I was also meeting secretly with Kara at that time. After a while the stress of all this maneuvering began to tell on me, as I had little talent for it. In spite of all my precautions, he caught me by surprise one night. It was on a street at the edge of the village, more of a lane than a street really, quite dark and with few houses about, only some old rotting sheds. I had left Marshlegs in the pasture that day to feast on the new spring grass and so was on foot, walking home alone from a healing that had been a long, difficult struggle and in the end a futile one. In spite of my best efforts, the baby had died.

Weary and heartsick, I wanted nothing more than to be quickly home in my own bed. There I could cry myself to sleep in privacy. Over and over in my mind I kept seeing that little baby's face turning blue as she fought for breath and seeing, too, her mother's look of anguish. Though others had little love for me, still I grieved for their griefs. I suppose it was part of the powers — and not always such a welcome one either — that I felt the pain and grief of others perhaps more even than my own.

I must have been very distracted not to sense his presence. Suddenly a voice next to my ear said, "Aha, now at last we are alone as we should be." Apparently, he had been hiding in the alley at the corner of a shed, waiting and watching there for me. I jumped back startled, angry with myself for having let down my guard. He stood in front of me, blocking my way and grinning, quite pleased with himself to have caught me that way.

As soon as I could collect myself, I said firmly, "I am very weary. It is late. I have no time for games, Jortho. Please let me pass."

"No, no, not so easily," he replied. I could smell the reek of liquor on him as he leaned toward me. "First, you must come with me to that little meadow just above the village. We have only to follow this alley and we will come to the path." Full of eagerness, he tried to grab my arm to compel me, then swore in frustration when he could not do so.

"Let me pass!" I said again, more sharply this time, for my weariness was telling on me.

Now he was angry at being so clearly rebuffed, the very thing I had tried so hard to avoid. "Witch-girl," he said through his teeth. "You lie down easily enough for dogs and wolves. Why not for an honest farm boy?"

I gasped at the ugly meaning of his words. Never in my life had I been truly angry before. Now, suddenly, anger rushed up in me like a flame, burning away all sense — a terrible raging beast leaping for the kill. It was straight out of the red heat of that anger that I answered him, with no compassion and no care for consequences, "Jortho, you revolt me. Your attentions are the plague of my life. I have endured them out of pity and for my brother's sake. If I wanted a man, you are the last on earth I would choose. As to dogs and wolves, that is an ugly lie. I have never lain with them, but I swear I would sooner do so than give my body to you."

Anger is a dangerous weapon. It finds its target all too well. Even in that dim light I saw his face contort with rage. "I see it is the Potter's brat you want and not a decent man like me," he snarled.

"Yes," I shouted back, recklessly mad now with this newfound anger. "Yes, and I would not let you touch me after being loved by her."

At that, he gave a roar of fury and shouted some
meaning to me. I saw that in one quick motion he ha
from his boot.

"No! Jortho, no! You know what will happen to you
him. Some sanity was returning to me. I was coming up
of rage, but his own madness was too great for him to heed my words. He
had forgotten all that he knew of me.

He swung the knife at me with lethal intent and fell back instantly,
blood spurting from his chest and his own knife lodged there. His eyes
went wide with hate and horror. With a cry, he turned and went lurching
and reeling away, leaving a trail of blood.

"Wait! Wait!" I called after him, horrified at the quick turn all this had
taken. "Let me help you. At least let me stop the bleeding." He gave an
animal cry of raw fear. I knew better than to worsen things by chasing
after him.

Lights began to go on in the windows of the closest house. A dog was
barking and I heard a voice call out. My own anger was all gone now. In
its place was an icy desolation. As soon as Jortho had stumbled out of
sight, I ran for home. Luckily, my father was asleep and the curtain drawn
across my parents' sleep space. My mother had been sitting up waiting for
me with some sewing in her lap. Sobbing, I threw myself into her arms.
"What do they want from me? Why do they hate me so? I cure them and
their children and their creatures. I gentle their animals. I keep their
village safe from wolves and hill-cats. I have never done them an unkindness. All I ask is to be left in peace."

My mother listened and stroked my hair, murmuring and trying to
gentle me just as I had so often done with creatures. At the end of my wild
tale she looked as if she were about to cry herself. She was shaking her
head. "A bad business, very bad. That boy's family — those are dangerous, angry people. Oh, my poor Tazzia, whatever will become of you?
The fate of the Star sits very heavy on your head, daughter."

Seeing how distraught she looked, I suddenly thought that my strange
existence and her great love for me probably brought her far more grief
than joy. With a deep sigh she stood up, took me by the hand, and led me
up to bed, helping me undress and covering me as if I were still a little
child. I was very glad my father had not wakened.

All my life my dreams had been sweet, often taking me to some
favorite place in the woods. That night I could find no peace in sleep. My
dreams were filled with screams and scenes of fire, the shouts of angry

_es and dark figures running in the night — all dread and horror and _rrible foreboding. When I woke in a sweat and lay listening, I could hear the river and sometimes a dog bark and the gentle sounds of animals shifting about in our barnyard and from far off the cry of a night bird, all ordinary sounds: only those things one could expect to hear at night at the edge of the village. Then, being so weary, I would sleep again and it would all come back: the screams, the shouts, the fire, people running to some terrible purpose.

At last I vowed not to sleep again and sat up with my back against the wall, eyes open, staring into the dark to wait for morning. In spite of that, I must have slept a little, for just before dawn I was roused by pounding and a woman's voice calling, "Liessel, Liessel, wake up!" I had a moment of confusion, thinking myself caught in my dreams again. Then I heard my parents' voices and leaned forward just in time to see my mother running to the door. She threw it open and our neighbor, Vendara, rushed in, frightened and breathless. Her clothes were barely fastened and her hair was standing up around her head in wild disorder.

"Quickly, quickly," she burst out. "They are coming to kill Tazmirrel. She must set out at once on the forest road." In a rush she told us that Jortho's father and brothers had come to her house saying that I was an evil and dangerous Witch, that having first seduced poor Jortho by my Witch spells and driven him mad with love, I had then stabbed him near to death out of sheer malice. Even now, he lay between life and death. They had come for her husband and her sons and were rousing the men of the village, for they were afraid to face me alone. "Hurry! There is no time! They will be coming soon with pitchforks and torches."

I had staggered to my feet. When she looked up and saw me standing there in the sleep loft, she added spitefully, "It was not to help you I came, but for your mother's sake." Then she rushed out, saying, "I must be home quickly before they find me missing. For mercy's sake, get her gone from here and do not say I warned you or it may cost my life." The door slammed behind her.

"Thank you and bless you," my mother called after her.

Even with this dreadful warning I was still innocent of any real fear. I moved about to no clear purpose, stiff and stupid with sleep, or rather lack of sleep. My mother, however, did not hesitate. She understood the danger well enough and instantly took charge, telling my father to saddle the horse at once. When he seemed uncertain, she shouted at him, a thing she had never done before. "Go! Now! Quickly! Man, have you forgotten how to saddle a horse?" Then, seeing my brother stumbling up from sleep, she yelled, "And take that one to help you!" This was my mother, who never raised her voice to anyone.

She pushed a pack at my sister, Ghira, saying, "Go fill this with food for the road and be quick about it." Then she shook me. I seemed to be the one still thing in that whirling household. "Get out of that sleep gown and quickly. I will bring you clothes. Your own are no use for this." She rushed off and came back with boots and an armload of my brother's clothes. These she thrust into my hands. "Hurry, girl. This time it is worse: this time they mean you real harm." Then she was gone to see to the preparations.

Still besotted with sleep, I struggled into those unfamiliar clothes and ran out to the yard as fast as I was able. The only things of my own I thought to take with me were my healing pouch, which I strapped on under the tunic, and a knife that my brother, Kerris, had made me when we were young enough to still be friends. This I slipped into my boot, or rather into his boot that I was wearing.

Dawn was just breaking, lighting up that strange scene. My father had already bridled and saddled the horse. My mother was strapping a pack to the saddle. My brother stood there looking hard and sullen, and my little sister, still in her nightdress, was crying. My mother, seeing me there, quickly tucked my hair up under my brother's cap, saying, "There is food in the pack and also some coins. That is all we have time for."

My father on the other side was urging, "Up! Fast!" He gave me a hand. "Go by the forest road. They fear that way and it may delay them. Ride as fast as you are able. Do not look back. For your life and ours, never return." That was more words than my father had spoken to me in years, save for that one time concerning Kara. I made ready to spring away. Already I could hear the shouts and cries of men hunting and the sounds of horses, but just as I turned to leave, I saw the flash of Kara's red hair. She was running desperately up the road toward us.

"Go! Go!" my mother urged, but I could not move, neither to race for my life and freedom nor to ride to Kara's aid. In a minute or two she burst in among us with my whole family pressing me to leave. Then I was able to move and help her swing up behind me.

"Go quickly, Tazzia," she said with ragged breath, "they plan to kill us both!" Now I swung the horse about to go, but already it was too late. The first of the men on horseback charged into the yard. Whichever way I turned there was a man riding up armed with a pitchfork or a cudgel.

Those on foot came up, panting and heaving, to fill the circle. I turned and twisted the horse about to keep clear of them. I knew my own power of protection was good against one or two, but I did not know how it would serve against a mob. I tried to turn so as to keep those who came near always in front us. For their part, though they seemed very eager for our blood, they were not so eager to be the closest to us. That was what spared us for a while. Those in back kept urging a speedy use of the pitchforks for our quick dispatch, while those who found themselves pushed to the front tried to push back, not wanting to risk striking the first blow.

Now, too late, I was fully awake and kept Marshlegs moving, in the hope of some space to escape. I knew this could not go on for long, Marshlegs being such a small horse and with two of us mounted on her. Still, I moved as skillfully as I could to stay them off.

At last, more filled with the daring of rage than the others, Jortho's father swung his pitchfork at the horse's head. She reared up with a snort of fear and I felt Kara loose her hold on me and slip away. I heard her scream, and when I swung around, some of the mob were already on top of her in a heap, my brother among them. I was ready to leap down to her aid no matter how hopeless when I heard my mother yell, "Hold tight for your life!" There was a loud crack, then a snort of terror as the horse sprang forward through the crush. This was followed by howls of pain and surprise and what sounded like the snapping of bones. Then in a few thundering bounds I was free of the crowd and soon past the edge of the village with the horse running fast down the forest road. The shouts and screams were quickly lost in back of me.

Never had I ridden so fast. I lay over the horse's neck, holding tight to her mane as clods of earth flew up and branches whipped past me. Terror had hold of me, terror was riding me as I rode the horse. I, who had never been afraid before, who had no experience of it and no understanding was now full in its grip. No way could I have turned back, not even to save Kara, though her screams still echoed in my head. Terror was all that existed. My mind had fled.

We went on till the horse slowed and finally stopped of her own accord. She was drenched with sweat, her head hung down, and her sides were heaving. I slid from her back and fell flat out on the ground, dropping down into a nightmare-ridden sleep, full of shouts and screams, my terror so mixed with Kara's death I could not tell if I myself were dead or living or being killed.

3

Witless and terrified, I must have wandered for days with the horse as my only guard or guide. Whatever happened there is all swallowed now in a blur of darkness. Apparently, there had been no pursuit, or at least none that had cut so deep into the forest.

My first true memory was of waking clear-headed and bitten with hunger. I was lying on a pile of damp leaves in a place that was totally unfamiliar to me. The sun was slanting through the trees. It was already well into the day. Marshlegs was standing over me, her breath soft and warm on my cheek. Suddenly, all that had happened rushed back at me, even Kara's death. With a will I held it off, biting my lip to not cry out. At least hunger gave me some hold on sanity. I had no wish to go plunging back into that darkness of the mind that had held me for so long in its grip.

Slowly I stood up, leaning against the horse's side for support while I brushed the leaves from my clothes and hair. As soon as I was steady on my feet, I groped for the horse pack. Nothing hung down from the saddle. I stared with disbelief at Marshlegs's bare side, where I knew my mother had strapped it on. Frantically I looked in all directions. Nothing! Nothing to be seen but rocks and leaves. Clearly, my food was gone, miles or days behind us or perhaps just a short ride back on the trail if only I knew for sure which way we had come. I thought it more likely lost in that first terrified burst of speed.

"Well," I said at last to my horse-companion, when the truth of it all had finally settled on me, "If I am to live, I must have food, and for that I must go where humans are." I was not altogether sure I wished to live. Truth be told, at that moment I would rather have faced a mother Oolanth cat in her den full of cubs than to see humans again. Having a good knowledge of such things, I even gave a thought to foraging for myself, but early spring is a hard season for that. Also, the roots and bulbs I knew best grew at the edge of swamps, and we were deep in the woods. Mostly, though, it was that I was too weak and too hungry to make that effort.

The track I had wakened by was obviously little used, being not much more than an animal track. There were no human signs about, but suddenly, from far off, I caught the sound of voices. My whole body began to shake with fear, that new feeling I had been so harshly taught. How I longed to stay in the shelter of the woods. Just as I thought that, my empty stomach cramped and the smell of wood smoke tugged at me.

With a sigh, I pushed my hair up tighter under my brother's cap, drawing the brim of it low over my eyes to hide my features. The clothes I wore were torn and filthy. I brushed them off as best I could. With some long thorns, I fastened the vest closed over the jerkin, hoping in this way to hide my female shape. All in all, I probably looked more like a beggar than an honest farm boy.

Having done the best I could with my poor, ragged appearance, I led Marshlegs over to a stump. There, with a painful groan, I clambered onto her back. We made our way toward human habitation, or at least toward the smell of smoke, with me wanting to press forward and hold back at each step. Marshlegs, untroubled by my newfound fear, ambled along easily. After a few bends our path intersected with a real road, a road such as would lead to a village or perhaps even a town. There was no clear sign of which way to go, but the smell of smoke came from one direction only. That was the way we turned.

The road there was wide enough for several horses abreast. We had gone no more than a few steps on it when I heard the sound of horses being ridden in haste. A loud, angry voice in back of me shouted, "Make way, make way for the Zarn's Commissioner!"

With no need of prompting from me, Marshlegs scrambled up the bank to clear the way. A group of men swept by us in a cloud of dust with hardly a glance in our direction. There were several guardsmen in black and gold as well as two or three well-dressed gentlemen riding at the center of the group. They filled the road with their passing, leaving no room for others. Had Marshlegs not moved so quickly, they might well have ridden into us in their haste. As it was, they left me coughing and coated with dust. Marshlegs picked her way back down to the road while I looked with care in both directions. It took some time for my trembling to cease, but I was certain now that human habitation lay before us and with it food.

Very soon the forest opened up to fields and farms. When we came to the top of a rise there appeared to be a town in the distance, or at least what I assumed to be a town. It seemed far larger than my little village or even the market village of Koorish, where we went each month to shop and trade. I could see a sizable cluster of buildings there and what must have been many streets. Surely in such a place there was food.

Then a terrible new thought struck me. What did it matter if there was food? My purse was lost along with my food pack. I had not one coin to rub against another and knew no one there to turn to. I did not even know the name of this town or how far it was from Nemanthi. When I had thought of leaving my village, it had certainly not been like this. I had never been in a town in my life and knew nothing of town ways. Whether I would beg or steal or have the good fortune to find someone who needed the help of a healer, I could not imagine. Whatever was to happen it must be soon. I had scarcely strength left to sit upright on the horse's back.

I went on now with little hope, but as my head was nodding forward one more time, something flashed on the road and caught my eye. Bending over, I saw several coins scattered in the dust. Weariness forgotten, I was on the ground in an instant, gathering them up. What incredible good fortune! They must have fallen from the purse of those passing gentlemen and not been noticed in their haste. Gold coins were something new to me. Very different from the dull, worn coppers I earned with my healing, they shone in the sun and felt warm and heavy in my hands. I poured them from hand to hand, liking the sound they made. Then I heard horses in the distance. Quickly, I slipped the coins into my healing pouch. Now I was no longer just a dusty beggar, I was a thief as well. No matter, I was too hungry to think on it for long. The bulge they made there under my hand gave a lift to my spirits as I rode along.

Soon there were others on the road. When the first of them came toward me, I could hardly breathe. I was almost sick with terror at the thought of what I carried. They passed, talking to each other with scarcely a look in my direction. Now I saw that I would have to learn to control this terrible new thing called fear. As each person approached me, my heart would begin to pound wildly. My impulse was to make a dash for the safety of the woods. Instead, I stilled my trembling by an act of will and kept my head low over my horse's neck. Several more men passed. Though they seemed to take scant notice of my presence, I heard the words "clod" and "lout" pass between them. After a few times of this, my fear lessened and some anger took hold. "Think what you will of me, you fools," I muttered under my breath, "as long as you let me pass in peace."

Now you understand, of course, that as a dirt-child growing up on my family's little farm I had never in my life been farther from home than the market village of Koorish, that being hardly an hour's ride away. I knew no more than that of the world and those who lived in it. In Nemanthi, I had little reason to think much one way or the other on my appearance or the color of my skin except in contrast to Kara's. I was simply a child of my village — though an unwanted one — and had the dark skin, dark hair, and dark eyes of my people. Even in Koorish, most of the folk looked much like my family and were probably related to us in some way. Save for the Potter folk, the only white-skinned humans I ever saw were the Shokarn tax collector and his retinue of guards, those creatures whose twice-yearly appearance struck such dread in the village. Aside from that, no Shokarn ever passed our way. To the Koomir, the Shokarn were something to be feared and avoided. They seemed to inhabit a different world, and the Koomir were like dirt under their feet. That much I had learned as a child.

Now, as I approached the town, I suddenly found myself on the road with folk of many differing hues, often lighter than myself, and many styles of face and clothing, most of which were new to my eyes. The closer I got, the more varied the crowd grew. There were even several Shokarn in evidence. Timidity and curiosity warred in me as I struggled not to stare at all this strangeness and tried to keep my own face well hidden.

Just at the edge of the town I came to a group of men who filled the roadway, leaving no room for me to pass. They were all looking at a notice or edict posted on a large tree and arguing loudly among themselves. I was too hungry and too close to food now and so had no patience or not enough fear left. Without turning aside, I was trying to slip past them on the edge of the road when one of them noticed me and called out, "Hey, boy, can you read this edict? The Zarn's men have just posted it."

I shook my head as if dumb of speech and tried again to pass, but another of those men blocked my way, saying, "You have not even looked at it." In that instant I saw once more the rough men of my village rushing at me with death in their hands. I was readying myself to bolt and so, no doubt, ruin my chances in that town when a voice from the other side of the crowd shouted, "Back away and give me some room, you ignorant louts. I will read it for you." Someone nearby pointed at me, saying to the man who detained me, "That one is but a farm dolt. How would he know how to read?"

With a grunt the man stepped aside to gather with the rest of them around the reader. Forgotten, I was quick to move on, not even waiting to hear what was written, though the words "...shall be put to death by whatever means..." came through to me clear enough. A shiver went up my spine, yet surely what was printed there was no concern of mine.

The town itself, whatever its name might be, did not look so different from Nemanthi, save that everything was larger and dirtier and some of the streets were paved. Those that were not were full of mud and flies, not so grand after all. Still, this town was large enough. I thought it must surely be possible to buy anything there, but I had no notion of the value of my coins, and that worried me. My hope had been to find some market in progress and seek out a vendor who seemed kindly disposed. I soon saw, however, that the market stalls were empty. The market square itself was rubbish-strewn and deserted. There was not even a food shop in sight. I was already feeling a sharp wariness in that new place and wishing myself elsewhere, far away from all those strange people, when an old tavern on the corner caught my eye, or more truthfully, my nose. The smell of food poured out of that place to blossom richly in the street. It drew me toward it. I knew I could go no farther.

In front of the tavern was a long tie-bar with several horses already fastened there. I simply laid Marshlegs's reins over it, not wanting to tie her. I knew she would wait there for me. As I was doing this the townspeople barely glanced at me. In fact, they seemed to look away. Perhaps it was my ragged appearance. They may have feared I would beg my dinner from them and wished to hurry by before I got up my courage for it, leaving me to the mercy of their less wary neighbors. Indeed, it was not so far from the truth. If not for my lucky find, I might have been forced to do just that. For my part, I wanted to watch them and see how they did. I had never been in a tavern before. I had a great fear of betraying myself as a woman by some unguarded word or gesture. In Koorish, women alone are not allowed in taverns.

My hunger pulled at me fiercely, and still I hesitated before the entrance, shifting from foot to foot. Then, suddenly, I felt another's eyes on me. I turned quickly and saw a young man who did not hurry by like the others. Instead, he stared quite openly, watching my every move. He reawakened all my fears. Though he did not approach or try to speak, he followed me to the tavern door. I could feel his eyes boring into my back and was hoping to disappear inside when the door was flung open and two guardsmen rushed out. The first of them shouted, "We may yet find the purse if we ride quickly." He would have knocked me down in his hurry if I had not flattened myself against the tavern wall.

"It was the Commissioner's haste that lost it to start with," the other shouted back as he swung onto his horse. With that they galloped off recklessly, rushing at a dangerous pace through the town streets in the direction from which I had just come. I scurried inside, very conscious of the coins hidden under my tunic.

With a quick glance about I chose a table in the farthest dark corner. I was hoping the serving-girls would notice me there and others would not. No one even looked up from their food or their board games or their noisy hands of cards. With a sigh of relief I sank into a chair with my back to the wall. From there I could survey the room. I sighed again. For a few wonderful moments I even thought myself safe. Then my watcher came in and seated himself at a nearby table. Had I been followed here after all? Was this Jortho's avenger? What did they want of me, anyhow? All I ever asked for was to live in peace.

I soon noticed that there was only one serving-girl for the entire tavern, and she was dashing from table to table. She passed me several times in her rush, her eyes sliding over me as if I were nothing but an old chair, and with as little worth. I despaired of ever being served. The smells of food were torturing me, yet I was afraid to call notice to myself in any way. Finally, just when I was on the verge of doing something rash, she was suddenly standing at my side, drumming impatiently on the table while I struggled to find my voice. Speaking barely above a whisper, I managed to order my humble bread and soup. She had to bend her head to hear me. Meanwhile, I was groping among my newfound coins. I gave her the smallest one, hoping it would suffice.

She looked at the coin in surprise, looked back at me, looked at the coin again, then glanced furtively all around the room before slipping it quickly out of sight. I had the unpleasant sense for just that moment of seeing myself through another's eyes, dirty and ragged and no doubt a thief. I could feel a mixture of greed and wariness spreading out from her in waves. With all that she said nothing to me, but gave me several coins in return.

While I waited, I sat with my head propped in my hands to keep myself from slumping forward on the table. The room began to spin. Soon the talk around me turned to a senseless rumble. The smells from the kitchen made my stomach clench and my mouth water. When she finally brought me my portion, I had to hold one hand steady with the other. I was fighting the impulse to shove all the bread into my mouth at once and down the burning soup in a few gulps. All this while that young man kept his eye on me so that even with the comfort of food, still I had no peace. That constant stare made my skin crawl and the hair rise on the back of my neck. For a moment I thought I had the sense of an intruding presence in my mind.

Just as I had begun to ease my hunger and was ready to ask for another round of the same — seeing how easily my coin had brought the last — there was a loud commotion at the entrance. The men who had been gathered around the proclamation now trooped in noisily together. They were talking loudly among themselves and to whomever else would listen. "Death edict, all girls of seventeen or thereabouts, all those born under the Great Star. Witch-brats, the lot of them, unnatural powers. The Zarn wants them done away with. Willing to pay a good price too, though I hear they are not so easy to kill."

Now the talk rose to a roar, with many shouts and exclamations. I had already noticed a stack of edicts on one of the tables but, of course, could not read them. Some of those were being passed about, though few there seemed able to read either. A man sitting near my table leaned toward his companion and muttered, "So, are we supposed to do the Zarn's killing for him?" The other growled in answer, "Well, I am very glad to have no daughters, of that you may be sure. Do they really expect us to start killing our own, then?"

With my head bowed over my bowl I kept myself occupied, diligently sopping up the very last of my soup. I felt stripped naked. At any moment I expected all fingers to point in my direction. My watcher, I was sure, had seen through to my true nature and would soon denounce me. Instead, he gave me a slight smile, almost of reassurance. Then, for the first time, he looked away.

Fearing to draw attention to myself, I did not call for another helping. I even tried to pull farther back into the shadows, but as the men scattered to find tables, the one who had first asked me to read noticed me in my dark corner. "Well, boy, come drink with us. It seems there is some hunting to be done, eh?" Plainly, he had already drunk a good deal himself. He was in no mood to be opposed. When I shook my head, he gave a roar of anger. Even so, I knew there was no way I could cross that room steady on my feet. Nor could I drink with those men and stay safe and silent in my disguise. He pounded on the table and shouted, "Too good for us, are you? Then we will have to come and fetch you. No one refuses to drink with Mainard!" He was struggling to rise, wanting, no doubt, to put action to his words.

The scene was about to become an ugly one. I was preparing to leap up and flee, hoping that speed and surprise on my part would be matched by drunkenness on theirs. Suddenly the young man who was my watcher stood up. Very deliberately he stepped between me and those men.

"So there you are, Cousin," he said over the noise of the place. "I did not notice you before in your dark corner. I hear your father sent you here with a fancy horse to sell. My father says I am to look at it. Come and show me what you have."

"Who are you?" I whispered urgently, getting to my feet but not moving a step.

"Outside. Come quickly," he whispered back. "You are about to be in more trouble than you can handle." Then he said loudly, "If you show me this horse before I eat, then I myself will buy you your next round of dinner. How does that sit with you?" With that he put an arm over my shoulders and forcefully guided me toward the door, right past all those men. He even waved to Mainard the drunkard as we went, calling out, "Thank you, Goodman. You have found my cousin for me. I had been watching for him, but this place is too dark."

I had no choice but to comply, yet I was much afraid of him. And still ... and still there was something in his manner that gave me confidence, some way he touched my mind almost as Kara had done. As soon as we were both outside, I said foolishly, "The horse is this way," as if we truly had some business to transact with each other.

He laughed and dropped his arm. "Come now, do I look to be in the market for a horse, especially a fancy one? I have scarce two coins to rattle in my pocket. Besides, I have been watching you. I know well enough where your horse is. I only needed some pretext to have you out of there and quickly. It was not a safe place for you at that moment and likely to get less safe very soon."

"Who are you?" I asked again.

"Bring your horse around to the back where none can see us. There we can talk with more safety."

When I hesitated, he said with some impatience, "Come, come, I am no lover of men who wants to grope with you in dark corners. Follow me and bring the horse."

As he turned, I could have leapt on Marshlegs and ridden off. I even had a mind to do so when I heard him say, "Do not be a fool." It was not clear to me if he spoke aloud or somehow in my head. Again I felt that tugging on my mind that reminded me of Kara. Full of fears and doubts, yet pulled in spite of that, I followed where he led.

In back of the tavern were the ruins of some old walls and even a small portion of roof. We had no trouble finding a dark corner, private from the eyes of others. Once there, he took my hand and drew it to him. Now I was very sure he meant some sexual mischief, yet I could not resist him as I had so easily resisted others. He slipped my hand into his vest and under his shirt. Then he pressed it to his chest. There I felt the soft, round breast of a woman.

With a gasp, I drew back, but my wrist was tightly held. In a very different voice, this person whispered, "You asked who I am and now you know. I am a star-brat just as you are, a daughter of the Great Star, born with powers."

My heart was beating wildly. Frantically, I shook my head, trying to pull free of this stranger's grip. "No use," she said, "no use denying it to me. I knew who you were from the first moment I saw you. I have been hunting us far too long now not to know the signs."

"No," I said, trembling, not understanding how she could hold me against my will. "No, why should I trust you? You are a stranger."

She gave a short, hard laugh that sounded more like a bark. "Why should you trust me?" she exclaimed. "Why? Because I have trusted you. Because what you just felt under my shirt could cost my life. You heard those men. You know what that means. If I wanted to betray you, I could have done it in there and collected some money as well. Besides, as this game is shaping up and likely to be played, strangers may turn out to be more trustworthy than family or friends."

I was still shaking my head. "Wait, wait, you must give me a moment to think. This is all too fast." I could still feel the soft warmth of her breast cupped in my hand, in such sharp contrast to her hard, lean face.

As if she understood, she took my hand back and pressed it again to her breast. "That is real. What you feel there is real. You must never forget it. On the other hand, you must forget it before we walk into that room again. There you must see me only as a man." She released my wrist. I stepped back rubbing it, still hesitating and ready to dash away.

"How do I really know who you are? How do I know this is not some trick or trap?"

She gave a hiss of impatience. "By the Goddess, use your common sense. We are both star-brats with our lives at forfeit. I held your wrist against your will. I can touch your mind. Who else could do that? Listen, girl, we have no time right now for trading words. We must be very straight and clear with each other, because those men in that room mean our death, and so shall every man in these streets very soon.

"Now, we will go back in there, a little drunk, but very friendly. We will talk of horses and prices and the stubbornness of fathers. I shall buy us dinner. Then we shall go elsewhere to make our plans."

"Why go back?" I asked in a shaky voice. "Since it is so dangerous in there, why not leave now? It would be safer."

"Far safer, without a doubt. But I have no wish to miss this meal, and by the look of it, you could use it, too. More important, my sense tells me something is about to happen. I have a need to be there. Now, Cousin, what is your name?"

I hesitated just a moment longer, then in a burst said, "Tazzia," as if in that way surrendering to my fate.

She slapped me on the back in the manner of men and said heartily, "Well, Cousin Tazzi, now we go in to win this turn. But before that, a little practice to improve your style. First, you must deepen your voice, start it from here." She pressed her hand to a spot below my breasts. "And you must walk with more weight on your heels." She pushed me away from her to watch how I did. "Step harder, yes, more angles, less grace, widen your shoulders, take more room." Feeling the fool, I walked back and forth under her critical eye. "Good, good, now remember all that. Then you will not be such an easy mark for mischief. We will practice more later. Now for dinner." She made ready to stride off, expecting me to follow.

I caught her arm. "What is your name? How am I to call you?"

"Oh yes, a thing of some importance. My birth name was Pellandrea. For now, for the world as it is, call me Pell."

"Pell," I said, testing the sound of it on my tongue. "Pell." I had never known a woman with such a name. "Pell, do you really have money to buy us dinner?"

"Well, let us say I borrowed a small negligible sum from the captain of those guards."

"You stole it?"

"An interesting question, Tazzi, a very interesting question indeed. Can you steal from someone who plans to be your executioner, your murderer, so to speak? Is that stealing? A question of morality, I suppose. Anyway, we shall dine very well on the captain's generosity, better than I have in days, in weeks really. Later, in some safe place, we can discuss morality." She leaned forward and whispered in a conspiring way, "And sometime you must tell me how you came by your gold coins. An inheritance perhaps?" I gasped. Pell held up her hands and said quickly, "Never mind, no need to know."

Lurching a little as if we had shared a private bottle or two, we re-entered the tavern arm in arm, with Pell saying loudly, "Well, your father is as great a fool as I would have expected. I would not pay half that much for such a horse. And she is lame besides."

"But that was only from a small stone caught in her hoof. You will see — tomorrow she will be better." I struggled to keep my voice low and steady.

This time, when we sat down together at my dark table, the serving-girl came instantly. Her eyes were all on Pell. Pell was ready. She ordered baked tarmar, spiced vegetables, roast potatoes, and honeyed suli-leaves, all with no hesitation, as if she had already rehearsed it in her mind. When the serving-girl asked, "No meat?" Pell laughed and said, "No coin," laying down the two coins needed for the meal and shaking out her empty purse. "We need the most filling for the least spent," she added. I had already seen her slip the rest into her boot. The serving-girl looked at us both with puzzlement, no doubt thinking of my gold coin. I avoided her glance.

When she left, Pell whispered to me, "I cannot eat meat any more than you can, but we must not let them know. It is a mark of our kind that we have speech with creatures." Our kind! Those words echoed in my head.

When the food came, the smell of it made me dizzy. I bent my head over the plate, not in fear this time, but to shorten the path to my mouth. Also, I wanted to put my face full in the way of those aromas. The serving-girl may have thought this cheap ordinary fare, since it had no meat. To me it was a feast such as we ate at home only on special days, once or twice a year.

For a while I lost myself in the pleasures of the food. I was thus absorbed when I heard Pell mutter, "Too soon by the Mother's Tit. I had hoped to finish my meal in peace." I looked up to see the Commissioner entering with his men and a whole troop of guards, the very ones, in fact, who had swept by me on the road. They dropped more edicts on the table that was already piled with them. Then, with much moving of chairs and benches, they all settled noisily at the table next to that one. Even the two who had rushed out of the tavern were back.

I could hardly swallow. My little stash of found coins burned like hot coals against my skin. More than the guards, the sight of the Commissioner set me to trembling. I found myself watching him against my will. In fact, dangerous as it might be to stare, I could not take my eyes off the man. I had never seen anyone so white or with such obvious power. Even the other men in the tavern were afraid of him. Their talk was suddenly subdued and they kept their eyes lowered.

Plainly impatient, he shouted for his dinner. The serving-girl rushed out to take his order, bowing several times. When she returned with his food, he looked at her strangely. As soon as she had set it down, he grabbed her wrist. His hand was instantly flung back and he could not hold her. "Ah, so you are one of those." With a quick sweep of his other hand, he caught the ends of her shawl, trapping her. I saw him pull her forward and say something in her ear. She gave a cry and tried to twist away. Now the whole tavern was alert and silent, watching the scene. Looking about, the Commissioner shouted, "Goodman, how old is this zuka?"

The owner of the inn came out instantly, wiping his hands on his apron. He looked nervous and fearful and bowed quickly.

"She is twenty at least, sir, twenty-one perhaps."

"How do you know that for sure?"

"She is my niece, sir, my sister's daughter. I know her age."

"Are you sure you are telling the truth, Goodman? She looks to be no more than fifteen or sixteen, just the sort we are looking for. It could be very hard on you if you are lying." He turned to the crowd and called out, "Is there any here that knows this young woman's age?"

"She was seventeen years just this month past," a young man called out from the back. People gasped. There were hisses and mutterings, but none came forward to deny his words. A woman near us said, "She has refused him three times. Now it will cost her life."

The girl meanwhile was struggling and crying out, "No sir, no sir, I have twenty years." She slipped loose of her shawl and leapt back.

Instantly, the Commissioner was on his feet, shouting for the guardsmen. They had her quickly surrounded. He called out to them, "Do not try to hold her. It is no use. Only block her way." The tavern was now in tumult.

Pell nudged me and whispered, "This is a fine turn, eh?" I had been watching so intently, I had almost forgotten her existence and could hardly hear her over the noise. Now I turned back to see her emptying my plate into a little leather pouch that she then slipped into her pack. Her own plate she had already emptied. "I hate to lose such a fine dinner, especially since it is already paid for. Now follow me closely and watch what I do. We must act fast and not get separated. We are going to leave here safely, Tazzi, and that girl is going with us." She was already on her feet and moving as she said this. Much afraid, I jumped up to follow. I had no wish to be left alone in that dangerous scene.

Everyone was pressing forward to see. Under cover of this commotion Pell slipped over to the table that held the edicts. There she tipped the lamp and poured some lamp oil on the pile of edicts, lighting it with a candle. Then she quickly pushed herself forward through the press of people, pouring a trail of oil right up to the Commissioner's heels. I think she even splashed some on his boots. Instantly, she stepped away from her flaming trail and began shouting, "Fire! Help! Fire! That young man over there has started a fire." She was pointing wildly at the informer.

Now the tavern was in an uproar, with people yelling commands and screaming and running in different directions. The young man tried to flee while others tried to block his way. "Seize him!" the Captain shouted to the guards. The Commissioner himself gave a shout of pain and surprise as the fire found him. He began leaping about with his pants aflame while guardsmen rushed to his aid.

Still shouting, "Fire!" Pell overturned chairs and benches and a few more lanterns for good measure. Then she grabbed my hand, saying, "Now!" We dashed forward into the chaos, heading straight for the serving-girl. She stood confused and terrified in the midst of it all. Pell grabbed her hand. The girl whirled toward us in fear, but Pell said quickly, "Come with me for your life. This is your chance. Is there a way out through the kitchen?"

Instantly, the young woman was moving. It was as if she had been spelled and all she needed was Pell's touch to release her. "This way! This way!" she urged as she dashed off, pulling us with her.

Together we plunged into the kitchen, forcing our way past those who were rushing out with pots of water to douse the fire. Stumbling on overturned furniture and coughing from the smoke, I struggled, with Pell beside me, to keep up with our guide. I could see no exit, but she flung open a door concealed behind a pile of produce boxes. We burst out of the smoke and confusion into the barely lit street. It was night already.

"Quick," Pell panted, slamming the door. "Help me." She began hauling boxes to pile against the door. We rushed to her aid, adding a log and part of a broken cart. That done, Pell turned to the serving-girl. "Your name and where is your horse?"

"Barrenaise is my name and I have no horse. I use my uncle's."

"Then where is that one?"

"I cannot take it, for he has no other."

"Then take a different one. There are more than enough."

"I have not the skill. That is the only one I know how to ride."

"Oh Goddess, save me from idiots!" Pell shouted, plainly at her wits' end. "Barrenaise, get on your uncle's horse or on another, it matters not to me, but do it instantly or we leave you here to die. I value my own skin and have risked it enough for one day."

"That one over there." She was pointing to a stocky gray cart-horse.

"Good! Get him and mount quickly while I free these others."

At my call Marshlegs had run up to me. Barrenaise and I mounted while Pell whipped out her knife and went along the pole, slashing reins on the guardsmen's horses and on all the others as well. Just as she swung onto her own horse, there was a shout as someone in the tavern saw what she was doing. Guardsmen came pouring out of the front doorway in a great cloud of smoke with their swords flashing.

"Follow me and do not for your life look back." Pell gave a spine-chilling howl like an Oolanth cat. The newly freed horses scattered just as the men lunged at them, too late. I was barely able to hold onto Marshlegs. Barrenaise next to me was struggling to keep her seat. That was the last I saw of the tavern that night. We went through the town at a mad pace, twisting and turning in the dark streets, trying to keep up with Pell. Her horse did not look like much, but what he lacked in looks he certainly made up for in speed.

From behind us came shouts, "Get them! Catch them! They went that way!" With my hands in the horse's mane I clung to her back, hearing horses behind me and never knowing if it was Barrenaise or the loose horses or if we were about to be overtaken by the guard.

Suddenly we took a sharp turn and the street wound up a hillside. I could still hear Pell ahead of me, or at least I hoped it was Pell. At moments I caught glimpses of smoke and fire below, but soon the noise faded behind us, the buildings thinned, and the pace slowed. Out of the darkness in front of me I heard Pell say, "We can walk now for a while and let the horses catch their breath. This is not a road many know of. Certainly no Shokarn guardsmen will think to come this way."

Instantly, my pace fell to a walk. I heard Barrenaise move up beside me. Pell was whistling and calling softly. Some of the freed horses trotted up to us, snorting and nickering. "Well, well, we are in luck," Pell said cheerfully. "Not only have we escaped with our lives this night, but with horses as well." She seemed more elated than frightened by this brush with danger. I was going though my own struggles with fear. Barrenaise, on the other side, was shaking and panting heavily. Her uncle's poor horse was stumbling along with his sides heaving and his breath loud and ragged. He, no doubt, was used more often for fetching eggs and flour than for outrunning the guard.

Soon the road narrowed till it became a winding track, wide enough for one horse only. We went for a while in silence along what seemed like a high rocky ridge. The moon had begun to rise, lighting the tall trees overhead. Shortly after that we reached a large boulder, where Pell stopped.

"We can rest here and finish our meal. After this the ride gets harder." I thought it already hard enough, but I kept my silence. Pell pulled a ragged blanket from her pack, shook it out, and spread it on the ground. "Our tablecloth." she said with a bow. "And now for our elegant dinner." She took out her little leather food pouch and shook the contents onto a plate that also came from her pack. To this she added two loaves of bread, a round of cheese, another of butter, some silverware, and a small bottle of quillof. "This is not the best-planned dinner because of some haste in preparation, but we do have a surprise." With that she drew out a covered bowl that she had wrapped in a napkin. This last item she opened and set down in the middle with a flourish.

Barrenaise gasped with surprise. "The Commissioner's dinner," she said in amazement.

"Well, I did not think he would miss it much. He has else to think on tonight. Eat now before it all gets cold. It is already a little scrambled from our ride." With a quick gesture Pell pulled her knife from her boot and stuck it into the bread. Speedily, we all sat down together on the blanket. Surrounded by horses, we ate our fill, sharing the bottle of quillof to the last drop. When we had finished what we could and packed the rest away, Pell said, "Now, you will follow me in silence. Keep your heads low over your horses' necks and try to break no branches." Again, she whistled and called and I could feel a strong mind tug.

A little ways past the boulder we turned and the woods began to change. The trees became strange and twisted. The low-hanging branches seemed to claw at us with a will. As we plunged into the deeper forest, the moonlight could barely reach through the thick growth. Light and shadow were oddly distorted and gave no guidance. I had to trust to Marshlegs to get me through and to Pell's knowledge as well. Barrenaise's fear was like a presence among us, but for me at that moment I had left fear back there with people. Exhausted, I put my head down on Marshlegs's neck and my arms on either side of it. I was fed, I was safe for the moment. I let myself be carried wherever fate and the Goddess saw fit to take me.

4

"Time for your help." My shoulder was being roughly shaken. I was sitting slumped on Marshlegs's back and woke to see a torch blazing and many horses milling about. We were in front of a small shelter tucked under a rock overhang. The one who shook me, this woman I knew as Pell, began unsaddling horses in great haste. The other one, Barrenaise, lay on the ground like a dumped grain sack, but alive and breathing. Pell, seeing my glance in that direction, said quickly, "She is no use for now. This night has been too much for her. We will take her in and cover her as soon as this work is done. Off your horse now and lend me your hands."

First Pell had me hold each horse's head while she daubed with dark stain at any light blaze or identifying mark. The horses were in a state of nervous agitation, snorting and shifting about, but Pell was able to calm them, talking and humming and petting as she moved among them. Goddess knows if I really helped or not. I was sleeping on my feet. I think it more likely that each horse in turn held me upright.

Next, nothing would do but that we must strip all the tack from the horses and conceal it in a pit near the shelter. Afterward we covered and disguised this pit with a careful crisscross of branches and then leaves. With every step I took I had to drive myself forward, all the while trying not to stumble and fall headlong into the pit. Pell, for her part, seemed to move with a tireless ease, talking constantly as she worked. "The guard does not take well to having their horses stolen — almost as serious a crime as killing guardsmen. Their tack is clearly marked in several places. It will take some work to alter it. Until that can be done it is best to keep it hidden." Personally, I cared not one whit why we did what we did, only that it be finished soon so I could sleep again.

When we were done and Barrenaise had staggered into the shelter between us and been covered, I fell face forward, still fully clothed, onto a mat Pell provided for me. I hoped to sleep at once, but soon Pell was shaking me awake again. With a groan of protest I turned to look at her. She bent over me, and as the torchlight lit her face I gave a gasp of fear, thinking some stranger stood there. She had put on different clothes and a mustache and so looked older and stouter by ten years.

"I must go back to Hamishair," she whispered. "There may be others there, trapped or in trouble. Stay within sight of the shelter till I return. These woods are tricky for strangers, easy to get lost in." She could have saved her words. I had no wish at all to venture out into those woods and thought I would gladly stay on that very mat till she came back. Furthermore, I thought her mad to ride again into such certain danger. I said none of this. I pulled up my covers and turned my face to the rock wall to try once more for sleep. The torchlight receded. Then the sound of her horse's hooves faded in the night.

When I woke next, it was to the tap-tap-tapping of a little hammer. It was full daylight already. Pell was sitting in the doorway of her shelter, if such could be called a doorway — actually it was more of a crude opening. She was already at work on a saddle. Barrenaise sat next to her, helping. Each time Pell spoke, Barrenaise looked at her adoringly, much like a dog that has found itself a kind master. I thought this a distasteful sight and so turned to look around the shelter instead.

This shelter appeared to be a rough, temporary place. A crude lattice of branches formed the outer wall, with stones heaped all along the base for support. There was a pile of coarse mats and bedding against the back wall on one side. Sacks and boxes were stacked at the other end. Above this, some pegs for hanging garments had been driven into a crevice in the rock face. In the other direction, at the furthest corner, a little spring seeped out from the wall and trickled out across some stones. Several crocks and jugs stood by it.

At the outer edge, near the entry, a little fire burned in the fire pit. In front of it, a crude table, consisting of a plank on some rocks, was set with a few plates, cups, and bowls, and what looked to be the remains of last night's dinner. Pots and pans hung from nails along its edge. That was all there was to Pell's shelter, but in spite of its roughness I felt a sense of order there. Each thing appeared to have a place and a purpose, to be set there with intention. I thought to get up and add my bedding to that neat pile, but must have dozed again.

This time, when I woke, the scene at the entryway was not near so cozy. Barrenaise appeared to have been crying. Pell was saying in a tight, angry voice, "I do not care one feather's worth for your uncle's fate. I hope that the young man who betrayed you was hung for starting the fire. I hope that the flames rushed up the Commissioner's pant legs to heat him in his most private place. As for you, what kind of a fool are you that you stayed there serving tables while that edict was being passed about?"

"But there was no one else to wait tables that night. My uncle promised he would protect me. And now we have burned down his tavern." This last brought on a new burst of weeping.

Pell sputtered with indignation, "Protect you? How? With that feeble little lie? He thought to protect you from the Zarn's edict with that nonsense? And you believed him? Even with a price on your head you believed him? Foolishness must run in the family. I had hoped to find others like me, but perhaps I have found more than I can manage." As Barrenaise was still crying, Pell shook her roughly by the shoulder. "Listen, girl, it was your uncle's tavern or your life, that was the choice. And besides, that fire probably looked far worse than it really was. Lamp oil makes a great show, you know, but not much heat. Anyhow, there seemed more than enough hands to put it out."

I was just thinking to myself that by now her uncle had likely been hung for lying and had no need for his tavern at all, when Pell threw down her hammer in disgust and shouted, "I risked my life to save yours. How long do I have to listen to your sniveling?"

Barrenaise sucked in her breath and stopped her crying by an act of will. She put out her hand to Pell. "Oh, Pell, you must not think me ungrateful. I know well enough it was your quick thinking that saved my life."

"Well, see that you use it with some sense, then." Pell stood up so impatiently she spilled her cup in the dirt. Barrenaise reached out quickly to right it. At that moment Pell noticed me sitting up. I was shaking my head to clear away the confusion of all that had happened. "Good, you are awake," she said quickly. "I was afraid you meant to sleep all day. We must talk together and make a plan of action as soon as possible."

"Did you really go back to Hamishair last night?" I asked. Clearly, there were only the three of us in the shelter, and I could sense no one else nearby.

"Of course."

"And what came of that?"

"That some are dead, and some escaped, and some have gone into hiding who may join us later. I am new in this place and so have few contacts. That made it hard."

The finality of her tone told me to press no further on that subject. Instead, I asked, "What is this place? Where are we?" What little I could see through the entryway looked very strange indeed, like no woods I had ever seen before.

"We are in a part of the Twisted Forest that none come to. It is thought to be haunted. Even with the edict we are safe here, at least for a while." Then her face seemed to soften suddenly. She turned back to Barrenaise, put a hand on her shoulder, and said in a gentler tone, "Sorry, Sister, sometimes my temper outruns me. I should not turn it on you or on any of us. It should be aimed at those men." Then she shrugged. "And what good purpose would that serve? Better to steal their horses and their money and escape with our lives. Let them be the ones to chew on their anger." At that she gave a sudden laugh. "Yes, money and horses and lives and even some dinner — not a bad piece of work for one night." Seeing me folding up my bedding and mat to add to her neat pile, she gestured toward the table. "There is some bread and cheese left from our adventures and a pot of gruel and dried fruit keeping warm by the fire." Then she went to pour herself another cup of tea and settled back to her saddle work. Barrenaise looked much relieved.

I took my portion gratefully and came to sit near them on a rock, this being the only kind of seat I saw there. Barrenaise had resumed her stitching with barely a glance at me and no word of greeting at all, though I saw her look admiringly at Pell several times when she thought herself unobserved. Pell had taken up her hammer again and worked in silence while I ate.

This was my first chance to really observe this Pell, this person who was a woman and yet not a woman, this person who had leapt so suddenly into my life. She was bent over the saddle, her thick brows drawn together in a single dark line of concentration, her shirt loose and open to the waist so her breasts hung forward in the light. I could see that her dark skin had been made even darker by the sun. She was thin and taut, as if everything in her had been turned to muscle and will. Yet she moved in an easy way, alert but relaxed in her body, as if for years it had been tuned to responding to her will. Her features were fine and clear. I suppose she might have been thought beautiful if anything was left for that, but too much had been pared away, pared down to the bone. There was no softness anywhere. Barrenaise, on the other hand, seemed just the opposite, all softness, softness everywhere. With her there was no outward sign of will, though I could feel it working underneath, a very different sort of will, devious where Pell was direct. I did not like this Barrenaise. Something in her very being made me itch with impatience. I sensed that she did not have much love for me either.

When I set down my bowl, Pell said instantly, "Good, now we can make our plans." It seemed as if she had been waiting for just that signal, though if she grudged me my meal she had given no sign of it.

Barrenaise set down her stitching and said quickly, "I must go back to my village to warn my sister and my cousins and our friends, for they are all in danger."

Pell leaned forward, immediately full of interest. "Yes, just so. Which village is that and where is it from here, or rather from Hamishair?"

"Athron. It lies south and a little east of Hamishair."

"Show me," Pell said eagerly, as she cleared a space in the dirt with her hand. She handed Barrenaise a stick from the kindling pile.

Barrenaise drew a set of lines, stopping now and then to rub one out and redraw it. Pell nodded as she watched. When Barrenaise finished Pell took the stick and added other lines.

"You must send someone to warn the young women of Ashire and Kernaka. Both those settlements lie further south like this and this," she said, pointing with her stick. "And they must send others to the villages of Menalli and Barthis. From there they must spread out to warn still others. Later, if possible, they should gather with us here. We will have to work out some meeting places and some signs and signals. Whoever goes to Ashire should look for Josleen or Megyair. Those are the only two I know in that direction, but they know many others. Yes, yes, someone must go to Ashire. Draw this sign or this one and they will trust you." Pell drew a six-pointed star in the dirt and then a triangle inside a circle. She looked at Barrenaise to see if she understood everything. Then she rubbed it all out with care and stood up, brushing off her hands on her pants. "We will find ways to slip around the Zarn's edict. They will end by driving us together, not apart. In that way we will become a power, the very thing they fear the most."

Barrenaise was looking up hopefully at Pell. "Come with me, Pell. You know so much more. It would be far safer." It was almost a plea. I knew she was afraid to go alone.

Pell shook her head. "Safer, perhaps, but not the best use of our time, and we have precious little of that. Besides, you know the way to your village well enough. I will set you on your path and make a sure place to meet, but I have other things I need to be doing. There are those north of here who must be warned and quickly, and they must be sent on to warn others. The game speeds up now that the Zarn has issued his proclamation. It has all moved much faster than I expected, much faster than I was ready for. We must set out running to catch up. I think we have a chance, though, for Hamishair lies close to the Zarn's main east-west road, and these places we will ride to are out of the way, much harder to reach. Hopefully, we will be there first. Yes, you will go south and I will go north. Tazzi will help me here." She said all this in such a tone of command that I found myself bristling with resentment. No one had ever ordered me about, not even as a small child, the result, I suppose, of having powers so young.

"It does not seem to me that we are planning this together," I said sharply. "Rather it is you who are the commander, mapping out our plans and issuing orders. We are to be the silent soldiers. You say what I will do. I have not even been consulted nor given my consent."

Those harsh words were out of my mouth before I had time to think. Barrenaise looked shocked. I braced myself for Pell's anger, but instead she answered me evenly, "That may be true, but you must understand, Tazzi, I have been thinking on this for a long time now, preparing for it and learning all I can. The Zarn has caught me off guard, but I knew that sooner or later the time would come when they would need us dead. Now that time is here. We must meet it quickly and in the best way possible. Later, when we have time, I will tell you my story and you may better understand. In the meantime, if you have any better plans spit them out. I am always ready to listen. But understand, I have no patience for games of pride or any other kind of games. We have no time for that. If you think my plan to be a poor one, say so now and say why and tell me what we should do differently."

"No, no," I answered hastily, "you seem to have it well thought out already." I was almost blushing and stammering with embarrassment. Then I caught Barrenaise smiling smugly.

"And you," Pell said, turning on her, "does your silence mean you agree or that you have no thoughts of your own?" Now it was my turn to watch Barrenaise's discomfort, though it hardly seemed fair as she had already voiced her disagreement. Barrenaise turned quickly to me. "And will you ride back to your village, also?"

I shook my head, "No, I can never go back. I am already wanted and marked for death there. Besides, it was such a small village, there were only two of us of that age. There is no one left to warn. Me they have driven away, and Kara they have killed." It was the first time I had spoken those words aloud. I bit my lip and clenched my fist against the pain.

Pell gave me a sharp look as if she could see into my head. "I have already said Tazzi will stay here and help me — that is if it is agreeable to her." This last she added with a slight mocking bow.

"Pell, you have had far more time to think on this than I have. I will do whatever you judge to be the best."

"Good. That will make things simpler, but do not hesitate to say whatever you may see. My eyes cannot be everywhere. Now, Barrenaise, my thought is that you should go south with your own horse, or rather your uncle's and two or three others. But first they must be well disguised. And before we go back out into the world, you both must be transformed."

She took up a pair of scissors and began to sharpen them with a stone. "You first," she said, pointing them at me. My hair had never been cut. It was long and thick with strong, stiff waves in it. I had worn it mostly in a single braid behind me. She had me stand before her. First she cut off the braid and dropped it on the floor. It lay there like a dark snake. Then, while I turned slowly, she cut my hair just below my ears in the style of young men, throwing handfuls of it into the fire as she worked. This made a choking stench that filled the shelter. It had us all coughing, but Pell ignored it, merely telling me to stand still or the scissors would catch my neck.

Meanwhile, she had set Barrenaise to grinding some berries in a bowl. When the cutting was done, Pell added some liquid to the crushed berries. This mixture bubbled up alarmingly. As soon as it settled, she brushed the bitter-smelling stuff into my newly cut hair, then rubbed the hair vigorously between her hands. I saw the palms of them turn red. After that she daubed some dark stuff into my eyebrows and down along my jawline and added some smudges under my eyes. All this time, as she worked on me, she nodded and muttered to herself. When she had me done to her satisfaction, she brushed the hair from my shoulders and handed me a bowl of water to see my reflection. I had to move this way and that to catch the light just right. Then, suddenly, a sullen boy with frizzy reddish hair and a shadow of new beard glared back at me from the dark, quivering water.

Pell nodded with satisfaction and said proudly, "Well, I believe your own mother would not recognize you on the street now." With those words, spoken in jest, the grief of my loss swept over me. Quickly, I set down the bowl before I dropped it. My mother! Would I ever see my mother's face again? I seemed to be moving further and further away from her. I did not even know if she still lived or if she had died on that terrible morning. And how would I ever know? Who would tell me now? Pell, seemingly oblivious to the desolation her words had caused, was already at work on Barrenaise.

When she had us both shorn to her liking, she went through her bags and baskets of clothes, holding them up against us for fit. Those that held promise she hung on the pegs. I was amazed. I could hardly believe this quantity of clothes, some even of fine cloth and make. I wondered how she had come by it all.

"I borrowed it here and there, knowing it would all come to good use," she answered readily, as if reading my thoughts. I understood that by borrowed she meant stolen, but I did not ask.

My brother's ragged clothes she rolled up "to be dealt with later." His boots were too large for me, but the cap she saved out, saying it did me very well. I was thinner than either of them, so Pell wanted to add some thickness to my slight frame. Barrenaise was wider than Pell and very full in the bust, so Pell found her a broad band to bind and flatten her breasts. We tried on this and that, rejecting more than we kept, till at last Pell had us clothed and shod to her liking, both of us looking like stocky farm boys. Barrenaise's breasts made no showing and my thin figure had been given bulk and substance. We glanced at each other and laughed nervously while Pell muttered, "Good, good, by the Goddess. That will surely fool them." When she had dressed herself in similar style she folded and put away most of the extra clothes with care, but selected out of it a small stock. These she stuffed into a saddle pack which she handed to Barrenaise. "Take this with you for the others. They may not have time to find clothes for themselves."

After that she had us walk back and forth for her appraising eye as I had done the night before. Finally, she pronounced us ready. "That will do for now. I would still know because I know, but for other eyes it is good enough. And one last thing, that name of yours — that will never do," Pell said, looking at Barrenaise. "No man has such a name. It will give you away in an instant. We could shorten it perhaps to Renaise, or change it to something else if that suits you better." When Barrenaise made a face, Pell said quickly, "Which would you rather safeguard, your name or your life? And besides, it puts the rest of us at risk if your disguise is uncovered."

"Renaise will do," she answered almost in a whisper, looking down at the ground. She seemed about to cry, quite at odds with her rough farm-boy appearance.

"Good, that is all settled, then." Pell took a stack of trail bread from a large crock buried in the dirt floor. She packed some in a little waist pouch and some in Barrenaise's pack. At a nod of her head we followed her out into the day.

It must have been past noon already. The sun was riding high, though still barely discernible through the thick covering of leaves. There was no clearing around Pell's shelter. The trees came right to the entrance. These trees, now that I saw them in the daylight, seemed repellent to me. They were all bent and twisted in strange, threatening ways and shapes, as if some disease or some foul wind had moved through this part of the forest. There was something unpleasant, almost loathsome, at the sight of them. It was easy to see why none came here. I shivered in spite of the warmth of the day and saw Barrenaise, or rather Renaise, do the same.

Before we left, it was necessary to pull the horses' shoes for, as Pell said, farmers' horses are seldom shod and guardsmen's always are. Also, shoes carry the owner's mark and number. Renaise and I were, of course, expected to help. Pell took tools from a wooden box hidden behind some rocks, under a low ledge. With these she showed us what to do. It seemed easy enough to me, but I found working with Renaise no pleasure. Her hands on the tools were clumsy and inept. I itched to take them from her and put them to better use in my own skilled hands. I said nothing, but I have no doubt she felt my impatience. All of a sudden she said scathingly, "You must be well accustomed to this kind of work from living on a dirt-farm."

There was such spite and contempt in her voice I almost choked on it. It was fortunate for us all that I could not inflict any real harm, or she might have regretted my skill with tools. "It seems a shame," I said back to her when I could breathe again, "that what you learned in that tavern was to wait on tables and to charm men, not skills that will be of much value here."

Pell looked over and said sharply, "It would be better if you both paid attention to your own work instead of trying to best each other. Take heed, Tazzi, you have broken a nail there and now it will be hard to pull." Pell herself worked swiftly and easily, all the while talking and petting and stroking the horses as she had the night before. She seemed to me more gentle and tender with horses than with humans.

When we finished, there was a pile of horseshoes and nails. Pell gathered them all up into a sack and hid them in her pit, saying, "All for later. Nothing should go to waste. Who knows when or how it will be needed." Before we could leave, Pell had Renaise rub dirt into the saddles she was going to use and so finish their transformation from the guards' smart issue to poor and much-used farm tack. "Now we go to the bog and let it work its magic on these horses."

When we mounted at last, Renaise sidled up next to me and muttered by my ear, "It is a wonder that poor little creature is strong enough to carry you such distances. She looks to be not much more than a farmer's cart-pony."

That stung, of course, for it was close to the truth. So I answered with equal venom, "It is good that yours is big and stocky considering the bulk he is forced to bear. Even so he was puffing fit to die after that first run."

Pell paid us no more heed. She rode out ahead, whistling and calling to our band of extra horses. Some of those stolen horses were sleek and well fed and looked to be of prize stock. Though Pell could have had her choice, I noticed that she still rode the same sorry-looking beast she had ridden the night before. He was a little cart-horse, not much bigger than Marshlegs, thin and angular with a blotchy, gray-brown coat, clearly no thing of beauty. As I was pondering this, Renaise pressed forward to catch up to Pell. I found myself riding behind them, trying to deal with this new thing called anger.

Pellandria was bad enough with her rough ways and her orders, more like the coarse boys who were my brother's friends than like any girls I had ever seen. In spite of this there was much I liked, or at least admired, there. Renaise, on the other hand, I found hardly bearable. Never in my life had I taken such a quick dislike to anyone. Everything she did cut me wrong, the way she moved or spoke, her little gestures, her simpering way of looking at Pell, and most of all her arrogance toward me.

There was no doubt that it was mutual. She had as little use for me. I think she saw me as a fool of a country girl, a dirt-child who had stayed in her village of cow dung and chicken feathers when she could have gone out into the big world and made something of herself. For myself I did not think much of this big world of hers if the town of Hamishair was any sample — an oversized refuse heap with rubbish left in the streets to rot.

If Renaise had not had powers, she would have struck me as very ordinary, just a plump, witless serving-girl with not a thought in her head who worked waiting tables in her uncle's tavern and was much puffed up with herself for little reason. Clearly, she could not have saved herself from so much as a mousetrap if Pell had not come to her rescue. At that moment I chose not to think what my fate would have been without Pell's timely intervention. All this grated on my spirit as we rode. It was like gravel rubbing in a boot. When I saw Renaise speak to Pell and then glance back in my direction I ground my teeth, imagining her spiteful and insulting words.

At last Renaise wearied and dropped back. I took this chance to ride up next to Pell and say some of my own feelings, hoping for her agreement. Instead, Pell answered sharply, "What does any of that matter, Tazzi? She is one of us. That is what counts. Nothing else is of any real importance." This only added to my store of bitterness. I said nothing more on the subject of Renaise and we rode on in silence.

By now we were well out of the Twisted Forest and rode under more normal trees. This at least was a relief. That unnatural growth had been oppressing my spirit more than I realized. Almost as soon as I felt the comfort of that change, our little track ended in a larger road, a road full of deep wagon tracks that looked much like the farm-to-market road between Nemanthi and Koorish. I could hear voices. All my fears came screaming back in force. Pell put a hand on my arm, saying, "Steady, Tazzi. Keep your calm." She beckoned for Renaise to ride up beside us. I glanced back anxiously for the extra horses, but they were nowhere in sight. I could feel waves of fear coming from Renaise on Pell's other side. At that moment I even felt some empathy for her.

"Listen now, both of you," Pell said quickly. "I want you to remember two things, two quite opposite things. You must keep them always in your minds. One is that you have powers. Driven to it, those powers will likely keep you safe, though for our purposes, of course, we would rather not have them shown. The other is that those we pass will see us as we seem, as we ourselves wish to be seen, as long as we maintain that appearance and do not panic. You have only to play that part, to be the person they think you are. Now breathe deeply and remember to keep calm at the center."

There were some riders coming toward us on the road, and two wagons that appeared loaded with people and possessions. It looked to be a whole family on the move. I tried to still the fluttering bird in my chest. It was beating its wings in a frenzy against the cage of my ribs. "How do humans live with this thing?" I whispered urgently to Pell.

"They are used to it. They learn from the time they are little," she whispered back. Then, as we approached the riders, she drew slightly ahead of us. "A good day to you all and good health," she said, touching the edge of her hat and giving a nod of salutation. The first man mumbled, "Good day," keeping his eyes lowered. To my surprise the other kept his silence, looking nervous and apprehensive, almost guilty. The old woman who sat in the lead wagon did not greet us. She had her shawl pulled so low it almost hid her face, and she kept her head down as if watching the road. From somewhere, somewhere quite close by, I could feel waves of fear as loud as an alarm bell to my inner ear.

"You are moving, I see. I wish you good luck in your next home." This innocent greeting of Pell's was met with a wave of agitation that flew through the whole group. A little boy in the next wagon began to cry. When his mother tried to hush him, the fear swelled out again, louder than before. I glanced at Pell. I could tell from the look on her face she felt it too. She flashed me a picture of a young woman lying hidden under the bedding of the second wagon.

Once past us, those others seemed eager to press on. I could hear them urging their oxen to move faster, though in my experience oxen have only one pace, that one being slow and steady. "Goddess bless your venture," Pell called after them.

"They had one of us hidden in the wagon," Renaise said breathlessly.

"Yes, and now that you have seen what guilt and fear look like on display, try not to imitate it. Those folk might as well be carrying a sign. I hope they get where they are going before they have to pass any that mean them harm."

I shuddered. "Are we to do nothing?"

"What can we do that will not frighten them more and endanger us as well? They are fleeing to save her. They will hardly turn her over to strangers, strange men at that."

We passed a few more farm folk on the road before we turned off onto another trail that took us back into woods, but I was never that fearful again. I was even able to touch my cap and nod and say, "Good day," as I had seen Pell do. Soon after we were on our new path I heard horses in back of us. I turned quickly, but it was only our free horses trotting to catch up to us.

For a ways the woods were thick. Then they appeared to be thinning. The ground grew damp and spongy underfoot. Soon after that we came to the edge of a marsh or bog. It was much like the one near my village where I often went to hunt for herbs and roots. At Pell's signal we both slid from our horses.

"This part is full of risk, for now we must strip off our clothes and so be naked a while, but I know of no other way, for the mud would soon ruin everything we wear." As soon as we had our clothes and tack and packs concealed between some rocks, we rode naked and bootless on the horses' backs, going as far into the marsh as seemed safe. The horses were reluctant. It took constant urging to keep them moving forward with the mud sucking at their hooves. When they would go no further, we slipped from their backs. Standing knee deep in ooze, we applied mud by hand to their necks and heads and backs and wherever else it was needed. We then had to go back for the others and were soon caked and coated ourselves, daubed beyond recognition. We looked like gray ghosts or the crude work of an unskilled Potter — such work as the Potters' children sell at fairs — come to life and staggering about.

All the while we worked, Renaise lost no chance at mocking my efforts or belittling me in some way. I defended myself in kind as best I could. We created such a brew of ill will with our traded insults that at last Pell turned on us both. "Enough," she hissed, "more than enough. I have run through my store of patience, which was not large to start with. Stop playing at being fools. Have you forgotten that there are men out there who curse our very existence, who would like to kill us by whatever means they could? Right now they are out searching for us. There is no need to help them by making war among ourselves. Our lives are hard enough without that. We may not love each other, we may not even like each other, at least at first, but we have a bond deeper than blood or family. Alone, we have not the power to hold against so many. Together, who knows what we can do?" By the end of this she was holding forth with passion, gesturing with both hands like a mad gray phantom. I felt a bubble of laughter swelling in my throat and swallowed hard.

Suddenly Pell herself grinned, cracking her gray mask. "And besides, what makes you think I find you both the most charming and delightful company? That I would have chosen you out of all others had I been free to do so?" She looked hard at each of us to make her point, then said forcefully, "I had no choice. The Goddess dumped you at my feet. I must make the best of it and so must you. Now please, if you have nothing good to say to each other, be silent. We must get done and be gone from here as quickly as we can." Chastened, we did not even look at each other as we worked in silence, rubbing the horses down with leaves till they were evenly coated in mud, and then tangling twigs and burrs in their manes and tails.

By the time we had finished and were on the road again it was late in the day, close to dark. We had done well. Those sorry-looking creatures could never have been mistaken for town stock or guardsmen's horses. From our hard work and the effects of the mud, they had lost all signs of gloss and care. Pell, after she had us safely on the right trail, rode back to cover our footprints in the mud as best she could. When she rejoined us, she was leading three horses on a long lead rope with gunnysacks tied over their saddles. The rest she must have found a place for along the way, as I no longer heard them in back of us.

For me this ride was a misery of discomfort. The clay had dried and cracked under my clothes, setting up a torment of itching that could not be scratched. There had been nowhere to wash but in the puddles of water that formed in the horses' hoofprints. With that and some dampened leaves we had done our best. When I saw the look of deep distaste on Renaise's face as she struggled into her clothes, I was tempted to mock her for her fine town ways. I bit back my words. She in turn said nothing ugly to me of looking like a true dirt-child, though she may well have been tempted. We rode mostly in silence. After a while our path began to widen, becoming almost a small road. By the time we reached the road we sought, we were at a true crossroad. Even so, it was hard to see, for it was dark now, with only enough earth glow to peer a few feet ahead of us.

"Here is where we part," Pell said abruptly. "I have put you on the road several miles south of Hamishair, heading toward your village. It is this crossroad you must come back to. There is a sign here for Menaltron in one direction and Hamishair in the other. That is what marks this place. You can tell that to any that should need to find us. How many days will it take you to go and come back? How many at the very most?"

"If I could ride openly and without fear, four, or perhaps five altogether. Having to be secret and not knowing what I may encounter, three down and three back, then at least one more to find and warn the others and get them on the road. Do not look for me before the seventh day." I heard the tremor in Renaise's voice and knew the effort by which she kept it steady. To my surprise, I felt not mockery but fear for her. It was a dark, lonely night to be out and a long road to go, with much danger on it.

"Seven days, then. We shall meet you here on the night of the seventh and again for the next four. After that, if you have not come..." Pell shrugged, then went on quickly. "Look for us after the turn of the night. We will be watching from trees, one on each side of the road. Hoot like an owl as you approach. We will hoot three times in answer if all is clear and it is safe to meet. If all is safe with you, hoot back three times. If not, hoot once and ride on. We will watch and try to catch you later or meet again the next night. Or, if we feel it is unsafe, we will hoot once and you go on. Is that all clear?" Renaise was nodding and Pell went on. "If the others can bring back more horses or supplies, all to the good, but do absolutely nothing that makes for more danger. This ride is risky enough. Ride well, Renaise, and come back safely with the others. Goddess go with you." They hugged each other, soldier style, without dismounting. Then Renaise was gone into the night, riding one horse and leading three others. Suddenly it seemed very large and dark out there. With my tongue glued in my mouth, I had not even wished her well. I felt a sudden ache in my heart.

Going back, I let Marshlegs pick her way and followed Pell in silence, each of us deep in our own thoughts. At some moment I heard horses behind us, but since Pell seemed to take no notice I assumed them to be ours. Suddenly, out of that silence, Pell said softly, "I cannot help but notice that you both have the disease of jealousy. It is another one of those things like fear and anger and hate that are part of the human inheritance and probably new to you. Not a pleasant feeling, surely, but you will have to learn to endure it with a little more grace and even to control it some. Besides, it is wasted on me. I am not worth it. My heart goes out to no one. What skills my hands possess can as easily be learned by another."

I made no answer. I could not imagine what Pell meant nor why she was saying this to me.

5

Pell was wrong, of course, about the skill of her hands. It was not just an ordinary skill such as anyone could easily learn. And she was right about her heart, but all that comes later on in this story.

The first thing Pell set out to do that next morning was to find safe hiding for the extra horses. She had us up and riding before dawn. My eyes were gritty from lack of sleep. My limbs felt thick, heavy, and unwilling. I was riding along behind her, head nodding, dozing with my eyes half closed, when she turned suddenly and said with a flash of anger, "Pay attention, Tazzi, and watch carefully where we go. It is important that you know, as well as I do, where the horses are hidden." After that she pointed out landmarks to me at each turning, a snapped treetop, a boulder in the shape of a horse. "How will you ever learn to find your way? You seem content to ride along after me, paying no mind at all to where we go!" Stung by the truth of her words, I opened my eyes wide, determined to remember each sign and mark.

We left the first four horses in a small, natural enclosure, away from the shelter but close enough to be quickly fetched if needed. The rest, about ten or twelve, I believe, we took farther off to a fair-sized clearing at the top of a hill.

Now I must tell you, this part was not easily done. The hill itself presented quite a challenge, especially on horseback. We had left our own two at the bottom. I was riding a stranger who was not at all glad to have me on her back. We had to urge the others to come with us. As Pell knew of no path up, we were forced to pick our way as best we could. For much of the climb, the ground was covered with a scatter of black, jagged rocks that slipped and slid dangerously underfoot. In places the hill grew so steep we had to dismount and stumble up on foot. By the time we finally pulled ourselves over the top, all of us, horse and human alike, were heaving and panting and drenched with sweat.

The clearing, after that hard struggle, appeared suddenly before us as a sweet and unexpected surprise, a place of magic. It was a soft, green bowl of a meadow, hollowed into the hilltop and seeming to fill it from one side to the other. The grass that grew there was unnaturally lush, of a brilliant hue that almost hurt the eyes. Everywhere the meadow was dotted with bright flowers, dancing and shifting in the breeze.

"What is this place?" I asked, still gasping for breath. "It is like nothing I have ever seen."

"It is the worn-down top of an ancient fire-mountain, or such is the local talk. I can well believe it from its strange shape. This is another of those places considered haunted, and so made safer for us by the fears of others."

I thought this hard way up was all the safety that was needed, but haunted or not, I liked its aspect far better than that of the Twisted Forest. There was even a pond at its center, bright blue under a bright blue sky, beckoning its invitation to us after that murderous ride.

As soon as the horses went to graze, we ripped off our clothes and ran to throw our filthy, clay-coated, sweat-streaked bodies into the cool water, shouting for the joy of it. Afterward we rubbed ourselves down with rushes and washed again. Pell was the most at ease I had seen her since we first met. She even gave us time to lie on the bank, drying in the warmth of the sun. This had been my first chance to bathe since my escape. I felt some of the horror of all that wash away along with the mud and sweat. I must have slept for a while in that charmed place, for all too soon Pell was shaking me awake.

As we went back to claim our own horses, I wondered again why Pell had left the best for others and kept such a sorry-looking creature for herself. As if reading my thoughts she said suddenly, "I would not trade Torvir for that whole pasture full of fancy horses." As she spoke he was rubbing his knobby head against her arm while she scratched fondly behind his ears. "He has been with me since before I left my father's house. He was my first companion when I was alone in the world. Besides, he is not what he appears to be, any more than we are. He can weave through the trees like a cat. He can run like the wind and never seems to tire, but to see him standing in a public place with his head hanging down, he looks like a broken-winded nag that could hardly go at a trot, a useful trick in my line of work. Besides, he knows everything in my head." I had been well answered without even opening my mouth. Utterly weary and ready for home, I climbed on my own horse without a word.

Riding back, Pell said with a sigh, "Now I can breathe easier. Even with my skill at storytelling, I would have been hard put to explain the presence of so many extra horses in the hands of two poor farm boys, especially since a fair number are missing from Hamishair. No one has ever come to the shelter or even near it. So far the woods have kept us safe, but now that we are all hunted fugitives there will be more risk in everything we do." She sighed again, more deeply this time. I understood now how much this matter must have weighed on her, though of course she had not said so. After that she seemed lighter and gayer. I could not say the same for me. Given a choice, I myself would have stayed in that green and sunny place, making my shelter there with the horses rather than returning to those unnatural woods. Riding back into them did nothing good for my spirits.

We had dismounted at the shelter and I was struggling to unsaddle Marshlegs when Pell said, much to my surprise, "You are staggering on your feet, Tazzi, no use to yourself or anyone. This has all been too much for you. I think you need some healing sleep. Go find a mat and use what is left of this day to cure yourself." This was one order I had no wish to argue with.

When I woke it was evening. Pell had already left. There was a small fire burning, with a pot of food and another of tea set by it. I was alone in that place, alone as I had never been in my family's home. There were no neighbors nearby, not a soul for miles. The wind outside was blowing wildly, causing strange rustling noises in the leaves, making the fire flare up suddenly and then as suddenly die down, sucked away to embers. I could hear my horse shifting about, or at least I hoped it was Marshlegs. She was all I could sense out there. Wind and the night's creatures and the absence of other humans — I had never been afraid of such things before. I made myself get up, pour a cup of tea, and put some fresh sticks on the fire. As I sat watching the flames and drinking my tea, the wind had a sad, mournful sound. It seemed to be calling to me.

This was my first chance to think by myself since fleeing Nemanthi. Suddenly it was Kara's name I heard in the wind. Her death came rushing back to me. With it came a terrible new thought. I could see now that it was Kara's death that had saved my life. Because they were so intent on killing her, I had gotten away with no pursuit. I could hear their shouts and curses again and see the flash of their pitchforks. With a frightful groan the cup slipped from my hands, cracking on the hearth. My life had been bought with Kara's. I could not get my mind past that thought. With another groan I went staggering back to the mat and fell face first on it. For a long time I lay there twisting and turning, beating my fists on the ground with the pain of that knowledge eating at me.

★

The next few days in Pell's shelter were like nothing in my life before. Tolgath's teaching had been kindly by comparison. Pell was teacher, trainer, taskmaster, and tyrant all in one. As her only student I was at her mercy, the center of all her attention, and she was being driven by the lack of time that lay so heavy on her. I thought she worked me harder than beasts being trained for the traveling animal troupe and told her so, but whenever I grumbled or complained she asked, as always, "Do you know a better way? Have you a better plan? Out with it, Tazzi. Spit it out." Then I would shrug and fall silent. I saw that she was even harder on herself. Under it all I could feel the concern that drove her. I could even feel some kindness there. In the end I would do as she asked, though she pushed me each day to the brink of rebellion.

Every morning Pell had me practice walking, speaking, turning, sitting in the style of men. "They must suspect nothing," she told me. "They must have no thought to look any further." At the most unexpected moments she would hurl questions at me as to who I was, where I was going and where I was from, what I was doing and planned to do. I was to answer in my new voice and without faltering, all with some practiced lies we had agreed on.

The simplest version of our story was that we were cousins, poor farm boys from the region of Manorath, near the village of Parthir, farm boys whose family farms had been sold for debt. Pell thought this a good region to choose. According to her it had been hard hit, first by floods and then by a long drought. Supposedly, we had come south to look for farm work or for opportunities in town, stables or kennels or the like, such as would suit our few simple skills. Having no coin for lodging, we had made our crude shelter in the woods.

Now you may think this all sounds easy enough to remember and recite, but not for one like me who has grown up 'scandalously honest,' as Pell liked to say. I was the kind who blushed and stuttered when I lied. Indeed, there had been no cause to do so until I started meeting in secret with Kara. It was not a concept that came easily to me — that one would choose to use words to hide the truth rather than to make it clear. Pell, on the other hand, acknowledged herself to be a practiced storyteller. She declared with pride that she could easily have invented a new life for us each day. It seemed a strange thing to brag about. I told her so, but she only laughed at me, saying, "I have lived out in that man's world since I was a girl of eleven. Not likely I could have survived this long on a diet of honesty alone. One might as well learn to do well what one has to do anyway."

Later she would draw maps in the dirt and drill me as to the placement of roads and rivers, the names of towns and villages. This would go on till I made an error. Then we would start again. Along with this we worked on the saddles and the tack. These we transformed from fancy, well-kept equipment — the best, in fact — to worn and shabby, much-used farm gear. Working diligently, we cut away or burned those parts that were owner-marked, adding pieces of worn leather in places and rubbing it all with dirt and rough stones. Pell was an artist at this kind of altering. She took as much pride in it as if she were doing a fine new piece of work. I also have skilled hands and so was quick to learn.

On top of all this, every night as soon as darkness neared, Pell would ride out on some mission of her own, leaving me alone in that place. Never again was it as bad as that first night. With practice I learned to fight down my fear and to shut the door on my grief. I have no idea if Pell slept at all, for no matter how early I woke she was already up and busy with some project. Often she was storing away sacks of grain and foodstuff in crocks buried in the floor. I knew well enough not to ask how she came by any of this.

On the third morning, I woke to find Pell standing over me. She had a look of longing on her face such as I have sometimes seen on the faces of men. When she saw me awake, she seemed embarrassed and quickly turned away. She would have stepped back, but I caught her hand. "Come sit by me for a while and talk. All we have done is work and drill. We know nothing of each other's lives. Surely, we have the right to a few words. Other things can wait a little while."

"Nothing can wait," she answered bitterly. "For some it is already too late." In spite of her harsh words, she allowed herself to be pulled down.

In fact, she crumpled to the mat with a loud groan, as if releasing some long-pent-up feelings. Even then she did not make herself at ease. Instead, she lay straight and stiff, keeping so far to the other side of the narrow mat that in no place at all did we touch. She was so still and quiet, I even thought she might have fallen asleep. Before I had a chance to feel my disappointment, though, she opened one eye at me and said, "Well, Tazzi, now you have me here, so you may as well tell me your life. At least tell me how you came to be in the tavern that day looking as if a pack of demons was on your trail."

Pell shut her eyes again. With her lying beside me, I talked. I talked and talked as I have never done with anyone but Kara. I told her most of what is written here. She listened with interest to everything I said, most especially when I recalled speaking with animals or told of the wolf who came to the village or the growth of my healing powers or how Kara and I spoke silently with each other and the games we played. This last she questioned me on so avidly that I grew embarrassed. But when I blamed myself for Kara's death and began to cry with terrible racking sobs, she gave me scant sympathy, not even putting out her hand for comfort. She would only say, "The dead are dead. Nothing will bring them back. Not all your tears can change that."

The coldness in her voice made me shiver. When I could not stop my crying, she sat up suddenly and said, almost with anger, "It is we who are living hunted with a price on our heads who must look to ourselves. Clearly, no one else will help us. Now with this death edict I will seek out the others to bring them to safety. That is my work. That is my life. I will go out in wider and wider circles and gather us together. I will do whatever is in my power for the living, but I will not mourn for the dead. No, Tazzi, I will not mourn for the dead and you cannot make me do so." She said this last part with such passion that she frightened me. Then she sat staring off into some far place. I thought her finished when suddenly, with all of that intensity, she turned her fierce stare on me. "These will be terrible years and they will be wonderful years, and who knows what we will make when we all come together." Then she gave a great sigh. "Oh Goddess, save us and spare us, this surely is a perilous time." With that she sank down again and shut her eyes. This time I thought her truly asleep. I even felt a moment of tenderness watching her there. Then suddenly her eyes flew open again. She looked straight up at me.

"So you were lovers, you and your Kara?"

"Lovers?" I could not catch her meaning. Lovers was for men and women and what they were to each other. I had never given that name or any other to what Kara and I had together or what we did.

"Lovers, yes, what else? It is plain enough from what you said. In Eezore, the Shokarn would call you Muirlla, woman's woman. It would be worth your life there even if there were no edict hanging from a tree to mark you. Among the Kourmairi they say Puntyar. Besides meaning women who are lovers of women, it means all sorts of filthy things, love under a rock, sucking the Witch's tit, left-handed daughter of bad luck, and much other loveliness, depending on which dialect is being spoken. Have you never heard it?" Puntyar — that was the word Jortho had thrown at me on that fatal night.

"Stop," I shouted, putting my hand over her mouth. "Our loving was fine and beautiful. It had nothing to do with such filth as that!" I was crying again. The wound had been reopened and some dirt rubbed in it. Yes, I had heard that word, had even heard it shouted at me, but had never guessed its meaning.

She shook herself free of my hand. "I am not disputing the purity of your love, only the quality of your wisdom. I am trying to warn you that others see it differently. Understand what you do and understand that it is forbidden. That is all I am trying to tell you."

"Will everything be taken from me?" I felt again that desolation that had swept over me when I thought of my mother.

"Perhaps, and perhaps there will be other things to take their place."

I shut my eyes, but could not stop the tears. "No," I said fiercely, "Kara is not a thing, and no one can take her place."

"Others will die besides your Kara, many if we cannot move fast enough. We cannot cry now for those who die. It will be hard enough in these next few years for those of us alive to stay that way."

"Pell, how can you be so hard? Do you love no one, no one at all? Is there no one you would cry for?"

"I love us all," she said abruptly, with hurt in her voice, "but not one more than the other. I love us all and plan to get us through this alive, as many as I can. You think me hard, I am hard. If Kara had been a little harder or a little faster, she might be here with us today. If I die tomorrow, waste no tears on me. You must promise me that. Go find the others and bring them together, for that is what we must do in these next few years. We can thank the Zarn for letting us know that we are many and for setting us in motion."

"But what have we done to them, Pell, that they want us dead? What have we done besides just be?"

"Since we have powers, that is enough for those who rule. That is enough to threaten them."

"They can have the power if that is what they want. I would trade all my power for Kara's life in an instant. What do I need with it? It is more like a curse."

"Poor Tazzi, it has all come on you so suddenly. I have seen it coming for a long time, for years. I knew they could not leave us be." Her tone had softened, lost some of its hard edge. She leaned forward and touched my face gently with her fingertips. Then, to my surprise, she kissed my forehead. Her touch, though it seemed meant for kindness, woke a quiver of pain and passion in me. I drew back to look at her and saw again that look of hunger and urgency. With a shiver I pulled her against me and was astonished to feel her stiffen in resistance. She even pushed me back with her hand, to be able to look into my face.

"Understand what you ask for, Tazzi. I can give you my body, but not my heart. That goes to no one till this is over — whenever that will be. If my body is what you wish for, it is yours, full of hunger and want. It has been so for days. I have been trying to curb it, thinking if I rode it to exhaustion it would leave me some peace and let me sleep. If you want more, if what you want is the heart-touch you had with Kara, then you need to look elsewhere. I do not have that to give. This must be very clear between us. I never want to think I have taken a woman without her full knowledge and consent, nor do I want her to think it can be with me other than it really is."

I pushed her hand away and leaned forward to silence her with a kiss. What I wanted at that moment was something to ease my pain — anything. If I could have that from meeting Pell's hunger with my body, then I was ready and she was welcome to it. As for hearts, I had no heart to give either. Muirlla, puntyar, now I knew it had a name. I had thought it was only a game we played.

This time when I tried to kiss her, she met me with a hard, bruising kiss of her own. We kissed for a long time, falling deeper and deeper into that kiss. Then she rolled me over and began to strip off my clothes with urgent fingers, saying, "Too long, much too long! One could die of this kind of hunger." I could feel her trembling. When she had me naked, I felt strange and uncomfortable under her scrutiny. "Shut your eyes, Tazzi. Forget yourself." I did as she said, feeling her hands on my body as she spread me out to her satisfaction. Then, starting at my feet, she began to run her fingers upward, very lightly at first and slowly, so slowly I shivered with anticipation, then faster and harder till she had me shaking and moaning, lost in pleasure. Suddenly she fastened her mouth to my breast and plunged her fingers deep inside me, deeper than Kara had ever gone. Before I could protest she had withdrawn and was rubbing me into a frenzy of pleasure till I wanted to beg for her re-entry, twisting about to catch her fingers. Then again, that quick plunge in followed by more teasing torture till I cried out, thrashing against her hand. Afterward I fell back, exhausted and soaked with sweat.

Pell's hands on my body had been full of knowledge. All had been done with such craft and skill that it made what Kara and I had shared together seem like childish fumbling, yet it did not fill my heart. Instead, it left me strangely empty, even sad. I reached for Pell. She shook her head and pulled the covers over me. "Time enough for that later. Sleep a while. I need you to ride out today. I think you are as ready now as you will ever be."

Ready, perhaps — she did not ask if I were willing. I fought again my hard battle with fear. Then I dozed for a while till Pell's restless energy drew me from sleep. She beckoned me over when she saw I was awake. I came to squat by her while she drew plans for me on the floor: where I was to go, who I was to meet, and where that one, in turn, was to go to warn others. Then she made me draw all of it over and over till I made no mistakes and could picture it clearly in my head, each fork and turning of the way.

"I think the guard will not have been there yet, because it is so far from here by road and these are only a few small, scattered settlements. Also I am sending you by a much shorter way, roads and paths that the Shokarn are not likely to know. Still, you must be very cautious in case they have already posted edicts in Delmorth or even in Thar's Crossing. Someone going to market in those towns could have carried the word home.

"You are to seek out Tamara. If any stop you or question you, say you are looking to buy a pig from Big Barthelli, a good brood sow, for that is what her father raises. I have drawn you the way there, but once you are close enough, you could find that farm by smell alone if nothing else.

"Remember not to panic. One of them alone cannot hurt you, nor even two or three. You have powers. Remember that. Keep it always in your heart. Wear it like armor. Your own fear is the worst enemy you have, worse than any man. Bluff, be clever, make things up. Only run if you have to and make sure you do that with a clear head. Here, wear this and show it to Tamara. She will trust you instantly." As she said that, Pell slipped a thong from around her neck. On it hung a pendant in the shape of a triangle inside a circle. It was the same sign I had seen her draw in the dirt that time for Renaise.

With a quick gesture Pell dropped the thong over my head and tucked the pendant under my shirt. When I started to question her, she said quickly, "Later, some other day. Now it is time for you to go. Only be sure to show it to her and she will know. And bring it back safely here to me." There was something strange in her face. When I tried to reach her thoughts, she shook her head. I could feel her blocking me from her mind. She gave me a sudden hard kiss and pushed me roughly out of the shelter.

There I was, thrust out in broad daylight, being sent off on my first venture. I did not even have the cover and safety of darkness. In spite of that I was feeling confident, almost eager. I was less afraid than might have been expected. This was the result, no doubt, of Pell's hard lessons and perhaps of my own struggles as well.

No need to describe here the roads Pell sent me by, only to say that they were narrow tracks more than roads and went mostly through wooded land. A few times I passed between plowed fields and had to cross real roads. Once we had to ford a rushing stream that wet Marshlegs to her belly. It would have filled my boots had I not put my feet up on her neck. I met few on the way. Many of those were furtive and hurried, not eager to engage or challenge anyone. For the most part, I was able to pass easily with a nod and no word spoken.

Just before dusk, with no worse incident than that stream, I located the settlement of Gaitherill. There, with only two questionings, I found what I thought from the smell of it must be Tamara's family's farm. A young woman was leaning on the gate. She was gazing out at the road toward the hills from which I had just ridden. There was a look of such longing in her face. The setting sun glowed in her hair, making a circle of rainbow light about her. In spite of that look, she seemed full of peace and innocence. It made my heart ache knowing what lay ahead, knowing what message I brought with me. I saw her as I myself had been just a few short days ago, leaning on my family's yard-gate, with no knowledge yet of fear and all that went with it. How I longed to turn around and go back with the words unspoken. She looked up at me with interest and I could sense her questions in my head.

"Are you Tamara?" I asked, swinging off my horse at the gate.

"Of course, who else would I be? My parents only have one daughter." She spoke in a light, teasing way, but I could feel her probing me, probably sensing that I was not what I seemed.

"I bring you a message from a friend." Saying this, I drew out the pendant from its place of concealment. It flashed suddenly in the slanting light.

Her eyes widened and she sucked in her breath. Her whole manner changed instantly, all mockery gone. "Is she ... has something...?"

"She is well," I said quickly. I could see the flash of fear in her eyes. "She has sent me here with a warning, for we are all in danger."

"Then you are ... oh yes, I see ... no wonder..."

"Is it safe to talk here?"

"Yes, only the pigs can hear. Tell me your news. I will listen for my family. If I start speaking of pigs, you will know we are no longer safe and are about to be interrupted."

While I spoke, she nodded many times. I told her of the edict and the danger to us all. Then I gave her Pell's instructions of where she was to go and who she was to warn. A look of surprise crossed her face. "Am I not to go back with you?" I shook my head. Tears sprung to her eyes, but she said lightly, "Ah well, I suppose she knows best."

Though I could not safely draw her a map, she seemed familiar enough with the places that I mentioned. When I finished, she said quietly, "So it has finally come to this. Pell warned us, but few would listen. Most thought her crazy. She wanted me to come away with her, but my grandmother was ill and dying, and then my mother had a new baby. She had woman troubles from the birth and needed my help at home. Tell me, please, how is Pellandria? Is she thinner? Is she wearing herself out? I wonder if she thinks of me still, the little pig-girl she left behind." She reached out her hand. "Can I touch it?" I held the pendant out to her. When she put her fingers on it, there were tears in her eyes. "Tell her I love her still," she said in a whisper so soft I was not even sure if she had spoken aloud.

"Was she from your village?"

"From the next settlement." Suddenly she withdrew her hand and straightened quickly. "I think my father is coming. We have been talking of pigs. You have not enough money for one of ours."

A big, burly man came around the corner of the barn. I could see him flush with anger when he spotted me. "Well, boy, what are you doing here hanging on my gate?" Then he turned on his daughter. "And you, are your chores all done? Have you nothing better to do than gossip with strangers?" Though he spoke to her gruffly, there was also a touch of wariness in his manner.

Unperturbed, she turned to smile at him. "The chores are all done, Father. This young man is here because he thought to buy a pig from us, but he finds he has too little money."

He looked me up and down, full of suspicion for all the wrong reasons. "So why are you still here, then? Go home. You have no more business at my door. Come back with enough money or do not come back at all." I did not think his belligerent manner would sell many pigs, but at that moment I suppose he was more worried for his daughter's virtue. He was so far off the mark it was tempting to laugh in his face — not that I would have been that foolhardy. Just then I saw his wife slip up in back of him. With a strange, pleading look she peered at me from behind the safety of his wide shoulder, but whether she was begging me not to take her only daughter away from her or begging me to take her quickly, I would never know, for at that moment her husband sensed her presence. He whirled around and shouted at her in a way he plainly had not dared to do with his daughter, "Go inside, you fool! What business can you possibly have with this stranger?" She scurried away with that anguished and unreadable look still on her face.

Tamara, not at all intimidated, put a hand on her father's arm. "Father, calm yourself. There is no cause for anger here. This young man merely came to buy a pig, but cannot afford one of ours. Surely his thin purse is more cause for his grief than yours."

At that he coughed and muttered and grumbled, kicking his heel in the dirt. I said quickly, remembering to keep my voice low, "I had no wish to cause trouble here, Goodman, and beg pardon if I have. My wife and I are just starting our little farm. I had heard from everyone that your pigs were the best, but I see I cannot afford one yet. I hope by next year we can manage. Can you tell me where else to try?"

He scowled at me intently, as if trying to decide something before he finally answered, "Try old Ranthair down by the edge of the bog. He has plenty of pigs for sale, though for myself I would not touch them. And go in the morning, boy, instead of sneaking around at night. Morning is when honest folk buy pigs."

I touched my cap and bobbed my head. "Yes, sir, thank you, sir. I will do as you say." He growled something unintelligible at me, turned, and stomped back to the barn. I wondered what he would think of me and my story the next day when he found his daughter gone.

As soon as he was out of sight, Tamara leaned toward me and said softly, "Thank you for risking your life to come here and bring me warning. The Goddess go with you and keep you safe." After glancing behind her, she touched my hand lightly with hers.

"And with you, too," I said. "Now please go quickly. They may come on you at any moment."

"At least I am warned," she answered. She seemed in no hurry to leave her gate. As I rode off, I looked back several times to see her standing there with the darkness of night closing about her. She raised her hand to me. When I was almost out of hearing, her father shouted after me, "Where are you from, boy?"

"The village of Tremuiri by the Orenth River," I shouted back at him, making it up on the spot. Let him chew on that one for a while.

The scene of Tamara at the gate had been so peaceful and pastoral and the whole trip, in fact, so uneventful as to make me almost forget the cause of fear till my small path was about to cross a larger road. Just as we were ready to step onto the road, Marshlegs jerked back. With a snort and a toss of her head she danced sideways for a few steps under the trees, so that I had to duck to save my head. Then she stood tense and alert. Sure enough, in a few moments I heard the sound of horses. Though I could hardly see them, it seemed like a large group of men, moving fast and with purpose. I stayed well hidden among the trees. Most of those men must have been speaking Shokarn, which, of course, I could not understand but suddenly, quite close to me, I heard one of them say in Kourmairi, "By the Gods, I hope we find a place for the night soon. I am sore all over from this ride. At this fool pace we will be in Thar's Crossing by tomorrow noon or before. If it is market day, we can put up these edicts in the market square and send them on with farm-folk to other towns. Maybe, in that way, we can save ourselves some hard riding."

Someone else answered out of the dark, "I will be glad when this is done and we can go back to the city. I find no pleasure in these country roads at night." They were soon past me, and whatever else they said was lost in the night. I rode hard for home after that, going as fast as I was able to in the dark, but twice more I almost crossed paths with troops of guards and once I heard what sounded like a large troop in the distance. It seemed as if the Zarn had his whole army on the move that night.

6

When I burst in on Pell, full of my news for her, she was sitting brooding by the fire. She looked up at me accusingly. "Already it has begun. We have been lovers only this once, yet here I sit up worrying for your safety."

"You might have done that anyhow," I said indignantly. "After all, this is the first mission you have sent me out on. You could have worried for me a little, even if we had not shared our bodies."

"Ah well, perhaps you are right. Now tell me everything. Did you find Tamara and warn her? Is she well? Did you show her the pendant?"

Handing the pendant back to Pell, I told her everything as it had happened, everything of Tamara and her father and the mock pig sale. Then I gave her a report on the large number of guards who had passed me on the way back. On this last she questioned me closely, though of course there was not much to tell. Then she asked again in a worried tone about Tamara. "Did she understand the danger? Will she leave at once? Did you have much trouble with her father?" She had slipped the pendant back in place. I noticed that she kept her hand pressed over it. There was a slight tremor in her voice, though she tried to cover it. She could not, however, still the waves of feeling that poured out from her.

"Pell, if she matters so much to you why were you not the one...?"

"Enough," she said sharply, holding up her hand. "Believe me, Tazzi, we cannot afford to care too much. They will break us with it in the end, break us in little pieces, or use our love to bend us to their will. That is just what my hardness is designed to guard me from. You see what happened to you because of Kara." At that moment it was Pell herself I could have cried for, though of course I knew better than to show it.

After a moment's silence, she stood up slowly. She seemed awkward and uneasy, looking down at the ground while she spoke. "What would you think of sharing a bed for the night? It has been so long since I have slept in a woman's arms, I have almost forgotten how to ask."

I was exhausted and thought we would fall instantly to sleep. Instead, we both tossed about with sleep evading us until I said, "Well, Pell, tell me your story, since you promised it to me and I have already told you mine."

She mumbled something unintelligible that I thought was a refusal, but then shifted so her arm was around me with my head on her shoulder. She began slowly, thinking it out as she went. "Mine is not a pretty story, not a pretty family tale, just the opposite. I myself never sought to gain my father's affections as you did. Quite the contrary, I always tried to keep clear of him. In addition to being angry like your father, mine had a craving for young female flesh. He had been able to use my sister at his will and thought to do the same with me.

"My powers came on me early, very early, earlier than most I know of. Let me tell you, Tazzi, you may sometimes think them a curse; for me they were a blessing and a saving, the only thing that kept me free of him, out of his hands. My father and I had our own small, bitter war going, almost from the time I was three. It was then he discovered he could not do his will on my body as he had done with my sister, Jeranthia. Young and unformed as I was, the more he found he could not touch me in that way the more he wanted to do so. Though my mother hungered for some touch and my older sister, already broken, would have offered her body to save mine, still he became obsessed with me and what was denied him. All he wanted was what he could not have.

"He would bluster and threaten and rage around the house, but in truth there was little he could do. Though his hands itched for it, he could not even strike at me with his switch as he did with all else on the farm — the animals, the hired hands, his other children, even his wife. The few times he tried taught him that quick enough. This galled him, I think, almost as much as the other. My brothers ... it was a shame about my brothers. They hated my father, all four of them, as much as I did. They should have been my friends and my allies. Instead, I think they hated me just as much for escaping the switch that fell all too often on their backs. It added to their anger that they could not touch me either.

"With my mother and my older sister I found some loving in that house, but their helpless terror tormented my childhood. Sometimes I even found myself being angry at them for it, wondering why my mother stayed. Foolishness, of course, or arrogance on my part. It is very hard, almost impossible for a woman to gather up her children and leave her man. How is she to make a living for her family on her own in any way but on her back? Even that is chancy. My mother had no skills and no way of gaining any. Besides, my father would, no doubt, have marked her as he was later to mark me. Moreover, her family and her village would have driven her back to him. If she had refused, she might well have lost her children. I suppose I must have known all that. Still, her helplessness galled me at times, as if she herself were at fault for it.

"I think the only thing that made my presence bearable in my father's eyes was my usefulness on the farm. My brothers were little help. Their anger and resentment made them lazy and careless, grudging at their tasks, shirking all that was not forced on them. I, on the other hand, worked hard and well, in spite of my youth. I grew quickly skilled at whatever I set my hands to, the powers no doubt helping to lend me strength. As I could keep away from him out in the fields or with the creatures, I took pleasure in the work, even some pride in it. Sometimes he loaned me out to work for the neighbors, pocketing some coins in this way. For me that was even better, as it gave me the peace of his absence.

"All this, at best, was only an uneasy truce. The friction between us came to a head one day when I was about eleven. Finding us alone in the house, something I was usually wary enough to avoid, he began shouting at me, insisting that he had father's rights. He said that as long as he fed and clothed me, I was his to use as he pleased, that I owed him that as my duty and should stop trying to avoid him. I think he was drunk that day as well as randy. That made him even more insistent than usual.

"For my part, I felt almost as much anger for having let myself be cornered by him in that way as I felt at the words themselves. Something turned in me. Something rose up in my heart. If I stayed, I saw years of the same ahead for me. 'In that case,' I shouted back without another thought, 'I will clothe and feed myself, for surely I am able to do so. I have been earning my keep here for years, better than all four of your worthless sons put together. Only for my mother's sake have I stayed in this house.'

"That was too much for my father. His rage or his drunkenness made him forget his caution. He gave a roar and tried to strike at me with all his might. Instead, by no effort of mine, he was blown out the door of his own house as by a great fist of wind.

"After that there was no way we could live together. I knew I had to leave, if not for myself or because of my father, then at least for my mother's sake, for our war was tearing her apart. The more she tried to shelter me from his wrath, the more she herself was made to suffer by him.

"It was time. I had no regrets. I thought with my reputation for hard work I would have an easy time of finding hire on neighboring farms. But when I left, my father rode out far and wide, spreading the word around that he had thrown me out of his house because I was a thief and a liar and lazy besides. He even said that the horse I rode was stolen from him. Not so! Torvir was mine, given to me by my mother's brother. But who would take a child's word against a man's? Because of all this I was shunned. I found no work, not even on those farms where I had worked before and they knew my worth. They may not have believed my father — after all, they knew better from their own experience — but they were not willing to cross him for my sake. I suppose he hoped hunger would drive me back into his hands again, more compliant this time. I would rather have died. Only once did I sneak back to my mother for food, but seeing the look of terror on her face and the way her hands shook when she filled my pack, I swore I would never do that again.

"The first food I stole I would much rather have earned, but I was given no chance. After that it became easier. I watched how the foxes did it and the rabbits and the rats. I learned some of my best lessons from them. After a while I lost any compunction I may have had. Having found no work and having grown hungry enough, I soon learned this new trade, not so honorable, perhaps, but still requiring skill. Indeed, I became the thief and the liar my father had marked me for, and very good at it besides. But not lazy, no, never lazy. I worked hard at this new occupation and discovered I had a gift.

"One of my first pieces of thieving was a set of boys' clothes stolen from a wash line. With these I began to pass as a boy. As I grew older I stole more clothes to fit my growing body and turned into a young man, that being an easier way to move with freedom in the world. I kept some women's clothing, however, for occasionally this was better suited for a particular piece of work. Sometimes the best way was to shift quickly from one to the other and so disappear almost in an instant.

"For that first year or two I was on my own, moving fast and learning to stay alive. Then, gradually, I began to meet others like me, others with powers. I began to understand that I was not the only 'unnatural one,' the only 'freak of nature,' as my father had been so fond of calling me. I knew then that 'we' existed, though as yet we had no name for what we were. By the time I saw you, I had gained enough experience. It was easy for me to see through your disguise."

I had been growing drowsy. Now, suddenly my curiosity was awakened. "Who was the first one? How did you know each other, or did she seek you out?"

Pell pulled her arm out from under my head, yawned, and stretched. "Are not you weary of all this and ready to sleep? Surely, I have been talking for hours."

"Only answer me this, then I will leave you in peace."

"I have your promise, then?" She drew me back into her arms. "The first one, eh? That would have been Jhemar. I remember it all very clearly. I probably had some thirteen years at the time, give or take a little.

"Sometimes I would sit at a Wanderers' campfire, out of loneliness and because they asked no questions. This night I thought myself the only woman in a circle of men, though of course I was in disguise, passing as a man myself. There had been a good deal of singing of old road songs, all pleasantly melancholy, to which I had added my own voice, keeping it as low as I could. There was also much drinking of yors and quillof. This I mostly avoided whenever possible, as it might make me careless, and I needed to always keep my wits about me. Now I want you to understand that since the Wanderers were good to me, I was as honest with them as I could afford to be. In their circles I was not a thief. I never stole from among them and told no lies that were not absolutely necessary, though as I have already said, they asked few questions and expected the same restraint from others. Also, I knew I could count on some food there and that helped keep me honest.

"It was getting late. I was yawning and thought to sleep soon when one of the Wanderers stood up, stripped off his shirt to wash, and to my amazement I saw, gleaming before me in the firelight, the breasts of a woman. My mouth fell open in shock. This woman, Jhemar, continued her washing calmly enough, ignoring my stares. But the men, of course, began to laugh and tease me, saying, 'What? A big boy like you? Have you never seen a naked woman before?'

"In my confusion I stammered, 'Yes ... no ... but...' as I blushed hotly. They, of course, were all slapping their knees and doubled up with laughter. When I had recovered and was able to talk again, I struggled to explain through their noise, 'It was only my surprise. It was so unexpected. How can one woman travel safe this way with a whole troupe of men?'

"There was a shocked silence when they understood my question. Mackero, the one who seemed to be the leader of this band, said with some dignity, 'I like to think that any woman can travel safe with the Wanderers, that, in fact, we would offer her protection. In that, we have our own code and are not like other men, not like the Ganja. To force love, to take another's will, is that not a form of murder? Now that you have sat by our fires and been one of us for a while, I hope you will remember that, no matter what the temptation to do otherwise. Let me tell you now and clearly, boy, if ever you force a woman against her will, you will not be welcome again in any Wanderer circle anywhere.'

"There were some threatening mumbles of agreement from around the circle. Now I was in total confusion and embarrassment. I could not imagine what to say to all this, except perhaps to jump up and strip off my shirt, which at that moment I was not quite ready to do. Mackero saved me by going on, 'Of course, this woman that you saw tonight is different. This Jhemar has no need of our protection. She has her own. No man can touch her against her will, and woe to him who tries. The more force he attempts, the more will come back at him to his own harm. But understand, boy, that knowledge is not for the world out there, not something to go flapping your lips about in the village pub. If you are to share our fire, you must also abide by our ways and keep our secrets.' He leaned forward to fix me with his eyes, wanting to make sure that, young as I was, I understood the seriousness of all this.

"'Yes, yes, I pledge you my silence,' I said instantly. 'I pledge it with my life, and I will take heed of all that you told me.' In my excitement I could hardly breathe. My heart was beating so fiercely I had to press a hand against my chest. 'She seems to have some magic, this woman. What else can she do?' I asked, trying to still the excitement in my voice.

"'She has a way with creatures better even than the Wanderers. I hear she can call them in her head and that she even converses with them there. I, myself, have seen her draw birds to her shoulder and coax a song from them, but say nothing of this outside our circle, is that clear? There are too many in the world out there who are jealous or vengeful and see evil in everything they cannot understand or control.'

"'Very clear,' I answered, 'and very true.' Now my heart was pounding so loud I thought surely they must all hear it. There was another like me in the world, and I was about to meet with her.

"Meanwhile, this woman named Jhemar had long since done with her washing and already left for bed. It took a while of stumbling among sleeping bodies and being cursed for my clumsiness before I finally found her sleep mat.

"'Jhemar, Jhemar,' I called softly, hoping not to wake the others.

"At last she whispered back angrily, 'Go away, boy. You were rude enough at the fire. They must already have told you it is no use with me. If you keep on this way you will soon wake the whole camp and have them all on your tail. Go away now.'

"'Please, Jhemar, I must speak with you.' I was almost in tears, afraid that I might lose this one chance. 'Please, please.'

"'Very well, then, come sit on my sleep mat, but try no foolishness with me.' Gratefully, I came and settled by her. 'Now, what is so urgent that it must be settled in the middle of the night this way?'

"'I was afraid that by morning you might have gone away. Give me your hand. It is better than words.' Like you, she hesitated, full of suspicion, but I tried to speak in her mind at the same time. She let me take her hand, and I pressed it over my breast.

"'Ah, so you go in disguise, also. But what has that to do with me?'

"'You and I have powers. I think you were born under the Great Star the same as I was.'

"'The Great Star?' She sat up now, fully alert. 'Can you repel harm back to the sender and talk with creatures and lift heavy things as with an extra hand? I thought I even felt something in my head, but I tried hard to shut it out. I had heard there were others like me. You are the first I have met.' She lit a candle to peer at my face, staring a long time into my eyes with that flickering light between us. Suddenly her whole manner changed. 'Well, well, what a wonder. Welcome, stranger who is not really a stranger, who is more family to me than my own family has ever been. Welcome indeed! I am very glad you persisted. Forgive my rudeness. Come share my mat with me so we can talk. We have much to tell each other.' Now she was sharing my excitement as well. I slipped in beside her. We talked all that night till dawn lightened the sky, trading stories and pledging to seek for the others.

"And that is what we did. We followed the rumors and the stories. We found others, many others, some hated, some in hiding, some loved and protected, cherished in their families for being special. And now the edict has been posted and the game has changed." As Pell spoke these last words the sky was indeed turning bright with the dawn, as if it were her story, repeating itself.

I lay for a while in silence, thinking of all she had told me. Then suddenly I burst out, "What are we, Pell? What are we? We have no name. We are nobody's children. Nobody wants us."

"Not so," she answered fiercely. "We are the Star's children. The future wants us." She leaned over to kiss me, and instantly our bodies were tangled with each other. This time, I determined I would be the lover and Pell the loved one. I used all the skill I knew already and all I had learned from her. Though I still felt a little clumsy and rough-handed, still I had the thrill of feeling her rise under my hands and hearing her cry out in pleasure. Before we were done the sun was shining in, touching our faces and flashing on my quick-moving hands.

After that, though there was little enough affection or gentleness between us, we used our bodies often for release from the fears and pains we lived with. Puntyar, Muirlla, whatever names they had, it was better than the loneliness of missing Kara, though of course it could not stop that, it could only dull the ache a little.

 $\mathbf{U}$ p till now Pell had come home alone from her nightly forays. This time she returned early and brought back with her two others, two who formed a strange contrast to each other. One of them was Jhemar, the very same Jhemar of whom Pell had just spoken, standing there in the flesh. A tall, mannish-looking woman with an in-turned countenance, she was so silent at first as to seem almost sullen. There was nothing in her of grace or ease, yet something in her presence inspired instant confidence. Zenoria, on the other hand, was lively and talkative, with a bright, open countenance, as sunny as her companion appeared dour. She was a small, restless woman, very dark-skinned, in size almost like a child, yet her hand in our handclasp was strong as any man's.

They had come with several extra horses. If not for the warning of Pell's owl hoots, I would have been much afraid. In fact, I had already leapt to my feet, dumping my work on the ground. I had been sitting by the fire, altering the last two saddles, feeling very much like the wife left home by the hearth. After our late night, I had slept a good part of the day, waking just as Pell was about to leave. She told me I was not to go out that night, saying that it was too dangerous with so many troops about and that first I needed more experience.

"And how am I to get that experience if you keep me shut up here?" I demanded indignantly. But secretly I was glad. That part of me that fought each time with fear was relieved to sit safe by the hearth. As soon as Pell left, I had set myself to cooking a big pot of soup out of whatever I could find at hand, hoping in that way to make myself useful. 'Grandmother soup' my mother used to call such mixtures. The aroma of that bubbling pot had soon filled the shelter, somehow keeping me company there in Pell's absence.

Now the other three had come to join me by the fire, or rather Pell and Jhemar joined me, drinking bowl after bowl of my soup. They were dipping in chunks of bread that Pell cut off with her knife. "Not stolen," she said with a grin as she reached out to offer me a piece speared on the blade. "Baked by a friend." It tasted like my mother's bread and so was both sweet and bitter in my mouth.

Jhemar looked up from her bowl and gave me a nod. "Good soup, almost as good as the Wanderers make." I understood from her tone that this must be the highest praise.

Zenoria ate with us in spurts, but when her energy or excitement grew too much to contain, she would jump up and pace about, sometimes going up and down the whole length of the shelter. At some moment she spun on her heel and came toward us, gesturing with both hands. "Do you know what the talk is in the taverns now? I have heard, not once but several times, that all the Zarns have issued a death edict on us. Not just the Zarn of Eezore, but all four of them, even the Zarn of Mecktash. It must be the first time in a thousand years all four Zarns have agreed on anything."

"And there must have been a good deal of bargaining back and forth between them to get to that," Jhemar added. "Maybe even some marriages made on it."

"All of them, eh?" Pell was nodding. "So, we are really something to be afraid of. Perhaps they know more of us than we know of ourselves. I would have given some good gold coins to have been a fly on the ceiling at those meetings and know what they say of us. It would certainly help us with our plans and our strategy." As she said this, she set down her bowl and jumped up. "Here, let us map out together what places we have already covered between us." With stick in hand, she began drawing one of her endless maps in the dirt as they talked. It was so long that she had to keep clearing new places to extend it this way and that.

"This whole countryside is crawling with guards," Jhemar said. "They are everywhere. It is hard to ride on any roads without crossing paths with them sooner or later, even on little-used farm tracks." She took the stick from Pell's hand and began making marks of her own. "We have seen them here and here and here, and a large contingent of them is camped here by the river, fifty or more, I would say. I think it is a base of sorts."

Pell took up another stick. "Tazzi saw them all through here when she rode back from Gaitherill last night. I have seen them in these places as well," she added, pointing. "They want this quickly done. They must be much afraid to think they need to send out such an army after a pack of young women, hardly out of wet-pants. Mark on there where you have already ridden with warnings." They went on for a while in this way, marking and talking, while I sat forgotten, drinking my tea and watching them. At last Pell stood up to ease her back. "The game changes, the wheel rolls faster and faster. With so many of us shaken loose we will soon need a better place to gather. Not here. There is not the room. Besides, I think the Twisted Forest grows more quarrelsome and recalcitrant with each new day, trying to block out intruders." They went on then to talk of possible places, none of which, for one reason or another, seemed to satisfy them. After a while Pell and Zenoria fell to trading stories, from which I gathered they also had known each other for some time. Jhemar sat silent and watchful, and I began to doze.

In the morning Zenoria was gone. She had ridden off on some mission of her own, having first taken the extra horses to hide with the others in the high meadow. Jhemar, however, was still there. Later, it seemed, she and Pell were planning to ride out together. Already they were bending over the dirt-drawn map. I had awakened hearing Pell say, "...fire." And Jhemar replying, "...need a healer."

Pell, sensing me awake, gave a nod in my direction. "Tazzi says she is a healer. She has even brought her healer's pouch with her."

"But is she some half-trained village Witch or a true healer? This will not be easy, and there will be more and more of it. I wonder if any healer will have the stomach for it in the end."

Stung, I got up and came to stand over them. "Since I was seven I have been the apprentice healer in my village and since ten, the only one. In that time, only twice have I lost a life to anything except extreme old age or violent accident where the Goddess had already set her hand and made her choice."

Jhemar looked up at me. "Well, what do you know of fire and burns?"

"Probably as much as any other healer. Houses and barns burn down in my village just as they do elsewhere. People are trapped or are burned escaping. I have done good work on burns and with little scarring left to mark the place."

"Good," Pell said, "or certainly the best we have with us at this moment." She bent back to her map. I felt myself dismissed, as if I had been a soldier reporting to his captain, not a woman answering her lover. Forgotten again by those two, I went about getting my breakfast.

Later Pell told me I was to stay at the shelter again come night, but she wanted me to ride to the swamp that day. There I was to gather whatever herbs and roots I might need for burns or infections. "Since there are so many guards about and you ride out in daylight, be very cautious. Try to stay out of sight and watch the trail behind you. I will send you a different way, slightly longer, but it will keep you off the roads altogether. Jhemar and I are going to sleep part of this day. We will need whatever strength we have for the coming night." She gave me careful directions, but again said not one word of where she went or what she did — not even a hug when I left.

Never in my life had I been ordered about by anyone, not even by my father — though he no doubt would have been glad enough to do so. And certainly not by my mother. With my mother, though she loved me much, there was always a tinge of fear and puzzlement in her treatment of me, the sort of wary respect a child sometimes gives to an adult. Pell, of course, had no such fear or respect. She simply put me to use in whatever way she felt was best. In spite of my moments of resentment, I was growing accustomed to her ways. I knew there was no unkindness meant, no intention to hurt under the brusqueness of her manner. She had far more knowledge of this dangerous game I was so new to. I had begun to think it easier to do as she said than risk having her ask me again, "Have you a better plan, Tazzi?" and finding myself with nothing new to offer.

It was a beautiful day to ride out, full of spring smells. I took no saddle and carried only a small waist pack. In this I stuffed some trail bread and some dried fruit and carried my knife for cutting and for digging. To bring back my harvest, I had two well-crafted saddlebags that lay across the horse's rump and hung down behind my legs.

If not for the Twisted Forest around me I might have enjoyed that ride alone. It was the forest that oppressed me at that moment more than my fear of the guards. This place seemed to grow increasingly malignant with each passing day. It was hard not to feel that this was meant personally for me, and perhaps it was. Still, spring was well on its way. Even in that blighted place, wildflowers and herbs grew in a carpet on the forest floor. Several times I stopped to pick some blue thistle or some perthali and even a little sweet-moss that was so rare in other places. With effort I kept my calm, even when my hair was caught and snagged or my back raked by some bent, clawing branch that seemed to have intention in its reach.

Altogether, I must say, it was a great relief when I noticed the trees begin to straighten to a more normal form and then to thin. Even Marshlegs seemed aware of the difference and went along with a lighter and springier step.

The swamp was much larger than I had realized that first time. It was like a vast, natural storehouse, rich in roots and edible spring greens as well as healing herbs. I gathered and gathered, enjoying the bounty, glad to replenish my store of medications and to be able to contribute some food for our table as well, food that was free and unstolen. I found much amairith there, which is good for burns as well as many other things. I even made a large gathering of diraithia, which I knew would be needed for pain, but found no ghero-root, which is thought to be the best for infection and of which my supply had run low.

In spite of the mud sucking underfoot, I soon found myself charmed by the sun and the soft breeze, the beauty of the flowers, and the sound of the reeds whispering around me. All this combined to fill me with pleasure until suddenly I had a fierce attack of longing for home. It came on me so fast and with such force that I abandoned my gatherings and threw myself down on the bank, sobbing loudly. How many days of my childhood had I spent in just this way, gathering healing herbs in the swamp and then later, riding out on Marshlegs with Kara. Oh, Kara! Kara! I think I lay that way for a long time. Fortunately for all of us it was only the birds and the butterflies who were witness to my folly. Later, as I sat on the bank eating my little meal and sorting my finds, I trembled to think what could have come of my carelessness.

When I returned later in the day, the others were already gone. Seeing that my soup was finished, I built up the fire and set an even bigger pot of soup to cooking with roots, greens, herbs, spices and a good flavoring of wild onions, all from that day's pickings. While that was heating, I prepared some herbs for salves, infusions, compresses, and pain easers. The rest of my gathering I fastened into little bundles and hung up to dry. In that fashion I kept myself busy until dark, feeling deeply comforted by this useful and familiar work.

★

It was not Pell's hoot that woke me this time, but an attack of pain so sharp I cried out, startling myself awake. Frightened, I sat up to listen. The night was dark and silent, the pain gone as quickly as it had come. I was alone in the shelter and could not imagine what had caused this. Then it came again, worse than the first time, so intense that I doubled up with a groan. As soon as the pain freed me, I leapt to my feet. I was terrified that Pell was in some mortal danger or that some fearful weapon was being aimed at the shelter itself. Again there was the silence of deep night. When the third wave of pain came, I was ready for it. I pressed my hands and face against the cool, living rock of the shelter wall and called on everything I had ever learned of shielding against pain. This time when it passed, I heard an owl hoot three times and then the sound of horses' hooves. With a gasp I stumbled to the shelter entrance.

Pell, reeking of smoke and fire, rode right up to it, only stopping a foot or so away. The air around her was thick with the stench of burned flesh. "Help me, Tazzi," she called out in a voice so hoarse and strained I could scarcely recognize it. A body lay across her saddle. It was from there that the waves of pain were coming. I jumped forward to steady the body as Pell dismounted. Then I helped her inside with her burden, lowering it to a mat as gently as possible. Charred clothing came away stuck to my hands and shirt.

"Quickly, quickly," Pell said as we both rushed out to help Jhemar, who had another body across her horse. This one I also helped to carry in, all the while fighting waves of agony, trying to keep myself braced against it so as not to stumble and fall or to cry out or double up with it.

Jhemar kicked the fire so that it flared up and gave us some light. Pell was trying to light the lamp. Her hands shook so that she could not strike the sparkstone. I took it from her and lit the lamp myself. By the light of it I could see her face all twisted with pain. "Filthy pricks," she said through her teeth. "May their flesh rot on their bones for this day's work. How could they do such a thing to another living being?"

I swung the lamp around to look at the two who lay moaning there, then gave a gasp and had to brace myself again. Nothing in my time of being a healer had quite prepared me for this. They seemed almost not human in their burnt rags of clothing; faces incredibly swollen, eyes puffed shut, coughing and gasping for breath, so blackened it was hard to tell what was soot and char and what was flesh. It struck me that this fire was no accident started by a pot of flaming grease or a chimney fire lighting the thatch. This had been done deliberately and by men's hands. Waves of dizziness swept through my body. I bit my own hand till the countering pain of that steadied me.

"Hold the lamp up so I can see," I said urgently. As soon as I could move again, I thrust the lamp into Pell's hands, then rushed to snatch up two cups. Quickly I poured out some of the diraithia from a pot I had set to cooling on the table. Diraithia is the most potent pain easer that I know of, and this batch was especially strong, as I had intended to dilute it.

"Come help me," I said to Jhemar. "We must get each of them to swallow some of this. As soon as it has done its work, then we can begin ours." We all three worked together, Pell holding the light and Jhemar propping up their heads while I tried to get some liquid into their mouths. Even so, it was no easy task. At each touch they groaned and cried out. Pell's hand must have been shaking, for I had to say several times, "Hold the light steady so we can see." All the while, I myself was fighting to keep the pain from tearing me apart. Later I found I had chewed my lip all bloody in this struggle.

Sometimes it seemed altogether hopeless. Almost as much liquid appeared to dribble out again as we attempted to pour in. One woman tried to push away Jhemar's hands with her own blackened ones and had to be restrained. The other, plainly more severely burnt, had hardly any life in her at all and no strength to swallow. Finally I thought we had enough forced down them to be effective. With a groan I leaned against the wall gasping for breath. Pell and Jhemar were both bent over, coughing.

For a moment all our frantic activity was suspended. The rasping breath of the burned ones sounded loud and harsh in that sudden stillness. Then, very soon, the diraithia must have started to bring relief, for suddenly I sensed an easing of the pain and I myself could breathe easier. Freed again to think and move, I became for a time the commander, the one who gave the orders, though it was not till much later that I even gave a thought to that shift.

"More light, we must have more light. Light more lamps, or if there are none, light some candles. Build up the fire, build it up well. Start another fire outside for burning their clothing. Yes, another, do as I say! Get some more water on to boil, the biggest pot you have. Bring me some water here. No, set it right here at hand where I can reach it. We must have clean, undyed cloth, as much as possible, torn in strips. Soak them in that solution of perthali and be ready to lay them on. Bring me the scissors, Pell, but first pass the blades through the fire to clean them. Good, now help Jhemar hold up this one's arms so I can cut away and peel off this charred clothing. Pour on some of that infusion to soften the crusted cloth. More! Quickly! Over here!"

Pieces of skin came away with the clothing. The stench of burning flesh was heavy in the air, thick and sickening. I heard Pell beside me retch and said sharply, "Get yourself under control. Take some deep breaths. We have no time for that now. Here, help me slip her onto another mat. That one is too narrow. Gently, gently, you are far too rough. And take every bit of that clothing outside to burn so it does not fester here. If the smell is too much for you, tie a cloth around your face to cover your nose and mouth."

For most of that night I was the one issuing the commands that we all three struggled to carry out: cutting away burned clothing, mixing medications, laying on new compresses, getting the burned ones to swallow a tea of amairith leaves to lessen the swelling and ease their throats and lungs from the ravages of the smoke, forcing them to drink as much as possible since burns weep and ooze away much of the precious fluid of life.

There was not a moment to stop and rest. I had no thought for the others or how I worked them, only of making the best use of them I could, until Pell began to falter and stumble. Jhemar said with rough kindness, "Let her sleep now. The worst is over. I will help you with the rest." Without a look or a word to either of us, Pell fell flat out on a mat. She was gone from this world between one breath and the next.

For a while there was a sort of exhausted peace in the shelter. Jhemar sat down with a groan against the stone wall, and I sank down next to her. Pell slept like the dead. The burned ones slept also, though fitfully, sometimes moaning and thrashing about. They were still breathing in that thick, raspy way. After a while Jhemar lit a jol pipe, something I had never seen a woman do before. The sweet smell of the jol helped to counter somewhat the stench of burning that permeated the shelter. She smoked with her eyes half closed and after a few puffs offered some to me. I shook my head. I was still struggling with receding waves of pain and afraid that anything might set it off again.

"Sleep, then," she said kindly. "I will watch them and wake you if you are needed."

"I cannot sleep."

"The pain?"

"How did you know?"

"How could I not know? I know the same way I know other things. I can read it painted in the air around you. It radiates out from your whole body in waves of red. You must learn to shield, girl. A healer cannot afford to take in so much pain."

"This is something new in my life, Jhemar. It was not this way when I was a healer in my village. I think what control or barrier I had was torn away by the sudden advent of fear in my life. It is as if some gate has been broken, loosing a flood of feelings. I have no knowledge of how to mend it.

"My skills as a healer are not from long training. Mostly I was self-taught, making my own discoveries of what worked best. Tolgath, the old village Witch, died in my tenth year just as she had begun some serious teaching with me. All I have is child memories or things I have taught myself. This is way beyond my powers. Who can I find to teach me this shielding, for clearly I cannot go on in this way? It will end in either madness or death."

Jhemar was nodding. "All true, all true. A Witch perhaps can help. Certainly none of us — we are all struggling with much the same thing ourselves."

"Us! Us! What is this 'us'? Who are we, Jhemar? *What* are we? Not until a few days ago did I even suspect there were others like me, except for Kara. What does it all mean? Is it a curse or a blessing? Do you feel the pain too?"

"So many questions. Does Pell not talk to you of anything at all?"

"Pell moves too fast. She has little time for talking when there are so many things that need doing."

"Yes, true, as you say, Pell moves fast and talks little." Jhemar took more puffs from her jol pipe and shut her eyes. I thought that was an end to it and leaned back against the wall. Shutting my eyes also, I tried to work on the pain as best I could. It felt as if someone were helping, drawing it out, soothing my nerves so that at last I could breathe easier.

After a while Jhemar gave a deep sigh. She said, as if we had just been speaking, "As to your last question, yes, I feel the pain of others, but not as sharply, I think, as you do. More than pain, what I pick up is the thoughts of others, too much, far, far more than I wish to hear. I suppose that is my special power, that reading of minds. It did not used to be so bad, but now it is getting worse all the time. Curse or blessing, these powers? That is always the question. I suppose this one seems more like a curse at the moment, because I am so at its mercy. That is why I am mostly silent. There is already enough confusion without adding my own voice to the uproar.

"As to what we are, I must have faith in the Goddess that she wants us here. We are some part of her plan and meant to exist no matter what men may think to the contrary. Beyond that, we are women with powers, derived, it seems, from the passing of the Great Star. What those powers are, we are still learning. Different ones of us have them in varying degrees, and they come on us at different ages. Zenoria, for instance, has good mind-touch with animals, the best contact I know of. On the other hand, she has little power for self-defense, whereas I myself am like a fortress. If their thoughts did not beat me down, I could probably stand off a whole troop of guards, so it is good for us to travel together. I worry when she is gone and have to hope that the squirrels and rabbits and her horse will keep her safe.

"As to the rest..." She turned to look me in the eye. "...all great gifts are two-edged swords, Tazzi. Curse or blessing — it depends on what we make of it. I can tell you this, though, we are something new. Even the Witches do not like us much. Whether we wish it so or not, they see us as some sort of challenge to their power. Others may call us Witches, but the Witches themselves know better. We are something different. For most of your questions, even we ourselves have no answers yet. We are living out the answers. That is what shapes our lives."

Jhemar gave a deep sigh, shook out her jol pipe, and leaned back once more. "There, that is more words than I have strung together since I first learned to talk." She fell silent and filled her pipe again. This time when I shut my eyes, sleep came instantly.

8

I woke quivering with pain. Jhemar was shaking me. One of the burned ones was screaming. I knew I had been hearing her in my dreams. Struggling over to her, fighting off my own pain, I gave her a heavy dose of diraithia, heavier than I thought safe. Even so, it took a while to do its work. I gave some to the other one as well, though not near as much. When I thought they could bear our touch, I had Jhemar help me with new dressings for them both, then sent her out to burn the old ones.

That done, they dozed for a while. I must have dozed as well, for I felt Jhemar shaking my shoulder again. "Please, Tazzi, I must have your help. I have done everything I can and nothing suffices."

This time I woke in confusion, not sure what was dream and what was real or how much time had passed. The same burned one was crying out again. Staggering through a nightmare of pain and weariness, I could barely drag myself to her. She was reaching out her hands for me. "Please, please, the pain is too much. Let me go. Set me free. Give me something to end this." The words went round and round in my head. It felt as if I had been hearing them for hours. Time seemed to have curled around and bent in on itself like a coiling snake. By the slant of the light I could see that it was late in the day. I shook my head in bewilderment. How long had this all been happening? Looking around for Pell, I finally found her hunched up in the far corner, her arms around her knees, her eyes hollow and smudged with pain. Clearly, there was no help to be found there.

Jhemar was watching me anxiously. Quickly I asked her, "Has this been going on all day? How did it get to be so late?"

"All day on and off, Tazzi. You have worked with her like one sleepwalking, doing what you could, but I think it only grows worse."

The burned one was looking up at me beseechingly from her swollen, red-rimmed eyes. "Please, please, for mercy's sake, for the Goddess, let me go. Why are you holding me here?" Her cries echoed from the stone wall of the shelter and went through me like knives. Jhemar came forward quickly. I had to lean on her or I would have fallen. I looked to Pell for some answer. For all her seeming toughness and hardness, she could not meet my eyes. When I turned to Jhemar, her eyes also shied away from mine. I was alone with the fearful weight of that decision, my own body so racked with pain I could hardly draw breath, much less think.

When the woman screamed again and then began an awful, wracking cough, it was the other burned one who raised herself slightly and said in a terrible, raw voice, "Look well at her, woman, and answer truthfully. Can you really cure her here, in this place, with what you have to work with? And if not, how long will you deny her release?"

In all that press to heal and save, this was not a question I had dared to ask myself. Now, though my stomach knotted and my teeth clenched, I made myself look. I was looking, not just at what I saw there before me, but at the days to come, days of agony that the diraithia could barely reach, the inevitable infection that would creep and fester everywhere beyond my control and then ... and then what...? She was still reaching for me, still begging with her bandaged hand, but less conscious and coherent. I knew, of course, what the answer was, knew it almost as soon as the question had been asked, and yet it was not easy to say the words. They stuck in my throat, a hard, dry block of pain. At last, in a choked whisper, I answered the second woman, "No, no, not as bad as those burns are. Not here with what I have to work with, nor with what I know or can do. Mother be my witness, I have already tried. If I give her much more for the pain, it means death, not sleep."

The other answered instantly in her harsh voice, "Then do it and stop delaying. For the love of the Goddess, do as she says and let her go so we may all have some peace at last. How often must she ask you? How long can you listen to her suffering and her screams?"

With shaking hands, I took the last of the powdered olinth-root from my pouch. This I added to the diraithia. By itself olinth is a mild sleep inducer, but mixed with diraithia the two together form a potent, deadly drink, though gentle and very quick. One last time I looked at Pell and

Jhemar. I thought I got a slight nod from each of them. With a twig I mixed the brew and saw it darken.

Trembling, I raised the woman's head. "You understand what this will do?" I asked, bending over her. For a moment she seemed too far away to comprehend. Then I saw her come back to herself by an act of will.

"Yes," she whispered hoarsely. She was fully alert for that moment, though I sensed the terrible effort it cost her. "Yes, do it, please!" She gripped my wrist with her charred hand. The strength in her fingers amazed me. Her eyes looked straight into mine as she drank. Shaking and sick inside, I kept my hand as steady as I could. I wanted to look away from her stare, but felt I owed her my eyes if that was what she needed. That might be the last thing she ever saw on this earth. When she had drunk this lethal brew to the bottom, she whispered, "Thank you for your kindness." Then she released my wrist and shut her swollen eyes. I eased her down.

She was going to die, now, right before me. It was not the first death I had witnessed, but surely the first I had caused. "Your name?" I whispered to her with sudden urgency. "What is your name?" Already she was slipping past me, though I could still hear her harsh, shallow breathing. "Jhemar, we have no name for her, no name to bury her with." I sat staring at the nameless one as if trying to call her back for one last word.

Pell and the other burned one had both fallen asleep again. Jhemar sat down opposite me. "No matter," she said softly. "Leave her be now. At least she will die among her own. At least we can give her that." We sat on either side of her, each with a hand on the body that no longer brought her pain and so did not mind the weight of a hand. We sat there silent until her breathing slowed and then finally stopped. Her body gave a last shudder. After a while I felt for her pulse and then bent to listen for her heart. I shook my head. Jhemar nodded. Neither of us spoke. We went on sitting as the day darkened. For a long time the only sound in the shelter was of our own breathing, until at last, out of that silence, Jhemar said, almost in a whisper, "You did all that you could." As if suddenly freed to cry, the tears began to roll down my face. Still, I did not move from there.

When she woke, Pell lit the lamps and came to feel for heart and pulse as I had done. After a moment or so she straightened and shook her head. "Gone, then. Well, I suppose it is better so. At least her suffering is over. We must bury her tonight." Though her eyes glistened, she did not shed a single tear. Instead, her face turned stony hard. "We must bury her quickly and well, bury her where neither man nor beast will find her."

"But, Pell," I said despairingly, "we do not even have a name to bury her with." I spoke as if all my grief could be compressed into that one small fact.

Pell shrugged. "Where she goes now she does not care if we name her or not. All that is show for the living, illusion to comfort us. For her it matters only that her pain has ended, not what name we use or what words we say over her body. For us it matters that we do this right. If men find her body, they will know she did not come here unaided and will set out to look for others. If animals find her, they will eat her and her bones will point the way to our shelter like so many arrows."

I shuddered. "Stop, Pell! Enough!" Jhemar pulled the cover over the dead one's face. The woman's silence was very loud between us in the shelter. I shook my head and said in a whisper, "How could one human being do this to another? I did not think such things existed."

"You will probably see worse," Pell answered harshly. "I have been gone from my father's house for almost five turns of the seasons and nothing surprises me any more. I think men are capable of anything."

Jhemar turned toward her. "Where can we do this? We do not have the time to dig a deep enough grave."

"Nor the tools. And the ground is hard and very rocky here, as I know well from digging that blessed pit." Pell stood for a while in thought, then said in a flat, controlled voice that had no trace of grief in it, "The deep part of the ravine. It is close enough, and we can fill it with rocks. It can all be done from above."

Jhemar shook her head. "Close, yes, but too rocky and steep for horses."

"All the better. It means none will go there by chance. With three we can carry her. We will manage, as we must."

The moon had not yet risen and the night was dark, but Pell seemed to know her way. Jhemar went next. I had only to follow after, setting one foot before the other and trying to keep step with them. We had wrapped her body in an old gray blanket Pell found in the bottom of one of her boxes. She had tied it securely for safe carrying, running a pole through the ropes for handholds. Even so it was slow going, struggling with that weight between us in the darkness. The way was narrow and the footing rocky and uneven, more like steep natural stone steps than like a path. It was hard not to stumble. Once my foot slipped, and I heard a scatter of gravel that seemed to go on forever.

"Take care," Pell said sharply. "We are climbing a high ridge. It would not do to fall into that ravine ourselves."

Soon my eyes became adjusted to the night. What I saw did nothing to dispel my fears. We were going up a thin spine, and there seemed a pit of endless darkness on either side. Several times we had to stop to set our burden down so we could catch our breath and ease our backs and arms. At least, I thought as we crept along, there are no trees here to claw at us and snag us in the dark. When the way began to flatten out, Pell said in a flat, practical voice, "Well, that should be far enough. I think there is an almost straight cliff below us here with little to catch on."

Jhemar wanted to say the Koormir words for burial before we pushed her body over. Pell said abruptly, "It is too dangerous out here. We must do this quickly. Whatever words need to be said can be said back at the shelter. If you believe in the Goddess, then you believe she is everywhere and will take her daughter home, with or without our words. Now, we must push the body far out so it does not snag on the rocks partway down."

Pell took her sparkstone from her belt pouch and lit a candle. That small light only made the darkness vaster. When she held it out, it was lost well before it reached the depths of the ravine.

"We need a torch," Jhemar said and quickly began gathering bunches of dried grass. She bound these to the end of the pole we had used for carrying. Pell lit the grass bundle with her candle, making a torch. Jhemar crammed it upright between some rocks, and suddenly light flared all around us.

"Now we must do this quickly," Pell said. We lifted the body, counted together to three, and at Pell's signal we pitched our terrible burden out into the darkness. There was a moment of silence, then a dreadful, heavy thud and the rattle of rocks. Pell held up the torch and leaned far out to look. "Good, to the very bottom. Now for rocks to cover. If I set the torch here, we can see." She forced the end of the torch into a rock crevice so that it cast its flickering light far down into the ravine. There, at the bottom, lay a gray bundle. After the first few rocks I turned away, retching. Later, when all was done, I had to be guided back. The sound of those rocks striking had been more than I could stomach.

When we returned, the other burned one was very much awake, more alert than I had seen her before. She had propped herself up slightly against some cushions and looked at us accusingly as we came through the entryway. "I thought you had left me to die here alone."

"Not so," Jhemar said quickly. "The other burned one died this evening. We have been to bury her, but we had no name for her, no name to send her home with."

"I could have told you her name, as we were from the same village. It was Shaleethia. Mine is Maireth, if you want to know. You will not have to bury me nameless if that time comes, but I think you will not have to bury me at all. I think I will live in spite of what they did." Her voice was harsh with anger and still raw from the smoke. Suddenly her body tensed, and her face grimaced uncontrollably with pain. Quickly I brought her a dose of diraithia and steadied the cup for her to drink. When she could speak again, she said bitterly, "Perhaps she was the lucky one after all. Perhaps that was the better way to go." I felt the effort it cost her to speak at all.

With a groan of weariness, Pell sank down on the pile of mats to pull off her boots. "Well, Maireth, you are under no obligation to live, but if you plan to die, please do it far from here and make your own burial. One body is enough to deal with this night."

I sucked in my breath and even Jhemar looked shocked, but I saw a strange, twisted smile pass across Maireth's face, or perhaps it was only a grimace of pain. "Pell, why must you always be so hard?" I asked her angrily.

"You think me hard? Let me tell you, girl, this is only the beginning. If you have no stomach for this, you will be no use at all for what is yet to come. In the long run you will see that my hardness is my greatest kindness. Now, Maireth, since you can speak again, tell us what happened to you both."

"No!" I jumped in front of Pell. "You will not make her talk. I forbid it. She is not ready for such an effort. It would endanger her healing."

"But she was talking on her own. It seemed little harm to ask a few questions."

"And then a few more and a few more. Soon you would have her on her feet pointing to places on the map. No, leave off, let her be. Do you just want the glory of rescuing them? Is that what matters to you, or do you want to see them live and recover? You told me to be a healer here. That is what I am doing, to the best of my ability. In this, I am the one with the experience and you must do as I say. If not, I leave her in your hands. You can begin right now by changing her dressings."

"But there are things we need to know."

"Yes, soon enough! Later! For now I forbid any more of this. Even this quarrel does her harm. Do as I say now or ask nothing else of me."

Calmly, Jhemar stepped between us. "You have each had your turn to give commands, now it is mine. Tazzi, go and sit down before you fall. I have no wish to start caring for you next." She gave me a firm but gentle push toward the mats. As Pell started to speak, she raised her hand. "No, Pell, not one more word. You both will be silent now and respectful of one another. Leave Maireth in peace while I heat up the soup. Then you will eat. We are all exhausted beyond reason. It is crucial that we have some food, especially Maireth and Tazzi. Healing drains the body, whether we are trying to heal our own or helping heal another."

I sat with my eyes closed and my head hanging down between my shoulders. The small, homey sounds of pot and fire were so comforting that I was starting to doze when, out of the silence, Maireth said, "All my life some have been jealous of my powers and given me grief for them, but never did I dream they would try to burn me alive for what I know." The terrible bitterness of her words cut into me like a knife. No more able to shield myself from that bitterness than I had been able to close out her pain, I gathered it up, storing it in my heart, adding it to what was already there.

Later, after we had eaten and I lay waiting for sleep, I heard Jhemar saying the words for the dead in Shaleethia's name. She had built up the outside fire and stood in front of it, a dark figure outlined by flames, intoning the death-chant with her arms raised.

9

Seven days had passed since Renaise had ridden home to warn others. Pell was sleeping late after our terrible night, the first time I had ever known her to do so. Jhemar had left with the dawn to rejoin Zenoria, and I had been up early attending to Maireth's burns. Now she too was sleeping, the most peaceful I had seen her. I was moving about slowly, stirring a pot of mush for our breakfast, when Pell leaned up on her elbow and said, "We go to the market today to see what we can find. Tonight we go to meet with Renaise."

By "find at the market," I knew she meant steal. The thought of going back to Hamishair, especially on such a risky project, made me sick with fear. "There is no need for that, Pell," I said quickly. "I have coins enough for anything you want."

"Save those coins carefully, Tazzi. They may mean our supplies this winter, sooner, perhaps. In fact, they may mean our lives, but we have to use them with care. Right now is not the time to flash Shokarn gold in the market. It would draw more notice than is safe and raise questions that I, for one, have no wish to answer. For bargaining and causing a distraction, take only those small coins you were given in change at the tavern." Pell climbed out of her bedroll and came over to sit by the fire. She served herself a bowl of gruel and began eating with good appetite while I looked at her in amazement.

"Pell, a woman died here last night, died in our hands, and we buried her nameless in a terrible way. No matter — you wake today bright as can be and ready to go off and steal at the market. I cannot understand you."

"You can, but you choose not to." She set her bowl down hard and took my wrists in a firm grip, forcing me to look at her. "What would you have me do, then? Scream? Beat my head bloody against this rock wall? Would that help her now? Would that bring her back to life? More important, would that help others not to be trapped as she was? I cannot relive yesterday. All I can do is my best for this day, and for each day as it comes. They want to kill us all, every one of us. I will do whatever I can to stop them, whatever is in my power for you or Maireth or any of us still living, but those who die are beyond my reach. At that door I stop and let them go, else I am no use here. You must learn to do the same. Otherwise you will die of grief and bitterness and so do the Zarn's work for him. Already I see those things eating at you." She released me then. "You have made us a fine gruel. Now, let us eat it in peace. In this game the next meal is never certain."

"I wish Jhemar were still here," I said stubbornly. "She could have gone to the market with you, and I could have stayed home caring for Maireth."

Pell gave a quick, harsh bark of a laugh. "Not Jhemar, surely. Anyone but Jhemar. With her reading of minds she is no use at all in the market. A market or any such public place would drive her mad in minutes. Now speak no more of this and eat your gruel. Remember, she said you needed your food."

With a sigh I surrendered again to Pell's will. We ate in silence for a while till she set down her bowl and poured us both some tea. "The market comes only once a week to Hamishair," she said, trying to persuade now that she had bullied me. "I seldom have the chance of such a good accomplice. I hope Shaleethia can forgive me for going the day after her death, but otherwise we wait another seven days. Who knows what that will bring or where we will be by then. For one thing, long before next market, we will be out of undyed cloth, very soon, in fact. I have no more hidden away here. And we need fresh food for Maireth if she is to get well. Besides, we may soon have other women here with us, many perhaps, many who will need what the market can supply."

"But how can I help you, Pell? I cannot lie without turning red and scrambling my words. As to stealing, I would probably fumble and drop everything right there before the market booth." I had been tormented with worry on this all the while we ate.

"Just so, you will be the decoy and a good one, or as they say among thieves, you will be the 'show' and I the 'hands.' All eyes will be on your fumbling. Do it well. Make sure you only arouse suspicion. Do not feed it enough for them to try to search you."

"Pell, did you learn all this alone, or were you taught to be a thief?"

She gave me a strange, sideways look. "Oh, at first it was just as I told you, I learned on my own, simply to live, to put food in my mouth. Then I was noticed in the market by one from the Thieves Guild. When he put his hand on my shoulder, I was sure he was a market spotter and was going to denounce me. I would have had to flee with the whole market on my tail, not a test of my powers I wished to make. Instead, he drew me aside and made me an offer I could not afford to refuse. More of that later. I will only say now that my debt there has long been settled."

"Does it not harm your powers to use them in this way?"

"Misuse them, I think you mean. Probably — though so far I have not felt it. I am very careful. I never steal anything for my own pleasure or amusement. I take only what I think we will need to live, never from those who befriend me and never much from any one place, nor do I steal from those in need. Sometimes I even leave them a little if I can.

"It is my skill, my gift — how can I not use it for us? You have your healing, and Zenoria her way with animals, and Jhemar her great strength and her reading of minds. I have this skill with my hands and my wits."

"But you are proud of it."

"Well, and should I be ashamed? Would that make it better? More honorable? Besides, this is what I have been given. Someone needs to do it for us. No, I will not be ashamed of what I have learned to do well, though I tell you truthfully, Tazzi, I will be glad when this is over and I can make my own honest living with my own two hands."

"You think this will really be over?"

"I must think it. That is the only way I can go on living." She set down her cup and stood up to go.

★

Now, at Pell's insistence, we were headed back to Hamishair, riding those roads again through a market crowd. Maireth had asked to be propped up against some pillows to watch our preparations. She had even made some comments on our appearance. Pell had me dressed in my usual farm-boy disguise. For herself, she had selected what she called her 'market coat.' It was a loose, roomy overcoat with layers of inner pockets for storage, yet giving the appearance of a very ordinary garment, such a coat as a portly man might wear. She lightened her face with powder, added a cap with side whiskers attached, brushed up and lightened her eyebrows. In the end, her own thin face took on the appearance of being thick, jowly, and of middle years. Finally she stood before us, just such a man as one sees at any market, the kind of man who would be buying a cart or an extra horse or looking over the tack.

When I had changed Maireth's dressing for the last time and laid her back down again, she took hold of my hand. "Promise you will come back, Tazzi. In the name of the Goddess, promise you will not leave me here to rot."

"I promise, Maireth, I promise I will come back." I was shaking. Who could say what would happen there? How could I promise her anything at all? Surely she must see my doubts.

"Bring me some fruit from the market if you can. I think it would help carry me back to life to taste some fresh fruit again."

"I will bring you some peaches," I assured her, hoping this was not a rash pledge. Truth be told, I would far rather have stayed there nursing her than to be riding back into that town again.

As it was, I tried to leave everything she needed within easy reach and gave her a last drink of amairith before we left.

"Remember," Pell told me as we set out, "do not panic and run. That is a good way to lose your power. Run only when it is necessary and you have chosen to do so. Keep your head clear. Watch everything all the time. Never become so engrossed that you neglect what is happening around you and especially behind you. And always keep in mind-touch with me. We do this quickly, no more than an hour or so in and out. Whatever we have not found by then can wait till next time."

As we came closer to town we rode apart, merely strangers going in the same direction. This proved no problem, since soon there was a whole throng headed for market. No one gave us more than a glance. Though we did not speak nor look at each other, I could feel the mind connection between us as strong as braided cord. As you can well imagine, for that whole ride I had been dreading the sight of the tavern. I thought to see it standing scorched and gutted on the corner. Instead, as we approached I saw it to be sound and whole, though apparently deserted. The windows were boarded up. No one went in or out or even lounged in front of it. Some of the tied ends of reins still flapped on the pole where Pell had cut them. I wondered where Renaise's uncle was hiding or if he still lived.

The market was large and noisy. It overflowed the market square on all sides and looked to have been in progress for some time. Even without

Jhemar's unshielded openness to minds, I found it bewildering. Uncertain, I wandered from booth to booth, trying to get the feel of the things and always very conscious of Pell over my shoulder. I knew I must begin somewhere and soon, but fear held me back.

I might have gone on in this way for a long while if the smell of a fish stand had not suddenly caught my attention. There were several large fish on display. Inspired, I lifted one, brought it near my nose, and gave a snort of disgust. "Pha! You call that fresh? I would not feed that to my dogs. I could catch fresher fish in the sewer that runs through my village." I stepped back quickly seeing I had overplayed my hand, for the fishman gave a roar of rage. He seemed about to leap over his stand and lunge for my throat.

Quickly I threw up my hands. "Only jesting, only jesting, Goodman. My apologies. My grandmother used to beat me often for the same sort of wit."

"Wit!" exclaimed the man next to me. "Witlessness, more likely. Never mind, Oranth, he is nothing but a farm dolt. What does he know of fish? He likely cannot tell the difference between fresh fish and pig dung. The smell is probably on his own hands."

"A thousand pardons, Goodman, I have the devil in me that will come out at the worst of times. Now these I know to be fresh," I said, turning to the girl next to me who carried a basket of peaches. I selected four and bargained loudly for them. Then, putting the other three in my pack, I took the choicest one and laid it down on the fishseller's counter, saying with a nod and a grin, "That is to sweeten your day, sir."

Next, I turned my attention to the eggseller. Taking three eggs from her basket, I said, "My old grandfather taught me this trick." With that I made a clumsy try at juggling. Instantly the eggs fell to the cobbles with a loud crack, splattering the nearest shoppers. I was quick to pay for them, bowing and apologizing several times to all those I had offended.

Now I had what I needed. A small crowd had gathered around me. They pronounced me the greatest dunce they had ever seen, calling others to witness my folly. People were turning to look. I tried to keep touch with Pell and hoped her work was going as well. With all eyes upon me I backed away, still apologizing, and bumped into a pottery stand. This set all the pots to rattling. One dislodged itself from the corner. With a quick turn I was able to retrieve it before it hit the ground. The red-haired Potter, a large, burly man, had jumped up from his seat and was staring angrily at me. He slammed down his hands on each side of the table to steady it.

"Sorry, so sorry," I mumbled hastily. I had no wish to mix with this man who reminded me so much of Kara's father, and also no wish to pay for anything else we could not use.

In this way I went through the market, moving from one small disaster to the next. I tried to keep my eye on Pell, though I dared not look at her directly. In my quick glances she appeared more portly each time I saw her. Once, she was standing before a fruit stand, munching an apple. Another time she was in earnest discussion with three or four other stout gentlemen who were similarly dressed. I was not sure if I had glimpsed a gathering of gentleman farmers or successful thieves.

I actually bought some foodstuff that was needed and made a clumsy attempt to pilfer more. My fumbling attracted a market spotter who approached and demanded that I turn out the contents of my pack. It was, of course, all honestly come by. He gave a snort of disgust. "Put it all back now and just remember we have our eyes on you."

"Yes, sir, thank you, sir." I scuttled away, but not so fast they would lose sight of me. In this manner I fumbled up and down the aisles, playing my part. In spite of the danger, I was beginning to enjoy this little game. I thought I was even acquiring some skill at it, I, Tazzia, who had been so painfully honest all my life. Having a price on one's head changes many things.

Finally, when I thought enough time had passed, I began heading for a way out, trusting that Pell was with me. The last booth at the far edge of the market had an array of trinkets and baubles. I saw nothing of interest there, but the old woman sitting at it looked as if she might be easily fuddled. I hoped that Pell was nearly finished. For myself, I was worn out with this act and wished to be done. Also, I was worried for Maireth and wanted to be safely headed home with her peaches. Why I even stopped at that booth I could not say, except that I had been drawn there. These were certainly not things I fancied, but I pretended to be much taken with a necklace of blue beads. I even started to turn away, as if to slip it into my vest.

The old woman had been staring off into space. She seemed only partly in possession of her wits, but before I could complete my turn she reached out and gripped my wrist. Her hand had such surprising force that I dropped the necklace back in its place. Then she pulled me toward her and leaned across the table to whisper in my ear with a fierce hiss, "Well, girl, you are not nearly as clever as you think, you and your friend over there. I have been watching you for some time now and trying to draw you here." I twisted in her grip, terrified at being held against my will. Clearly, she had seen past my disguise. The market spotter moved toward us, but she waved him away with her other hand.

"Do not struggle so, Little One. It draws attention, and we need to talk. I am not what I appear to be any more than you are, and have no intention of giving you away. In fact, I wish you no harm at all and perhaps much good. Both of you are in need of help and guidance." I could sense Pell watching this scene, but keeping her distance. The old woman went on with her harsh whisper, "Bargain loudly with me for these beads while your friend finishes her business here, then go separately to the quillof stand, for it is the closest one to the woods. Buy yourself a mug of quillof, but do not drink much of it. You are already two young fools. I do not wish to deal with two young fools who are also sotted. Meanwhile, I will close up my business here, such as it is. When I pass the booth, you will follow me into the woods. Keep separate from each other and not too close to me. Hopefully, if any notice you following, they will think you go to rob a helpless old fool and not concern themselves too much. When we are well into the woods, you will follow closely. I have secret paths and am quick about it. Once at my hut we can talk freely, but not before."

With those words she released my wrist. I stepped back and rubbed it while I watched her, ready for any sudden move. I had only that moment and no more to decide whether or not to trust her. Much in our lives and safety might hang on my choice. I tried to enter her mind, but darkness blocked my way, a strong, skilled shield. Then curiosity added itself to the scale. How, and by what force had she drawn me to her and held my wrist? How had she seen through our disguise? Why did she keep her silence? There was something here worth exploring. With a quick glance I touched my eyes to hers and gave her the slightest nod. Then I picked up the necklace again. She gave me a slight nod in return and told me an outrageous price for the beads.

I drew back as if in surprise and said loudly, "What!? For this trash! They are glass, most likely, not even real stones and poorly crafted at that. I have far better at home. It is only that the light on their color caught my eye. I thought to have them for my little sister, but not for that much money, old woman."

"Go away," she screeched at me. "Would you cheat an old woman of the food to her mouth, you worthless scum? Glass, are they?! These are the last of my family's treasure. You would have me give them away and starve, eh? Put them back, then, if you cannot pay a decent price. I can

see by your clothes that you do not have the money. Put them back, I say!"
By now we had all eyes on us. Many were jesting and jeering and urging
on one or the other of us. All this time, I sensed Pell going on about her
work and thought her coat must be full as a store.

At last we settled on a price. I put the beads in my pack, pushed
through the crowd, and sauntered off to the quillof booth as if quite
pleased with myself. There I ordered a mug of quillof, though I had no
taste for such stuff. Behind me I heard the woman muttering and com-
plaining loudly to all who would listen. Pell came soon afterward, but did
not speak to me or take any notice in my direction. Instead, she struck up
some talk with a group of men from the market. This talk, directed by Pell,
soon turned to the strange fire at the tavern and the mysterious disap-
pearance of the owner and his star-brat niece, as well as two strangers and
quite a large number of horses. Those men had several interesting ex-
planations for all this. Some arguments even broke out on the matter.
While I listened to this talk, I rubbed my wrist. It still hurt where the old
woman had gripped me.

Soon afterward the old woman herself passed by us, trundling all her
belongings in a small cart. Secretly I gave most of my quillof to a thirsty
plant that grew next to the booth. Then I raised my mug, pretended to
drain it to the bottom, and set it back on the counter, all a waste of our
good coins. I was hoping somehow to get back the money for the beads,
as surely I had no use for them.

It was hard to keep the woman in sight. She certainly moved fast for
one so old and encumbered. I had mounted quickly and ridden off. Soon
I could sense Pell riding behind me. I knew she was trying to draw me
back, pulling at my mind, but I was set on a course I could not alter. The
way branched several times. Soon I was hopelessly turned around. Not
even for my life could I have found my way back. I hoped Pell was not
so easily lost. This road or path was narrow and even more twisted and
overgrown than the one to Pell's shelter. After a short way I was forced to
dismount or be swept off the horse by branches. Several times I lost sight
of the old woman in the tangle ahead. Just as I was sure we had been
abandoned in that strange forest, I would catch one more glimpse of her
back.

After a while the nature of the forest began to change. The trees grew
larger and there was less underbrush to bar the way. When I was able to
mount again, Pell rode up next to me and said with barely restrained fury,
"What is this madness, Tazzi? All this way I have been calling you to halt.

You never even turned to look at me. You just went on following that old hag as if your life depended on it. Have you lost your senses? Are you bewitched?"

"Pell, up till now I have followed you everywhere. I have done all that you said. Now, for a change, I am asking you to come with me. But let me tell you clearly, I go to meet with that one, whether or not you choose to come. This is something I must do for myself. Listen, she knew who we were and did not betray us. I believe she is a Witch. There are things I need help with where you are no use at all. She may be that help for me." So strong was the pull that I said all this without stopping or even slowing much.

"She is indeed a Witch," Pell shouted after me. "I have no doubt of that. And she has laid a compulsion on you. Witches have no liking for our kind. We may be riding right into some sort of trap. Why should we trust her?"

"I trust her as I trusted you that night in spite of my fear, and for no other reason but what I feel. Go back if you do not wish to be here. I can go on alone." It was amazing that I was talking so to Pell, but at the moment I hardly noticed it.

She rushed to catch up again and laid a hand on my arm to stop me. "By the Goddess, Tazzi, you certainly are like one bewitched. No, I will not let you go into this alone. Two are better than one, and I can more easily resist her charms."

"Please yourself," I answered. "Come if you wish, but do not try to stop me." Feeling so strongly pulled, perhaps I was really charmed as Pell had said, but I had no intention of turning back now, not after having come so far and certainly not for prudence. "Now see what has happened with all our talk, we have lost her again." With no more words, I rode on. Witch and wagon had vanished while we argued. I threw an angry look back at Pell and was met by her sullen glare.

Soon we came to the edge of a large clearing, ringed by a circle of the tallest trees I had ever seen. From beyond it I could hear the sound of running water though I could not see its source, and right at its center was something that appeared to be a shelter or, if looked at in another way, was only a thicket or perhaps some confusion in the natural order of things. I was sure we had lost the Witch until by circling this 'thicket' I saw her wagon. It lay hastily concealed, tucked under some bushes. Pell sat on her horse, her face full of mistrust, but I dismounted. By the end of my second circling around I understood that this strange growth in the center of the clearing was a ring of very large stumps. They had been haphazardly roofed over and were surrounded by a thick growth of brush, ivy, and thornbushes. It was then that I noticed a thin wisp of smoke rising from somewhere in the strangeness. Whichever way I looked, however, I could see no door or entryway till a dark-haired woman stuck her head out through the tangle. She beckoned us in. After some groping about in her direction, I found the way. I had to push aside ivy with both hands in order to duck in through a low archway made of twisted branches. Pell came in after me. She stood staring about suspiciously, as if ready to back out again at any moment.

Somewhat fearful myself now, I looked around. The house — if indeed such a thing could be called a house — was in no way reassuring. In my little village of Nemanthi most houses were one or two rooms, often with a blanket hung between for privacy, and sometimes a loft above. All was easily seen; there were no dark, hidden corners. This one was all hidden corners and darkness, and nothing was easy to see. The huge stumps jutted out into the central space, some appearing to be used for storage and some for rooms. The spaces around them and behind them were full of dark places. There was scant light from outside. What little came through had a strange, greenish cast from the leaves. Light from a single lamp threw twisted shadows about in that uncertain space or suddenly flared up, catching some odd detail so that it leapt forward with startling effect. Now I, too, was full of uneasiness. Remembering Pell's warnings, I thought perhaps I had led us right into a trap with my willful haste.

"Where is the Witch?" I asked the dark-haired woman. I could see no one else there. Of course, someone could easily have been hiding in one of the dark corners or one of the stump chambers that spread in all directions.

"What Witch? As you can plainly see, there is no Witch here. Have you lost your way? You should be more careful in these woods. They are not kind to strangers." The woman had come to stand before us. Her long black hair, streaked with silver, stood out around her face. When she shook her head it appeared to have some life of its own, like a tangle of snakes. Her face, though deeply lined, had a sort of agelessness about it and seemed to shift and alter in that flickering light. "There are many Witches in this world, none of them easy to find. What is her name, girl? Why are you looking for her here?" Her words, and in fact her whole manner, seemed full of challenge and mockery.

"She never said her name. She only said we needed to talk. We followed her through the forest to this place. I know her wagon to be hidden in the bushes outside."

"There is no wagon here that I know of. I think you were careless and did not pay attention to the way."

I could feel Pell's anger rising. She stepped in front of me and said, loudly enough for anyone to hear, "Enough of these games, woman! Where is the Witch? Let her show herself if she wants to speak with us, otherwise we leave. Personally I have no wish to be here at all and no desire to speak to her. I came only because of that one's foolishness." Pell turned and pointed disdainfully at me.

At that moment, I happened to glance at the hearth and saw on a bench beside it a patterned kerchief with wisps of white hair attached, as well as a ragged shawl and a cane. I poked Pell and nodded in that direction. "Perhaps we have not lost her after all," I said boldly.

"How observant of you." The woman laughed and bowed. "Ah, yes, welcome to my home. I do not have many visitors here, and so you must excuse my poor manners." Then, looking directly at Pell, she added, "And, yes, I am indeed a Witch. What else would I be? Surely not the witless old hag you saw at the market. And you, young woman, are both rude and not so good a thief as you think yourself to be, not if these old eyes can spot you so easily."

Pell shrugged. "Perhaps those old eyes are sharper than they seem to be or not so old after all."

"Perhaps so. Well, now that you have found me out, sit down and make yourselves comfortable. Let me pour you some tea." She was suddenly as full of good humor and bustle as any ordinary housewife.

While she went to poke at the fire, I sank gratefully onto a pile of cushions by the hearth. Pell continued to stand, with a frown on her face that drew her brows together in a single dark line. After a few minutes she began to pace about, saying, "What do you want of us, woman? Why did you bring us here?"

"You think I want something of you, eh? Perhaps I have something to offer you, instead." The Witch paused as if considering this, then nodded. "Yes, I want something, but not in the way you might think. I want to know what you are, and what you will become. I want to understand this new thing. The passing of the Great Star was the end of the Witch-kills. In a way it was also an end to Witches, or at least to Witch power. I think it was the closing of an old time and the beginning of a new one. What that means or what it will bring I cannot see, however much I try to look into the future. I have heard rumors for a long time of some new power in the land. Now, suddenly, edicts spring up like mushrooms on every tree. Reading them, I thought to myself, they must be something to see, these young women, if from this far away they can disturb the Zarns in their cities. Yes, I have heard rumors, but you are the first such creatures I have ever met. I want to talk with you. Also, I want to help you if I can."

"Indeed? Well, that little game of yours was a fine beginning. Why should we trust you? What help can you be to us?" Pell spoke sharply, as suspicious now as I had been with her.

"In a world where so many hands are raised against you it is good to have some friends, star-brat, especially some with power. Also, we Witches are no friends to Zarns for what they have done to us."

"I see little power here, Witch, and I want you to understand, we are not your weapons against the Zarns."

"My poor, foolish girl, whether you like it or not, your very existence is a weapon against the Zarns. Why do you think they wish to kill you?"

"Witch, what is your name?" I was growing tired of this exchange. My neck hurt from looking back and forth between them.

"Alyeeta is how I am called."

"Well, Alyeeta, my name is Tazzi and that is Pell." With those words I took off my brother's cap and laid it on the bench beside her scarf, as a sign of trust. "You are both welcome to your arguments, but I am weary and thirsty. You offered me a cup of tea. For that I would be most grateful. I think Pell may be afraid of your tea, but I will only ask you not to spell me with it. There is a young woman, severely burned, who is in my care. I must be back to her before nightfall. Now her life is in your hands as well as mine."

"One of those from the barn?"

"How did you know?" Pell asked quickly.

"I know more than you might think. I have been watching all this for a while. So you have saved them. I came on the scene too late to do any good and thought them both dead in that inferno."

"One is dead, the other badly burned."

"An ugly way they do their killing, those guards. But then, I suppose you are not so easily killed. If you wish, I will come sometime soon to see to her burns."

I saw Pell stiffen, but I said quickly, "I would be very grateful for your help. This healing may be beyond my powers."

Alyeeta sat down in a chair nearby, poured our tea, and turned her dark eyes on me. Now she was really laying on a charm. I found I could not resist her stare. It felt as if my very soul were being drawn out of me, pulled up to the surface. At that moment she could have had that or anything else of mine for the asking. In a rush of words I told her everything: of the burned ones, and my attempt to heal them, and the pain it cost me. I also told her of Shaleethia's death. Suddenly I found I was twisting my hands as if to break my fingers. In a burst of grief and anger I cried out at the end, "I am a healer and they have made a murderer of me. With these hands, with medications made for healing, I have taken another's life. Had I but waited one more day you might have saved her."

Alyeeta reached out and laid her hands firmly over mine to still them. She was shaking her head. "Not likely. Show me in my head." I stared at her. "Shut your eyes, Tazzi. See her burns again and show me. You can do it. It will be painful for the moment, but you will have your answer." I did as she said, gritting my teeth against the pain, going back and trying to see everything, even things I had been barely conscious of at the time, sinking into the memory until she said, "Enough."

When I opened my eyes she was looking at me with such compassion it made me want to cry. She still held my hands. Now she shook her head again, saying, "Not much chance there. Not from what you have just shown me. Not even with months of healing in a clean, safe place and someone always with her." Suddenly she released my hands and sat back, as if also releasing me on some other level. "No, I could not have saved her, nor could you, believe me. You did your best. The fire had bitten too deeply. Do not eat yourself up with it, child. That one is gone, let us look to heal the other."

Pell had accepted her cup of tea, but not a seat. She held herself tense, as if ready to spring away at any moment. Alyeeta turned her attention in that direction. "Well, Pellandrea, will you talk with me now? Please forgive me my little games. I have lived alone too long to be easy with others in my space, but I am neither a fool nor your enemy. I could even be a useful friend — if not for you then for Tazzi. There are things she needs to learn, things she needs to know if she is to survive as a healer."

"My name? How do you know my name?"

"I know many things, Pell, and nothing at all. Tell me, then."

Pell sighed deeply and set her cup on the bench. She stared down at Alyeeta as if trying to decide. Then, with a sudden motion she turned away and began pacing back and forth. I raised my hand to stop her, but

Alyeeta shook her head. "Let her be. She must come to this in her own way." We both drank our tea, watching Pell in silence. For a while her restless steps were the only sound in that strange place. Then, just as suddenly as she had turned away, she came back to stand before us. With a quick gesture she flipped off her hat with its attached hair and whiskers, tossing it on the bench next to mine. Then, with much care, she shrugged her way out of her coat and leaned it against a pile of wood by the hearth. It settled there stiffly, almost standing on its own — a strange, lumpy shape that looked like a wide, short, headless man. Watching this, I realized that Pell could not have sat on the floor cushions in that garment. Without it she looked suddenly thin and unprotected and very vulnerable as she sank down with another sigh. She passed her sleeve across her face. Part of the powder came away. It left her face streaked light and dark, as if just at that moment she were emerging from a different skin.

"So, Alyeeta," Pell started slowly, seeming to draw the words up from some deep place, "you want me to trust you. You say you want to help us. Well, let me tell you, there has been little to trust these past few years, not even one's own family, that least of all. We have only each other. That bond is very fragile still, just beginning. The rest is like quicksand." There was a terrible grieving in her voice. I had never seen Pell so close to tears.

When she stopped, Alyeeta said gently, "Tell the rest." All trace of mockery was gone. She leaned forward in her chair, her eyes intent on Pell. At that moment she looked almost as old as she had pretended to be.

Pell nodded and went on. Once she had decided to talk, the words flowed out of her. She told it all: the discovery of powers, leaving home, finding the others and the network forming between them, the dangers of the edict, and her hopes for the future. "And in the end we will gather together," she finished passionately. "We will find ourselves a safe place in this world." There was silence for a while, then she sat up suddenly and said in a very different tone, "Well, Witch, I have trusted you with things no one else knows, no one who is not one of us. Our lives are in your hands. Perhaps I am a great fool."

"And I have brought you into my home that no one who is not a Witch has ever set foot in till this day. At this moment, Pellandrea, we are in each other's hands. Something is making and shaping here among us." I saw a strange look come across Pell's face at those words, a look of hope and grief and wariness, combined with much else I could not read.

While they were speaking I was intent only on them. Now, suddenly, I sensed another's presence in the room and looked around nervously.

With a start, I saw what appeared to be a part of the wall detach itself from the side of the shelter and walk toward us. Mouth open, I watched in amazement as a black, shaggy mountain-pony materialized out of the gloom. As much at home inside as any dog might be, it came to rest its head on Alyeeta's shoulder. There it snuffled softly in her ear till she fed it some hard crackers from a crock by the hearth.

"My companion, Gandolair," Alyeeta said with a smile, as if introducing a friend. "His presence helps ease the loneliness here." Pell made a slight bow. I held out my hand, which the pony lipped gently. Alyeeta had finished her tea. She stroked his head for a few moments in silence. Then she stood up suddenly and said in an abrupt manner, as if dismissing us, "So, Pell, you must tell me the way to your home if I am to come there and help heal this girl."

Pell's face hardened. She sprang to her feet also. Everything between them changed in that instant and the air felt thick with threat. "No! No one goes there without me. You can come with us or not, but I give no one directions to that place."

"Well, I had not thought to be leaving quite so quickly, but never mind, girl, I will see it easily enough in your head." Alyeeta's face was also closed and hard. The mockery was back, with even an edge of contempt to it.

"You will not," Pell said fiercely. The look on her face frightened me. They stared at each other in silence, Pell with her hands on her hips. I could feel the air trembling between them and my head hurt with the pressure. Their silence at that moment rang louder than shouts. Suddenly Alyeeta gave a cry and raised both hands to her head. Her mouth was twisted in pain. In quick succession I saw many looks pass over her face, first of surprise, then rage, then fear, and finally triumph followed by amusement. "So, I see," she said at last, "something new has indeed been born on this earth. Something new in our time that has never been seen before. I wonder what this means for Witches." She looked Pell slowly up and down and added, "If that is how you wish it, then I will follow when you are ready to leave." With those words she made a slight bow that had both mockery and respect in it.

Pell stood staring at her a moment longer, then she shrugged and seemed to drop her guard. "No, what does it matter. What you already know could see us ten times dead. For some reason Tazzi trusts you. If we are going to work together, if I am ever going to trust you, I may as well start now. Here, you may read it in my mind." She let her arms fall to her sides and stood very still, looking into Alyeeta's eyes and leaving herself open, more naked than if she had stripped off all her clothes.

"Ah," said Alyeeta after she had pondered in silence for some time, "a good place, the twisted part of the forest where most are afraid to go. Even those who know the woods well often lose their way there. You have made a fine choice. If, in some ways you are a young fool, in others you are no fool at all. Well, if you are still willing, I will go with you now." Pell nodded. Her face looked pale and strained.

While Pell went to get her saddlebags to repack the contents of her coat, Alyeeta took up her pouch. She had me follow her and hold it open as she went from shelf to crock to cupboard for what she needed. Finally she put on her shawl and her kerchief with the white hair. Then she threw ashes over the fire. At the entryway she turned to Pell and said as one might to a child, "Hold your face still now." Then with a cloth she wiped away the remainder of the powder and added softly, "Stripes are not a good disguise out there."

I glanced back as we rode away. Alyeeta's house looked like a tangled thicket in a clearing again, and no smoke came from the chimney.

10

My mother had raised me to return honorably and with care everything we ever borrowed. In my whole life I had never stolen so much as a matchstick. Yet there I stood in Pell's shelter, all dressed in stolen clothes, surrounded by stolen wares, and about to eat stolen food. And so life changes!

We had just returned from our thieving trip to the Hamishair market, bringing back with us Alyeeta the Witch as well as a whole cargo of stolen goods, the contents of Pell's extraordinary, expanding coat. Pell, in a high good humor, had insisted on having me try on different bits of the new clothing to see what did best for me. She kept turning me this way and that for Alyeeta's inspection. Maireth, freshly bandaged, sat propped against some cushions, watching silently and eating slices of the peach I had brought back for her. All this, I believe, was more for Pell's amusement than for any real purpose. The shelter itself looked much like a market stall, with everything from her packs lying scattered around us in colorful disarray: clothes, boots, wooden bowls, another lamp, a jar of lamp oil, potatoes, apples, more peaches, a bolt of undyed cloth that Pell swore she did not steal but bought from the weaver for honest coins, two knives, bread, cheese, berries, and a small blanket.

Pell herself looked almost playful, a strange altering of her lean, hard face. "Tazzi, I must tell you, you were a marvel today, wonderful, inspired, better than I could possibly have imagined. In fact, by the Goddess, you are the best fool I have ever followed through the market, though I think we cannot play that same show there again. Too many would remember. Next time they would be watching and waiting to catch us." I looked down at the floor, blushing in discomfort at this high praise for being a thief's accomplice.

"Give me back my necklace," Alyeeta said suddenly. "It is worth far more than your few coins and is much too fine for a crude farm girl."

"Good," I said, grateful for this distraction in spite of the insult. "I surely have no need for it, and it cost far too much besides." I fished in my pouch and held out my hand with the beads. I was glad enough to be rid of them, though seeing them now in the lamplight there was something alluring in the depth of their blue, something that seemed to draw me in.

Alyeeta laid some coins in my palm, quickly took up the necklace, and slipped it over her head, saying, "You have no knowledge of true worth."

"Count the coins," Pell said sharply. She had been watching all this intently.

I did as she said, then held out my hand again. Alyeeta looked reproachfully at Pell. She sighed, shrugged, gave a little laugh, then put more coins in my hand, one at a time, until I nodded. "I thought at least to get something for my work," she said to Pell with a grin.

★

On the way back to Pell's shelter the three of us had come by yet another of her meandering paths. To me it seemed to wind in circles and bend back upon itself. I did not question. I simply held to my horse through the tangled growth and the steep ups and downs, following her mindlessly just as Pell had so often accused me of doing. I was too exhausted by that day's happenings to care, and even dozed a little when I had the chance.

For her part, Alyeeta kept up a low, quarrelsome complaint, grumbling about everything: the roughness of the path, the steepness, the rocks, the rub of the saddle, whatever came to mind, though her surefooted little pony had no trouble with the way. Pell would hush her impatiently. For a while Alyeeta would be silent. Then, at the next hint of difficulty she would commence again. It was as if she had put on the voice with the scarf and the white hair, mumbling and muttering to herself as much as to either of us. If I had not seen with my own eyes that strong-looking, straight-backed, black-haired woman, I would have sworn this was a decrepit old crone we traveled with, one whose bent body could not bear the hardships of the trail. I was struggling not to laugh, but Pell was in no way amused.

113

"It is dangerous out here, not a place for clowns and fools," she snapped as Alyeeta started up again.

By the time we reached the shelter it was already the edge of dusk. There were just a few streaks of red from the dying sun visible through the trees. I was much relieved to be safely back before dark. Pell, for her part, was thoroughly aggravated and out of sorts, while Alyeeta looked amused and pleased with herself.

Once there, Alyeeta took on a different style. She went striding about outside, looking at the shelter and poking at it with a stick. "Well made and well hidden. Yes, yes, very well. Even a little spring here, I see, and all tucked into such a secret part of the woods. You must have very special powers for the Twisted Forest to welcome you this way. Most it keeps out or drives back. Yes, well done. I could not have done better myself."

Pell could not tell if she was being mocked or praised. Her eyebrows were drawn together again in one dark line. She appeared to be struggling to keep her temper. I felt caught between anger and amusement at seeing her so tried. Finally she muttered some answer and went off to see to the horses.

As Alyeeta was setting out to do yet another turn around the outside of the shelter, I took hold of her arm. "Alyeeta, please come look at Maireth," I pleaded.

"Ah, yes, the burned one. This is all so new and interesting I had almost forgotten what brought me here." She took up her healing bag and followed me in.

The stench of festering struck me the instant we entered. Maireth had lit the lantern and was sitting propped up, watching the door. "This time I thought you had truly deserted and left me to die here alone in spite of your promise. Look, it is already dark." Her eyes were reproachful, her voice bitter and full of accusation.

"Spirit, anyhow, that is a good sign," Alyeeta said as she came over to peer down at Maireth. "Give her some of this for pain, and let us get on with it."

"These are for you, and Pell has more," I said, quickly setting an offering of three peaches in Maireth's lap and beginning to slice a fourth one for her. "And I have brought back another healer for you, one who has ghero-root and other things we need, as well as more skill than I do." Even as I said those words, I hoped in my heart it was true.

Maireth looked up at Alyeeta with a grimace. "This is the healer you brought?" There was no mistaking the contempt in her voice. I glanced at

Alyeeta. She did indeed look very strange, nothing to inspire confidence. From the ride her kerchief had slipped sideways. The wisps of white hair were all askew, giving her the appearance of a tipsy and very unreliable old crone. I whispered to her to take off her disguise.

"Ah yes, I forgot," she said, untying her scarf and dropping it carelessly on the floor. When she shook her head, her own wild hair came tumbling down. I saw the look of surprise on Maireth's face. While I was watching Maireth, Alyeeta turned to searching though her bag. "Make a fire quickly, Tazzia," she said with impatience. "We need hot water. This infection is running away with itself, as anyone with a nose could easily tell." In a few quick motions she had cleared the table of Pell's things. Then she lit a cone of thiur-paste to burn against smells and infection. After that she laid out the contents of her bag with care.

Now I was the one who scurried about taking orders, building up both fires, hauling and boiling water, ripping cloth into strips, and holding the light where it was needed. All the while I watched everything Alyeeta did and tried my best to remember. I followed her around as if I were again a child of seven helping Old Tolgath on a call. Alyeeta worked fast and in silence. When it came time to scrub away some of the scabs and corruptions, not even a strong dose of diraithia was enough for the pain. Maireth cried out and tried to strike at us. "Hold her hands or bind her wrists with one of those strips," Alyeeta said abruptly. "This must be done right if she is to heal cleanly."

Maireth ground her teeth against the pain and took fast, harsh breaths. When it grew too much for her to bear she dug her nails into me, but did not cry out again. I had to lean on the wall to steady myself against her pain so I could hold her and not pull away. At last Alyeeta gave a great sigh. "Done," she said as she laid on new compresses. Then she nodded, turning to me. "Now the healing will come right." Afterward she turned to Maireth and added, "You may not think so now, but later you will thank me for this."

Maireth released her grip on me. She spat off to the side, spit bloodied by her bitten lips. "May the demons bite off your tits, Witch!" she snarled to Alyeeta through her teeth. "It will be a long, cold day in summer before I thank you. You are a torturer, not a healer."

Alyeeta stepped back unconcerned, drying her hands on her skirt. "And this one," she gave a nod in my direction, "this one was probably much too gentle with you. Those burns must be cleaned of putrescence each day." Then she gave me a sudden grin. "I think your patient will live, Tazzi. No one so rude and bad-tempered dies easily."

Then, with one of those sudden changes of mood, Alyeeta stepped forward again. With a very different look on her face she began moving her hands about in patterns I could not understand. She cast no spell or signs that I could see, but at moments she would stop, shut her eyes, breathe deeply, and cup her hands over a burned place without actually touching Maireth's body. She would stay that way, utterly still, till a strange, deep hum came from her that resonated back from the stone wall of the shelter and even set the cups to ringing. At those moments I would feel such a pull of power as to make me unsteady on my feet. Maireth had mysteriously lost all will to argue. She lay back motionless, her eyes open wide, staring at nothing. As suddenly as she had begun, Alyeeta stopped. She stretched her hands far from her body and shook them as if shaking off some noxious liquid. "That is the real healing," she said to me. "I can teach you that if you want, but it is not easy."

I nodded, still shaken from Maireth's pain and from her blaze of anger. I was also dazzled by Alyeeta's performance. Alyeeta reached out and pressed her fingers to my forehead. It was like cool water flowing through me. When I looked at her with surprise, I saw again that look of absolute compassion in her eyes, so different from the mockery that was often in her words. Softly, almost in a whisper and as if for my ears alone, she said, "Truly you are a very good healer, Tazzia. You have done your best here. It is only that you carry too much pain. I can also teach you how to let loose of that. Otherwise it will burn away your talent, and your heart as well." Then she said loudly, "Take that filth outside and make sure to burn it all with care. Then wash thoroughly with hot water and perthali before you come back."

By the time I returned, Pell had come in. Alyeeta was stirring something over the fire, and Pell sat watching her with a strange, brooding look on her face. Maireth in turn was watching Pell while running her hands over her own face and breasts. Suddenly she burst out in her raspy voice, "I suppose I should be grateful to you for saving my life, but I am not so sure I want it. Now I will be scarred from these burns to mark me like a brand as one they hunt, scars that will make me easy prey. Since the Goddess saw fit to keep me among the living, I suppose I must get used to it. I am glad there is no mirror here. I might be tempted to look and then regret it. Men used to tell me I was beautiful. No one will ever bother me with such rubbish again." The bitterness of her voice was like a sharp nail scraping up and down my spine.

Pell stood up and walked over to her. "You may not believe this now, Maireth, but someday you will wear those scars with pride, wear them like a mark of honor. You will show them in remembrance to your granddaughters when you tell your stories."

Maireth made a strange sound in her throat that might have been a laugh, a curse, or a cry. "Easy enough for you to say," she growled, "since they are mine to bear, not yours." Then she said, more thoughtfully, "Perhaps I will be able to thank you later."

Pell shrugged. "Later or never, it matters little." She turned to us. "Well, what do the healers say? Is she well enough to answer some questions? Her tongue and mind seem sharp enough."

Before either of us could answer, Maireth said curtly, "I can speak for myself. I am not a child in your care. Ask whatever questions you please, Pell."

Pell sat down cross-legged by Maireth's mat. Alyeeta faded into the shadows. I drew a mat over to the wall so I could sit leaning against it. When Pell, hunched forward and listening intently, began her questioning, I made little effort to follow the story, though some of it still came through. From what I remember, Maireth and Shaleethia were both from the village of Karthi. It seems they scarcely knew each other, but for safety their families had sent them together to the market of Ghomarth, by ill chance on the very day the death edict was posted. All unknowing, they had stayed late to enjoy their rare time away from home. On the way back they had been stopped by the very guardsmen who carried the edicts. Frightened, they had dropped everything and fled to a barn for shelter, a shelter that all too quickly became a trap.

"Shouting curses and threats, the guards formed a circle around the barn. I watched through a crack in the wall while one of their number made a spiral of some greenish white powder right up to the barn. The others picked or dug a wide ring down to the dirt and cleared it of leaves and grass. When the powder was lit, it made a roar like the winds of a winter storm, and a wall of flame shot up all around."

"Fastfire!" Pell sat up suddenly and spat out the word like a curse. "The thing they use when they lay siege to a fortress. They tip their arrows with it and also keep a circle of fire around the walls. This is a war being waged against us. How did you survive? Not many can survive fastfire."

Maireth did not answer. There was a long silence. When I looked at her I saw she was staring ahead strangely, not conscious of Pell or of any of us. Her eyes were wide and empty. She seemed to be looking back into the fire itself. Even trying to shield myself I could see pictures of it in her mind and feel some of that heat. When she began to talk again it was as if someone else spoke through her. "I kept telling her to stay down flat, but she would not listen, she would not listen to me. Now she is all burned. She is dead and gone, all burned. I kept telling her to stay low, but she would not listen. What could I do?" The hair went up on the back of my neck at the hollow, lifeless sound of her voice. She said this over and over as if to some unseen judge, until Pell shook her gently and asked, "Where have you gone, Sister?"

"Nowhere," Maireth answered impatiently, as if none of this had happened. "I am here answering your questions. What else do you want to know?"

"How did you survive?" Pell asked again.

"There was an old stone part to the barn, some of it underground. I tried to get Shaleethia to stay there with me, but her fear drove her to run about in search of exits."

Pell was shaking her head. "I wonder, I wonder if together you could have stood them off. It seems once we are afraid and turn our backs to run, too much power is lost. Perhaps if you had both held your ground, you could have faced them down."

"And perhaps not! You were not there. What do you know? If there had been three or four, we might have managed, maybe six, even, but they came on us so suddenly, ten or more. Besides, Shaleethia had little power, not much at all. I wonder if she was truly one of us or only of the right age for their edict or if her real powers had not yet come on her. Even if we had stood our ground, they still would have used their fastfire, only then we would have been out in the open with no hope of shelter."

Pell was shaking her head again. "Fastfire, eh? There is no way I know of to fight it, but perhaps we can find something. I must talk to Jhemar." With that she jumped to her feet and began pacing around, suddenly infused with angry energy. "So, fire is their way around our powers. What else will they think of to use? Men have always been good hunters. Perhaps we are no more to them than some exotic wild new quarry to use for sport. They will compare methods with each other till they have learned the best way to bring us down. We must move quickly. There is little time."

Alyeeta suddenly stepped out of the darkness. "Well, is that not always the way of it with humans? What they cannot understand they must destroy. There is nothing new in that. Now that is enough questions for the moment. Let the girl eat her peaches in peace. She needs them for healing. Come show us what you carried away from the market in your coat. That coat, by the way, is the best of its kind I have ever seen. I shall have to make a copy of your design. It could have many uses."

★

When Pell tired of displaying her newfound wares, she began methodically packing them away. Maireth had long since signaled me to help her lie down again and was sleeping soundly, her breathing easy for the first time. I still could not accustom myself to stealing, and said as much to Pell. Without stopping her work to look at me, she answered, "Well, Tazzi, as you can see it is not so simple for fugitives to find steady employment in this world. You will have to learn to live by a whole new set of rules or not live at all. That is the choice they have forced on us. I, for one, do not intend to die or at least not die easily, so for now I will live however I must. I have no objection to earning my bread by the work of my hands if that is possible. If not, then my hands have other uses. Speaking of bread, however gotten..." She cleared one corner of the table and set on it a loaf of dark, fragrant bread and a pale yellow round of cheese. As she took the knife from her boot and began to hack thick slices into three piles, Alyeeta was quick to gather her healing things together at the other corner.

We had not eaten since morning. At the sight of food my mouth began to water and my hands tremble. Clearly, I was not ready to die even if I did not have Pell's easy scruples. When Pell finished her work, she pushed a pile in my direction. I began stuffing it in my mouth, bread and cheese together. Alyeeta had stood silent all this while, watching us intently. She made no move now that she had rescued her things from the shower of crumbs Pell made with her knife.

Pell looked up at her. "Well, Witch, will you share some bread with us, or do you think stolen bread is tainted to the taste?"

"I was not sure you intended to invite me," Alyeeta said coolly. Then she sat down suddenly and fastened Pell with her stare. "Girl, I have lived in this world a long time. I have baked bread and borrowed bread and begged bread and stolen bread to keep breath in this body. As long as it is fresh, I have never noticed any difference in the taste. Do you think, at your green age, to teach me something of surviving on this earth, or to teach me anything at all for that matter?" She reached for a bowl and heaped on her share. "Stolen bread goes stale like any other and is best eaten fresh, though my appetite may not be as crude as some." She turned and looked at me.

I felt my face flush under this assault, but Pell answered tartly, "I do not think you have much to teach us of manners, considering the welcome you gave us in your home."

Suddenly the bread turned dry in my mouth and hard to swallow. I gulped down some tea and said angrily, "Can we not have some peace in this place? You both sound not much better than that rabble of men at the tavern."

Pell looked at me in surprise and Alyeeta said sweetly, "We are just getting to know one another."

Feeling the fool between them, I flushed again. Without another word I gathered up my bread and cheese and went out quickly into the night. There I found myself a comfortable rock and sat cooling my hurt pride. I ate slowly, listening to the first owls of the night calling to one another from the hills.

When I came back in, Pell and Alyeeta were deep in talk together. Neither one looked up nor spoke to me. Feeling no need to join them, I drew my mat over to the far edge of the shelter and lay down. I hoped only for sleep, but that took a while in coming. Suddenly I felt Alyeeta's eyes on me with a stare I could not fathom. It made me shiver, as if a cold wind had blown across my soul. Clearly, they were talking about me. I turned angrily to face the wall and pulled up the covers to shut them out.

In spite of the sound of their voices, I must have slept then, for I woke with Pell shaking my shoulder. "We go to meet with Renaise," she told me.

I sprang to my feet. We were quickly ready, for I had not taken off my clothes, not even my boots. Alyeeta said she would stay to watch with Maireth. I had no need to ask Pell if she trusted her.

All to no use. We waited in misery through the long, uncomfortable hours of the night, each in our appointed tree. As well as being stiff and chilled, I was filled with guilt and apprehension, afraid for Renaise and ashamed of myself. At that moment her unpleasant voice would have filled me with the greatest pleasure. I found myself hungering for her grating words and her annoying mannerisms, if only to lift the terrible burden of that guilt. After all, annoying habits are not good enough reason for dying a terrible death. All through our watch I saw in my head dreadful scenes of fire, and pictured Renaise burned as Shaleethia had been. I longed to speak to Pell and had to force myself to keep my silence.

Several times we heard owls, though none of them were ours. Twice, men on horseback passed beneath us. With the darkness already graying into dawn, we rode back weary and discouraged, to find Maireth still sleeping soundly and Alyeeta dozing by the fire. Her pony lay on the floor beside her with his head on her lap. I looked at Pell. She shrugged and signaled me to bring our mats outside.

There, in a little shelter of bushes, we reached out to touch before we slept. We found in each other's bodies the comfort we could not find on the road. It was there that Alyeeta sought us out later in the day. I woke to see her peering down, as if she had just discovered something interesting but slightly unpleasant. Pell drew me to her with a protective gesture she had never used before. It was instantly clear to me that she intended Alyeeta to find us this way. Two dogs and a bone, I thought angrily as I wrested myself free of Pell's grip and jumped to my feet.

"You did not have to go off and hide," Alyeeta said with her mocking smile. "If the earth itself had shaken I would have slept through it after that hard ride you took me on."

Later, Pell left on one of her searches, and my education with Alyeeta began. It seems they had agreed that Alyeeta was to teach me what Pell could not. They had decided my fate between them without consulting me, as if I were a small child with no sense or will of my own. Yet I knew I could say no. My moment of anger flared and passed. What does it matter? I thought. It is something to do, it passes the time, and I have no better plan. I had been uprooted too suddenly. Kara was dead, and all that had meaning in my life was gone. Not driven like Pell, I was mostly content to let myself be used by her. Why should I care if Alyeeta used me as well for some purpose of her own?

But Alyeeta, for reasons I could not comprehend, was determined I should learn to read and write. This was harder than all Pell's teachings, this making of letters and the meaning of them. I could not grasp the shape or purpose of it. It was like nothing I had ever learned. The trying of it made my head throb and ache. I thought myself likely too old to learn and not smart enough besides. Alyeeta, however, was patient, far more than I would have expected, more than I myself would have been. Nodding with approval, she told me to trace the letters over and over in the dirt till mind and hand together grew accustomed to their shape. My fingers cramped, my eyes crossed, and I had six elbows. When Alyeeta went to tend to Maireth, I wanted to throw the stick down and shout, "I cannot understand! This is bending my mind! Why are you forcing this on me?"

Instead, I struggled on, hoping for light, for ease. There was nothing else to occupy my time. I could see that in spite of her bitter words, Maireth had given herself over to Alyeeta's care in a way she never had with me. She did not need me for that time. It was with a strange mixture of relief and regret that I saw myself dismissed as a healer and so freed to learn this new thing I could not learn.

★

We went back to our vigil that night with no incident and no Renaise, but the third night, on our way home, we had our encounter. I was riding behind Pell in my usual semi-doze when suddenly she stopped her horse. I sensed the riders only a moment or two before I heard them. It sounded as if there were many, and they were riding fast. I made ready to charge up the bank into the woods, but Pell laid a restraining hand on my arm. "Too late for that now. It would only worsen things. Just remember that you are a very humble and not overly bright farm lad."

Several guardsmen swept round the corner at us as we guided our horses out of their way. I thought they might rush right past us. Indeed, they almost did so, when their leader called for a halt and for a torch to be lit. He held it up to examine us. I squinted and cast my eyes down in the sudden bright light. "Well, what have we here?" he said, thrusting the torch so close I could feel its heat. "These two look to be local farm boys. Maybe they have some useful knowledge." He turned to Pell. "Well, boy, we are hunting star-brats for the Zarn and hear there is a whole nest of them in some part of the Twisted Forest, somewhere near here if word be true. What can you tell us?"

Pell bobbed her head several times as if bowing, keeping her eyes averted as she spoke. She appeared to be painfully aware of her low station, as well as dazed and confused by this display of magnificence before her. "Well, sir, yes, sir, if I may speak, sir," she stammered with apparent difficulty, "I have heard such talk at the market, though I myself, of course, have never seen any of these creatures. It is said they have their lair high up in the hills near the ever-burning grotto, but none has the courage to go there. There are many dangers in that part of the forest." She pointed the opposite way from her shelter. When the leader moved away it was my hope to see them all sweep off down the road that direction, but after a few minutes of hurried consultation with the others he turned back to us. I thought we were surely outsmarted when he said, "Since you seem to know so much, perhaps you can guide us there yourselves."

Pell began to shake. "Oh, no, sir, please, sir," she said, almost groveling. "I have only heard rumors. I do not know the way. We never venture into that part of the forest. It is said that the trees there feed on flesh, even on men and horses, and that the paths lead into one another like a maze so that one cannot find a way to leave. God's truth, good sirs."

"God's truth, eh? If all die there, then who has lived to bring back these stories, and how can these star-brats survive there?"

"They have unnatural powers, sir. Some even say they are in league with the forest itself."

"I think you are either lazy or afraid and so have just spewed out this mouthful of lies to us. Turn your horse around, boy, and show us the way to this flaming grotto you speak of."

Pell began to blubber and stammer as if in terror, "No, sir, please, sir, it is said the ground there is unsteady and bubbles underfoot. It will mean our sure death and yours as well. Please let us pass, sir, for already we are late for our work and our master will be very angry."

The first man said sharply, "I think I smell some treason to the Zarn in this." He rode forward as if to lay hold of Pell. I tensed in readiness, but another rode forward to block his way. "Lazy or lying or not, they are only two superstitious fools. They might well be more hindrance than help, especially mounted on those farm ponies that will wind much sooner than our sturdy horses."

Just as I was feeling some hope from those words, one of them turned to me and said with malice, "And you, boy, what do you know of this? Are you always so silent? Are you voiceless or witless or what?"

"I ... I...," I stammered as my voice choked up and my face turned red. I could feel Pell in my head saying over and over, /Stay calm, play dumb,/ saying it soothingly as one calms or gentles a frightened animal. I slowed my breathing and let my eyes go out of focus, staring at the ground. I allowed my fear and my struggle with it to show. "I am not very bright, sir," I managed to mumble at last. "My cousin here is the one with the wits. He always speaks for us both. At home they tell me to be quiet when we go out, that he will be smart enough for both of us. Excuse me, sir. I am talking out of turn, sir. They will be angry ... now I have..." I let confusion and embarrassment overcome me altogether, not too difficult to do as I lapsed back into speechlessness.

The men began to talk and laugh among themselves. Pointing at Pell, one of them said, "So this the wit of the pair? The talking brain?" The others all thought this a great joke as I had hoped they would. They seemed ready to let us go, seeing we were of so little use, when another of them said, "They have not a brain between the two of them. I wonder if they are really human. Perhaps they are only walking clay, mud-boys. I wonder if they would bleed on a sword point." With a grin, he made as if to draw his sword.

Pell cringed visibly and said in a pleading, supplicating way, "Please, sir, please, permit us to go on. We will be beaten for being tardy and fined besides. We were to be there at dawn for the planting and now we are already late. Besides, it is not safe to linger on this part of the road."

I was tensed again, ready for anything, when one of the others called out, "Come, Thorin, let them be. There is nothing of worth to be gotten here. We are wasting time with these dimwits. You may as well ask questions of a horse or a pig."

Bowing and muttering her thanks repeatedly, Pell backed up her horse to clear the road, with me beside her. As the guards spun around to leave, I saw the flash of Pell's knife just for an instant, like the flash of light on water. Then it was gone and she thrust her hand in the pouch of her loose overshirt.

As we watched them ride off, she muttered, "Careless and stupid, unbelievably stupid to have let them come on us unawares. My old master would be ashamed of me. He would no doubt have threatened to cut off my fingers for such carelessness, or, better yet, my useless ears. I thought at any moment we would be unmasked, or worse."

"Pell, how could you have let that happen?" I asked reproachfully.

"How could *you?*" she asked back instantly. She had a funny little smile on her face.

It took a moment for the import of her question to sink in. "You knew?"

She gave a slight nod. "It was a whole troop of them. After all, they did not drop from the sky on silent wings."

"But that was so dangerous. How could you...? Why did you...?"

She shrugged, turning her hand palm up. "You said you wanted experience. Better to get it with both of us to deal with them than with you alone and surrounded. And now perhaps you will stay awake on the trail and not always trust your life to me. Besides, it was useful. We have learned far more from them than they have from us. They search for us too close to home. The time has come. Soon we will need to move."

I was shivering, chilled with fear, but Pell slapped me playfully on the knee. "You did very well as my idiot cousin, very well indeed. It is a good

part for you, full of possibilities. We should work on that some more."
They had hardly ridden off, and already she was jesting.

"Can we go now, Pell, or do we wait here for their return?"

"Let us ride up to that rise and see which way they go. Then I would
be only too happy to ride fast for home."

As we rode off, my fear dissipated. I thought of their smirking faces.
Anger, that other wonderful new feeling, flared up in me. "Does it not hurt
your pride to grovel and whine and plead before them?"

"No, not at all. I enjoy the game. I take pleasure in their contempt and
their arrogance. It only sweetens the purse."

"The what?"

She tapped her pouch, saying, "Later, when we are safe. That is the
dessert. I trust you will have no scruples about it this time." We had
reached the high point in the road. Pell turned to watch their dust. "They
are not turning off into the woods this time, but very soon, with more men
and more pressure to find us, they will begin to do so. Now it is time to
be off this road before that man of wits chances to discover his missing
purse."

We slipped off the road into one of Pell's many little paths. As we rode
home through the brightening dawn, I was so awake and alert for every
sign that my ears ached from listening and my eyes burned from not
blinking. The back of my neck was stiff with fear, as if at any moment a
hand might land there. At last, when there was a wide enough space, I rode
up next to Pell.

"Pell, are you never afraid at all?"

"All the time, Tazzi. After all, I am not the one who rides along half
asleep. But I have lived with it longer than you have and learned how to
use it. Fear is not an enemy. It is a warning of danger, a signal. It is, in
fact, a friend to keep you safe in a dangerous world. But it is a very
powerful friend. You must keep it at your side as a friend, not let it ride
you or drive you or take control. It will try. It is a friend that will test you
often.

"You know how cats use their whiskers and snakes flick their tongues
to tell them what is out there in the world? You must grow whiskers of
fear at the nape of your neck where your eyes cannot be, and all up and
down your back. Then the guardsmen cannot ride up on you that way. In
truth, I think you left me to watch for us both, eh? I am sharp, but I am
only human, Tazzi. You must learn to be your own eyes no matter who
you ride with." I shivered again. I could not imagine making friends with

that terrible new feeling that clenched my stomach and froze my will and drove me to mindless flight.

When we came in, Alyeeta and Maireth were already awake. Zenoria and Jhemar were there with them. They all looked up at us expectantly. Pell shook her head and tossed the purse on the table. I thought she would start telling our tale. Instead, she drew Jhemar aside. I heard her say, "Fastfire! They are using fastfire against us. We must find something that stops it."

Jhemar was shaking her head with a very troubled look on her face. "Not much chance of that, Pell. Others have surely tried it before us."

"Tell me, then, must we just let them go on burning us alive? Is that all we can do?" Pell was shouting now.

Jhemar went on shaking her head, looking down at the ground as if lost in thought. Suddenly she looked up again and grabbed Pell's arm. "Wait! I remember playing with permegeant as a child. Once I put out our hearthfire with my little games. I gained myself a lot of trouble for it, I can tell you that. Perhaps with something added it could be of use to us in this."

"Permegeant, eh? Then we must find some source of fastfire to work with. I wonder if..."

"Not possible! No one would do that for us."

"The Wanderers, perhaps...?"

"The Wanderers least of all," Jhemar said with finality.

Their voices lowered then, and so the rest was lost to me. As they were deep in conversation, it was left to me to recount the night's happening. Zenoria picked up the purse and tossed it from hand to hand. The coins made a sort of music. Maireth was watching me intently. I could see fear and hatred flash back and forth across her face as I spoke of the guards. At the end of my telling, she said grimly, "Perhaps they were the same ones."

★

The next night we had hardly gotten ourselves stationed when I sensed something on the road. Pell's hoot was answered by another. Soon I heard the muffled sound of hooves that had been wrapped in rags and a voice whispering, "Pell, Pell." Pell made an answering hoot, and in an instant we were both out of our trees. There were four others besides Renaise, but we took no time for names. "We must go quickly," Renaise said in a hoarse whisper. "We are so late because we have been trying to evade pursuit."

"We met them on the road last night not far from here," Pell whispered back. Marshlegs and Torvir slipped out of the woods to join us. As soon as we mounted, Pell led us off into the trees. It was a strange, silent ride. I could feel the fear of the others thick and heavy around me. When we reached the shelter, only Maireth was awake, with the lamp lit. She was sitting up against the wall. As we came in she drew the blanket up, almost covering her face. Her eyes above it stared out defiantly.

Renaise stopped in midstep. "Who is that?" she asked suspiciously.

Maireth made no answer, but Pell spoke for her. "She is one of us. They tried to burn her to death in a barn. Her name is Maireth."

I could make out the still forms of Jhemar and Zenoria sleeping in each other's arms at the far edge of the shelter, but could not see Alyeeta. Suddenly Renaise sucked in her breath in fear and jumped back. A strange figure stepped out of the dark, a wild-looking woman with black hair like a tangle of snakes and her eyes full of shadows.

11

Alyeeta! Alyeeta! How to explain this Witch who was still very much a woman? This woman with the powers of a Witch? How to speak of my time with her, more demanding and intense even than my time with Pell, gentler and yet more brutal, time that stripped me down and turned me inside out, humbled me and gave me back to myself full of pride and power. Alyeeta, who taught me what I had refused to learn and made me glad of it and taught me much, much more besides.

Pell and Alyeeta — they sat up half the night arguing over me. I heard Pell say, "I thought to train her to be my second here. She has just begun to be of some use, and now you want to snatch her from me. And for what? For nothing! For nonsense! The shielding from pain, that I can understand, that is useful, though I think you could do that here in a day or so without taking her away. After all, there is much else she needs to learn here of mapping and tracking and woodcraft. She can hardly find her way through the woods by herself yet. But this reading and writing — of what use is that to our survival? What do we need with it?"

"I see that what you yourself do not already know is of no worth to you," Alyeeta answered sharply. "Such is the ignorance and the arrogance of youth. There is so much more she can learn. She is too valuable to the future to be shut up here and wasted in this way."

"And what future will there be if we cannot save ourselves now?"

"And what will that future be worth if you blight it now in your mindless impatience? I have not that much longer to live and a whole convent's worth of knowledge to pass on, knowledge that you and your daughters and your daughters' daughters will need in that future, knowledge that I cannot even write down to give you because none of you ignorant girls can read, as well as books and more books that are closed to you and so will be lost to the future. Later may be too late. I too have little time." Alyeeta had a strange kind of hunger gnawing in her voice.

"Tazzi belongs here," Pell answered, sounding both angry and frightened. "I found her and saved her. What right do you have to take her away from me? Besides, she does not want to learn this scribbling of yours and has already told you so."

I felt ripped apart in this conflict and at last jumped up, shouting, "Stop! Enough! I will not have you fighting over me as if I were some trophy from the spring games that you each think yourselves entitled to take home."

They both looked at me in amazement, then looked at each other and started to laugh, surprised and amused that the trophy had come alive and was speaking on its own. Others in the shelter were muttering and grumbling in their sleep. Those two may have gone on for the rest of the night with their argument, for all I knew. It did not cross my mind to make my own choice and so settle it all. Instead, I dragged my mat and blanket out into the woods, far enough away not to hear them. Even the Twisted Forest with the wind hissing through those unnatural branches was preferable to the grating of their voices. Even the sounds of owls and bats gave me more comfort. By morning, when I came back, it had all been decided. I was to ride away with Alyeeta.

"But who will care for Maireth?" I asked with concern.

"Renaise's cousin Arnella," Alyeeta told me, making it clear by her tone that everything had already been decided. "She was also the healer in her village and is glad to be of help here. I have shown her what needs doing. Besides, Maireth is out of danger and beginning to mend." In this way was my fate decided.

I went to gather my few belongings, thinking as I did so that I had hardly met this Arnella and knew nothing of her healing skills. The rest of Renaise's companions I met hurriedly just before Alyeeta rushed me out. She seemed to be afraid that Pell would change her mind.

As we left, Pell tried to draw Alyeeta a map of the way back. Alyeeta gave a snort of contempt or amusement. "No need for that. Even if I were taken from there with my eyes bound over I could find my way home again. When the time comes that Alyeeta cannot find her own place in the world, then that is the sign to dig her grave, for then she is truly dead."

Pell shrugged and turned to me. She pressed on me food and clothes and a pack for carrying them. In the doorway she gave me a rough kiss. When I was mounted, she slapped my leg and said, "Learn well everything you can, Tazzi. She is right that you can be more useful that way, and you were right that she can help us."

Pell was my lover, yet she sent me off with no more than this, no mention of when we would meet again, no endearment, no words of missing me. It was clear she had no love for me, only for my usefulness, and so had bargained me off to a Witch. Well, she had warned me. For her part she had been honest. And still I had not been prepared for such coldness. I felt the pain of it deep between my legs and the blade of it in my heart. I missed Kara again as if the wound of that loss were fresh made. My only consolation was that Renaise was lying safe asleep in the shelter. She was not to be some terrible weight of guilt and fear always to be carried in my heart. Pell, of course, took no notice of my turmoil. She was already busy making plans with Zenoria for the care of the horses.

Jhemar was to ride with us to learn the way. At the very last moment, just as we were turning to leave, Maireth called out for us to wait. I had thought her still sleeping and not wanted to wake her. She came stumbling out of the shelter, leaning heavily on a stick, the first time I had seen her walk. With her painful, awkward gait she came to stand directly before me. "I know I have seemed ungrateful, but now I want to thank you before you leave, though of course there is really no way to thank you enough for all your care." She looked me in the eyes for a long moment, then pressed something cool into my hand. Without another word to me she turned to Alyeeta and lifted Alyeeta's hands from the reins, though she had to lean against the horse to do so. Holding the Witch's hands in her still-bandaged ones, she kissed them both, saying, "Healing hands, hands of the Goddess." Alyeeta's eyes opened wide with surprise at this. With those words Maireth turned and hobbled back into the shelter, still with the aid of her stick. Alyeeta and I stared at each other in amazement. I knew the pain that little foray had cost her, as I could feel its echoes in my own body. My gift I did not look at then. I slipped it into my pocket for later when I was alone.

★

How we got back to Alyeeta's clearing that day was a wonder to me. It was nothing like following Pell. I puzzled if Jhemar got much use of it, though she diligently scratched some marks with charcoal on a piece of bark and noted the angle of the sun whenever she was able. If she could make any sense of this way, she was certainly more skilled in the woods than I could ever hope to be. Alyeeta, in the lead, went silently. She would ride a little way, stop, look about, cock her head, and listen as if to some inner voice. Then she would proceed, sometimes in the same direction and sometimes changing course. When at last I asked what she did, she answered with impatience, "Easy enough for any fool to see — I picture my home and try to feel which way it draws me." I had to trust that she could find her path back in this way, else we were lost in this forest that "fed on men and horses."

So we zigged and zagged this way and that. After a while, I simply sat my horse and watched the day flow by, not caring if we rode up or down or stopped or went on. The woods soon lost their taint of evil and seemed full of spring music. Suddenly, for no reason I could comprehend, I felt a rush of joy in my heart for the first time since Kara's death and my own terrified departure.

As I had not the guiding of us nor even the skill to mark the way, and we went mostly silent, I had much time to think as we rode. I decided I would let Alyeeta teach me all she knew of healing and of shielding from pain and of such matters, but that I had not the wits for reading nor for writing. The trying of it bent my brain painfully. Besides, I saw no use in it. No one in my village knew more than a few words of this sort. They lived well enough without it. I would waste no more time on this effort and determined to tell Alyeeta so quite clearly. I had even resolved to do it that very day, as soon as Jhemar had left.

Even so, it was not till long after Jhemar had ridden on, not till I was seated by Alyeeta's fire with a cup of tea in hand, and she was standing with her back to me searching her shelves for some books, not till then that I found the courage to say, "Alyeeta, teach me whatever else you think I should know. I will work hard with it and do my best. But spare me this struggle with the written word. I have no mind for the learning of this and see no use in it. Besides, no one in my family ever had such skills."

She set down what she was holding with a hard crack and whirled around to face me, making a sound in her throat like a growl or a snarl. "Goddess be my witness!" she shouted. "They want to stay as dumb as the dumb beasts they live among and be no better treated. With such thickheadedness how can they ever hope to build this new world they will need?"

Alyeeta came to sit before me. She gripped my wrists with such force the tea shook in its cup. Her eyes bored into mine, trapping me. I could neither move nor look away. In a voice that seemed to come from the very walls themselves, she said, "Tazzia, you will learn to read and write. If I teach you nothing else this time round, I will teach you that. I will free you from this prison of ignorance you live in. After that, all other knowledge will be open to you. And when, Goddess willing, there is peace again in this poor land, you will teach others of your kind. It is not for you alone we do this. Never speak to me of it again, only set your mind to the doing of it." I was trembling with the force of her passion and could find no answer.

When at last she released my eyes and my wrists, she sat back and said in a gentler tone, "If you find it so hard to learn, I must not be a good teacher. We will have to look for new ways. As to being a dirt-child, the child of peasants, believe me they learn as well as any other sort. That is what the Highborn would have you believe, that peasant children are some sort of witless animals. Not so, their own daughters are just as hard to teach or just as easy.

"Before the time of the Witch-kills, when Witches still had some power in this land, there were Witch convents. I was mistress of one such. Before the time of the Witch-kills, Witches were all educated women. We learned in the convents, and we taught there. It was the only place a young woman could get some schooling, poor as well as rich, Witch and non-Witch alike. Along with Witchcraft, which we taught only to those with the gift, and healing, which we shared, we had knowledge of all the herbs, a knowledge of plants and animals and of all the natural world, even a knowledge of the stars and the heavenly bodies and the paths on which they moved. We Witches are all scattered now. Who are we to leave it to, this great store of knowledge? Young women in the Zarn's cities have no place left to learn, but I will pass on to you as much as I am able, and you, in turn, will pass it on to others. In that way not everything will be lost." As I saw her face age and soften, I knew she was looking back into that other time. For the first time, I wondered with a shiver just how old Alyeeta really was.

All was silence for a while. I sat very still with my tea cooling in my cup, not wanting to draw her attention back to me. Suddenly she seemed to return to the present. She said, as if we had just been speaking, "As to uses, child, think of it, you could not even read an edict that spelled out your death though it was nailed up before you on a tree. That does not leave you well prepared even to save your own skin, much less to build a new culture, and that is what you will be forced to do. You might have preferred to remain the healer in your little dirt-village. It is no longer your choice. Ready or not, you have been shaken out into the world.

"Now, give me your cup, for it has all grown cold. And smile a little. You look to be made of stone. Come, come, am I as bad as all that?" Her face was suddenly friendly and warm with smiles.

"Alyeeta, you frighten me, as you well know," I answered curtly, not wanting to be so quickly melted.

"Ah, so you are afraid of me, Little One. Well, no doubt that is to be expected, but it will soon wear off. Let me tell you, it is a two-edged blade, this fear. I am afraid of you as well, and that will not change. There are not many things that frighten Alyeeta the Witch, of that you may be sure."

I was about to object when she raised her hand to silence me. "Listen to me well, Tazzia. You and your kind, you are something new in the world, something never seen before. Star-cursed or star-blessed, you may all be young fools, but still untrained, you have powers we Witches only dream of. The Zarns should be trembling in their beds. There is a thunder rumbling under the earth that will shake their power. Not all their edicts can save them. They will hunt you down as best they can, they will even kill some of you by whatever tricks they can learn, but most of you will survive." She paused, shutting her eyes as if looking inward. Suddenly she threw back her head and laughed, a strange, wild cackle like the old crone she sometimes played at being. "Well, indeed, well, well, well. So that is why She sent me to the market at Hamishair. Three times that morning I threw the pebbles, and three times the pebbles told me the same thing, to set up my little booth at the edge of the market. Whether we wish it or not, Tazzi, our fates are bound together by the will of the Goddess."

There was silence again. I sensed her looking out to some far place, or perhaps deep into the future. When she finally spoke, it was as if another Alyeeta spoke through her with the strange, hollow voice of an oracle. "When your powers are trained you will make changes in this land, great changes, but perhaps it will take your daughters or your daughters' daughters to tie them all together. I will not live to see the end of whatever is started here, but I will see a good beginning and have my part in it. It is no wonder the Zarns do not lie quiet in their beds and that they send their armies out to hunt for you. Danger, they see red danger before them and think to cut you down, but they will not succeed. They cannot read you well enough." Alyeeta's face had changed again. She jumped up. There was a mad look on her with the firelight leaping in her eyes, and her hair rising around her head like snakes uncoiling. She gestured wildly with her hands as she shouted, "Fire and blood and change, that is what I see!" She shouted this three times as if casting a spell, then seemed suddenly to come back to herself.

As if freed from her own spell, she sat down again quietly and said in a brusque but friendly way, "Well, you said I frightened you, and now, no doubt, I have frightened you even more. Enough of this. Let us set to teaching and learning, but first let us eat. Sometimes I forget the body must be fed. Look about if you like while I start the pot. This is to be your home for a while."

★

And so began my new apprenticeship, exciting, painful, confusing, sometimes bright and tearing as a flash of lightning, but never dull. The one sure, predictable thing about Alyeeta was that she was never predictable. That much I could depend on. All else was in the hands of change and chance.

There was that side of Alyeeta that was mocking, belittling, and seemed altogether devoid of sympathy or kindness. To try to do her bidding at those times was like trying to dance on knife blades that move and twist underfoot. When such a mood came on her, I would go to sit by the stream. Sometimes I went with her little pony, Gandolair, turning to him for shelter and for comfort, and soon we became fast friends. Luckily, she did not often show that side to me, or if she did it was not for long. Otherwise I might have tried to find my own way back through the Twisted Forest.

There was another part of Alyeeta that had a depth of caring, of compassion, a well of love and gentleness the likes of which I had found only in my mother. And beyond that, when she spoke of the Witch-kills, I sensed a core of grief and loss and pain in her greater even than my own. That I counted as a bond between us. In spite of that, I soon learned that she could not resist a clever, wicked word, not even if it left me cut and bleeding, could no more resist than a child can resist offered sweets. If it went through her mind and seemed witty, it had to come out of her mouth. Later she might make a careless apology in passing, something almost as hurtful as the first cut. Many times I came close to tears. Then I had to grit my teeth and try to forgive her so we could continue our work.

As a teacher, Alyeeta was as relentless as Pell in her own way. There was a passion in her to pass on what she knew, though the powers of the Star-Child and the Witch are differently shaped. Pushing and insisting, she often grew impatient with me as if it were almost too late already. There were times when I saw myself running as fast as I could with a hound snapping at my heels, surely not the best way to learn, as I tried to tell her. Then, abruptly, just as I was about to rebel, she would relent, flash me her compelling smile, touch my hand, and beckon me into her best chair while she made me a cup of tea. She might even cook me a special treat for which she knew I had a fondness.

Of all of it, the thing that most distressed me about Alyeeta, frightened me in fact, was her bitterness, her terrible, unrelenting bitterness, most of it directed toward "those humans," as she called all non-Witches. She had contempt for them as well, as if they were a different sort of creature from her altogether. I never knew where I stood in that naming and cursing, on which side of the line, or if she forgot at those moments that we were not the same thing. Oh, Alyeeta! At times I thought her house was the place I most wanted to be in the whole world. At others I wished myself well out of her sight and her power. Yet I did not leave. Looking back, that is what comes clear to me. I did not leave, though surely I was free to. No, I was far too curious, too bound by that curiosity. I think I was bound in other ways as well, though I did not understand that then.

And truthfully, there was much to stay for. There was far more praise than impatience. Except for shielding, anything to do with healing I learned quickly. It was so different from learning from Tolgath. There, I was to do only as she did. With Alyeeta there were reasons and theories and a whole body of knowledge attached to each thing she taught, as well as magic and power, a going outward as far as the stars, as well as a going deep inside.

Only in my war with written words nothing had changed, nothing improved. It was like struggling to peer through a fog. For brief moments the eye strains at a hint of this or that shape, a branch, or maybe a piece of roof-line before it is all swallowed again in a thick white blur. So it went on for days till I finally went to Alyeeta in despair, head splitting and tears running down my face. "Please, Alyeeta, please let it go. However much I try I cannot open my head to it."

I cringed, expecting a torrent of mockery and insistence. Instead, I saw a look of pain in her eyes. She drew me to her and pressed her fingers to my forehead. Under that cool touch the ache subsided. "There are other ways," she said, almost in a whisper. "Other ways, though I did not wish to use them." I thought she sounded sad, and very tired. Much later, at the turning of the night she cast a spell, a spell complete with candles and incense and strange, repeated words.

How to explain that moment, that mix of amazement, fear, and awe, that sudden flash of lightning illuminating all the landscape, ripping through the fog. It was an ordinary morning two days after Alyeeta's little spell. I was trying one more time, though with scant hope, to make some sense of this cursed writing. Suddenly those meaningless tracks and scratches in the dirt became letters. The letters became words. All of it hummed and buzzed with meaning as thick as a hive of bees, hummed like the secrets of a spell cracked open before my eyes. The letters swam in my tears. I threw back my head and howled. I had been blind and suddenly could see.

Rushing to the shelves, I snatched down the first book that came to hand. When I opened it the words jumped out at me, jumped off the page shouting their meaning. I turned page after page, laughing and crying in that torrent of words. Then I dropped the book and ran out to find Alyeeta.

She turned instantly. Her back had been to me as she bent over, planting in her little garden. "Alyeeta, Alyeeta!" I shouted as I ran out to her. With no explanation I pulled away her hoe, threw it down, and grabbed her hand. "Come, come, please come," I cried, tugging fiercely at her. Though she grumbled and tried to resist, she had little choice. Once inside I grabbed up that first book and began shouting the words as they jumped out at me. Then I dropped that book and pulled out another and then another, reading faster and faster in a sort of frenzy or fever. The power! The power of it, a fire blazing in the wind. Had Alyeeta not shaken my shoulders I might have gone on snatching down books and shouting words out of them till there was not one book left standing on the shelves. "Stop! Enough! Tazzi, Tazzi come back! You are like one possessed!"

When my wits cleared I saw Alyeeta staring at me with such concern that I sobered instantly. Blinking and shaking my head, I looked in amazement at the books scattered about the floor and piled at my feet. Alyeeta, seeing me safely back, said with her usual mockery, "Well, girl, this is no doubt a miracle to rejoice in, but it seems a trifle greedy. Perhaps you could begin by eating up one book at a time." Only later did I come to understand how precious, how valuable, how absolutely irreplaceable these books were to Alyeeta, books all written by hand with such pains-taking care, treasures that in my frenzy I had scattered on the floor.

Together we replaced them, each in its special place, all but the first one. With that one we sat till darkness came, heads bent and almost touching, drinking tea and, together, teaching me to read. When night fell we lit the lamp and went on, not even stopping to eat.

Have I already said that Alyeeta was unpredictable? Sometimes she seemed to me perversely contrary. Suddenly, without a word, she shut the book. Annoyed at this interruption, I looked up to see her staring at me so strangely my stomach clenched in fear.

"Alyeeta, what is it?" I whispered. "What is it?"

She looked at me a moment longer in that strange way, then said as if making a solemn pronouncement, "Books are good and fine for what they are, but remember that not all knowledge or learning will fit between the covers of a book. Remember that life itself is lived elsewhere."

I stared back at her, my eyes hard. My new game had been spoiled. I felt as if I had been snatched back from flying and dashed to the ground. Anger flared up in me. "Alyeeta, are you never satisfied?" I shouted. "You told me to learn to read and write, forced me to it, in fact. Now the way is open for that. What more do you want? By the Goddess, Witch, what more do you want?!"

"Much more," she snapped back in her mocking tone. Then, before I could think of a sharp and mocking answer, she said again, "Much more," almost in a whisper, said it with such sadness that it stopped my tongue.

I looked at her in surprise. She was staring down at the floor. I was completely mystified and at a loss for words. When she spoke at last, it was so softly that I had to lean forward and strain to hear her. "Books have been my friends and company for a long while. I know about books. I live with them. I have for years. But I am also a woman of flesh and blood. Books are not enough ... there is more to life..." When her words ran out there was a silence again in which I scarcely dared to breathe. Then she looked straight into my eyes, took a deep breath herself, and said, "Tazzia, I would like to be your lover."

This was so unexpected that I gasped in surprise. I was too astonished to speak. I could not imagine it, what with the great difference in our ages, our knowledge, even our origins. What would she want with me, a green girl, as she so often said, or for that matter what would I want with her? Even as I thought this a shiver of desire ran through me. With that I felt the pull and power of her wanting. I saw it in her eyes and so set myself to resisting. Suddenly I felt that power withdraw, felt Alyeeta close in on herself. She turned away and shut her eyes to not compel me with them, waiting silently, even bowing her head, as if she who had such power was herself the supplicant there. I took so long to answer that she was forced to speak at last. There was even a quaver in her voice when she asked softly, "What think you, Little One? Can you say me yes or no, or do you need more time to think on it?"

It was that quaver that decided me, that humble hopefulness. It went straight to my heart. And then I thought again, as I had so often since Kara's death, What does it matter, what does any of it matter? It is only a way to pass the time, to go on living. "If you wish it," I said aloud, hoping that Alyeeta had not heard my thoughts as well.

"And what do you wish?" she asked, looking at me again, no power or pressure with her gaze, only questions.

"I am curious. Besides, what harm can there be in it?" Not a very passionate response, surely.

I saw a look of hurt cross Alyeeta's face, then she laughed and appeared to ease. "Ah, well, no doubt there are worse reasons to be lovers." She seemed about to move toward me. Instead, she paused, looked me in the eye, and asked with much seriousness, "Are you sure, Tazzi?" I nodded. She gave me more of her deep, probing stare and asked again, no doubt to give me my last chance of escape, "Are you very sure?" This time when I nodded she leaned forward and kissed me. I was amazed at the softness and magic of that kiss, and even more amazed at the waves of passion and longing that rushed up my body.

When she sat back again I could hardly breathe. To regain my composure and get the ground back under me I asked, using her own mocking tone, "And when do you want to begin with our little adventure?"

"Now!" she said forcefully, clamping her hand around my wrist and standing up. Suddenly this was no game. I stood up with her, my knees shaking so they could hardly hold me, and my heart pounding. There was a wild roaring in my ears.

★

The lamplight was fading already in the brightening dawn by the time I slept at last. How can I write of what happened between us there, of what Alyeeta shared with me? It was so wild, so different from anything in ordinary life, such a pushing of the senses beyond what I knew or could contain that even now I cannot remember it clearly. Yet I know that never, never, not even if I live to be an old, old woman will I forget it — colors bursting up from a well of darkness, colors never seen before that had no names, and sights and scenes rushing past with every new wave of feeling that surged up my body. Time seemed to stretch out and bend in, filled with brilliantly lit images and quivering bands of light. Then colors and brightness and even light all folded in upon themselves and returned to the darkness, the darkness that is of the beginning, the central core, the deepest source where only feeling is. Then feeling became so fierce that soon it burst again into color and sound, the sound of new things finding voice, the sound of old, old things that have always been. And through it all the feelings of the body, each part and every part and all of it together being called to life by Alyeeta's hands and mouth till suddenly the sound that filled my head and the shelter and the clearing and perhaps the world itself was the sound of my own voice crying out.

What I do remember clearly is Alyeeta bringing me back, gathering me together, all the pieces, Alyeeta folding herself around me to hold me close and safe in the gentle pressure of her arms.

★

While we were loving I forgot our difference in age and all our other differences as well. Both willing and afraid, I had gone with Alyeeta into that dark, glorious place. There, differences had no meaning. But later, when I woke, suffused with loving and wanting to be held again, the bed was empty. It was not Alyeeta the lover I saw when I looked around for reassurance. It was an old woman, puttering at the fire, hobbling about and muttering as if to herself. She had even put on her kerchief with its rim of white hair, and already it was askew. When I came over to the fire, this old woman cocked her head sideways. She looked at me strangely, with no hint of recognition, and said not one word for my ears. She only went on muttering to herself. I could not catch her eye. It was as if all we had shared had been my madness or a dream.

Annoyed, disgusted, and most of all hurt, I watched this performance in silence for a few moments. Then I burst out angrily, "Alyeeta, why do you make fun of old women in that way? Someday we shall all become old women."

She straightened suddenly, threw off her kerchief, and said in her sharp way, "So we shall, and some much sooner than others." Then she pursed her lips and looked at me quizzically for so long that I felt uncomfortable under her stare and wished I had kept silent. "So that is what you think, eh, that I make fun of old women? Not so, Tazzi, you mistake me. Why should I do that when I am one myself, older than you can imagine?"

I looked at Alyeeta — straight-bodied and dark-haired — and shivered again. What was she truly? What did I know of her, this woman who had consumed me body and soul in the night, what did I really know of her?

"Make fun of old women?" Alyeeta continued with amusement. "No, that is not possible, my dear. That is not my way. Just think, more than half the wisdom of the world resides in old women. What I make fun of is the world. The world sees old women as ugly and quarrelsome or witless, useless, and harmless, and, above all, sexless — remember that, dry as the riverbed in the summer drought. That is what I play with, not old women but the way the world sees us. It is the best disguise, the best cover under which to move safely. Who looks closely at an old woman? They are all alike. Who cares what she thinks or does? The old fool, she is hardly human. Dressed this way I can pass anywhere. It is as if I do not truly exist among the living, as if I had become a cat or a ghost or a chair. People will say in my hearing or do before my very eyes the most amazing things, things I would never witness in this present guise.

"Ugh," she said suddenly. Hunching up one shoulder and dropping the other, she instantly turned herself into an old hag. One side of her face was drawn up in a grimace, her eyes crossed, her body bent and twisted sideways. "Even looking like this I could have more wisdom in my head than ten pretty young men, but who would ever guess?" she asked, leering and squinting up at me.

"Alyeeta!" I shouted in exasperation. On waking, my body filled with pleasure, my first impulse had been to put my arms around her in love and gratitude. Now I drew back from her, repulsed and almost afraid.

She grinned at me. "You see how easy it is? I suppose I should not tease you so, nor Pell either, but it is so hard to resist, especially with Pell. She is so young and serious, so puffed up with herself, so full of grand ideas. It is as if the whole weight of her world, or, rather, the fate of a people, rests on her shoulders. She is the commander, the general. She will bring her people together and herself lead them to a land of promise and safety." Alyeeta drew herself up and with passionate gestures said in Pell's voice, "And who knows what the future will hold when we have all come together?" At that moment she sounded so much like Pell at her most solemn that I exploded with laughter. Then, suddenly, I was angry for Pell's sake, seeing her so easily ridiculed.

"And she will do it, too," I said fiercely, myself sounding much like Pell. "She has the power and the vision to shape a future for us."

"Oh yes, she has, of that I have no doubt," Alyeeta answered, her voice thick and slow with sarcasm. "She does indeed have the power and the vision and strength and courage and love and much else besides. I have no doubt that she will bring her people together and get them to safety and build something new in this old world. Nonetheless, she is also a green girl, too much puffed up with her own importance and in need of a little trimming down."

"Oh, Alyeeta!" I burst out. "Why do you hate her so? It makes my heart ache to watch you two together, to hear how you speak to one another."

"Hate Pell?" She seemed genuinely surprised. "No, you mistake me again, Little One. I envy her, admire her, even, but hate her? Never! She is too much what I myself would like to be."

I thought she mocked me still and so spit out angrily, "You are only jealous of her."

Alyeeta's face changed. She looked thoughtful, almost sad. Then she said, very seriously, "Yes, in that you are right, Tazzi, quite right. I am jealous, not proud of it, but it is true enough. Pell will make it all happen. She will have her dream, and it lies before her, while we Witches have lost ours. It is all behind us now, lost in the Witch-kills, gone with the passing of the Great Star. We were able to come together enough to fight the Zarns and survive and save our lives, some of us at least, but what we built and made, the glory of the Witches, that has been destroyed forever. We are scattered and alone now. We do not have it in us to rebuild what was. The Witches who ran the convents and were a power in every city are now living scattered in huts in the woods, muttering to themselves with their books for company. Yes, I am jealous. Nonetheless, Pell will have her dreams, and we Witches will help make it happen."

"We?" I asked, surprised.

She shrugged and turned away, but not before I saw a bright edge of tears in her eyes. With a sigh I picked up her kerchief and laid it gently on the bench.

★

Things had moved so rapidly since I had left Pell's shelter that I did not remember Maireth's little offering till many days later. Then it surprised me by falling out of my tunic pocket to lie shining up at me from Alyeeta's dark, dirt floor. I picked it up and saw in my palm a pendant in the shape of a circle inside a triangle inside another circle. It had a yellow-green stone at the center that stared at me like the eye of a cat.

The coolness of it quickly warmed in my hand, and I felt a tremor of power run up my arm. I slipped the thong around my neck. As the warmth of the pendant settled between my breasts, I thought that perhaps Maireth was something more than she seemed. Wearing it, I even felt protected or guarded in some way.

Alyeeta, when she noticed, looked at it strangely and asked with a gesture of her head, "Where from?"

"From Maireth," I said quickly, as if defending something.

"Ah, I see," Alyeeta answered. She asked no further questions and made no comment, though I often saw her glance at it strangely, as if it held for her some challenge or a puzzle.

★

Alyeeta the lover, as she let herself be known by me, was very different from Alyeeta the Witch. The Witch was clever and sharp and bitter and cutting and, above all, critical. Alyeeta the lover was full of such tenderness and kindness and sweetness, had such knowledge of my body it seemed as if she had studied it like a craft. She gave me pleasures I could not have imagined, though never again was it like that first night, neither the terror of it nor the blinding beauty. For myself I could only give her back my girlish, untrained fumblings, but she accepted whatever I had as if it were a great gift and opened herself to me.

Alyeeta the Witch was something else. The moment she was upright, she resumed her mocking ways. Nothing was said of what had passed between us in the night, no more than if we had merely lain down together for lack of another bed space. When I questioned her on this one day, she looked at me thoughtfully with one of her long silences till I wished I had held my tongue. At last she answered slowly and with no trace of mockery in her voice, "Understand this, Tazzia, for I will not say it again; I love you, I love you more than anything in my life, even more than Gandolair. You have given me hope to live when I was ready to leave this body and this world. You have given me joy in places I never expected to meet it again in this life. You have given me the pleasure of watching something new shaping and forming, something of more worth than all the old, weary games I have already seen played out. All that is true, more perhaps than you can understand, more surely than I have words for. But I cannot change myself altogether. I am still Alyeeta the Witch and my tongue is still sharpened on both sides, though sometimes I myself bleed when it cuts you."

I nodded as I listened, tears in my eyes and my hands pressed between my breasts to hold all of that fullness in my heart. I did not think she made such a confession lightly or was likely ever to make it again.

★

Days went by. Strange to say, I seldom thought of Pell or of the shelter and what happened there. It seemed very far away, in a different world, in fact. I worked hard at what there was to learn, especially the reading and the writing now that Alyeeta's spell had opened the way for me. I even made some progress with the shielding. Alyeeta said it was the lovemaking that had broken through, though who knows where the truth of that really lay. She also told me that I would be a better healer for it. However it may have come about, something had changed. I even started being able to do for myself what Alyeeta had done for me with the touch of her cooling fingers on my forehead, to tap and use that river of coolness that is part of the Mother's healing side. So with my learning and with helping Alyeeta at her chores and sometimes sharing her bed for a time of loving, our life together began to settle into a sort of pattern. Then, one evening when I went out to relieve myself, I was startled by the sight of a man stooped over a small fire in Alyeeta's clearing.

12

It frightened me that I had not sensed the presence of this man. From the look of his fire he had been settled there in the clearing for some time. In truth he seemed not to have a presence, none of those waves of energy and being that go out from living things and most of all from humans. Ragged and dirty, he looked up sideways at me with no light of wits behind his eyes. Feeling instantly repelled, I was about to shout that there was an intruder when Alyeeta herself stepped from her house. On seeing this stranger she made a slight bow and said, quite formally, "Welcome to my home, Hereschell, and welcome to Soneeshi as well. I am glad that your circle brings you round to my little clearing again. These are interesting times, as you no doubt have gathered."

He appeared to take no notice of her, but made a slight nod in my direction. Alyeeta looked at me with one of her unreadable smiles. "Ah, yes, a Ganja," she said mysteriously. "But not really a Ganja, as you will soon discover." I could make nothing of all this, but felt some insult in the use of that strange word and the way Alyeeta spoke of me to such a one. This Hereschell made no answer, but dished himself up something from his pot and went with it to sit on a rock. Alyeeta settled near him. They leaned close together. If they spoke, it was not in words that I could hear.

Suddenly I felt a chill go up my spine. I turned quickly to see a gray wolf lying at the edge of the clearing. She was almost hidden in the brush, head up, eyes alert, staring straight at me. It was instantly clear to me that wolf and man were together. Why Alyeeta would be interested in such a man I could not fathom, but as long as he was harmless, he held no further interest for me. The wolf, however, drew me. She pulled at me like a compulsion or a binding spell, yet as soon as I took a single step in her direction she made ready to leap away. Instead of pursuing futilely, I settled myself against a tree and set to calling silently to the creature. At first she only turned toward me and whined. Then she got up, came a few steps, and lay down once more. Silently, with no aid of words, I called again and yet again, putting all I knew of creatures into that call. At last, after several more stops, she came the whole way, dropped to her belly in front of me, and lay her head in my lap. A rush of warmth went through me as I sank my hands deep in her ruff. There was a gasp of surprise that seemed to have come from Alyeeta. I never even looked up. At that moment nothing mattered but the wolf. I felt at peace in my body and at peace on the earth, blessed as if it were some aspect of the Mother Herself that lay under my hands.

Until long after dark I sat there, with no thoughts and no cares. I was content just to breathe with the animal that lay against me and be warmed by her warmth. Only when Alyeeta tapped me on the shoulder did I come back to myself. I had forgotten her, and the man as well. When I glanced up, I saw him standing by the fire watching me. For an instant there seemed a spark of mind in his look. It was the illusion of the firelight, perhaps, for as soon as he caught my glance I saw again that blank stare of idiocy.

"Come," Alyeeta said to me. "It is late already."

"No," I answered quickly. "I will sleep here by the wolf."

"No," Alyeeta said firmly. "You will come with me. Let her go for now. Hereschell needs her." Though she gave me a clear command, still there was an odd deference or hesitancy in her manner. The man made a sound low in his throat. With that the wolf got to her feet. Before she left, she took my wrist in her mouth and very gently pressed her teeth into my flesh, as clear a farewell as any human handclasp. Then, with a bound, she was gone, and I saw her again on the other side of the fire.

Spell-dazzled, I let Alyeeta take my hand, lead me in, and lay me on her bed. She sat down beside me and leaned forward so that a wing of her wild, coiling hair fell across my face. "So," she said in a whisper that was almost like a hiss, "so, you have this great power with wolves, eh? Soneeshi goes to no one but Hereschell, not even to me." Her tone, as so often with Alyeeta, was an odd mix of love and admiration and envy and some strange kind of anger. "You think you have power, do you, girl?" she continued ominously, "I will show you something of power tonight. You will ride the winds with me this time."

A sudden shyness came over me. "No, Alyeeta, he might hear us," I whispered urgently, thinking of the stranger in her clearing. She ignored my words as if I had not spoken. And indeed I had no will to resist nor any real wish to do so. There was a force in her that frightened me and thrilled me and made my breath come rough and fast. When she began stripping off my clothes I moaned, moving this way and that to help her.

This was to be different from other times, that I could sense. Her barely controlled wildness made me tremble. "This time you will feel everything," she whispered fiercely in my ear. "Everything! And you will remember it all." She straightened suddenly to light the lamp, saying, "I want to see what I am doing here. I want to light up my work." Then, quicker than my eyes could follow, she drew some lengths of cord from under the bed. Before I was even aware of her intentions she had me bound to the bedposts by my wrists.

It startled me when I found myself helpless against those restraints. "Release me, Alyeeta," I said angrily. "What sort of game are you playing here?"

"You will find release soon enough, Little One, soon enough, as soon as I am able," she said, laughing as I twisted and struggled against those ropes. "But you must be patient. It may take me a little while. Do not be in such a hurry for release. Enjoy your little time in bonds. Give your power over to me for this moment. You will find it a great pleasure to be unburdened in this way."

I was ready with a sharp answer, but when she leaned forward and dragged the soft coils of her hair along my body, brushing me everywhere with that featherlike touch, I could feel myself melting. With a groan I surrendered to her will, only to find that in another swift motion she had tied my ankles as well. So now I was bound hand and foot, naked on her bed while she loomed over me fully clothed, dark and oddly distorted in the quivering light of the lamp. She stood in such a way that she was mostly in shadow.

I had indeed given over my power, or it had been taken. When she began running her hands up and down my body, I ceased to struggle. "This time you will remember everything," she whispered again. I could sense her mind probing mine for my secret places, and for a while gave myself over to enjoyment. She used her hands, her mouth, her tongue in such a way that I no longer knew if it was one who worked on me or many, with many hands and mouths. I lost the boundaries of myself in that wash of feelings, but each time I came close to release, begged for it in fact, she slowed almost to a halt. Each time, when she started again, it was very, very slowly.

This seemed to go on forever, with me floating in some timeless place. Then suddenly all changed and shifted. The sensations were too strong, too sharp to bear. I struggled again against my bindings, gasping, "Too much, Alyeeta, too much! Stop, have mercy!" At my first cry her hands stilled. Her face, when I looked up at her, changed before my eyes. It took on a different aspect, lost its fierce, hungry look and turned remote and distant, or so it appeared from what little I could see, half-shadowed as she was. It seemed a stranger who stared down at me. I shivered and grew afraid. "Who are you? You are frightening me!" I gasped.

At that she straightened and said in her most mocking voice, "Oh, so the girl who is not afraid of wolves is frightened by a little loving." She crossed her arms with her hands tucked up into her armpits, hidden away as if she meant never to use them again. I felt all her passion and power withdraw from me, tucked away with her hands. "Do you want me to stop, then?" Her voice seemed to come from a great distance.

I shook my head, needing her hands, her touch, regretting my quick words. "No, no, go on. Only be a little more gentle," I said, almost in a whisper. She made no move and no sign that she had heard. By the way she stood now, she blocked all the light from her face. I could only see her outline, dark against the glare of it. "Please, please go on, Alyeeta," I heard myself begging to this shadow woman. "Please touch me again," I said, louder now in my desperation.

Still she did not move. Never in my life had I felt so naked as I did at that moment, lying bound and unclothed on Alyeeta's bed, with no hand on me and no mouth. I was alone with my longing, stretched out, shivering with desire and fear, my own face and body clearly lit by the lamp while Alyeeta stood in shadow. "Please, Alyeeta," I begged again. "Please touch me. I had not really meant for you to stop."

"But those were your words," she said coldly. Since I could not see her face and so read her mood there, I thought she might be so angry as to never touch me again. I thought she might even leave me in that condition, to die of desire. My whole body was swollen with it. I could feel myself pulling toward her, straining at my bonds, my back arching with want, a terrible ache of need between my legs. "Please," I said, pleading one last time, putting all my need in that one word.

With a sudden motion she shifted the lamp so that now her face was all in light, and just as quickly she tucked her hands away again. "Can you see me clearly? Watch my eyes," she said in a strange voice, as if speaking a spell. "Watch my eyes. Do not look away even for a moment. Watch my eyes."

I watched her eyes. I had no choice. I watched as her eyes traveled up and down the length of my body. Everywhere they touched me it felt like the touch of hands, but deeper, much deeper, hands inside my skin as well as on it. With all my senses quivering I followed those invisible hands. At moments I even saw my body through her eyes, my body laid out before her, flickering bronze in the firelight. At that time I had never been to the ocean, but later, when I was to feel the pull and swell of Her tides, I remembered that night in Alyeeta's bed when only her eyes touched me. Suddenly she leaned forward and put her face between my legs. At the touch of her tongue I cried out in release. The wolf howled an answer from her place in the clearing.

★

My first sight on waking that next day was of a toad sitting on the bedpost. It regarded me so thoughtfully with its hooded, gold-flecked eyes that I was tempted to nod and wish it good morning. I was alone there in the bed, my body pleasantly sore and languid. Man and wolf were gone, that I could sense. Alyeeta sat in the far corner of her house talking rapidly and in low tones to another woman. I lay listening. No matter how I tried I could not catch the meaning of their words, and so thought they spoke in a different language. Then Alyeeta said clearly in Kourmairi, "She is awake now." This other woman stood up and walked over to look at me. I thought from her manner and from the way Alyeeta spoke with her that she must also be a Witch.

In appearance she looked older than Alyeeta, though I knew by now how little appearances meant with Witches. She was very thin, thinner than Pell, not thin and frail with age, but thin and hard like a branch of garzwood such as farmers use to make their fences. Nothing can pass through garzwood. It only hardens more with age. That was my first impression of Telakeet, that she would get harder and more impenetrable with age. She wore her gray hair short and tight like a cap or helmet on her head. Her face was dark and deeply lined. There was nothing soft or gentle there, nothing kind or forgiving in the unrelenting stare she turned on me as she peered down into my face. "She does not look to be so much after all, certainly nothing to frighten Zarns and set old women to chasing after her," she said in a tone even more acid than Alyeeta at her worst.

I flushed with anger, pulling the covers up tight around me to protect my nakedness from her hostile stare. Alyeeta said something sharply in that other language. The Witch laughed and answered rudely, "Well enough if you like them that way." Then she turned back to me and said, "I am Telakeet, the Witch, and we will soon meet again." With that she scooped up the toad from its post, slid it into her pouch, and was gone, slipping out of the room like a shadow before I could sit up to see her better.

Alyeeta came to sit by me, stroking my warm, sleep-softened flesh and looking hungrily at me. I shook free of her. "No, Alyeeta, enough. You will swallow up my soul. We have other things to do." I was glad I could find the strength to resist. In truth, it was myself I was fighting as much as Alyeeta, for I could easily have sunk back upon that bed and fallen under her hands again. I did not think this was what Pell had sent me here to learn.

"Yes, true, it has been such a long time since there has been some good loving in my life that it is a danger. I could get drunk with it and lose all sense. We must get you ready. When Hereschell returns, you are to go with him and take a message to Pell."

"Hereschell?" I said with surprise. "But how will he know the way?"

"Do you know the way? Did you mark it well when we came? Could you find your way back alone?"

Embarrassed, I had to shake my head at all her questions.

"Do you think I would send you into the woods with someone who would lose you there or betray you to the guards or bring you some harm?"

I shook my head again.

"Good, then it is settled."

"But he is dumb," I burst out, angry at having to state so obvious a truth.

"Dumb means silent, not stupid," Alyeeta answered sharply. "He still has eyes to see and ears to hear, and the wolf is his nose. I know of no one better in the woods." She sounded offended at my words.

A sudden cold fear gripped my heart. "Alyeeta, are you sending me away?"

"No, child, it is already too late for that, far too late. I am sending you both together because Hereschell cannot go alone among those women with a message, and you cannot find the way by yourself. You can come back as soon as it is done." With that she handed me a note that was folded and sealed, saying, "Keep this safe. Open it and read it to Pell when you get there."

"What does it say?"

"You will find out when you read it."

I got up and dressed myself with ill will and dread in my heart. When I went out, it surprised me to see the day already well on its way. At least the wolf would accompany us — that much was a pleasure to be held onto.

★

The heavy silence was oppressive, yet what was there to say to one who could not answer? One who was mute and witless, though he held my life in his hands? It wearied me to even try to think of such a conversation. And as for speaking in thought, more response came back from rocks and trees than from this man. So, with Hereschell always in front and me coming doggedly behind trying to keep pace, we rode a long time with no words through a narrow, wooded way. This seemed like no way I had been before, but I did not try to judge, I merely followed. In spite of my hard lesson with Pell, I paid no heed to how we went. It felt to me as if all power in the matter had been taken out of my hands. Besides, exhausted as I was by my work with Alyeeta, and, truth be told, by the lovemaking as well, one tree or rock or hill looked much like another to me.

It had been well into the afternoon before we set out, with the sun already slanting low. This meant traveling in the dark or, worse yet, camping on the way. Considering the company, neither of these prospects pleased me, but when I had suggested we delay till morning, Alyeeta would not hear of it. I wondered if it was to humble me, or to teach me something, that she had sent me traveling on the road with a fool, and a silent one at that.

At first Soneeshi ranged close by, sometimes to the left and sometimes to the right, but mostly within sight of us. It gave me much pleasure to watch her move. Often she seemed more like a swift, gray shadow than a being of fur and bone and flesh. For a while she disappeared on her own affairs and was gone so long I began to worry. When she appeared again, a silent gray shape moving far to the left of us, I felt a surge of joy and relief. I looked at Hereschell's ragged back bent before me, and in spite of my hard feelings toward him, I thought, anyone who has such a way with wolves cannot be altogether worthless.

"Anyone who has such a way with wolves cannot be altogether worthless." The words were said aloud as if in that instant they had been plucked from my brain. Hereschell had turned back to look at me with a grin on his face and sharp, mocking wit in his eyes. I could have fallen from my horse in amazement. I would have been no more surprised if it had been his horse that spoke those words to me.

"You saw into my head," I said angrily, feeling both tricked and intruded on.

"Yes, I can read minds when I need to. You and I thought almost the same thing at the same time. It is true that Soneeshi comes to no one else but me, not since Corbin died. You may be a rude Ganjar, but there must be something more to you as well."

"And you speak. I thought you silent," I said stupidly, trying to cover my confusion.

"When it suits me I speak."

"Why did Alyeeta not tell me?"

"Because it is for me to speak or not to speak, my choice to make, not Alyeeta's."

"But why, for what purpose, do you play the fool?"

"It saves me a great deal of nonsense with the Ganjarin to pretend that I am dumb. Also I learn many secrets, some of them valuable to Wanderers. You cannot imagine the things that are said in front of me by those who think me stupid as well as silent."

I blushed at those words. I was in an agony of embarrassment now for the things I had said to Alyeeta in front of this man, and even more for the things I had thought. Damn her, anyhow — she could at least have silenced me.

"I feel in you a great confusion of regret for all you have said and thought of me. Why bother? Regret is for the real fools. The way to go is forward. Let us tell each other stories and enjoy this ride we have together, since for the sake of the wolf I have chosen to speak to you, something I do not do for many Ganja, very few, in fact. Or perhaps it is not for the wolf, but for the sake of our friend Alyeeta who shared love with a young fool so many years ago. Either way it is an honor, and you may take it as such." He nodded his head in a slight bow.

I stared in amazement at this man, dirty and ragged and with his hair all in mats, who spoke like a Highborn lord in disguise, such as those in the childtales told in our village. He stared back at me with such fierce intelligence in his eyes that it made me want to look away, but I determined to hold his glance.

"You are not a Ganja," he said at last. "Alyeeta is right about that. You are something new, something worth studying, perhaps."

"And you," I said, stung by his arrogance, "you are not a fool and you are not a wolf, however you may seem. What are you, then?"

"A Wanderer."

"Ah, yes. Wanderers used to pass through our village sometimes. Pell has spoken to me of the Wanderers."

"So then, I suppose, you know all about us." I heard such bitterness in his voice that it startled me.

"I know what is said," I answered curtly. "Now tell me what you think to be the truth."

He had turned back and was looking straight ahead. As he was silent for so long, I thought he would not deign to speak to me again. I could not help but notice how straight he sat his horse now that he no longer played the fool. Finally, out of boredom, when this renewed silence had gnawed at me long enough, I asked, "Who takes up a Wanderer's life and for what reason?"

I was still not sure he would answer till finally, without turning his head, he said, "Different ones and for many different reasons. The younger son of an uppercaste Shokarn family, for instance, one who can expect to inherit little or nothing, not the house, nor the land, nor the money, nor the title, and yet is untrained for a trade and so must live on his older brother's charity. Such a one sees no expectations before him and may find a Wanderer's life more promising. Or the youngest child in a peasant's hut where there is already a crowded table. That one may be left in the hills for the wolves or the birds-of-death. When the Wanderers find such a child they will take it to raise in their own way. Many a mother has prayed, in spite of her fears, for the Wanderers to pass through. Or think of the young woman sold by her family in marriage, or not even in marriage, to a man she abhors. What can she hope for from such a life? With the Wanderers she can slip free of her fate. Or the woman who sees before her years of being beaten by her husband and finds some way to escape her marriage, yet must flee her village as well. The villagers will only send her back to be beaten again, even if it means her death. Such a one may come among us and find protection in 'the Code.' Then, of course, the Wanderers themselves come together and make children who may become Wanderers as well."

"And you?" I asked, thinking he might be one of those Highborn younger sons.

"I was one of those left for the wolves."

Left for the wolves — I hoped that might mean some story that would last us the rest of the way. It was almost dark by then. In the gloom before us I could barely make out the piece of road we would soon need to cross. Just as we were starting down the last steep part of the path, the wolf growled and crouched low. Instantly Hereschell swung his horse about, squeezed past me on the path, and signaled me to follow him back up the slope to the safety of some large rocks. There he leapt off his horse, scrambled up the largest rock, and lay flat out on the top, turning his head this way and that as if sniffing the wind. The wolf was still growling low in her throat. Except for that, there was only the silence of night around us. Then, far off, I heard the sound of horses. With a chill of fear I dropped off Marshlegs and pulled us both behind the shelter of the boulder to wait for those men to pass. Instead, they seemed to stop and gather on the road below us. Soon I heard horses coming from the other direction as well. Hereschell dropped down beside me and said with disgust, "By the Mother, do they mean to camp below us right at the crossing?" We listened for a while in silence. It seemed as if rather than leaving, more and more riders were joining them.

"Come," Hereschell said at last as he swung back onto his horse, "there is no use waiting here. Who knows what they plan to do? We will go back and camp in a little valley I know. In the early morning we will ride across the river instead of going by the road." All my worst fears had come true, but it no longer mattered. As I rode up next to him he said, "Good thing we were not in the middle of crossing that road with such a mob of them coming from all sides. We Wanderers do not have the same powers of protection you are blessed with. For myself, I prefer a more peaceful way to pass the night than playing chase with men and horses in the dark."

★

We camped in a tight circle of boulders with just room enough between for the horses to pass through, such a circle as might have been made by the Old Ones and left for us to puzzle on. I was afraid the firelight would betray us, but Hereschell hid his fire well. He dug a little pit for it in the sheltering curve of the largest boulder, the one that towered far over our heads and hid the stars in that direction. While we sat huddled together in this shelter he boiled water, cutting into it chunks from a large lump of hard, gray stuff. After a time, of stirring, this turned into a gray gruel. Though the smell was pleasant enough, the sight of it near took my appetite away. "Eat," he said gruffly when it was done. "It is better than it looks. If nothing else it is hot and filling."

I forced myself to take the first taste and soon was holding out my bowl for more. "What is it?" I asked, thinking this something Pell might find useful.

"Korshi," he told me. "The Wanderer's trail food. It is made of fruit and crushed tarmar, cooked long together till it forms a thick mush, then poured into big pans to cool, harden, and dry in the sun. After that it is cut into blocks such as the one I used tonight. Korshi is the best food for the road, easy to make, light to carry, long-lasting, and, most important, good to the taste." He looked at my outstretched bowl that waited for yet another helping. "Did I not say it tastes better than it looks?"

It surprised me how comfortable I felt, sitting by a fire with this stranger, the very thing I had most feared. The wolf had come to lie between us, and we each had a hand in her ruff. "Tell me your story, Hereschell. Since the wolves did not eat you, someone else must have carried you off."

"It is not the wolves who eat abandoned babies, but the birds-of-death. As to my story, if you really wish to hear it, it was one of the Wanderers, a woman named Liera, who found me, but she was no more my mother than many others. Those who had milk nursed me, and others carried me about strapped to their backs. When I grew old enough to move about on my own, I went from mischief to mischief, curling up at night like a puppy to sleep in whatever warm spot I found, sure I would be fed and cared for. The Wanderers taught me as best they could whenever I stayed still long enough to learn. I was loved and cuffed by whoever was about, cuffed gently but often, for I did not listen well. They moved constantly and I went with them, carried on some strong back. That was the only life I knew. Then, when I was about four years of age this happened." He raised his shirt to show me a long, puckered red scar that ran from his chest under his arm and halfway down his back.

I gasped, barely able to stifle a cry. "The Wanderers did that to you?" I asked with horror, having already seen far too much burning.

"Oh no!" he said quickly. "No! Never! The Wanderers may be rough and careless at times with the children they gather, but they are never cruel. It would go against 'the Code,' the Cerroi, the Great Wheel of Fate. No, I did it to myself while rushing about. Running where I had been told to walk, just what I had been scolded for so often, I stumbled into the fire and fell across a smoldering log.

"This was not my first accident, only one of many, but it was by far the worst, and beyond Wanderer skill to mend. Besides, they were moving on again and could not be so burdened. They did what they could for me, then took me to an old Witch in the Crom Hills for healing, trading her a supply of yima for that service.

"That Witch was a good healer, skilled and patient with my burns, but she had scant patience for a small boy's wildness. She grumbled and scolded constantly, though I had already been much tamed by my accident. Still, she never beat me, though many times she threatened to, especially when I forgot what she told me before she had even finished speaking, or when I lost or broke something of value to her, something I was not supposed to lay my hands upon.

"She taught me as best she could some of her healing skills and knowledge, hoping, I suppose, to make an apprentice of me. It was there at her fire that I first met Alyeeta, and even then she was not young. What an impression she made on that small boy so long ago.

"By the time Corbin came through with his knife-sharpening business, the Witch had wearied of me or decided I was hopeless. She traded me off easily enough for a wolf cub. Corbin had a litter of them from a wolf bitch who had died in a hunter's trap. The Witch said the pup was less wild and more tameable and altogether more useful than I was, but Corbin was well pleased with the trade. He had long wanted a child for help and for company. I seemed strong and sturdy enough for his hard life. So, on a nod and a handshake I became apprentice to a sharpener instead of a healer. I had no regrets in the matter, then or ever.

"Corbin became mother and father and teacher to me, the first human, I think, to whom I gave my love and trust. He trained me to keep his fire and cook and help with his knife sharpening. For the first time ever in my life I did my best to listen and be good. Together we went up and down the coast, stopping at Koormir settlements to ply his trade. Of the wolf litter, we traded them all but one. That one became my companion and teacher in the woods and the passion of my young life.

"We lived so for a few years, going south in the winter to Wanderers' Gatherings and north in the summer for work, sleeping mostly under the stars when the weather allowed. I had the wolf for blanket and pillow while we lay by our fire with Corbin telling me stories of his life and all he had seen. For that time I was quite content with my lot and thought I had fallen on great good fortune.

"Then, one fall, Corbin grew very ill with something neither of us could cure. A terrible, deep cough shook his body and wracked him with pain. We met with a band of Wanderers who said they would take him south with them for the winter and care for him and cure him. They told me I was welcome to come as well, but not the wolf. They were afraid for their little children. None of our arguments could change their minds. I had to make a hard choice. With the heedlessness of youth I chose for the wolf, thinking I would meet with Corbin again in the spring.

"I waited for him in our appointed place long after the time we had set. It was the Wanderers who came at last to meet me, not Corbin. He had died that winter. I was grief-stricken, and in some way blamed the Wanderers for his death and for my absence from his side as well. In truth, what choice would I have made had I known I was never to see him again? Would I have left the wolf?

"For a while after that I had no wish for human company. I gave away my tools and with them my trade and went away with the wolf, far from the lives of people. She taught me how to live: how to watch and listen, how to smell what travels on the wind, how to walk soft and silent in the woods, how to move swiftly. Every few years she mated and had cubs, but in the end she always came back to me with them. When she grew old she left me one from the litter. She and the others vanished in the night. That one is Soneeshi, the gray shadow that follows me now." She looked up at him at that moment as if she understood his words.

When he leaned forward to put on the pot for tea, I thought suddenly of Alyeeta. "Tell me, Hereschell, how old is she really?"

"Soneeshi?" he asked.

"No, Alyeeta," I said impatiently, thinking I was at last to have an answer to this mystery.

He laughed and shook his head. "Alyeeta — do you think because I shared a bed with her for a short while that I shared all her secrets as well? You should know better than that. Alyeeta takes what she wants and gives what she wants. She does not answer to anyone."

Rebuffed, I said sharply, "You are a man of intelligence. Does it not bother you to play dumb? When I first met you, you seemed so ... so..."

"Witless," he said with a grin. "How easily we are fooled into seeing what we want to see. How afraid we are to look further. The shambling fool, the vacant village idiot, witless, helpless, harmless." He slouched forward, let his head fall sideways, mouth open, jaw slack, eyes staring past me into nothing. Then with a laugh he straightened again and stared right at me, through me, in fact. At that moment I felt as if a wolf in man's shape looked into my eyes.

"But why wish to appear less than you are?" I insisted.

He shrugged as if it was of no account. "For much the same reasons Alyeeta sometimes chooses to appear as a mindless old hag. The good opinion of others does not concern me much, but my safety and the ease of passing among them does. Also, as a single man, wandering alone, I could be seen as a threat and a challenge. Ordinary men are like bristling dogs on their doorsteps, protecting what they think is theirs against all comers, even when there is no real danger. Believe me, Tazzi, I could use my wits to make them respectful and afraid, for I have some tricks and a little power at my command, or I could use my sham of witlessness to make me seem harmless. The second is easier. It takes far less effort and less energy to maintain. If it fails, I can always fall back on the first.

"They are all familiar with Hereschell. As a known fool, I can go where I choose. They think me no threat to their safety, and so are less threat to mine. The Kourmairi villagers are to me like cattle whose fields I must cross. Do I care what the bull thinks of the quality of my mind, as long as he does not block my way with his horns or think to charge at me? Besides, I give them a chance to feel superior. They are able to pity me, and that makes them generous, thinking, no doubt, 'My lot may be hard, but at least I am not like that poor creature.' Often they feed me and house me out of that guilt and pity."

"Would it not be better to be a knife sharpener than to live off the crumbs of pity?"

He laughed. "Ah yes, to have honest and honorable work. Well, to tell you the truth, the pay is about the same. Besides, I have no more wish to be bound by work than by place. But have no fear. Your precious Kourmairi are not coin-out-of-pocket for my sake. They save their hardest brute work for me since I am mindless, and they think of their food as charity. I always do more than I am paid for and am left in peace with my own thoughts. If I wish to use my wits or be my true self, I go to a Wanderers' fire circle or to a Gather. There I can sing my songs and tell my tales, speak my dreams, match wits with the best of them, and so be known and remembered for who I truly am. For the rest, humans are no more to me than cows or pigs, save that they are far more dangerous."

His words were such a mix of mockery, bitterness, and longing that I grieved for him. "And have you never wished for a home, a fixed abode, somewhere that is yours?" I asked.

"Never. The earth is my home; the sky is my roof. I can make a nest anywhere. If I stay too long in one place, something in my spirit begins to wither and die. Then I wake one morning to find my feet on the road no matter what I leave behind. Those with fixed homes do not grieve for me. Why should I grieve for them?" He stood up abruptly. "Enough! For a man of silence I have filled this night with words. It is time to sleep. Morning comes all too soon." With that he took the pots from the fire and began kicking dirt over the embers. We were suddenly swallowed by darkness. But I had heard my story and so slept content, curled up by the wolf with my head on her flank.

As we set out next morning, Hereschell signaled me to ride up next to him. "You ride as if blindfolded, dumb to the way, yet you are no city girl. Do you know nothing of the trail?"

"I knew the woods around my village, knew them well in daylight or darkness and at any season of the year, but that is gone now, gone forever, and all this is strange and new to me." I had not meant to let my grief leak through in that way. The words sprang from my mouth before I could stop them.

He looked at me with concern, but his voice was stern. "No matter what you have lost back there, you have chosen to live. That is not a choice you make only once. It is a choice you need to honor and make again each day. To survive you must learn to find your way wherever the fates have thrown you. Otherwise you make a choice to die, though death may not collect you right away."

For the rest of the ride he taught me to see: to observe the shape and form and texture of the land that rose and fell under our horses' hooves, the type of trees and vegetation, the shape of the rocks, the slant of the light, and, most important, how to find the subtle markings where the paths crossed or turned, markings I had never noticed before. He did not say, but I knew they must be Wanderers' markings and was touched that he was sharing them with me. By the end of that morning's ride I knew more than from all my rides with Pell. Hereschell had opened the book of the roads for me as Alyeeta had opened the book of words.

★

When we rode in that morning Pell was standing before her shelter, arms crossed, anger blazing from her eyes. "Why have you brought a man to this place?" she called out to me in a voice full of rage.

"Alyeeta sent him to guide me back with a message," I answered quickly.

"Then you are a miserable, useless fool that you cannot find your own way. I knew I should not trust that Witch. She could have come herself or left her message home. I need no man here. You have shown him our secret paths and ways and now we are no longer safe. What does Alyeeta know of our lives? What does she care?"

I was about to protest when Hereschell himself spoke in a voice hard with contempt. "Alyeeta knows better than you who to trust and who not to. She has played this game for many more years than you have lived and kept herself alive through the Witch-kills. You think yourselves so secret and so special. Let me tell you, young woman, none of the paths we came here by are unknown or new to me. Most of the ways you go by are Wanderers' paths. There are few places in Yarmald or in Garmishair either that Wanderers have not been before you. You flatter yourselves with your cleverness, yet you leave your traces everywhere. It would not take a wolf's sharp nose to track you down. A simple farm boy could find you if he kept his wits about him."

I saw Pell struggling for words. "Enough! Enough of that," she shouted back at him when she could speak. "I need no man riding into my dooryard to teach me how to live. I have seen enough ugly death already at the hands of men." She was shaking with rage.

At that moment Maireth rushed out of the shelter and stopped short in surprise. "I know this man. He worked on my father's farm, but I always thought him a mute and simple as well."

"You saw what you wanted to see," Hereschell said coldly.

"No," Maireth answered sharply. "I saw what you wanted us to see, and that is different."

Hereschell turned to me and said in a voice full of bitterness, "You see why I said it was easier to pass for dumb and witless than to deal with the Ganjarin as equals?" He turned his horse, clearly meaning to leave.

"Wait, Hereschell, wait. Listen to me, Pell, he knows things that are useful, things we need to know. He can help us." Now I was shouting too, desperate to make her hear.

Pell whirled on me, about to answer, when Jhemar rode in and swung off her horse with a shout of greeting. "Hereschell, friend-of-the-road, what are you doing here? I did not think to see you till this fall's Gathering, and surely not to see you in this place." As she rushed up to him, he leaned down from his horse. Their hands met in a complex and elaborate dance of greeting. Then she stepped back to look at him and slapped him on the leg. "How goes it, Brother? You look just the same. What brings you here among us? Surely you are not leaving just as I arrive. I would consider that a great insult and a greater loss, especially since I hear you to be favoring us with speech this day."

Hereschell's face was tight with anger. Looking straight at Pell, he said with hurt dignity, "Yes, and it has been a grave error, as your captain can explain to you." Again I was amazed at the pride and presence of this man who looked like the most ragged of beggars.

Jhemar looked at Pell in bewilderment. Pell looked back and forth from Jhemar to Hereschell, the struggle in her heart written plain on her face. Suddenly her face went calm and clear. She stepped forward and said quite formally, "Please forgive my ignorance and my rudeness. You are welcome in my home." With that she made a slight bow and held out her hand. Hereschell sat his horse, hesitating, searching Pell's face as if for signs, not riding off, but not reaching out either. Pell did not draw back her hand in pride. She waited quietly, hand outstretched. There was a kind of stillness all around her. In all the time I was to know Pell, I doubt if she did anything that I admired more than the way she stood there that day, proudly and humbly holding out her hand, waiting to see if her apology would be accepted.

At last I saw Hereschell's face soften. He held out his hand to meet hers, a simple handclasp this time, but filled with meaning. "Well," he said with a slight edge of mockery, "there have probably been gentler meetings, but this is the one we had. I hope your welcome is as generous as your rudeness. It may be worth staying for."

Pell laughed suddenly, her usual good humor restored. "We promise to do our best here, myself most of all."

At that, Hereschell swung off his horse at last. Pell reached to take the reins, saying gravely, "Please make yourself easy here. Let me see to food and water for your horse."

Hereschell answered with equal gravity, "I leave my friend in your capable hands."

When I finally slid down from Marshlegs's back, my shaky knees would hardly hold me upright. Only then did I notice the many curious new faces that peered from the shelter or from between the trees, watching this scene. Among them I noticed Renaise's sister Thalyisi, her cousins Arnella and Ethrin, and her friend Tzaneel. In that mass of strangers they almost looked to me like friends. Later I learned that

Renaise's ride home had gathered at least ten or twelve new ones, among them Josleen and Megyair, Pell's friends from Ashire. Those two and several others had met Pell at the crossroads a few nights after Renaise's return.

The greatest surprise of my homecoming was to see Maireth walk out to greet me without the aid of a stick. She still limped slightly, her hands were bandaged, and there was a blaze of puckered red across her face and neck, but altogether she looked far better than I would have expected. It seemed as if Alyeeta's salves and Arnella's healing had worked some sort of miracle after all.

★

That night Renaise and her sister Thalyisi made us such a feast that I was sure there had been another raid on the market. The shelter was crowded now with new women. There was no room at the overloaded table for everyone to draw up a mat or rock, so most simply sat themselves in a circle on the dirt floor. No one took their plates outside. Curiosity was too strong a glue, and Hereschell was certainly an oddity among them. Much to my discomfort, many of them stared at him quite openly.

It was not till we had all gathered to eat that Pell thought to ask me for Alyeeta's message. I took the folded note from my pouch, broke the seal, and read what was written there, as surprised by those words as anyone in that circle.

"From Alyeeta the Witch to Pell of the Star-Blessed, this is to ask if you would come with all your women to my shelter. The other Witches wish to meet with you there to see how we may best work together for our mutual aid and benefit. Come if you can the day after the morrow. Please to send your answer back with Hereschell. Tazzi will write it for you. As it must be, Alyeeta of Eezore."

There was a buzz of excited voices from around the table. Pell was watching me with surprise. "Are you sure of what it says, Tazzi? Did you memorize it all correctly?"

"No, I memorized none of it," I said with pride. "I never saw it before this moment, not until I broke the seal. I read it to you word for word, exactly as Alyeeta wrote it."

Pell leaned forward and stared at me intently as I passed the paper to her. While the others talked excitedly, she reopened the note and gazed at it for a long while, mouthing the words. When she looked up at me again there was a strange, hungry look on her face. "So you can really read," she said in a voice so low it was almost a whisper, a voice that had in it a mix of wonder, envy, admiration, and even an edge of anger. "Who would have thought it possible in so short a time."

"Oh, Pell, I could teach you too," I said eagerly.

"No," she answered quickly, shaking her head and sounding almost frightened. "No, when there is peace, when we are in a safe place, then it will be time enough for me to learn such things. For now it is good that you can read and write. Alyeeta was right. It will help to keep us safe." Then Pell turned back to the others as if nothing had passed between us. "So the wheel turns," she said loudly. She had a wolfish grin. "We ride out tomorrow, unless there are any of you who think we should not go. Either way, Tazzi will write our answer." This was followed by some discussion back and forth, but in the end all were agreed that we should meet with the Witches.

After that there was much talk around that table, but at first Hereschell was almost silent, full of stiff dignity, not at all like my easy comrade of the trail. Then I told the story of our ride and spoke of his wonderful block of food. Renaise begged to see this Korshi. Suddenly she was sitting next to him, asking questions, with Thalyisi on his other side. Hereschell was talking as if to an old friend, while the brick of Korshi passed from hand to hand being explained and commented upon. I saw Pell's face light up when she held it. "Food to travel with, food for traveling light and far," she said, nodding.

Later I dragged my mat outside, thinking I would rather try to make my peace with the trees than endure the stuffy confines of the over-crowded shelter. When I lay down to sleep, Pell and Jhemar and Hereschell were still squatting by the fire, heads bent together, talking of guard strength and troop movements and where the edict was already posted. I could tell from the smell of it that they had some Korshi cooking in the pot. From their talk, I thought they would soon be drawing maps in the dirt.

Suddenly I heard Hereschell's voice raised in anger. "No! Never! No Wanderer would touch fastfire! We certainly would not pass it on to another for their use. We are not killers nor do we aid others in killing, least of all with that most terrible of weapons."

"Not for killing, Hereschell, I pledge you my life on that. We would never use it on another, not even the Zarn himself, but we must have some to discover a way to quench it. Please, Hereschell, help us. Who else can we turn to?" Pell was almost pleading.

"Never!" Hereschell repeated emphatically. "Say no more. Let that be an end to it." After that their voices went back to a murmur. I fell asleep wondering how Pell would manage. I knew her well enough to be sure she was not done with this project.

13 I woke with Soneeshi licking my hand. Beyond her, in the dim grayness of dawn, I saw Hereschell mounted and ready to ride. But I have not written our answer, I thought in a panic as I struggled to free myself of the bedding.

Hereschell rode over and looked down at me with amusement. "There is no need of a written note only to say yes. Dimwitted as I am, I can remember that much. If speech fails me, at least I can nod." He spoke low, mindful of the many sleepers.

Grinning at his mockery, I settled back gratefully into my bed. "I suppose I wanted to please Alyeeta with my writing," I said ruefully.

"And she no doubt wanted to show off your prowess. I, for one, was much impressed with your reading last night — something I have never learned. But surely there is no need for you to leap up so early to write that one word and surround it with many others just for show."

Looking up at this semblance of a ragged beggar, I was suddenly struck by how much I would miss this man, this fool that I had thought it an insult to be sent out with. "Thank you, Hereschell, for everything you taught me. And thank you for your patience with my own witlessness."

"Thank you, Tazzi. I had not thought there was much left for me to learn, least of all from a Ganja, but I was wrong."

"And I thought Alyeeta sent me out with you to teach me a lesson — to punish me in some way."

At that he threw back his head and laughed aloud, forgetting his attempt at silence. "I think that Witch sent us out with each other to teach us both a lesson," he said with a grin. Then he paused and looked thoughtful. "That

Pell — you could have done worse. She is not half-bad, very capable, in fact. She will get you through all this if anyone can do it."

"And what of all those things you said of her yesterday?"

Hereschell shrugged. "Wanderer pride," he answered lightly. With a nod he reached down to touch my hand, while I reached mine up to meet his. For a moment he looked me in the eye with his wolf stare. Then he turned to go.

"Will I see you again?" I called after him, feeling bereft.

"Only if our paths cross," he called back without turning. "If it is the will of the Cerroi." Soneeshi whined and licked my hand again. Then, in a flash of gray, she vanished into the forest. Instantly the morning mist closed around them both, muffling the sound of their footsteps. After that I settled back to sleep till the sun rose.

★

Later, on entering the shelter, I saw I had walked into a heated argument with Pell and Maireth on one side of it and Zenoria on the other. The rest of the women stood ranged around them in a loose circle. Pell had evidently had a change of heart or done some thinking in the night, for she was saying angrily, "What do they mean, commanding us in this way? Let them come here. There are many more of us. Why should we all gather ourselves up to go to them?"

"Because we have given our word on it, and Hereschell has already left with the message," Zenoria countered, with some heat. She must have come in the night. With her hands on her hips, she was standing in front of Pell, looking tall and proud in spite of her short stature. "It would take too long to change all that and get them to come to us, even if they consented, which I doubt. Besides, what can we offer them? How can we fit any more into this shelter? Look at it. The space is too crowded already for those who are here." Pell was about to begin again, when, with a sudden, impatient gesture, Zenoria turned to me. "And what does Tazzi think? She has been there. Let her say."

I was startled, unused to making decisions, far more comfortable with following. I was about to shrug and shake my head. Instead, I found myself looking around Pell's shelter, which had been so orderly and well organized when I left. Seeing the chaos of clothes and bedding and belongings, and even unwashed dishes mixed in with the rest, I answered on impulse, "We should go to Alyeeta's. There is room enough for all of us and more in her shelter and her clearing."

Pell stared at me in silence, as if weighing many things. Then she said abruptly, "Good, then that is settled. We must make ready to leave immediately."

I was amazed at Pell's sudden change of mind. I was even more amazed that I had so boldly opposed her will in this way. She seemed not at all put out, but drew Renaise aside to speak to her. Meanwhile Zenoria set off with three other women, all strangers to me, to gather and make ready some horses.

To my surprise it was Renaise who organized our departure, restoring a measure of order to the shelter, making sure we had supplies with us and trail bread for the road, seeing to it that each woman had clothes and bedding ready as well as a cup, a bowl, and a spoon of her own. Scolding or shouting as was needed, but mostly issuing commands in a clear, firm voice, this was not the Barrenaise I remembered from that time in the tavern, not the soft, helpless serving-girl who had ridden back with us that night. Or perhaps, I thought as I stopped for a moment to watch her, the skills learned there were far more valuable than I had realized.

More than Renaise had changed in my absence. It seemed as if everything there had changed. There were at least five and twenty women, maybe more, maybe thirty camped in the shelter or outside it with their gear and clothes and bedding strewn about in all directions. Most of them were not known to me. Many, I suppose, were from Pell's contacts, and three were burned ones, though none burned as badly as Maireth had been. Later Maireth told me that she had wanted the Witches to come to us because she and the other burned ones could not travel yet.

I moved through all this bustle and chaos feeling like the stranger, the outsider among them. I was unnerved by their noise and rendered almost helpless by the confusion around me, as I had become accustomed to the silence and order of Alyeeta's shelter. Of all those new women whose names I heard, most I forgot almost as soon as I heard them, but not Kazouri. That name I remembered. Who could forget the woman who went with it? I was standing at the shelter entrance, surveying the scene with some dismay, when this giant came striding up to me from outside. She clapped her big hand on my shoulder. It felt as if a hill-cat cub had landed there.

"So you are Tazzi," she said in a booming voice, "the one that went off to be Witch-taught. Well, it does not seem to have harmed you much. I am Kazouri, Jhemar's friend. I used to train her father's horses. We left there together. I went wherever someone would pay me to tend horses, and Jhemar went to follow the Wanderers." She looked like a big burly man, even taller than Jhemar and much broader in the shoulder, a walking mountain of a woman. I would not willingly have put myself in the way between her and something that she wanted. Her dark, bushy brows and thick features reminded me of my father. She had a wide, infectious grin that spoke of good nature, but even so, I was aware that the hand on my shoulder covered half my arm and could probably have lifted me off my feet with ease. "I am looking for Pell or Renaise," she said urgently. "We have just brought in four more women, one of whom is injured. I must see what is to be done with them, as Jhemar cannot venture into this uproar."

"There are already so many here I cannot remember one from the other," I answered with some resentment, but I stepped aside quickly to be out of her way.

"Well, girl, there will be many more before this is over. At least twice this number are hidden in places nearby, and there are other gatherings that Pell keeps contact with to the north and south of us."

I might as well have been gone a year, I thought. As she spoke, I had a sense of the whole land in motion, rising and shifting underfoot, guards and Star-Born changing places in a strange, deadly dance. Then her eyes lit on my pendant. I saw them widen slightly. "Ah, so you are one of those," she said with a quick intake of breath. She made a slight bow and was gone through the entryway in one long stride. My arm and shoulder ached from the weight of her hand and burned with a strange heat from her touch. The look in her eyes had surprised me. Puzzled, I put my hand over my pendant and felt the familiar warmth filling my palm. I resolved to ask Maireth some questions when I had the chance to thank her for her gift.

Hoping to be of use, I went to see to the injured one. Arnella and another healer were already there caring for her. They had no need for me. As I had already gathered my things, or, rather, never unpacked them, and no longer knew the workings of the camp, I stood about at a loss for what to do. Suddenly Pell came up and put her arm around me. She had not spoken to me the night before, except in reference to Alyeeta's message, not one word of affection or interest. I drew into myself, withdrawing from her embrace. With a gesture at the scene around us, I said coolly, "I see much has changed in my time away."

She nodded. "And there is more change to come, much more. Things are moving faster and faster now. This meeting with the Witches is only another step. And you, have you learned much? From your own experience, is Alyeeta to be trusted? You yourself seem to have changed in ways I cannot yet understand." She gave me a hard, calculating look and drew me to her for a rough kiss.

I pulled away to where I could look her in the eye. "Yes, Alyeeta is to be trusted, as much as any of us," I told her. "And yes, I have changed. I have changed in ways I cannot yet explain." I was not even sure myself all that I meant by those words.

★

In the end, after much discussion and argument and some confusion, it was decided that only fifteen of us would ride out to meet with the Witches. Some of the other women were off on their own missions. Maireth, Renaise's cousin Arnella, and two other healers were to remain with the burned ones. More burned ones were in hiding and expected at the shelter soon. Renaise suddenly found herself freed to go with us when Kazouri said loudly, "I will stay here with Thalyisi to watch over the camp. I have no need to go and be lied to by a pack of Witches." Zenoria and several others had already left to fetch our horses. Jhemar only came in to join us at the end when Zenoria and the others had returned.

When we were finally gathered, those who were going were in a state of nervous excitement, charged like the air before a storm. Even the horses had caught the fever. They danced about between the trees, tossing their heads and nickering to each other. On sudden impulse, before we were even out of sight of the shelter, I urged Marshlegs forward, pushing my way past Pell and the others.

"What are you doing?" Pell shouted at me. "You could not find your way here. Do you think to find your way back?"

"Yes!" I shouted back at her. "I have learned something of the trail from that man I rode with — much, in fact." I had not planned to do this and was as surprised as Pell, but tried to keep a good face on it all.

"Do not play the fool," she shouted again. "You will lead us all in circles in these woods."

The sound of disgust in her voice made me shrink back into myself. Though I was about to answer again, in truth I could feel my own assurance slipping away now that I had made that rash gesture. Then I heard Jhemar say, "Let her go, Pell. You push her forward and hold her back with the same hand. With Hereschell's teaching she surely has learned something of use. Wanderers are the best teachers for the road and

Hereschell is the best of the Wanderers, having learned much of his skill from wolves."

"Well, see that you do not lose us on the way," Pell said grudgingly. Then she dropped back to ride with Jhemar, while Zenoria rode up next to me.

After a few turns of the road, Zenoria leaned toward me. She spoke close to my ear so the others could not hear. "You will be our eyes and watch for the trail. I will be our ears and listen for the guards or any other travelers on the road so that none can come on us unexpected."

I nodded, grateful for her kindness. After that I was free to focus on the way. So intent was I on the trail, I scarcely heard a word said around me. My eyes ached from watching for every little sign Hereschell had shown me, and my head throbbed from the strain. When there was confusion ahead and all else failed, I stopped and did as Alyeeta had done, reaching out before me with all my senses, especially those senses for which we have no name. But it was not Alyeeta's shelter I sought ahead of us. It was Alyeeta herself. I would picture her and hear her voice. I let that pull me forward. The others stopped respectfully behind me and waited till I nodded and went on. Even Pell refrained from mocking comments.

In this way we crossed the river, passed through the little valley where Hereschell and I had camped, and finally came to the road. It was clear that a large number of guards had gathered there and camped as well. I rode back to Pell, who was examining the signs. "From here on it is yours," I told her. "This is as far as I know the way."

"Then you have lost us for sure," Pell answered curtly. "This road is not known to me, nor is any of this way by which you chose to bring us." She was scowling furiously at me.

My heart leapt up and my mouth went dry. I looked at all those I had betrayed in my eagerness to take charge. As I was about to grovel apologies, Jhemar rode up and shook Pell's arm. "Enough foolishness, sister. That is not kind. Praise her for her good work and lead us the rest of the way. That first part may have been new to you, but you know this road as well as I do. Besides, a guard camp is no place to be playing jokes."

I looked in surprise from one to the other of them. Pell shrugged and grinned. "Sorry, Tazzi, you were so very serious, I could not resist that bit of wickedness. " She rode up to hug me, then drew away and held my shoulder to look me in the eye. "Well done," she said with a nod — only those two words, but for me the whole world was in them.

Later she turned back and asked, "How is it that you learned in one morning what I could not teach you in all our rides together?"

I was stung by her tone and said sharply, "I learned because Hereschell took the time. He taught me with care and patience and did not mock or belittle or insult me as you did."

Jhemar was laughing and slapping her leg. "Well spoken, by the Mother, well spoken! This one is not shy in answering."

Pell looked like a storm cloud with her brows knotted together. I held her stare and would not look away, though inside I trembled. Suddenly she laughed, too. "Well, this new one is coming of age. Maybe she will be of some use to us after all."

★

We reached Alyeeta's clearing just before dusk, only slightly delayed by my pathfinding. This time the entryway was easy to see. The ivy that had covered it before had been woven back upon itself. A warm little quiver of light reached out through it. Eager for the sight of Alyeeta's face, I rushed in first, then stood there blinking, blinded by the lamplight.

"Well, she looks no more promising this time than the last. Why would you want to waste valuable Witch time on such unlikely material, answer me that?" Those were the words that greeted me on entering Alyeeta's shelter. I had no need to see the face to know whose voice that was.

Another voice answered from the gloom. "Telakeet, do you plan to waste, use up, and expend your whole store of charm on this first meeting, or will you save some of it for another time?" This was followed by a musical laugh that made the hair rise on the nape of my neck.

By then I was able to distinguish Telakeet. She was in a chair by the hearth, with a stout stick resting against her knee. I swung to face her and was gathering myself for an answer. Quickly, before I could respond to her insults with my own, Pell stepped between me and the source of my anger. She put out her hand in greeting and said quickly, "I am Pell. This is Renaise and Tazzi, whom I see you know already, and Josleen and Megyair and Tzaneel and Jhemar and..." She was trying to name us each in turn as we crowded into the shelter, or rather poured in, seeming to fill up all the space. Telakeet ignored Pell's hand and glowered at us.

As soon as we had all squeezed inside, Alyeeta appeared from one of her stump chambers. She was clearly flustered. "Well," she said tartly, "I know I said to come with all your women, but I had not expected such an army."

"And this is not the half of them, Mother," Pell answered with amusement. "We left twice this many or more at home. Even so, we had to throw the pebbles three times, and then three times more to see who would be chosen for this honor."

I leaned over to whisper indignantly to Pell, "There is not a word of truth in that last part. We did not throw the pebbles even once."

"I know," Pell whispered back, "but the way it all happened was so dull. Who could tell that story with any pleasure?"

Just then Telakeet leaned forward. "And so you are Pell," she said, pointing with her stick. Ignoring Alyeeta, she seemed prepared to continue her tirade with Pell as its focus.

Pell threw up her hands before her in mock horror. "Please, Mother, spare me your flattery. I have no need for it at the moment."

Before Telakeet could begin again, the other, the one who had laughed in that astonishing way, stepped forward. She seemed to change as she came out of the shadows. I could see that her yellow hair was almost golden in the light and her eyes were bright blue. She had a Shokarn fairness of skin that startled me. Her countenance was fresh and open. She appeared as bright and sunny as Telakeet was dark and stormy, yet there was about her something that made my skin crawl. One could not look at her clearly or directly. She slipped out of focus. The air around her seemed to bend and shiver. She looked young and yet not young, beautiful, yet plain or almost ugly, tender and gentle, yet mocking. Her handclasp was both warm and cool. Looking into my eyes, she said softly, as if speaking for my ears alone, "So you are Tazzi. You are indeed very lovely. That one with the sweet tongue and pretty manners is named Telakeet, and here I am called Shalamith, though in other places I have other names."

"Tazzi and I have already met, as you heard me say," Telakeet burst in rudely.

Shalamith went on, ignoring this interruption as if it were no more than the buzzing of a fly, "Ever since I first heard there were young women of power I have wanted to find some, especially after the Zarn's edict. It is a great pleasure to be meeting you at last." With that she even made a slight bow.

I could feel the mockery in her voice and see it in her smile, but there was music in her, the sensuous grace of the snake and a kind of golden glow about her. If Telakeet was all rudeness, Shalamith was all charm. I found myself bowing in return with a large, foolish grin on my face. I knew her charm to be Witch's artifice, but I would gladly have left my hand in hers forever. In fact, if she had asked me for it at that moment, I would have given her the hand off my arm or the foot off my leg with pleasure. I would certainly have given her the heart out of my breast. All this time I was very much aware of Alyeeta just at the edge of my vision, watching me; Alyeeta, whom I had rushed in to see and had not even greeted yet.

As the heat rushed up my arm and into my face from Shalamith's touch I heard a low growl, almost like a beast. Telakeet said in a deep, gravelly voice, "Leave off, Shalamith, let the girl do her own thinking. Mind-bending, as you well know, is a far worse crime than rudeness."

I saw Shalamith change again as if water had rippled through her being. She withdrew her hand and stepped back, her face suddenly closed and unreachable. "I only meant to test her powers and see how susceptible she was." She shook her head, then laughed again in that way that made me shiver as if someone had run their fingernails across my soul. Clearly, she thought me far more susceptible than Pell, whom she ignored. One part of me felt outraged at being so used. Another longed to hold her hand again, to have her look into my eyes again. It was as if the sun had withdrawn its face from me. Then Alyeeta stepped up next to me and put her arm around my waist. She slipped her hand up under my tunic so that the warmth of her palm cupped my breast. Instantly Shalamith's charms faded like the moon at dawn.

At that moment Telakeet said something to Shalamith. She spoke so low I could not understand, or perhaps she was speaking in that other language. Shalamith answered sharply, with no music in her voice this time. Suddenly they were in a contest of power, trying to stare each other down. The air around them quivered with force. The rest of us shifted awkwardly from foot to foot till Alyeeta said in a loud, commanding voice, "Sit down, all of you. You are crowding my space like so many circling wolves." She swept the gathering with her eyes. All of us obeyed, even the other Witches. Somehow we all found space on her cushions. Her shelter seemed to stretch and reshape around us.

Alyeeta leaned back then, her side pressed to mine and her eyes half-closed, while Pell told how we had all gathered and how many more there were, this time all of it the truth. From time to time Alyeeta nodded, seeming half-asleep. Then suddenly she sat up straight, all mockery and alertness again. "All ignorant green girls you are bringing together. Who will teach them and train them and guide these powers of which they know so little?"

Pell turned on her. "Are you speaking to undertake this useful task, Mother?"

"A thankless one, more likely," Alyeeta said with asperity. "Who knows if they are even capable of being taught?"

"And that is the mark of a good teacher, the one who teaches well those who are not easily taught."

There was no pleasure for me in listening to Pell and Alyeeta trade words. It was more like hearing two stones rubbing and grinding against each other than like ordinary human talk. I cast a look about, but no one else seemed to take notice or to care. In the end, Alyeeta rolled her eyes to the ceiling and lifted up her hands. "Goddess, why was I the one you sent to market when so many others could have been chosen?"

"Oh come, Alyeeta, you would not have missed this on your life," Shalamith said with her great shining smile. Pell laughed aloud. For once it was Alyeeta who looked discomfited.

When our stories of the present had all been told, Telakeet and Alyeeta fell to trading tales from the time of the Witch-kills, terrible, bloody stories of death and destruction. It was almost as if they had forgotten we were there, or perhaps they spoke with intention for our ears, though for what lessons I could not imagine. Telakeet talked with great bitterness. Though it did not make me like her more, still I began to better understand her sharp tongue, to see how it had shaped and grown. The others listened wide-eyed. Hearing their tales, it was clear to me that the Witches were far older than they seemed, Alyeeta especially.

Shalamith said little, but watched from the shadows, once in a while making a face of distaste. After some time of this, she sat up suddenly. The light flashed on her face and in her golden hair. "Enough of all that blood and death and fire! There is more than enough of it out there. Why bring it in here to us? Now is the time for music." With that she drew a small ferl from her pouch, the smallest I had ever seen. Moving forward into the light, she began to strum and sing. If her speaking voice had charm, her singing voice had magic in it. I think she could have summoned a flock of birds with it or melted city gates. None of us was immune, not even Pell. We all sat up and leaned toward her like flowers toward the sun. Even Alyeeta and Telakeet left off their talk of old battles. Shalamith's voice reached into the very core of my being, and I gave myself over to it as to a lover. We might have stayed listening forever in that charmed circle if Telakeet had not finally thumped on the floor with her stick. Pell sprang up suddenly as if released. She said in a loud voice and with deliberate rudeness, "Well, Witches, why are we here? I cannot think you summoned us all on that hard ride to be insulted or to be charmed, entertaining though they both may be in their own way. I must suppose this gathering serves some other purpose. It is late. We will soon grow weary. The time has come to talk."

"You could at least have waited for the end of Shalamith's song," Alyeeta said accusingly. "Have you no manners?"

"None at all," Pell answered instantly. "I was born lacking them. Besides, we may as well wait for the snows of summer to fall or the flowers of winter to bloom. Shalamith's song has no end, as you well know. Now, if there is nothing more to talk of, we may as well go home again, for there are others there who need us."

At that Alyeeta sat up, all seriousness. "Well then, as you say, the time has come to talk."

After looking all around, Pell sat down again, but slowly, as if ready to leap up at any moment. I felt an unreasoning anger toward her. I wanted Shalamith to go on singing forever. When she stopped, slipped away her ferl, and slid back into the shadows, she looked like an ordinary woman of indeterminate age. All that golden glow was gone, as if the light of a lamp had been suddenly blown out. My heart ached with longing for her music.

Now the real talk began in earnest. It went on for most of that night. Much was decided there among us, all of it to Pell's great satisfaction. It was agreed that we would move our camp to Alyeeta's clearing, since the space both in her shelter and around it could accommodate many more. For the moment, at least, the other Witches would stay there also. From there the Star-Born would begin gathering and assembling, as well as training. The final plan was for us to move west and north together, going toward the coast and as far away from the Zarn's troops as possible. There we hoped to find some place to settle, at least for the winter. Alyeeta, for her part, seemed to have such a place in mind, though clearly at that moment she did not choose to divulge it. For the time being, Pell's shelter would remain a healing place for the burned ones. Unfortunately, we could expect more and more of them in the future, and it was plain they would need a calmer place to mend and be cared for than the center of a busy camp. If she was willing, Arnella was to stay and care for them there with Ethrin's help.

Toward the end of this I began to doze. For me the talk turned to a murmur, like wind in the trees. Suddenly I heard Pell say loudly,

"Alyeeta, where are we all supposed to sleep?" She was standing again, surveying the scene.

Alyeeta stood up so quickly I almost fell sideways. I must have dozed off leaning against her. "You are not 'supposed' to sleep anywhere. This is not a town hostelry. I am not equipped to accommodate whatever passing mob chooses to lodge here. This is my own small private shelter. It is possible you may stretch out there where you are sitting and sleep against your neighbor. If that does not suit you, you may find lodgings outside in your cloak next to your horse. For myself, this day has been a long one. I need some sleep and some healing dreams." Saying this, she began dousing the lamps and pouring sand around the edges of the fire. Soon only a small handful of flames still burned at the center of the hearth.

I stood up slowly, stupid with weariness. When Pell, who had been attending to others, began to move toward me as if with intention, Alyeeta quickly came and took my hand. "You I can find room for in my bed," she said loudly.

When I lay beside her, wrapped in her arms, she whispered eagerly, "Things are moving, Little One, moving and shifting. The Zarns are right to be afraid. The wheel turns faster. We will have to learn to ride the chariot or be crushed beneath it. I feel some larger shift coming. Even now it reaches out. Somehow we must be ready, though for what we do not know. We must be ready for something we have never seen before, a good trick if one can manage. If I have been bored in my life before, I think I will never be again. I may die without tasting the luxury of boredom again. So be it. May we all have the courage and the wits for what is coming." In all this she sounded so much like Pell I had to bite my lip not to laugh aloud. Then she pressed me against her. I could feel the heat rise between my legs and words no longer mattered. Later, before she let me sleep, Alyeeta had me tell her the whole story of my ride with Hereschell and how he was received at Pell's shelter.

★

In spite of their constant sparring, Pell and Alyeeta seemed to have come to some agreement over me. After that first night, they shared me fairly between them, exchanging a look or word or a slight nod to indicate who had claim, as if I were some baggage to be traded back and forth and had no mind or will of my own. Still, I had my choices. I could have said no. But what did it really matter? I got my pleasure. One body was as good as another. Alyeeta was far more loving and caring and tender than Pell,

175

but I felt Pell equally entitled. Somehow I did not much care. It was all distraction anyhow. Whichever of them wished to claim my body was welcome to it.

That next morning, I saw Renaise going about the clearing with a ball of string and some little stakes, as if measuring everything for use. When Alyeeta rushed out indignantly to ask what she was doing, Renaise answered calmly, "Trying to lay out this camp to the best of my ability."

Alyeeta was bristling visibly, her voice full of acid. "Remember, young woman, that this is still my clearing."

"I understand very well that it is your clearing, Alyeeta. Now we can be here or not be here; it cannot be both ways. If we are to be here, then this camp must be better organized than where we are now, for your sake as well as ours. Believe me, you would not be pleased to have your clearing look as Pell's shelter does at this moment."

Without another word to Renaise, Alyeeta turned on her heel and stormed back into her shelter, saying to me in passing, "Respect and gratitude are surely not among the gifts of the Great Star." I almost choked on my laughter, but managed to keep a straight face until she passed. As I watched Renaise going about her self-appointed task with such skill and confidence, I realized she had become someone to reckon with. Seeing her stand up to Alyeeta in that way, I even felt some grudging admiration for her.

For that next week or so there was little rest for any of us, and less sleep. I suffered under the double burden of being the object of others' passions. Pell had far more stores hidden away than any of us knew. New storage had to be set up, and all that was not needed for the healing space had to be moved carefully by backpack and horse pack without arousing suspicion or endangering our new camp. This was no easy task, I must tell you. And I no longer had the shelter of being a follower. I was a leader and a guide now, responsible for the safety of others. Goddess knows, though, there were moments when I longed to let my head nod forward and have my horse follow after the next horse's tail. Now there were women who followed after me in that same way. I had to remind them often to pay some heed to where they went and to watch for signs. And Mother help me, I had to remind myself to have some patience with their thoughtlessness.

I went back and forth between Pell's shelter and Alyeeta's so many times that now it all seems blurred together in my memory. But one time comes clear to me. I can still see a picture in my head of that woman seated in front of her wagon. I did not come on her unexpectedly, of course, for I no longer traveled in that head-blind way, but went with all my senses alert. She had set up her little camp in the 'Y' of the road where she could catch all comers. With her cards spread out before her, she was seated cross-legged on a blanket as if to read her own fortune or another's. Behind her, tucked under the trees, was her travel-wagon, gaily painted with bright decorations of yellow, red, and orange — such a wagon as I had sometimes seen used to sell from at markets instead of a booth. Next to it her little dappled horse dozed in the shade, head hanging, eyes half-closed.

This woman looked up at me expectantly, as if I were the very one she waited for. Though I knew myself to be well disguised, still I felt a chill of fear rush up my spine. Her appearance was so strange and striking, it was hard not to stare. Her loose, brightly colored shirt revealed a large tattoo covering her shoulder and running up her neck. A many-faceted blue crystal hung on a chain between her breasts. Her earrings were like flashing crescent moons against her dark skin.

Suddenly, with a start, I noticed she had drawn in the dirt in front of her the very sign I wore hidden under my tunic, a triangle inside a circle inside a triangle. I was not quick enough to hide the shock and surprise that crossed my face. Hastily averting my head, I touched my cap, mumbled, "Best of days to you, Goodwoman," and made ready to pass quickly by. This seemed some sort of trap laid out before me.

Instantly she was on her feet, her cards scattered in the dust. I had the feeling that she meant to leap before my horse to stop me if that proved necessary. "You know that sign," she said quickly. "I saw it in your face." When I could not form my answer fast enough, she went on. "You do not say yes, yet neither do you say no, so the answer is clear enough. Come sit by me a little and I will tell your cards."

"I have no money for such things," I protested in my deepest voice.

"Not for money, then, but only for friendship. The road grows lonely at times. And save your deep voice for others. With me it is wasted."

"I have no time either," I said, really frightened now and impatient to be gone.

"Quickly, someone comes and we must talk," she whispered urgently. "Let me lay you out a hand." She had taken a firm grip on Marshlegs's reins. I saw I would not get free of her without a scene. Reluctantly I dismounted and came to stand by her while she deftly gathered her cards and laid out another hand. I could hear horses now. "Come sit by me," she hissed. "And be interested." I noticed that she had rubbed out the sign with her foot, though in my mind I could still see the shape of it in the dark, fresh earth.

When the others came on us we were bent over the cards together. They were two men, farmers by the look of them. They hesitated a little, then the boldest of them asked, "Can you do our cards next, Auntie?"

"Last hand of the day, good people. I have to go tend to my old mother, but if you come back tomorrow I will be here, in this very place. Vanhira-of-the-road, who is never wrong about past or future. The present, of course, is yours to tend to yourselves. Or better yet, look for me at the next market in Hamishair." They made as if to stay and watch, but she shook her head and waved them away. "What is in the cards is for that person's eyes alone and for no other." By the time they left I was trembling and soaked with sweat.

As soon as they moved off I made ready to rise, but she put out her hand to hold me. "What do you want, woman?" I growled at her. "You have detained me long enough."

"Give me a moment only to read the cards. Then if you are still in such a hurry, I will not hold you." I gave a reluctant nod. In her card-reader voice she intoned, "I see you carry a heavy fate. In your past there is a great star that leaves a blazing path across the heavens and scatters powers here below. You are one of those on whom the powers have fallen, am I right?" She tried looking in my eyes, but I evaded her and said curtly, "Go on, I need to be on my way."

Deftly she turned new cards now, peering into each one as if it held some truth, while she said, "I see here two others under that same star who must remain hidden until dark, two who have not the use of words and for whom I have no names. They need horses and a guide to take them to safety. I hope you understand the meaning of the cards, for that is all they tell me now." With a sudden, practiced sweep she gathered up all her cards and stood up. "Your course is clear, then? I will be here until someone comes. Look for me back in the woods a little, away from curious eyes."

"Answer the owl when it hoots three times," I told her as I sprang onto my horse. She nodded and closed her hand over her crystal, as if for protection. That is how the "silent ones" came among us. Vanhira knew nothing of them save that they were Wanderers' children. Later, Jhemar told me their story as she heard it on the road, though even she had no names for them.

Other new women came to us as well, a few at first and then more and more till it seemed like an endless flood, with food and shelter and all the rest needing to be provided. As word spread that there was a safe place to gather, those who had been waiting began to come out of hiding. Some, having been given directions, rode in on their own horses with spare clothes and food and other goods. More often they were brought in by one of us, ragged and hungry as I had been, frightened and distrustful as well, or burned or wounded in some way. Some crept in through the woods past our sentries, wary as wild animals at first. All had their stories, those who were willing or able to talk, stories as much in need of telling as the one I write here. Some told of families who had hidden them and kept them safe and sometimes died for it, some of families who had hated and betrayed them and even tried to kill them, often at an early age. There were those who had been on their own as young as Pell or younger and others who just now had come out of hiding in their family's secret storage places.

All of us who rode back to move Pell's goods — our goods, as she liked to remind me, and in truth they were often put to use as soon as we brought them in — also searched for survivors on each trip. Now I no longer avoided those signs — those stars and double triangles and circles within each other — as I had that first time, but watched for them, watched intently with my senses as well as with my eyes. We ourselves even drew them in the dirt at crossroads and resting places, leaving a little X of sticks to recognize our own. Later we would come back to see if there was another sign drawn next to ours or over it, or if we could sense someone watching and waiting there for us. It was then that I began to understand the work Pell had done, the web of contacts she had woven over the years.

Sometimes I felt lost, drowning in that flood of strangers. Not Pell. Pell seemed to be everywhere at once, doing what was needed for each one. And when the press of numbers grew too great, she chose three of the women who had come in with Kazouri and sent them west with Josleen and Megyair as guides. They were to seek out a friend of Hereschell's, a Wanderer woman named Yaniri, who had settled down in her old age. Pell was hoping we could set up another gathering there with her. Sick from the turmoil of the camp, Jhemar went with them. Though the Witches had begun to teach her something of shielding and focusing, still she needed some relief from all the troubled thoughts swirling through our camp.

★

Some days later, as we were bustling about noisily in the clearing, cutting brush and stretching canvas to set up new shelters, I suddenly felt the hair go up on the back of my neck. I looked up to see an old woman watching us from the edge of the clearing. How long had she been standing there, watching quietly, unnoticed by anyone? How had she slipped in so easily past our sentries? Her stillness and her stare made me afraid. Though she said nothing, I felt called and went to stand before her. There was something in her presence that commanded respect and obedience. Short, stout, and solid, she stood with her feet planted wide apart as if rooted in the earth. In fact, with her brown skin, brown hair, and brown clothes, all of the same shade, she looked like a piece of the earth itself. Her somewhat hooded, gold-flecked dark eyes that stared unblinking into mine made me think of Telakeet's toad in human form, wise and ageless.

I bowed before her, saying, "Mother, how may I help you? Are you looking for someone here?"

She regarded me seriously and intently for so long before answering that I began to shift nervously from foot to foot, though I could not free myself from her piercing stare. Then, with a sudden grin she said, "I have been looking for someone all my life. I suppose I am as likely to find her here as elsewhere. So you are one of the new ones. I am sorry to have missed our meeting, but other matters..." Then she stopped speaking and openly stared at me, looking me up and down again, with no cruelty, but with not much kindness either. I felt myself being examined for use. Even my mind felt forced open by her scrutiny. It was a relief to suddenly sense Alyeeta's presence next to me. She had slipped up silently and now put her arm around my shoulders like a protection, saying, "This is Tazzi, who is destined to become leader among these young women, when she learns to fill out the promise of her powers. And this," she added with a slight bow toward the old woman, "is Hamiuri, Mother of Witches, who is guide to us all."

"Not so, not so," the other answered with a smile. "I am no one's mother, only that I no longer care to hide my age as some do. But never mind all that now." With a sudden gesture she took my hand in hers and said with compelling warmth, "Come, child, sit by me if you can spare some time out of all this busyness to trade words with an old woman. I would like to know more of this new breed. I have three with me who escaped from the city. Thinking to shelter them with Alyeeta, I brought them here, only to find you are already forming a tribe or an army in this place. You must tell me how all this has happened."

On the other side of me Alyeeta whispered in my ear, "Trust her. Tell her all she asks, as best you can. She truly is our 'Mother.'" Then she dropped her arm from my shoulder and was gone as suddenly as she had appeared. With my hand in Hamiuri's, she seemed not near so threatening or formidable. Indeed, in her changed mode, she had almost as much charm as Shalamith. I went with her easily enough to a mossy place at the edge of the trees.

There I talked and talked, trying to answer all her questions. Finally I had to call over Renaise and Zenoria to help me. Then Pell herself came to sit by us and soon others were there, adding their stories and being questioned. After a while all the women in the clearing were sitting in a circle around Hamiuri. It seemed as if she had drawn us together by intention. Suddenly she stood up and turned to look at us all, this small brown woman who was like a mountain of power. "This is your first council meeting, take note of that," she said in a loud, commanding voice. "And now, you must choose a leader to see you through these hard times that are still to come."

That was how the choosing began. It was Hamiuri's plan we followed. First we said our names around the circle so we would know clearly who it was we were choosing. Then we made each three choices. When it was over, Pell was named most often as one of each woman's choices, if not the first, for that might be that woman's friend, then at least the second or the third. No other woman was named so often or even near to it.

That done, there were roars of approval and a burst of loud, boisterous talk till Hamiuri clapped her hands for silence. When all was still, she asked, "Is there any voice raised against Pell as leader? Speak now, for this is your chance." She swept the gathering with her eyes. As no hand was raised and no voice spoke out, Hamiuri said with great seriousness, "Understand, all of you, that you have, with no questions and no doubts spoken, chosen a leader this day. Now, Pell, you must stand up and speak so they can hear if they have made themselves a good choice."

14

It had all happened so suddenly. The look of surprise on Pell's face was almost comical, but she got up slowly, giving herself the chance she needed. By the time she was on her feet and facing us, she looked to be in command of herself and of the scene as well. With a slight bow toward Hamiuri she said, "I thank you, Mother, for your guidance here." Then, turning to the rest of us, she went on, "And to all of you for your trust in me. With the help of the Goddess I will try to live up to it. I must tell you, however, that I only agree to be leader for now and to issue orders here in the hope that soon there will be no need for such a leader or such orders. I want nothing more than to find a place where we can live in safety. For myself I plan to grow old and fat and lazy in that place. Yet I see a long, dangerous road for us between here and there."

Having said that, Pell looked about, her eyes sweeping the clearing as if in search of something. Then, seeing a great old stump, the width of a small table and the height of a woman's knees, she went striding over to it. Watching her, I felt a sudden swell of love and pride in my heart. Leaping up on the stump, Pell raised her arms for attention. As soon as she had it, she called out to us, "If you are going to make me speak, then you must all come where I can see you."

Quickly we rearranged ourselves. When we had finished shuffling around and there was silence again, Pell went on, "Ever since I first began to understand who and what we were, I have dreamed of this day, of seeing us gathered together in our numbers. And now, by the Goddess, what am I to say to you all? I have nothing written, of course. Even if I did I could not read it. Like most of you, I am a poor farm girl with nothing but my wits and these strange gifts." With these few words she had everyone's notice. Women were leaning forward, totally silent, listening intently to her.

"As to those gifts, none of us asked for them. They are the gifts of our birth. Wondrous as they are, they must sometimes seem to you as much a curse as a blessing. It is these gifts that have brought down the wrath of the Zarns on our heads and driven us from our homes. The high and mighty who rule this land see us as some kind of threat to their power. And so we must be, or they would not have posted their edict. Yet what we are or what we might become is still unknown to us. As to the powers, even we ourselves do not know the full extent of them. That is what we hope to discover here, sharing with each other and helped by the Witches. We have different powers and they seem to come on us at different ages, though some, I believe, like mind-speech and speech with creatures, are common to us all.

"Those powers are our bond. Never forget that. It is for them that others seek to kill us. No matter what your passing quarrel with another woman, remember that bond. It matters more than all your differences. That might not always be easy. Pain has not made us all lovely or loving to be with. But in the end, believe me, it is all you have left in the world of family, friends, lovers, village, tribe, people, future, or hope — only that bond with each other."

Though, as Pell said, she had no prepared speech, she went on for a while in this way with ease. She spoke of plans and strategies, of the Zarn's likely intentions, of that terrible new feeling called fear and how to use and control it. She spoke of much else besides. The words flowed and flowed, as if all this had been waiting there in her head for years. At the end of it Pell raised both arms and shouted, "No matter what else happens, remember, the Goddess made us as we are. We are Her children! She wants us here!" There was wild cheering and stamping from around the circle at those words, and it went on for some time. Then, in a quieter tone Pell added, "Now, I shall choose captains from among you for each function. They shall choose their seconds. You must listen to them as you would to me."

By the time the choosing and naming was done and Pell had jumped down from the stump, she was shaking and soaked with sweat. Shouting and cheering, women rushed forward to embrace her. I was just readying myself to plunge into that mob and save her from the crush of too much affection when I saw Kazouri's broad bulk striding forward, making her a path.

That evening I had a few moments alone with Pell as we went together to bathe down at the stream. "Lucky for me I was taught something of making speeches by the Thieves Guild," she said as she stripped off her clothes. "Otherwise I might have died of embarrassment. That Hamiuri is a fox. She looks to be someone's sweet old grandmother, but I wager she could spin the whole world on her little finger if she set her mind to it. She has turned me into something I had no thought to be, and made me work for it besides." Pell sounded half-vexed and half-pleased. She gave me a funny, sideways grin.

I shook my head. Never, not for one moment, not since she had first fixed me with her compelling stare, had I thought of Hamiuri as someone's sweet old grandmother. "She was right, Pell. It was a thing that needed doing. And, without question, you were the natural one to choose."

"Really?" she said, cocking her head at me. Then, with a sudden laugh and a throw of her hip she had me in the water, still in my boots. With a shout I sprung out and leapt upon her. Wet and half-dressed, we rolled about on the mossy bank laughing and struggling. For that moment we were just two girls playing together instead of the newly chosen leader of a hunted people and her second-in-command. Later, we even found time for some loving on that soft, damp ground.

★

After Pell was picked as leader, she set to organizing, in a more deliberate way, all that had been done before by chance or assumption. For a while, a sort of peace and order settled on the camp. It was the first time since leaving home that I had some sense of safety, or at least I had it until Rishka's coming shattered and blasted all that, turning everything upside down.

Yes, it was true, I was chosen to be Pell's second there, and it frightened me. I thought many others more able. All those I would have named, however, had some urgent task that needed them. The rest were too new, too green. And so, almost by default, that post fell to me.

Renaise, of course, had been put in charge of the camp and the food supply, doing what she already did so well. She chose her sister Thalyisi as her second there. Alyeeta was asked if, with some help from me, she would organize the healing — the teaching of new healers, the gathering of herbs, and the making of ointments — to which she gave her grudging consent. The system of watchers and sentries had fallen to Zenoria, as she already had charge of the horses. Now that she was learning enough of shielding to make crowds bearable, Jhemar had been chosen, in her absence, to be our ears, spying at the fringes of towns or markets, in taverns and in quillof booths, keeping us informed of what was happening out there in the world. She was also to train and organize others as spies, any who had a special talent for the hearing of silent speech. Kazouri, Jhemar's giant friend, was appointed to be our trainer, to make our bodies fit for whatever lay ahead. That one, as I soon found out, had no pity and was blessed with a voice that could make the very stones jump out of the ground. For the next few weeks, even the laziest of us were driven to lift, stretch, run, and climb till we were panting and sweating and begging for mercy. Kazouri herself, of course, made it all look effortless. New women, as they came in, were to be assigned to one or the other of us. In that way they found their places in the structure of the camp.

Meanwhile, the Witches were teaching us what they could. Learning from Witches made Kazouri seem like the 'Mother of Kindness' herself. They drove us all, poking and prodding to understand our powers. Often we were in tears with pains in our heads and our bellies as new things sprouted from us that, as yet, we could neither comprehend nor control. Sometimes, I think, they prodded at us as a curious child prods at a bug, to see what makes it work, to see if it will crawl away and hide, or fly away, or turn its pincers back in anger. Alyeeta did not drive me quite so hard, perhaps because she had already done so, or perhaps because she loved me too much, as Telakeet so often said. She even had her moments of kindness. You can believe that Telakeet made up for that with a vengeance, singling me out for her attacks.

Into the middle of all this, Josleen and Megyair returned, bringing word that a camp was being set up at Yaniri's. They said we could now begin sending women west. As long as they could work together, they agreed to continue being guides. Those two seemed to do everything in unison and to gain strength from it. I found them a cheerful contrast to the frequent rancor and bickering of the camp.

Jhemar came back a few days later, looking troubled. She rode straight up to me and handed me a square of much-folded paper that she had hidden in her sleeve. "Does this say what I think it does?"

I spread it out on the ground. Another edict! My eyes blurred and my stomach clenched in fear. "It says that any who help us will be put to death," I told her, shortening the message to its essential meaning.

"As I am not much of a reader I thought to bring it to you. I found it on a tree at the edge of the woods, somewhere between here and Hamishair."

Pell and several other women had gathered around us. Pell was nodding. "It only puts in writing what was already fact," she said with a shrug, "and it makes our task a little harder."

Even in the midst of all this work and learning, there were also friendships being formed. Of the three escaped Shokarn, Ashai, Sural, and Irdris, that Hamiuri had brought with her, only Irdris spoke Kourmairi well, though her speech was strangely stilted and formal, almost foreign-sounding to my ears. (For the sake of this story I have shortened their names here from their long, embellished, Shokarn ones.) Ashai had some book knowledge and Sural an air of competence, but it was Irdris whom I was drawn to at once, perhaps because we were so different. She was, I suppose, everything that a Kourmairi dirt-child is taught to fear and hate. In appearance she was the fair-haired, blue-eyed daughter of the Shokarn Uppercaste, looking like the guards or like the Zarn himself, from what I have heard, and raised in the midst of every ease and privilege. Yet, instead of hating her, I found myself admiring her. I liked the quiet, centered way she moved about the camp, always watching, observing everything, doing work that must have been new and hard for her. I never saw her complain or try to put her tasks on others.

We began by exchanging a few words in passing. When she saw I was willing to be friendly and did not treat her as an enemy, she began to relax, occasionally giving me a shy smile. She even offered to teach me some Shokarn if I wished. I think I was the first Kourmairi she talked to for more than necessity. As I discovered later, she was shy with us, not overly proud as others thought. Soon we found ourselves sitting next to each other by the evening fire, exchanging bits of our so different pasts. I would be trying out my new words of Shokarn, rapidly gaining confidence with her help. I felt us becoming closer and closer. It was like having a sister again, or perhaps something more. Who knows where this might have led if everything had not been so suddenly disrupted by the coming of the 'Wild Ones.'

Rishka, Rishkaria, Rishkazeel — trouble by whatever name she chose to use. She came soon after Tamara had left. Poor Tamara, she had ridden in looking about her with such joy and expectation in her face, turning her head from side to side, clearly searching for someone. I was amazed to see her there. When she saw me she called out gaily, "Pig-boy, where is

Pell?" knowing me easily enough in spite of my changed appearance. I called back that I did not know, as did several of the others whom she asked. I had just set down the saddlebag I had been stitching to go and talk with her, when I saw Pell striding across the clearing. Tamara jumped off her horse and ran into Pell's arms, joy written plainly on her face for all to see. Pell, as she passed me, had such a mix of love and pain in her expression that it tore at my heart. After they embraced, Pell put her arm around Tamara's shoulders and walked her out of the clearing. As they left I heard Tamara saying in a high, excited voice, "Oh, Pell, I could not wait any more for you to come. When Zenoria brought us some horses I made her tell me how to find you."

Later, when Tamara rode away again, she stayed at the far edge of camp, her head bowed and her face averted. There was nothing of joy or lightness about her any more, nor did she call out to me or to anyone as she left. Soon afterward, Pell walked through issuing orders in a voice like thunder. None of us dared approach her for anything. Looking neither left nor right, she walked on into the woods alone. Afterward I heard that Tamara had been sent west to Yaniri's. She went with Josleen and Megyair, who were just then leaving with their next group.

All of us were unusually subdued after Pell's abrupt departure. We went on about our work, but with low voices and no spirit, until suddenly one of our watchers rode in, coming so quickly we all looked up, instantly alert. "There are four women riding fast this way, not even in disguise. They did not stop for the guard, but pushed right past her. The one in front is riding like a demon. They look to be Muinyairin from their dress and style!"

Muinyairin! Up till now, though many of us had been strangers to each other, at least we had all been Kourmairi, all, that is, but the two silent ones who were Wanderers and the three Shokarn who had come in with Hamiuri. Though Pell had often spoken of the Muinyairin, still they had not seemed real to me. They had a fearsome reputation. From the sound of it, these seemed only too ready to give truth to it.

Arnella was standing next to me. I was about to send her to ring the warning bell when the first of these Muinyairin charged into the clearing, only moments after the sentry herself. This wild thing was brandishing her sword and shouting what I took to be war cries, though of course I could not understand the words. Three others followed after her, almost as fearsome. Women jumped up from their work and rushed about shouting in confusion. The two silent ones ran off into the woods, their terrified screams being the first sounds we had heard from them. In an instant the whole camp was in chaos.

With Pell's absence I was the one in charge. I yelled for the riders to stop and tried to grab the bridle of the first horse. I could as easily have caught a fistful of wind. That horse was well trained and swung its head to one side to avoid my hand. The rider swept by so close the tail of her horse lashed across my face. Now the bell was being rung. Many were shouting for Pell, since clearly I was of little use. Even when Kazouri tried to stop them with her great bulk they dodged her hands easily enough and charged on. I looked to Jhemar for some help, but she was doubled up with her arms wrapped around her head as if struggling to shut out a raging clamor.

Suddenly, just as the wild ones were making their second or third turn around the camp, Pell reappeared from wherever she had gone to hide her pain. The look on her face was one of anger set in stone. With arms outstretched, she stepped directly and very deliberately in front of the first one's horse. I gasped with fear. That horse reared up and came to an instant halt less than a foot away from her. Only a very skilled rider could have kept her seat. The three companions stopped also. With Pell in charge, the others from the camp moved forward cautiously to watch.

The first of these wild women shouted rudely to Pell, "Out of my way, fool, or you will be trampled. I am looking for the chief of these women." Much to my surprise, she spoke Kourmairi. Though her words were arrogant, she looked somewhat discomfited at having her horse stopped so easily by another. She even glanced about uncertainly.

Pell was shaking her head. "We have no chief here," she answered coldly. "I was chosen leader a few days ago and could just as easily be unchosen. Now, what do you mean riding in here in this way and disrupting our camp?"

"Where is your Chief? I will only speak to the Chief."

With a look of disgust, Pell began to say again, "We have no..." Then suddenly I saw her stance and her whole manner change. Right before my eyes she became 'the Chief.'

At the same time, the other seemed to go through some change of her own. Accepting that she had been stopped and bested in this way, she said suddenly, "Then you are my Chief."

Pell had drawn herself up very tall. In a voice I did not recognize, she said, "Yes, I am your Chief. You will dismount immediately and act with respect in my camp." Pell took the reins in her hand so there could be no question of compliance and went on in a thunderous voice, "I do not tolerate this sort of insubordination here. And you, also!" This last she said with a quick nod of her head to the other three riders.

Instantly the first woman leapt off her horse, followed by the others, who had been watching her closely for a sign. To my surprise, this loud savage put her hand over her heart, made a deep bow, and said to Pell with respect, "My deepest apologies if we have troubled your peace. We come to join with the women here. Having been blessed or cursed with powers, we are no longer welcome among our own people. I am Rishkazeel, and this is Zareetzi and Daijar and Noshira."

"Well, Rishka, that is better," Pell said, still trying to maintain a haughty manner, "though here we do not bow so low. Now, you and your women are welcome to stay in this camp as long as you obey me in all things. First of all, you are never to ride in on that road again. Also, you are never to go about openly as women in the world out there. You can cut your hair or hide it away, but you cannot wear it long in that manner. And you are never to go mounted in this camp again unless you are riding back with an urgent message. Is that clear? Is all of that understood?" Rishka nodded and Pell snapped suddenly, "And who told you of this place?"

"Heraki-the-Wise," Rishka said, bowing again.

"Well, a curse on her wisdom, then. She should have told you to come here quietly and with caution. Perhaps I should send some of my women to visit her wherever she lives. You may have compromised the safety of this place if you have been seen coming here and so put us all in danger of our lives."

Rishka looked at the ground and bowed again, really low this time.

"And stop that cursed bowing!" Pell shouted with extreme annoyance. "Once will do. Here we bow only once a day."

Alyeeta appeared suddenly at Pell's shoulder. "I am glad you came back and stopped her. If she had ridden one more time around my shelter in that way I should have found it necessary to turn her into a bat or a beetle."

Rishka stared in surprise at Alyeeta. "You are a Witch," she said contemptuously. "I had not thought to find Witches here among the star-cursed."

"Indeed I am," Alyeeta answered, staring with open hostility at this newcomer. "I am a Witch, and this is my shelter and my clearing. The very ground you stand on has been spelled by me, so have a care and try to find some manners, if that is possible for a Muinyairin. You are likely more use to us as a woman than as a bat, though who can be sure of anything in these strange times?"

By now Telakeet and Hamiuri had joined us. Most of the rest of the women in the camp had gathered round, seeing that the wild ones were no longer a mounted threat. In fact, I think all of us were there, all but the silent ones, who were still in hiding, and Ethrin and Irdris, whom I had sent to find them and, if possible, bring them back. Off in the woods that way, they not only endangered themselves but the rest of us as well.

Telakeet pointed at Rishka, saying in her spiteful way, "Well, the Muinyairin have not improved much since I last met with them, and this one looks to be a good sample of their ways."

Hamiuri glanced at the others for only a moment. It was Rishka who held her stare for a long while, so long that Rishka herself was forced to drop her eyes. She asked in a much-subdued voice, "What do you search for in my face, Mother?"

Hamiuri was shaking her head. She said almost in a whisper, seeming not to answer Rishka's question but some question of her own, "Wounded, so much pain, the walking wounded." Then to Telakeet she said sharply, "Curb your tongue, Sister. You only add oil to the fire." Without another word she turned and walked away, bowed over as if by sadness.

"Witch, I have no need of your pity," Rishka shouted after her, more daring now that Hamiuri's back was turned.

Pell took a deep breath and shook herself as if shaking off some bone-deep chill. "You have no need of anyone's pity, and be assured that you will get none, but for as long as you are here you will treat our 'Mother' with respect or you will answer to me."

"Tribal Mother? That dowdy old creature? Where are her marks of rank? She looks more like the rag pickers in towns I have ridden through than like a person of power."

"Have you forgotten that I am Chief here?" Pell roared. "If you cannot curb your tongue, I will have your fancy sword melted down and reshaped as a chamber pot for all to use. As to power, pray to the Goddess you never give her cause to use that power on you. Now you will come with me and my captains, and we shall decide where to put the four of you to use." Rishka started to bow again, then stopped in confusion. She stared at the ground as Pell spun on her heel and strode off without a look or another word to any of us.

"Trouble, nothing but trouble, like a bone caught in the throat," Telakeet muttered, making a nod of her head in Rishka's direction as she turned to leave. "They should throw her back out to the wolves or let the Zarn have her. They deserve one another." For once I agreed with Telakeet, could not have agreed with her more.

While the rest of the women wandered back to their tasks, the new ones and those of us who were captains followed meekly after Pell. I noticed that one of the wild women, Zareetzi, or Zari, as she later came to be called by us, dogged Rishka's footsteps as if for protection, all the while looking about her fearfully. Seeing that, I sensed that under all their bluster, those women might be as wary of us as we were of them. Even that thought did not make Rishka one bit more likable.

The place where we gathered was a little clearing on the high bank above the stream, well away from the turmoil of the camp. Pell gestured silently for us all to sit. This was my first real chance to look at those wild women, the first moment they had been still for long enough. They were lighter than most Koormir and much darker than the Shokarn, with very dark, straight hair. They were not dressed in dull farm-boy clothes as we were, but in layers of bright, ragged finery: vests and tunics in many styles of embroidery, brilliantly colored sashes, and strings of beads with jewelry flashing at their ears and wrists. They wore their hair long, some in tiny braids decorated with feathers, shells, and beads. Though they looked very strange indeed, still it saddened me that soon all that rough beauty would have to be hidden.

Renaise was sitting on one side of me, very stiff and tense, staring hostilely at Rishka. Zenoria, on the other side, seemed quite at ease. She leaned toward me and said in my ear, "Save for their style of dress, they do not seem so different from us, these Muinyairin. Perhaps they are the Kourmairi's wilder side. And then it may be I think that because I am part Muinyairin myself. My grandmother came from one of the northern hill tribes in the Drylands. She even taught me a few words of the language."

It was amusing to watch Pell as leader, caught between her usual position of first among equals and that of having to play tyrant-chief for Rishka's eyes. More than once I had to cover my mouth and turn away or risk being disrespectful to my 'Chief.' In spite of all this, we managed to make a plan. After much questioning of the new ones and some consultation among ourselves, it was decided that Rishka, because of her great skill with horses, would work with Zenoria. Zari would help there, too.

191

Daijar would join Kazouri as our 'trainer' and be her second there. Noshira was to learn more of healing from myself, Arnella, and Alyeeta and also add her store of knowledge to our own.

Through all this, Rishka acted with some respect toward Kazouri and Jhemar, though I noticed that Jhemar herself kept as great a distance as possible between them. But I saw a look of disgust cross her face when she heard Zenoria was in charge of the horses. No doubt she thought she could do much better. Her expression for Renaise I can hardly describe, only that it made me want to leap up to her defense. Worst of all was the look she turned on me when she discovered I was second there to her precious 'Chief.' At least in front of Pell she knew better than to match her evil looks with evil words.

In spite of their outlandish appearance, the other women seemed civil enough now that they were off their horses. Zari, in fact, seemed timid, almost fearful, still clinging to Rishka's side. Daijar struck up an instant rapport with Kazouri. As I went off with Noshira, or Noshir, as we called her, to look for Alyeeta, I could already hear them comparing training styles. Yes, the others we could deal with in spite of their strange appearance, but not Rishka. Telakeet was right. It was clear that Rishka was nothing but trouble. I would have been glad enough to throw her back to the wolves, though in truth, not to the Zarn's guards. No, not even Rishka would I have fed to the Zarn's guards.

As I walked away I could feel her eyes burning into my back, furious with resentment that I, a dirt-clod, was second to 'the Chief' and so to be obeyed. I knew there was to be no easy peace between us. For my part, I wished to the Mother that this one had found her way into some other camp. Truly, there was some special enmity between us.

Though on the surface calm and order were restored to the camp, I was never to feel comfortable there again. Always I sensed Rishka's presence or felt her angry eyes fastened upon me. If she had a chance and Pell was not within hearing, she would say some cruel and insulting thing whenever we chanced to pass, things far worse than any Renaise had ever said. This time I knew better than to complain to Pell. Renaise also came under attack. One good result of all this was that Renaise and I became uneasy allies. We would come together to complain of Rishka to each other as we could not to Pell. Only when I was out of camp on a search mission or sentry duty did I feel free of her. Even then, there was some sort of pull that made me uneasy. It was like having a sore from a saddle that is always being rubbed and so never has a chance to heal.

Strange to say, but then maybe not so strange — maybe only sad — what I could do for others I could not do for myself. I found myself ending everyone's troubles but my own. As Pell was frequently away and I was second there, it mostly fell to me to settle those disputes and conflicts that so often arose among us now. Truth be told, I enjoyed doing it and even gained some skill at it. I think it reminded me of the gentle, caring child I had been before bitterness began eating up my heart. I would shut my eyes and listen intently to each person's story with some inner sense. When they were done I would see the solution as if written before me on a wall, a solution that would bend to both needs and blend them, leaving no one the loser. Others went away well satisfied. They praised my fairness and my skill. But for myself, in this painful conflict with Rishkazeel the Muinyairin, I saw nothing when I asked for guidance but a blank wall.

★

Spring had turned into summer. The heat had become oppressive, especially in the middle of the day. Even in the shade of the great trees we sweated and complained. Most of us were grateful for the chance to go shirtless in the camp, glad for that time at least not to have to pretend we were men. Not Rishka. I never saw her shirtless, not once, at least not till that day when I came on her accidentally by the little stream that flows below Alyeeta's clearing. The sound of running water must have masked my approach. She was undressing to bathe, bending over to take off her boots. Her back was covered with a crisscross of scars and welts, some still crusted. I sucked in my breath. She must have heard my gasp, for she whirled on me.

"What are you staring at, you fool?" she snarled, catching me open-mouthed. "Have you never seen lash marks before? Why do you always go about gawking and gaping like a country girl in the city streets? Did they send you here to spy on me? If so, you may have seen more than you bargained for, eh?"

I stepped back speechless before her savage questioning, a hot flush rising into my face. We stared at each other a moment in hostile silence. At last I collected myself enough to say with some attempt at calm, "I am no spy. I came here to bathe, hoping to be alone and out of the clutter of the camp. Since this place is already taken, I will go elsewhere." I tried to keep my voice steady, but inside I was shaking, wanting to turn and run from so much rage.

"Are you afraid?" she sneered at me. "Do my scars make you ill? Let me tell you how I came by them, since you are so curious." Her voice was like oil. I was trapped by her stare. I could no more move my feet than if I had stepped knee deep into swamp mud. "All this that you see," she went on, "happened before I fully came into my powers. By the Mother's Tit they came slowly, those powers, different ones at different times, the power of self-defense last of all. This last beating, this one that is not yet healed, was because they could not bend my will to marry some fool twice my age. They wanted this match because he was rich in goats and horses and so would do honor to my family. Why he wanted me I will never know. I certainly gave him no encouragement — just the opposite. But there I was, about to be sold for horses like a pile of trade goods. Not only did they want me to go with this horse-tick and lie beneath him for the rest of my life, they wanted me to go willingly, to be polite and submissive. And since I showed no sign of that, after they struck their bargain they thought to soften me with the lash.

"It was my older brother who was doing the beating, as I had worn out my father. I had just rudely told this brother where he could stick a horse's cock. He was in a thundering rage. Among Muinyairin men it is considered a disgrace if they cannot control their women. He was laying on the lash with a vengeance. Suddenly this great flame of fury rushed up in me. Through that haze of red I could see my brother lying on his back, streaked with blood. His arm was bent above his head at an unnatural angle. I ran, leaving him there screaming in pain. I have not seen him since, but I hope I haunt his dreams as he haunts mine. It was on his horse that I fled my people as soon as I could gather the others."

She went on, the words flowing out almost as if she had forgotten me, raw pain in her voice in place of anger. "All my life it has been that way. I was raped by my uncles when I was little, to teach me submission. For as long as I can remember, I was beaten by my father, mostly for not being a proper woman, sometimes for being a Witch, and always with my mother's encouragement. She would say his hand was too light. 'Harder, Husband, harder, you are too kind. No wonder she strays.'

"You wonder why I did not leave? I did, I ran off many times. Always other tribesmen returned me to my father, tied me up and brought me back as if I were his goods. Even those who were my father's enemies did this, for they counted themselves honorable men, not thieves. Of course, that always meant another beating. And in truth, where was there to go in the Drylands that was not some tribe's marked territory? And where else is the child of the Muinyairin to go in a world that despises us so?"

The despair in her voice tore at my heart. At that moment I did not hate her. I could have cried for her instead. Her face twisted with pain as she said, "No one will ever touch me that way again." Then she looked straight at me as if suddenly remembering that I was there and snarled, "But why am I sharing these things with a chaka?" This last word she spat out between her teeth with disgust. I had never heard it before. Later I discovered it to be one of the Muinyairin words of insult for the Koormir. A polite translation would be horse-droppings. It was no worse, I suppose, than the words of insult the Shokarn and Koormir heap on each other and both of them use for the Muinyairin.

Later I got a small jar of ointment from Alyeeta. I took it to Zari and put it in her hand. "Some of those wounds are beginning to fester. Use this on her back. It may save her from a bad infection." She looked at me in surprise, but I was gone before she could question me.

After that moment of openness, Rishka was even more hateful than before, as if to ensure there would be no other such moments. From then on I was far more cautious of where I went, and actively avoided her when I could. Of course, it was not always possible. We all had work to do and things to learn. One evening some of us, Rishka and myself among others, were sitting in Alyeeta's shelter around her little fire, listening to the Witches speak of the uses of charm and illusion and even trickery if needed. Shalamith was talking, holding forth at her shining best, when suddenly Rishka jumped to her feet, shouting, "Sometimes all this stealth and subterfuge seems like cowardice to me. I would rather use the skill of my sharp sword, draw blood, and be done with it."

Shalamith turned her radiant smile on Rishka. "Such a shame that your powers deny you that pleasure."

Alyeeta looked up from the other side of the circle. "And what would that gain you? A head to display on the end of a pike in the manner of the Muinyairin, some bodies to be disposed of by others later. I wonder if the heroes of great battles ever think of those who must follow after and cart away their bloody leavings. Swords are messy. Besides, what you call stealth and subterfuge are also skills, not to be scoffed at. There is nothing pretty or glorious in heaps of dead bodies left lying about, flesh rotting in a cloud of flies. Believe me, I have seen it all and more. Besides, if you had not the powers that stop your striking hand, the death you court so avidly might be your own."

"I am a Muinyairin. My sword and training would not fail me," Rishka said haughtily.

"Indeed, girl," Alyeeta answered with amusement, "you think you would only come up against clods and butchers and fools with no training of their own?" With that the Witches all burst into loud laughter. Even Hamiuri joined them.

Rishka turned deep red and whirled around to leave. Tzaneel, Renaise's friend, who had been sitting next to Rishka, put out a hand to block her way and said to Alyeeta, "We have all come here bitter and in pain, hated and hunted by others, denied sometimes by those who bore us. Why should we not want to taste blood on the end of a sword? What gifts of love can we possibly bring to the world, or to each other, for that matter?"

"Somehow you must." To my surprise it was Shalamith who spoke. Her glow seemed to be dimmed by sadness. "If you cannot find your way to that love it will all end the same, all go down in fire and blood and death. There has been more than enough of that already." It was the first time I had ever heard Shalamith speak a serious word.

"Ask the Goddess for healing," Irdris said softly, almost in a whisper. "She heals all our wounds when we let Her."

"No gods for me!" Rishka shouted, whirling on Irdris now. "I will worship no gods. I would tear down all their altars if I could."

Filled with quiet power, Hamiuri's voice came to us out of the darkness. "The Goddess is different from men's gods. She does not force you or demand your worship. Instead, She invites you to join the dance. The only punishment for your absence is your absence. And you cannot tear down Her altars, child, for the whole world is Her altar — yours as well, if you will have it."

Rishka had turned back to face us. "Mother," she said to Hamiuri, anguish in her voice now instead of her usual mocking arrogance, "Mother, this is no childish anger. I saw my lover killed before my eyes. Men of my own people thrust their swords into the 'sacred' fire, then held them high for the blessing of their gods before they cut her throat. After that they hacked her body half from half. They would have done the same for me with their god's blessing and told me so, save that they had already bargained me in marriage to some old man. That is what I know of gods. There is no worship left in my heart, and precious little love."

Hamiuri seemed about to answer, then shook her head and turned away. "Humans!" Alyeeta spat out in disgust. "Always humans."

Rishka's pain burned in me like a fire. It was my own story told again. At that moment, in spite of all she had ever said to me, I wanted to go to her and give her comfort. Of course, she would not have let me. She would not have let any of us near her. Very slowly, all the while she was speaking, she had been unfastening her shirt. Now she said, "I not do this for pity, only that all of you should understand." Then she dropped her shirt, turning slowly so that each of us in turn could see the ruin of her back by the flare of the fire. There were gasps and then a long, shocked silence. No one dared voice a question. Finally Rishka picked up her shirt and went out.

At last Alyeeta said slowly, as if to no one, as if to the night itself, "Goddess have mercy on us all."

15

Rishka's moments of openness seemed often to be followed by more bitter rage, and so it was after that time around Alyeeta's hearth. A few days later I chanced to come to Alyeeta's shelter one morning in search of a book or some advice on healing. Instantly I saw that I had stepped into a fierce argument between Rishka and Alyeeta. Irdris seemed to be the subject of it. I heard her name mentioned several times.

I was about to step out again as quickly and quietly as I could and leave them to it, but Alyeeta spotted me. She raised her hand, saying, "Wait, Tazzi, I need to speak with you. Rishka and I will soon be done here." I stood there feeling trapped. There were at least a hundred places I would rather have been at that moment than caught between Rishka and Alyeeta.

Rishka, for her part, appeared glad for an audience. Her anger, in fact, seemed fueled by it. She burst out with malice, "Irdris is like a soft white slug, boneless and gutless. Why should *I* be the one to teach her to ride, her and her two Shokarn friends? Why not Zenoria or Tzaneel or another of those chaka?"

"We have already been over this ground three times at least," Alyeeta said tersely. She was plainly out of patience and wanting Rishka gone. "Why argue this with me? Go take it up with Zenoria or Pell."

"You only like Irdris because she can read your moldy books," Rishka shot back.

I saw Alyeeta bristle at this. "Whom I like and why I like them is my own affair and none of yours. Talk to Pell if you are dissatisfied. She is the chosen leader here." That much she said aloud. In her head I heard her say, /Go back where you come from, demon-brat, if you do not like it here./

I heard it as clearly as if she had spoken aloud. Rishka, however, seemed to take no notice. She had the bit between her teeth and was running fast with it. "No use to talk to Pell. She is worse than you are with this Irdris. She tells me Irdris is my 'sister' and I must treat her as such, that in fact all women here are my sisters. Let me tell you, that one is no family to me, that Shokarn slug. I might hate the men in my family and wish them all painfully dead and soon, but they are more kin to me than those soft white things, those girls of Eezore. They cannot even hold a horse between their knees. They have to be taught to ride like unweaned infants. I was riding before I was five and had my first horse by six. I can fight and ride as well as any man. What are they good for, those koribi? I will never call such women sisters. They are no kin to me." I could tell from this ugly outburst that Pell was no longer the revered 'Chief,' but had become common clay like the rest of us.

Alyeeta was gathering herself up. When she spoke, her words were thick with sarcasm. "Those are all good skills such as are useful to us here, but I think you will find there are other skills among us just as useful. In such close quarters sometimes even silence is as useful a skill as good horse handling, though it might prove hard for you to learn. I doubt if any here would have the patience for trying to teach you. Now I am done with this. Enough!" She turned to me as if to make clear that she was finished with the matter.

Angered at this dismissal, Rishka shouted, "You are not so special. There are many like you in my tribe. You are nothing but an old Witch. You even..."

"Indeed," Alyeeta said menacingly, turning back toward Rishka. There was a look on her face such as I had never seen before on any human — more like a fox or a hawk, perhaps. She narrowed her eyes in a threatening way. Her smile froze my blood. Stretching out the first two fingers of her left hand, she slowly raised her arm to point at Rishka while intoning words I did not understand. This clearly was a spell. There was a moment of frozen silence at the end of it. Then Alyeeta dropped her arm and said in her normal voice, as if she had just taken care of a piece of business, "Enough of words. That one needs some time for thought."

Rishka, meanwhile, had fallen silent in midsentence. Though her mouth moved and her eyes bulged with effort, not another word came from between her lips. Considering all the harm she had done me with words, I might have been tempted to laugh at her plight, but the look on Alyeeta's face made me keep my peace. I had no wish to be silenced in the same manner.

Alyeeta now stood, hands on her hips, looking back and forth between us with something clearly working in her head, while I stood rooted to the spot, helplessly wishing myself elsewhere. Then, flashing her demon smile again, she said, very slowly and clearly, "If you wish to regain your speech, Rishkazeel of the Muinyairin, you will make yourself subject to Tazmirrel and do her bidding here. Follow where she goes, do as she does, and obey her in all things. Pay heed to what I have just told you and remember it well, else next time it may be a month before you favor us with speech again. Now go! Take yourself out of my space and out of my sight!" With those words Alyeeta stretched out her arm again. Her hair lifted and coiled about her head, and blue sparks seemed to flash from it. Once more, she was pointing her first two fingers at Rishka.

Seeing Alyeeta thus occupied, I took my chance of escape and slipped out by another way. Whatever she wished to tell me would have to wait. Much as I loved Alyeeta, I could not face her at that moment. Also, I had a terror that she might try binding Rishka to my side by some further spell.

Once free from there I ran all the way to the stream, as if pursued by a pack of demons. Clothes and all, I threw myself into the water. After that I lay on the bank for a while, basking in the sun and trying to forget all that I had just seen, or at least to lessen its hold on me. I have often wondered how different my life might have been if Ashai or Arnella or one of the others had gone to Alyeeta's shelter that morning instead of me.

For the rest of that day I occupied myself as far from there as possible, working for Renaise, washing clothes and bedding down by the stream. I had hoped to stay well out of the way, but Zenoria found me easily enough. She came riding up with an anxious look on her face. "Do you know where Rishka is? I was told you were the one to ask."

"Not here, thank the Goddess," I answered, more sharply perhaps than I had meant to. The last thing I wanted to do at that moment was to think of where Rishka might be or, in fact, to think of Rishka at all. What I wanted was to have Zenoria and her questions gone. I longed to be left alone again with my washing. Instead, she slid off her horse and came over to squat by me where I was scrubbing on the rocks.

"Please, Tazzi, I am worried. No one seems to know where she is. She has not been to teach the new ones their riding."

I cringed at those words, put down my soapstone, and turned to face her. "Zenoria, listen to me. You must not let her teach riding, at least not to those three new Shokarn. She hates them, hates them with a fury, especially Irdris. I fear she will do them some harm."

"Not teach? But she is the best rider among us."

"Zenoria, you must believe me in this."

"Tazzi, what happened today? There is such strange talk in camp. Something about Alyeeta..."

I sighed and sat down. Plainly I was to have no peace from this, so I told her all that I knew of what had happened that morning in Alyeeta's shelter. At the end of it, much to my surprise, she shook her head and said, "Poor Rishka."

"Poor Rishka, indeed!" I exclaimed. "She provoked Alyeeta unmercifully and brought it all down on her own head." I answered all the more hotly for feeling forced to defend Alyeeta where I myself found her indefensible. Worst of all, I felt in some way tainted by this, as if I had had a part in it instead of doing my very best to avoid it. I knew Zenoria already distrusted the Witches, thinking them strange and frightening, though she had often said that Alyeeta was the least strange of them all. All this would do nothing to gain her trust.

She was shaking her head. "Surely with all her power Alyeeta could have found some other way to deal with Rishka."

"You were not there! You do not know! That woman is a monster and hates us all!" I burst out.

"Oh, Tazzi, how can you say that? Think what has been done to her by men." Then she stopped as if considering something and said slowly, "So that is the silencing Zari spoke of."

"Is it all through the camp, then?"

"Well, they know something happened. Alyeeta was loud enough for many to hear, at least at the end."

Now my feelings were all in confusion. I suppose it should have given me pleasure that others knew Rishka was to be under my orders. Instead, it turned my stomach. As I saw again Alyeeta's outstretched arm and pointing fingers, a chill of fear rushed up my back. As to the silencing itself, instead of feeling joy in it, I remembered Rishka as she had stood in the firelight, shirtless before that circle of women. In some way my heart went out to her. Then, when I remembered her words from that morning, I thought a little silence was perhaps a blessing after all.

At last, convinced I knew nothing more, Zenoria went away to look elsewhere. I had some peace again, but not for long.

It was Zari who found me next. I was resting there in the late afternoon with all my work spread out drying in the sun. She was out of breath and looked very troubled.

"I have been told of Alyeeta's spell," she said quickly. "I have heard that Rishka has been made your 'creature.' Please do not hurt her in that way. She has already been hurt enough, hurt far too much."

"She is not my 'creature,' as you put it, and I have no intention of hurting her at all. This was all Alyeeta's idea, certainly not mine, though I must say Rishka brought it on herself, every bit of it."

"Please," said Zari, looking at me beseechingly, "you do not know, you cannot understand what horrors she has already been through."

I felt a sudden anger flare up in me at this gentle, timid woman pleading for Rishka's sake, Rishka who hurt others whichever way she turned, who had punished me with words at every chance. "How do you know what I can understand?" I shouted at her, "or what I myself have been through?" I wanted to shake her by the shoulders. This was the second one who had come to speak for Rishka. Who was there to plead for me in my pain? Then I saw her recoil from my anger, staring at me with tears in her large, dark eyes. Suddenly I felt embarrassed and ashamed.

"Here, come help me fold these clothes," I said quickly. "The sun will soon be gone. I promise you I mean her no harm, though she has certainly done me enough. Can she speak again? Did she send you here to beg for her?"

"No! Oh no! She would never never do such a thing." Now there was fear and confusion in Zari's face. "I came here on my own. Please, I beg of you, do not tell her I spoke to you in this way." She was so full of agitation, I put a hand on her arm to calm her.

"Trust me," I said gently, not sure what it was I pledged myself to do or not to do. Then I made a motion of my head toward the clothes and she nodded. In silence we gathered and folded and stacked. She helped me carry back the baskets till we were within sight of the clearing. Then she set hers down and ran off, vanishing like a deer into the trees.

When I returned to my shelter it was almost dark. I had delayed as long as I could. Light streamed out at me through the lattice of branches, so clearly someone was there before me. I entered, fearing, of course, that it was Rishka. To my surprise I saw her lying on my mat, stripped naked, legs slightly spread, arms at her sides. Her face was a wooden mask, her eyes dark pits as if they had sunk into her head. "Have your will with me and get it done with," she said in a cold, dead voice almost before I had stepped through the entrance. "Since this is the price of having my speech returned I will survive whatever you choose to do. Worse has already been done than you can possibly invent."

I stared at her, puzzled and then incredulous and finally with horror. When at last the full import of her words came home to me, I flushed deeply, a painful heat rising from the back of my neck into my face. "Oh no! We do not...," I stammered, "I do not ... This was not what Alyeeta meant..."

"I have no wish to give offense, only to say that I accept my lot. After all, I let myself be humbled by Alyeeta's silencing and have been given over into your hands. Now that I am in your power I assume you will use me at your will. I have not, after all, been very kind to you."

I was shaking my head wildly. Now I better understood Zari's fears. Hers must be a culture that used sex as punishment. Rishka went on in that voice that chilled me to my soul, "There is no more will left in me to fight. I have fought all my life and been beaten for it over and over. Suddenly today I thought, Why? And to what end? What use? What is it all for? Let them do what they will with me. If this is the price of staying with the tribe, then I submit myself to you. After all, what can you do to me that has not already been done and worse? So let us get on with it. I am not an untouched child."

I looked at her lying there, waiting for her fate at my hands. I thought of how often, when she mocked and tormented me, I had wished her helpless. Now she lay before me, more helpless than I could possibly have imagined, ready to submit to whatever cruelty I could invent, yet it gave me no pleasure. In fact, the flat, dead tone of her voice pained me more than all her cutting words.

My own past resolves of vengeance melted away. I saw Zari's lovely, stricken face before me and began to shake, hardly able to stand on my own feet. As she saw me swaying, Rishka moved over on the mat. My knees gave way. I fell flat out next to her and began to cry. This was something she had never seen me do, no matter how she had tormented me, though I knew she had often reduced others to tears.

I cried and cried, cried as if to end all crying, cried for myself and for Kara and even for Rishka, who thought I meant to rape her, and for her unknown lover, whose life had been cut away by swords, and for little Zari, who knew too much, and for Pell and Tamara, kept apart by the Zarn's war. I wept for all of us at that moment, even Renaise, even Telakeet, who was so bitter and had lost so much.

After a while Rishka put her hand on me to stop me or to comfort me. Gradually my crying eased. I turned to her and slowly put my arms around her, saying gently, "I have not been set up as your master, only assigned as a guide. I want nothing from you and wish you no harm." She lay in my arms, stiff and passive, not resisting my embrace nor yet yielding to it. For a while I stroked her hair and her arms, very careful not to touch her back. Softly I said her name over and over, to bring her back from that cold, dead place where she had gone. In just such a way I had once held a fawn in my arms while it died of an arrow. This went on for so long with no change that I thought she had fallen asleep. Then, suddenly, a great shudder passed through her whole body. Sobs came after that, great, violent, wracking sobs that seemed to well up from some unimaginable depth. Soon she began to throw her body about, crying as if those wild sounds were torn from her throat by torture. I struggled to hold her, fearing she might do herself some harm, but she seemed to have no knowledge of me or of the shelter or even of her own body and how it moved. Sometimes she cried out as she thrashed, shouting, "No, no, leave me be!" and then, "Never, never, no matter what you do!" Once she screamed and tried to bite me. Through it all I held on with no sense of time, no memory of any other place. At last she began to still. Finally her crying ceased, and slowly she came back to herself.

I thought she would strike out at me then. Instead, she looked at me with surprise, her eyes all swollen, gone soft and out of focus. Tentatively, she reached out her fingers and gently touched my face. Very moved, I responded in kind. After that she made a slight motion and I made another in return and so it went till soon, to my great surprise, we were touching in the manner of lovers. Not the brutal rape Rishka had pictured, no, nothing like that, nothing even hard or passionate, but slowly, all slowly and tentatively, trading a touch for a touch, and then waiting and then another touch. We were sending careful signals to each other and receiving them back and maybe hesitating or maybe sending back something a little stronger, a little firmer, and then waiting again. In this way we moved toward each other slowly, ever so slowly, but building, moving, drawing energy, swelling and rising until just as night turned toward morning, we both reached release together in a great shuddering cry that must have wakened half the camp.

★

Of course, things were not to be so easily mended between us nor a lasting peace made. For the next few days Rishka followed me around, dutifully doing as I told her. Zari followed Rishka even more closely than before, giving me puzzled looks that were a mix of gratitude and envy, as if Rishka and I were truly lovers. For that time, at least, Rishka was contrite, being carefully polite to others and avoiding Alyeeta altogether. Then her spirit began to rise. She could not resist sharpening her tongue on me again. Fired with passion, I learned to answer her in kind. It was during that time that we really became lovers, though it was never again to be kind and gentle — far from it. It was like a sword fight, all flashing edges. I had found someone who could meet my bitterness and grief with rage and no pretense of love. I threw myself over and over against her hardness with a kind of twisted joy. It satisfied my demons, fed them, and made them grow so that with each passing day, I myself became more and more like Rishka. I even gloried in it. I saw Alyeeta watching with concern and flaunted our passion before her. I can say "our," for it was clear to me that Rishka met my furies with her own and had the same hard joy in our coming together.

At last Alyeeta summoned me to her shelter, as I knew sooner or later she must. I was ready with a whole stock of clever, cutting words and asked defiantly, "Are you angry with me for my Muinyairin lover? You were the one who sent her to me."

"Yes, in truth I was, and I have come to regret it as all things done in anger are sooner or later to be regretted. I only meant for you to tame her a little, not to fall prey to her madness yourself. But how can I be angry at you, Little One? I am an old, old woman and you are very young. How can I begrudge you your youthful passions? I only love you. I do not own you.

"You are a great gift in my life, Tazzi, one I could not have hoped for or imagined. Who would dream that Alyeeta the Witch could have learned to love a human, and at my age. No, no, child, I am not angry with you, only glad for your existence and a little fearful for you at this moment. As to Rishka, if you could love her past some part of her bitterness, it would be a blessing. As she is now, she is of little use but for making trouble. Instead, I fear you yourself have become infected with her sickness. It is a dangerous business. Take care of your heart, Dear One. Protect yourself. It could all turn on you in a moment."

I was not sure what she meant by that warning, but I found myself being gently kissed and firmly escorted out through the hanging ivy before I could gather an answer. I had come to play a good, rousing game of knives or cudgels and had been disarmed of my anger right from the start. Later I thought Alyeeta must have carefully planned it so.

After that I wandered in a daze through the clearing where others seemed so busy, till Pell came up and took my arm. "Tazzi, I need to speak with you in private for a moment," she said in a low voice.

"So you do also want to warn me to cease my evil ways?" I asked mockingly.

"No, only to speak for myself and say my own truth. It might be better to go where there are not other ears."

"This will do well enough," I said, stopping deliberately in the way, where others had to step around us in order to pass by.

"Very well, if you wish it so," Pell said coolly. She looked at me silently for a moment, as if trying to gather the words, then spoke quickly. "I only need to say that your bed grows too complicated and too crowded for me. I need that part of my own life to be simple. Right now the rest of it is hard enough."

"It seems you have your own complications," I flung back at her. "I have seen Renaise in and out of your shelter often enough."

"What you think about Renaise and me is true, but at least I am not such a fool as to sleep with someone I am in love with."

I recoiled from this verbal blow that hurt all the more for having been unintended. Pell looked stricken as the meaning of her own words came home to her. "You warned me," I said softly. "You warned me many times."

"Sometimes no warning is enough. Sometimes I tell myself that I should take no pleasure till all this is over, but I have tried and it is too hard. Goddess hear me, this is a lonely piece of work, even in the middle of this crowd." She shook her head. "Sorry, Tazzi, I knew of no gentle way to tell you."

I shrugged and turned away. Women were looking at us curiously as they passed. As I watched Pell walk away, I thought that I had never seen her try to do a deliberate unkindness, nor had I ever seen her take one single step out of her way to avoid doing one.

Of course, I felt some hurt from this rejection and quickly added it to my already full store of hurts. But in truth, my body burned so for Rishka that there was scarcely room for any other feeling. And in all honesty, I was no more in love with Pell than she was with me. She was my captain, my leader, my chief. I would follow her anywhere, even at risk to my life. Besides that, I think we were even beginning to be friends and comrades, at least inasmuch as Pell was capable of being friends with anyone at that time. But we had never been passionate lovers. At moments, of course, I had had my illusions. Yet underneath I knew it had always been a thing of the flesh only, something that left me more lonely than satisfied when it was over. And in truth I was not in love with Rishka, either. It was only a strange sort of madness. You cannot be in love with a brand that has burned its name into your flesh and will do so again and again.

That evening Renaise sent me down to the spring for water and then sought me out there. Another one today, I thought, as I saw her coming toward me. I had just been settling the jug on my shoulder for the walk back. She came to stand before me, hands on her hips. "Do you perhaps have some time to talk?"

"Tell me if this is going to take long and I will set down my jug."

"I hear that Pell has finally put you out of her bed. No wonder, since you are making such a scene of yourself all over camp with that 'wild thing.' She should have done it sooner." Her tone was full of contempt and mockery. She even had a sort of gloating look on her face.

I did not respond in kind. I merely nodded, swung the jug off my shoulder to rest it between my feet, and said quietly, "What you hear is true, Renaise." Whatever her feelings toward me, I had made my own peace with Renaise. It had happened while waiting through those long, hard nights so filled with guilt and anxiety when I wanted nothing more than her safe return.

She looked at me in surprise, having no doubt expected a sharp retort. Instead, I said flatly and with no forethought, "The truth is, as long as this strange war goes on, it matters little to Pell who fills her bed, only that it be someone."

Instantly I saw from her face that, as Pell had done with me, I had given Renaise far more hurt with my thoughtless honesty than if I had spoken words whose sole intent was to cause pain. I quickly put out my hand. "Sorry, Renaise. You may not believe me, but I did not mean to hurt you. I only spoke a simple truth that both of us have had to live with. Perhaps we should do as Pell says, make peace among ourselves and suspend our small war till the larger one is over. Later we can fight again if we need to."

She looked at my hand a long time, then said thoughtfully, "I have always been jealous of you, Tazzi. You seemed to have so much power and I so little. Also, it frightened me that you were a healer. I thought only Witches were healers and I was afraid of Witches. But most of all I saw how Pell favored you. And what was I? Nothing but a serving-girl."

"I have been jealous of you also and not kind," I said, reaching for her hand. "Peace, Sister."

She hesitated a moment longer, then, very slowly, laid her hand in mine. "Peace, then. I suppose it is only a truth you spoke that Pell can love no one till this is over. Still, it hurt. I cannot help what I feel for her and will share her bed for as long as she will let me. Perhaps sometime we could ... you could ... I would not mind if..." She stopped, blushing deeply and stammering with embarrassment, but I could easily read her thoughts.

I shook my head, touched by her offer and struggling not to laugh. It was no doubt the most generous offer anyone had ever made me, and probably the funniest. I knew it had not been easy for her to say even that much. "No, no, it is all for the best," I said quickly. "Alyeeta and Rishka are all I can handle — more, in fact." I did not tell her that Pell already had one she truly loved. If she chose not to know of Tamara's place in Pell's heart, she would not learn of it from me. My careless words had already been cruel enough. In the end we walked back up to the camp kitchen in companionable silence, trading the weight of the full jug back and forth between us.

After that I saw Renaise differently. Whether she had really changed or my way of looking at her had changed or both I will never know, but from then on we were friends of a sort. It pleases me to write of this, for I think the only sane and decent thing I did during that time of madness over Rishka was to deal honorably with Renaise. Later, that was to serve us both well.

Life went on, death threatened, but whatever else was happening out there in the world, whatever endangered our lives and our future, Rishka and I continued whirling round and round each other in that wild dance that was love and that was not love, that was madness, that was obsession, that was closer, perhaps, to hate. I could have thought it to be a spell laid on us or a compulsion, had I not known how much the Witches themselves all opposed our being together. They would have been only too glad to unspell us if they could have. Each one of them had spoken to me in her own way, and to Rishka also. For the most part we brought out the very worst in each other, not the best. We were like two boulders that had rolled down opposite hills and collided. Crushed and bruised in the encounter, still we were unable to pull ourselves apart.

And yet there was another side to all this. It was her pain that called to me as well as her rage, cried out to me to be mended, drew me like a magnet — pain so like my own that sometimes I could not tell where the boundaries between us lay. She touched me as no other lover could, and in places that had been closed and sealed over. There were even moments of sweetness, almost unbearable sweetness that drew me back whenever I thought to break away. Yet whenever that sweetness turned to closeness and I thought to trust it, it would as quickly turn again to rage, slashing and burning, destroying all that had been built between us. It was as if we were locked in mortal combat and all our loving was a war, with those sweet times only a little truce before the next battle.

And yet ... and yet ... where does the truth really lie in all this turmoil of the heart? There were some more-normal times when we simply went about together and shared our tasks for the sake of each other's company. I noticed that Rishka did not try to bait Alyeeta any more, that, in fact, she avoided her whenever possible. So there, at least, Rishka had met her limit. Sometimes we even talked in the way that lovers do and told each other our stories, or at least Rishka told me stories of her life among the Muinyairin and I told her some tales of my early childhood. Of Kara I did not speak, nor of my own escape. Though often I thought to tell her my story, so like her own, something always held my tongue, a voice in my head saying, Of what use? How can she hear you? Her heart is too burned out to care. Also, I remembered Pell's coldness when I cried for Kara, and could not risk encountering that again. Instead, I added Rishka's bitterness to my already full store.

The contempt in which others in the world held the Muinyairin had with Rishka turned to vengeful pride. Even when things seemed pleasant enough, something would suddenly strike her. She would look about strangely and say to me, "See how they all avoid me? Jhemar, especially — she keeps a distance of at least six horses between us at all times. And those silent, frightened girls who try to hide whenever I pass — do they think I plan to eat them alive?"

"Rishka, sometimes your pride makes a fool of you. Jhemar avoids you because she is an empath, more than any of us. What is in your mind hurts her. As to those girls, those silent ones, they saw their people murdered before their eyes, butchered by riders who rode into their camp, much as you first rode in among us, shouting and with swords flashing. I know from the one who hid them that their own people were all killed for sheltering them. Do you blame them for being afraid?" Except for Alyeeta's silencing, this was the first time I had seen Rishka with no words and no answer.

In spite of her bristliness, she made herself useful in the camp. She was in truth as good a teacher as Zenoria had said. A few times I even went to watch her teach. The contempt and loathing she had spewed out in Alyeeta's shelter she did not allow herself in the practice ring. Zenoria was right, there she was fair and patient and very capable. Her skills as a rider were matched by her skills as a teacher. Even watching her with Irdris I could not have reproached her, though Irdris herself, while trying hard to do her very best, must have been a trying student. In spite of Rishka's best efforts, Irdris never learned to ride well. She could not sit her horse comfortably. Far from merging together as one being, it always seemed as if she and the horse had collided accidentally and might part again at any moment. The look on her face was usually one of slight surprise, as if this chair she had been sitting on had suddenly grown legs and decided to walk away with her on it. In spite of this she could talk to horses better than any of us, except perhaps Zenoria and myself. Horses would follow after her, sometimes even with their unwilling passengers. But that is a different story and for another time.

Those moments of normality and peace between Rishka and myself were always short-lived. Our own private tempest grew so fierce that Alyeeta felt obliged to speak to me again. "You do yourself some harm with this, Tazzi. The best in you is being bent and twisted."

"You are only jealous," I answered spitefully. "You cannot bear to see me loved by another." I knew the words were ugly and untrue before I spoke them, but I could not stop. Some demon that seemed beyond my power drove me.

Alyeeta looked at me sadly and shook her head. "No, Tazzi, not this time. There is nothing here to envy, only something to grieve for. Believe me, it is not out of jealousy or hurt pride that I say these things, though I am quite capable of both. It is for love of you, for your own sake that I speak and tell you what I see. That young woman has a deeper pit of rage and pain and bitterness in her than you can imagine. She will draw you into it if she can. You are susceptible to her, for she has tapped your passions in a way no one else ever has. I see you eating poison with both hands like a starved beggar. Do you expect me to stay silent?"

I was angry at Alyeeta for telling me what I already knew and did not want to hear and would not listen to, so I said rudely, "It no longer matters to me what you think or say." As soon as I said that I felt again a chill of fear and remembered her pointing fingers.

Alyeeta drew herself up tall and said coldly, "Be careful, Tazzi, you risk something far worse than my displeasure if you continue in this way."

I could not be sure if this was a threat or a warning. Either way it mattered little, for, of course, I did not heed her words. In the end none of it mattered anyhow, for our small private lives were soon swept away in the rush of larger happenings. Later I shuddered to think what might have befallen us both had we continued on our course.

★

One evening, when Rishka was off on a mission in search of some Muinyairin said to be in hiding, I found myself prowling about the camp. Not willing to lie alone in my shelter, waiting to see if she would come back in want of some loving, or come back in a fury, or come back at all, I wandered restlessly till Jhemar called me over to the fire. She had camp watch for the night and so asked me to sit up with her and help her stay awake.

I went, but I went warily, coming to squat beside her. "Do you also want to preach to me about Rishka? If so, you waste your breath."

"I? Preach?" she answered with a laugh. "My own head is so full of tangles, how would I know to tell another the right road to take. The night is long, sitting watch is tiresome. You are the only other one about. I thought perhaps to have some company, to tell some stories or smoke some jol."

"Excuse my edginess, Jhemar, but when so many hate her it is hard to know what will be said to me next. She sees how you keep your distance as if you find her loathsome."

"Hate her? Surely not. I think it is the pain of her Muinyairin pride that makes her see things so. There are some here who are frightened of her, and she herself helps that along. Some are angered by her ways and she helps that even more. But hate her, no, that is something else altogether. Not me, certainly. How could I hate her? I pity her. I know too much. I can read all that has happened in her life as soon as she comes near. Yes, I keep my distance. Being near her causes too much pain for me. Not all the shielding the Witches try to teach me can shut that one out. When I get too close she comes cutting through like a knife. And you, how can you stand it?"

I shrugged. "Her pain is so much like my own pain, I swim through it like water. How can it hurt me?"

"It hurts you, Tazzi, but you choose not to see it." Quickly she held up her hands. "Now that is all I will say on the matter."

"So she is to be blamed and shunned for her pain and so more pain added to it? When I think of the things her father did to her all those years ... Sometimes I think fathers are the curse of our lives."

"Not mine," Jhemar said quickly, as if glad of a different topic. "Not mine. My father was my first true friend and I miss him still." As she spoke she was lighting the jol pipe she held in her hand. I relaxed and sat back to listen, putting Rishka out of my mind for that moment.

"My father thought me very fine," Jhemar went on. "He tried to teach me everything he knew, though my mother interfered when she could, saying such knowledge was unsuitable for a girl-child. It was my mother, poor misguided woman, who wished to make a lady of me, a losing game if ever one was played. You can see I was not cut of a cloth for that. But I was her only daughter. Who else did she have to work her dreams on?

"Already at twelve I had reached my full height, with hands like a farmer's, and the feet of a horse. I had grown too fast. I never knew where my limbs were until they collided with something fragile and, of course, valuable. My poor mother, she tried, but what was she to do with this great creature? She could not beat me into a different shape, nor did she attempt that again after the first try. Instead, she used her tongue. Until I learned not to care, that tongue hurt more than a lash and left me more helpless. If she could have cut off my fingers and toes so that the stubs could be forced into little white gloves and dainty slippers, I swear she would have done so. Instead, I did us both a great kindness. I left. But I know my father must still grieve for me as I do for him."

While I was still dealing with the surprise of all this, she went on to tell me some childhood story from before her time with the Wanderers, and suddenly I understood. "But you are a Shokarn," I exclaimed, sitting up to better see her. "But your skin ... your speech...?"

"I would be as white as Irdris if I lived in a house in the city. And speech is easily learned. By now I feel as if Kourmairi is my native speech, but I can also speak some Muinyairin, and much of the Wanderers' secret tongue as well."

"But you never speak Shokarn, not even to Irdris."

"It is not my favorite tongue," she said abruptly. "It brings back too many memories." Then she quickly went on to tell me some tale of the Wanderers while I leaned back again to listen. I was used to Jhemar's silence, and so was amazed at her skill as a storyteller and charmed as well, but underneath I sensed an uneasiness, some trouble eating at her. At last her words stopped, and she sat staring into the fire. I could feel a great weight on her, yet nothing came clear.

"Jhemar," I finally said, "what is it that sits so heavy on you?"

"Eezore," she answered, still staring into the fire. The way she said that word, it sounded like the tolling of a heavy bell. Then she looked up suddenly, straight into my eyes, and said again, "Eezore! There is some civil strife there between those who are high and in power, and we, the Star's children, are in the middle of it all. In some way, we are the cause of it. It is hard to get a clear picture of what is happening there. We only get rumors, bits and pieces. One thing, however, is very clear. Many, many of us are trapped behind those walls. I think Pell plans to move against Eezore while they are in conflict with each other, thinking this may be our only chance to crack open the city."

"To do what?!" I exclaimed, sitting up straight and staring at Jhemar. "Move against Eezore, the city of the Zarn? She must be mad! Does she think to take this bunch of half-trained girls and go up against a walled fortress city of many hundreds, defended by the guards?" Irdris had told me enough of Eezore to have formed a very frightening picture of that city.

"Keep your voice down," Jhemar said quickly. "None of the others know yet, only myself and Zenoria. Pell has spoken to no one else."

I was shaking my head and could hardly breathe from the shock of it. "Eezore," I repeated numbly. "She thinks to go against Eezore. Well, she is even wilder than I had imagined. No wonder you are so full of dread. With your city knowledge and your Shokarn speech, you would be very useful in such an enterprise. For myself, of course, I know nothing of cities and can speak only what little Shokarn Irdris and Alyeeta have taught me. Surely I would not be one of those chosen to go to Eezore." Jhemar nodded but made no answer.

After that we spoke little, but sat watching the fire, each in our own thoughts. Soon Noshir came to replace Jhemar, and I went off to my shelter to try to sleep. The dreams that came to me that night were strange and very troubling.

★

There is what we say and there is what we do. Sometimes they are the same, as close as twins. Sometimes they are not even acquainted with each other. So it was when I spoke of Eezore, saying I would not be one of those to go. The great walled city of Eezore, source of all our troubles, lay in the path ahead of me like fate or like a mountain. No words of mine could move it. We say what we want to say and sometimes what we need to say, but in the end we do what we must.

16

For those next few days, rumors of Eezore hummed and buzzed among us like a hive of angry bees. Every rider coming in brought with her some new story — tales from the market or the road. Each one was more unlikely or fantastic than the one before, so they soon tangled with each other, full of contradictions. In the end nothing came clear, nothing we could base our plans upon.

In the midst of all this, much to my amazement, Maireth rode into camp. She had come with Josleen and Megyair. They had just escorted some burned ones to Pell's shelter. Though I was overjoyed to see her up and riding that way, I was also much concerned for her health. She, however, was not to be persuaded to go back. She had come to learn the healing of burns from myself and Alyeeta, saying we knew much more of that than Arnella did. In spite of my worries, she insisted on staying. She even spoke of going to Eezore to rescue the burned ones there.

As I had little time at that moment for teaching, or for healing either, Alyeeta took on most of the task, going at it with such a passion that I could almost feel jealous. She had already taken on Ashai, the new Shokarn, teaching her reading and writing as well as healing. I noticed how Ashai watched her, much as Renaise used to watch Pell. Seeing that, I even felt some of my old discomfort. Now, whenever I came into Alyeeta's shelter, either Ashai or Maireth or both were likely to be there, and sometimes Irdris as well, sitting in the corner bent over a book.

By now every woman in the camp knew, or at least suspected, that Pell meant to mount some kind of raid against the city. That added much heat to the talk. Pell's own contacts in Eezore seemed to have fallen into some deep crack in the earth. When she tried for mind-touch with them nothing came back, nothing but silence and darkness, or sometimes an edge of pain. In a constant fret of worry for those of us who might be trapped there, she threatened to go to Eezore herself and seek out the truth of it all.

Jhemar and I both tried hard to dissuade her. I echoed Jhemar's arguments that all had to do with tactics and strategy, saying we could not afford to lose her to the city at this time. In truth, I begged her not to go because I had such a terror of that place. It was very different from the fears I had already learned. It was a terror I could not have explained to anyone, and it haunted my dreams. The thought of Pell in that city filled me with dread.

Often it seems as if we draw to us the very thing we fear the most, and so, of course, it was I myself who drew Eezore even closer. It had already been a bad day among us, the worst, I think, since we had come to camp there in Alyeeta's clearing. Then a sentry rode in saying that someone had come with a message. When I heard that two of the Star-Born were in hiding at the edge of the woods on the Tarmaine-to-market road and needed a guide to bring them safely in, I leapt at the chance. Pell, Jhemar, Zenoria, and Kazouri were all away at that moment, so I was the natural one to go. Even if they had been there, I think I would have argued for the chance. Leaving Renaise in charge, I was up and gone from the clearing like a horse bolting through a broken fence, glad for any excuse to be free from there in spite of the danger.

The camp had been getting hotter and more crowded with each day. The full weight of the summer's heat had finally settled on us. Even there, deep in the woods, everything was dry and dusty, the leaves hanging limp and gray in the still air. Clothes, if we wore them at all, turned wet and clung to us like korbi leaves. If we went naked, our bodies ran with sweat that dripped into everything we did. There was no breeze and little relief, even at night. Worse than any of this was the threat to our water. The little stream that ran below Alyeeta's shelter was being sucked drier with each passing day by the heat. Its few remaining pools had to be saved for drinking water for us and for the horses. There was nothing to spare for washing. Sweat-encrusted clothes had to be worn again and again. Our dirty bodies gave off a rank stench and clouds of flies settled everywhere to plague us. In fact, the whole camp reeked. I joked sourly that we could have been found by smell alone.

Tempers were short and quarrels broke out easily. As much as possible the Witches kept clear of us. Since Pell was mostly gone, it fell on me to keep the peace, no easy task, since there was little peace in my own heart. Renaise and I even set to snapping and snarling at each other, something we had not done since we had settled our old quarrel, a poor example surely for those who looked to us for guidance.

Altogether, I rode away from our camp with the sense of freeing myself from a deepening bog. Things were no better on the road, however. Even before I reached the appointed place, I could smell smoke. Soon there were signs of fire and the hoofprints of many horses milling about. A sense of awful doom hung over that spot. I waited in hiding for a while, making the call of a tzatzi bird at intervals. Finally I turned for home, as eager to be safely back as I had been eager to be away. I went as fast as I dared, carrying a terrible weight in my heart for the fate of the two who had not been there to meet me.

Long before I reached her I saw the old woman, and I sensed her well before that. She was sitting under a tree with a basket of apples for sale. A shiver of apprehension went up my spine. There was nothing unusual in the sight of an old woman selling something by the side of the road except, of course, that she had not been there when I had passed by such a short time before. Certainly her apples would not have stopped me. They looked old and wormy. I could easily have found better apples lying under any farmer's tree. I might have ridden by hastily with hardly a glance, if not for the circle of bent willow branches in the dust before her. Inside this circle was a triangle, also of willow, in the middle of which she had set her best apple, a golden one to catch the eye. I looked at her to try to read her expression. Even in that stifling heat she had herself covered with a fringed shawl that hung low over her forehead and almost obscured her face. Nothing could be read in its shadow.

This time, though my heart was beating fast, I did not try to slip by and ride on. Instead, I swung off my horse and picked up the central apple, kicking apart the willow twigs as I did so. "What is the meaning of that sign, Goodwoman?"

"If you do not know, then plainly it is not for you," she answered me tartly, shaking her head so the fringe of her shawl moved as if in its own breeze.

Watching her closely, I took a bite from the apple. At the same time I slipped my pendant out from under my shirt, leaning forward so that it would swing and catch the light. She looked up. For that moment her face was clearly visible. I saw her eyes widen, but only by the slightest nod did she acknowledge what had just passed between us. Yet, in that glimpse of her face I had seen a kind of plea or hopefulness.

"How much for an apple?" I asked loudly to cover our silent exchange. I found myself studying her for meaning. Surely it was no accident that she had set herself in my path.

"Why not buy the whole basket, young man. You could save me the trouble of sitting here. It is tiresome being hot and dusty, and too few pass by. I will make you a good price. Then I can go home."

I shrugged, thinking I might as well take back some apples. She named a very low price and I tossed her a coin. At just that moment I felt the hair go up on the back of my neck. I froze. There was no time to try to hide without arousing suspicion. I had stepped away from my horse and for that moment turned my attention on the old woman before me, instead of remembering the road at my back. I cursed myself silently, thinking what Pell or Jhemar would have said of my carelessness. Forcing myself to move against my fears, I quickly slipped my pendant back inside my shirt. I was about to pick up the basket when three guardsmen rode up, reeking of smoke. They looked at the apples and nodded to each other.

"How much for those apples, old woman?" the first of them asked impatiently, pushing past me to the basket as if I did not exist.

"They are already sold to that young man," she answered calmly, making a nod in my direction.

"For how much?" he asked again.

She named a price, far more than I had paid. The guardsman gave a grunt and reached in his pouch. "Give him back his coins, woman. We will give you twice that." He dropped some coins on her mat. Then, turning as if seeing me for the first time, he said, "Here, boy, pour those apples in my saddlebag and be quick about it. We have a fast ride ahead of us to catch up to the others."

With lowered eyes I picked up the basket. It was all I could do to keep my grip steady, but I had no wish to be crawling about on my hands and knees after fallen apples. My skin prickled from the nearness of the guard. The acrid smoke burned in my nostrils. He even brushed against my hand with his as he opened the pack. The path of his touch felt like a brand or a burn. That was the closest I had ever been to one of them. Without a word he buckled his pack shut and leapt on his horse. In a moment they were gone as quickly as they had come. The other two had never even dismounted.

I found myself leaning against a tree to support my shaky knees, but the old woman had managed to keep herself calm throughout. She even remembered to make a little bow and call after them, "Thank you, good sirs." Under her breath she mumbled, "Not a bad price for wormy apples." They had ridden off leaving us in a cloud of dust. It now settled like a thin layer of mud on my sweating face. The old woman stood up, shook out her skirts, and spit deliberately in front of her. "The curse of the Mother go with them. May She pluck off their hides. May crows pick their flesh from their bones. They have just been at some ugly business. I think they grow more dangerous every day. I suppose I should be glad they paid, instead of pilfering as they have taken to doing lately. After all, one does not argue with a spear or a sword for a few coins. The Zarns have loosened a plague in this land." She shook her head, and at that moment her shawl slipped back from her face. There, in the middle of her forehead, dark red and puckered, I saw what I thought to be a caste brand.

Quickly she replaced the shawl and said angrily to me, "What are you staring at, fool? Have you never seen a brand before? Yes, I am branded, branded like cattle, like horses. That is how they do to ordinary folk there in that city. I am owned by Eezore. If the guards had seen that it would have cost my life. And first they would have taken me back for torture. If you choose to report me, you can get a fine reward. I think, though, that you yourself may have your own reasons for not calling back the guards, eh?"

I had gone on staring stupidly into her angry face until she said that last about the guard. Then I was able to pry myself loose from my tree and found the voice to ask, "What is your game, woman? Why the sign of the circle?"

"To show off my best apple," she said with a shrug.

"Then I need to be on my way," I told her, eager to mount and be gone from there.

Instantly she reached out her hand to stop me. "No, no, not so quickly. Do you know the old Witch? 'The Old One'?"

"What old Witch?" I asked, full of suspicion now. "There are many old Witches in the world, far more than all the apples in your basket."

"'The Old One,' 'the Old One,'" she repeated impatiently. "She was Witch-healer in my village when I was a girl. I have things to tell of Eezore that someone must hear, and quickly. Her I would trust. What do I know of you?"

"And what do I know of you either, seller of wormy apples, that I should trust you or even be talking to you here. What is her name, this 'Old One' you seek?"

"Among us she did not have a name, even then. She was always just 'the Old One.' I hear she is with the young women now, those star-cursed ones. You know the sign and wear one yourself. You will know where to find her. Go fetch her to me quickly. Eezore has closed and sealed its gates. Many are trapped within. Help is needed. That is all I will say for now. Go! Go! Time is wasting, lives are in danger."

Now I was filled with indecision. Hamiuri must be "the Old One" she spoke of. Who else could it be? This woman had really come from Eezore. That much was clear from the mark on her forehead. If she could tell us the truth of that place, perhaps Pell would not have to go there herself to find it. "How do I know I can trust you?" I asked again.

She gave me a nod, reached into her shirt, and drew out a talisman on a chain. It was much like the one I was wearing. This she slipped off and pressed into my hand. I looked at it in surprise. Then I looked back at her.

"No, no, it is not mine. I am indeed the old woman I seem to be. It is my daughter's, a token of trust. That should bring 'the Old One.' Now take it and go quickly. Put that in her hand. You must fetch her to me. Tell her I will wait near here at the Nathron crossroads, hidden in the little glen by the stream. Tell her the woman who waits for her was once the child Askarth, from the village of Larimeer, the one who was her apprentice for a year."

"Come with me, it will be faster," I said, suddenly throwing away all caution. I so much wanted Pell to hear news of Eezore before she did something rash on her own.

"No, I tell you, I go nowhere till I see her face. Do not fail me! Make haste! Even now lives hang in the balance. And bring me a horse, a stout horse that can carry my weight. Also let it be a gentle one that will make the ride easy and not throw me to the ground."

"You have no horse?" I stared around in surprise. "How did you come here?"

"Hidden in a farmer's wagon after the guards had already searched it. You think they would let me ride out of the city gates, the branded servant of a Great-House? The gates are closed, I tell you, the city is sealed. They search all who pass. If they had caught me they would have been glad enough to question me with tongs and a torch."

Suddenly I felt the press of her urgency. I slipped the chain around my neck and heard the pendant click against my own as I swung onto Marshlegs's back. "If it is still light, listen for the call of the tzatzi bird. If not, listen for the owl that hoots three times and then three more. Be ready to go at once. If there is any falseness in this it will cost your life, woman, I promise you that." An empty threat if ever there was one. She must have known that if she really knew us at all. I rode home in haste, feeling as if Askarth rode on my back, urging me on.

As luck would have it, Hamiuri was out hunting herbs. She was not pleased to see me when I tracked her down. Even Hamiuri seemed to be infected with the soul-rot of the camp. In no hurry to come with me, she stood there shaking her head. "Do I remember Larimeer? Yes, I remember it well enough. One of those many manure-ridden villages that are full of fools who hate Witches, yet need a healer for their cows and their brats. I cannot recall Askarth. Perhaps she was one of the little girls who threw rocks at me and called me names and then came sweet as egg-pudding to fetch me because her mother was birthing again. And why did I do it, tell me that? Why did I put up with any of it? Because I thought I should use my art and my skill for some good purpose. I was fool enough to think Witches should do some honorable work. They had taken everything that mattered from us during the Witch-kills, everything I would have been proud to turn my hand to. Girl, you had better believe that I would never do it again. Never! For all I care now those villages can rot in their own ignorance and sink back into the dung heap they came from. Now tell me again what this Askarth had to say."

So I had to repeat again what little there was to tell. I had never heard Hamiuri speak in this way. Her words were so bitter she sounded more like Alyeeta or Telakeet at their worst. She even spit and said "humans" with contempt in her voice as Alyeeta so often did. All the while I was trying to urge her to hurry. "Please, Hamiuri, please. She said to come as soon as we could."

With deliberate slowness Hamiuri gathered her herbs in her baskets, muttering, "Since when do I hurry myself for humans? What have they ever done for me?" After that I kept silent, only helping with the basket. At last I had her moving in the right direction.

Pell must already have gotten word. When we returned, she was there waiting for us with Torvir and two extra horses, both of them stout and gentle. She helped move Hamiuri along, though that one grumbled mightily at having to ride.

"My bones are too old to be moved about so fast," she muttered as we helped her up. As soon as they started off I went to arrange for four others who were to follow, staying well hidden and keeping watch in case of trouble. Zenoria and Daijar had already left to track the guards, going to see if those two young women were still alive and could be freed from their captors.

When everyone was finally organized and on the road I threw myself down on a mat, exhausted. Renaise came to rub the weariness out of my back and shoulders, and so we made our peace. There was even a little breeze that came at evening time, bringing with it a measure of relief.

That night the wind rose and the heat finally broke in a steady, driving rain. By morning, water had made its way through the leaf-and-branch thatch of my little shelter. I was wakened by water dripping on my face. Outside I could hear the stream running again. When I crawled out, stiff and wet, I was greeted by a noisy, joyful chorus of frogs and birds. The sun was just beginning to break through. Everything was bright and sparkling from the rain. Most of the camp was still asleep, but Hamiuri and Askarth were already up, or perhaps had never slept. They were sitting side by side at the cookfire, drinking tea. With their heads bent together, talking and laughing like old friends, they looked to be of one age, just two old women together. Then I remembered that Hamiuri had already been old when Askarth was still a child, and I felt again that familiar chill.

Renaise was up next, organizing a long-overdue washing of dishes, pots, and clothes. Soon she had us in a line, carrying jugs of water up from the stream and filling every available container. Before we had even finished, Pell called a meeting, going about the camp beating on a pot to bring us together. Yawning, stretching, and grumbling, we ringed the speaking stump in several rough circles.

Pell spoke first, climbing on the stump and raising her hands for silence. "This woman," she said, pointing dramatically to Askarth, "this woman has brought us word of how it is in Eezore. She has just now come from the city." The moment she said "Eezore," she had our full attention. The restless shifting stopped instantly and all eyes were fixed on Askarth.

Hamiuri stepped up next for just a moment. "Trust this woman and listen closely to what she has to tell you. I can speak for her. She was once my apprentice and I have known her all her life."

Then, with Pell's help, Askarth clambered up on the stump. Once there, she threw back her shawl and turned slowly so we could all see her face. There were gasps from those watching. "In case any of you are wondering if I speak the truth of Eezore, you can all see it clearly branded on my forehead," she said loudly, as if throwing out a challenge.

After that she spoke at length, repeating herself, pleading with us to go to Eezore and save those who were trapped there. She went on and on, saying far too much for me to try to repeat it all here. The sum of it was that some of the most powerful families in Eezore, uppercaste Shokarn, were resisting the Zarn's edict. They had barricaded themselves in and were refusing to turn over their daughters to the Zarn's guards for destruction. Instead, they were sheltering them and other young women as well in their Great-Houses, those houses within the city walls that had their own separate walls and gates and also their own guards. Most such houses were well supplied and could probably withstand a siege. The Zarn was apparently reluctant to launch a full-scale attack, thus provoking a civil war he might not win since he usually relied on these same Great-Houses for much of his support. Yet he found himself with both feet in the fire. He could not let his orders be defied in the very heart of his stronghold. It seemed that his plan was to wait them out, starve them out, in fact, till they began one by one to capitulate. All those houses were ringed by the Zarn's guards. People, if they could slip past the Great-House guards, were allowed to leave. They were even encouraged and helped as long as they were first searched by the Zarn's guards and proved not to be the star-crossed in disguise. But none could return, no supplies or help of any kind could be sent back in. I listened to all this, thinking how right Jhemar had been. Eezore was indeed at war with itself and we, the star-cursed, were at the very center of it, a bone being fought over by snarling dogs.

Just as Askarth was about to begin her recital again, Pell interrupted, calling out to her, "And what is all of this to you, Goodwoman? Why have you risked your life to bring us this word?"

"Two of them are mine, one that I raised myself who is like a daughter to me and one who is my blood-child, though she does not know it. I want to see them safely free of that city and soon, but that will take help and horses. Is that answer enough for you?"

"More than enough, but we must make plans to crack open the city and free all the Star-Born who are trapped there. Understand me, Askarth, I am not taking my women on a raid into Eezore just to free your two daughters. How can you help us? If, as you say, the city is locked and sealed, how can we breach it? How are we to free them and escape with our lives? Surely we cannot all come in as you left, hidden in a farmer's wagon."

At that there was nervous laughter from the women around me. Unperturbed, Askarth said loudly, "I can show you the way in, but will say no more now till there are ears to hear." Instantly there was silence again. After looking all around slowly as if to make sure we could maintain it, she went on. "There is an old forgotten tunnel into the city. It starts by the Bargguell, the great garbage heap outside the wall, and runs under Eezore at least as far as the Central Prison. The tunnel was once used for taking out the bodies of executed prisoners, but has long since fallen into disuse. It has been blocked off with huge boulders that must be removed from the outside. There are smaller tunnels that lead into it. To one of these I have the gate key. At another the gate is more rust than iron. My grandfather was a jailer in the Central Prison, as was his father and his grandfather before that. He taught me many things. I may be the only person left alive that knows of the tunnel. Believe me, there are many secrets in that city that would surprise even the Zarn himself." Askarth fell silent after that and stepped down.

Pell jumped up to take her place. "This plan is as full of holes as a fisherman's net. Even if we succeed in getting into the city and past the Zarn's guards, how are we to get past the guards at the Great-Houses? How will they know to open for us?"

"They will know," Askarth assured her quickly. "They will be ready."

"How? How is that possible, since none can pass between?"

"Birds," Askarth said angrily. "Birds can fly where feet cannot pass. That is all you need to know. They will be ready for you. I tell you that on my honor, on my life."

"And how are we to leave afterward?" Kazouri shouted, her loud voice booming from the back. "Once we have raided the city, that tunnel will more likely be a deathtrap than an escape."

Askarth opened her mouth, but no words came. There was a silence followed by louder and louder muttering. Pell looked around the circle as if searching for an answer there. Suddenly Shalamith stepped into the center of the circle so that all eyes fell upon her. She raised her hands for silence, and sparks of light flashed from her fingers. "I will open the West Gate. That will be my part in this," she said in a clear, musical voice that seemed to fill the clearing.

"You, by yourself? You will open a sealed gate?" Pell asked in disbelief.

"Do you doubt my powers, girl? What do *you* know? I could make you turn somersaults in the air if I chose to do so."

Alyeeta came to stand next to Shalamith. "I will help you from the outside. I have no doubt you can get it open. Keeping it open long enough, that will be hard."

"How do you plan to do this?" Pell challenged.

"How!" Alyeeta exclaimed with her mocking laugh. "How! That is for us to know and you to see. Just do your part, and we will do ours. Make sure to get yourselves there alive at the right time. Then you will see what Witches can do."

There was a buzz of excitement. Pell's face was flushed, and her eyes were bright. Now, now she will begin to shape our plans, I thought. No one had spoken against it. It was clear to me that we would stage a raid on Eezore, though from some kind of stubborn folly I still thought I would not be one of those to go. The final questions had been answered. As I looked about me at that circle of ragged young women standing around a stump in a dusty clearing in the woods, and thought of them trying to invade the Zarn's city, the very center of power, I did not know whether to laugh or cry or shout at them all for their madness. In the end I kept my silence on it.

In the midst of Pell's talk I suddenly heard Ashai shouting with fear. Her few words of Kourmairi rang out over and over in the clearing. "Help! Come quickly! A man here is!" Women grabbed frantically for their clothes. When I looked around I saw Hereschell slipping through the trees with the gray wolf, Soneeshi, at his heels.

"Nothing to fear," I shouted to the circle. Quickly I ran to calm Ashai and then to meet with Hereschell. "Why did you come sneaking in like that past our sentries instead of letting them bring you to us?" I asked him angrily. "Look what confusion you have caused!"

"How did I know who you would have on sentry duty and if they would know me and let me by? After all, I am a man and so not be trusted. I thought it easier to simply come here. And you should train them better. If it is so simple for me to slip past, then Pell has been careless at her work."

I had more angry things to say. Then I saw he was grinning, clearly pleased with himself. I had no wish to add to his amusement.

"Ah, you," I said with mock annoyance. "You could slip through a fishnet if you wanted to. If you have something to tell Pell, tell her yourself. Now what is it that brings you here this day?"

"I hear you have plans to move against Eezore."

"So there are rumors about?"

"This was no rumor. This was a message sent to me."

"Then you mean to help us?"

"Yes and no — after all, Wanderers are all fish who slip through the fishnets. They must be careful. It would not do to be tagged by one side or the other."

"Still, you will help us in some way or you would not be here."

"Oh yes, without a doubt, I will help you in some way. Among other things, I have knowledge of that city that you need. We Wanderers do not always go in and out by the Great Gates and let ourselves be counted. We have our own ways."

"If the Wanderers helped us more openly, would harm come to them for it?"

"Perhaps, but not likely. I cannot go into the city of Eezore with you, that you must understand, nor can I be too plain with what I do, but mostly Wanderers are left to go their own way. Not even the Zarns want to pinch the Wanderers too hard. For the most part Wanderers stay out of Ganjarin affairs, but they are the very devil when roused, and slippery besides. I think the Zarns have enough on their hands at this moment without seeking to engage the Wanderers."

I could still hear Pell's voice from the circle, spinning out plans. "Hereschell," I asked urgently, "is this madness? Can she do this thing? Will the Star-Born all die in that city? Is Pell a fool?"

He raised both hands. "Easy, Tazzi, I am no reader of the cards. It is not one of my talents. But in the first place your people are not easy to kill. Let us remember that. It gives some comfort. And then, of course, there is the advantage of surprise. The Zarn will not be expecting such a raid. I am sure the Zarn, in all his power, does not look to this raggle-tag to invade his city. He believes his enemies are being hunted elsewhere. He will not think to find the hunted suddenly become the hunters right inside his walls. Also, I trust you will not stand and fight like a troop of guards. Hopefully you will slip through their city as swift and silent as sewer rats, gone almost sooner than you are seen. You could learn some lessons from those long-tailed folk. As to Pell, you are a better judge of her sanity than I could ever be." Each time Hereschell said the word "you" I could feel my heart start pounding wildly and my throat constrict. Then I had to remind myself that I would not be one of those to go. I had planned exactly what I would say to Pell in the matter. Likely she would leave me to manage the camp in her absence, as I would be of no use to her in Eezore.

Out of the corner of my eye I had glimpsed the silent ones creeping around the edge of the clearing as we talked. To my surprise they did not run and hide at the sight of Hereschell. Instead, they advanced in a zigzag course in his direction, coming stealthily, but with clear purpose. He must have sensed them, for even as he spoke he turned slowly. I saw a look of shock and recognition cross his face. "So they are safe here with you. We did not find their bodies with the others and thought they had been taken by the raiders."

As they crept up on him I told him how they had come to us. "Ah, that Vanhira," he said, nodding, "she was always a brave one. I wonder who brought them to her and how."

Holding hands, they came to stand and stare at him, knowing and yet not knowing him, ready to run at any moment yet drawn by some flicker of memory.

"Take them away with you, Hereschell," I whispered, "take them far from here. Hide them safe with the Wanderers where they can heal and remember slowly. In this place they are a danger to us and to themselves as well."

He nodded again, watching them with a terrible sadness on his face. "I suppose we Wanderers are in this thing one way or the other, whether we will it or not. Johalla, Illyati," he said softly, naming them for the first time in my hearing. They came forward slowly, reaching out cautiously to touch his sleeves and then his hands with tentative, questioning fingers.

★

A little later Pell came to look for me. She seemed full of energy and resolve, amazingly cheerful for one about to ride off into the jaws of death. "Come to the mapping, Tazzi. I need you to know as much as possible of the city. Good thing that Irdris has taught you something of Shokarn speech. On the way to Eezore I trust that you will cover the rear of the line while I cover the front." Before I could say even one word of my planned speech Pell was gone again, gathering others for this mapping.

This time Pell was the learner as Askarth and Hereschell between them laid out a giant map with sticks, rocks, pieces of string, and whatever else they could find to add to the scratched lines for marking the walls, gates, streets, and Great-Houses of Eezore. Even the Zarn's palace itself was marked there, as well as the passages that lay beneath it all.

Irdris and the other two Shokarn, Ashai and Sural, added their own lines and pebbles to show us how the streets and houses they knew connected to each other. The others milled about, asking questions and squatting down to see better. Even Maireth was there among them. For me, hard as I stared, the lines remained only lines and the pebbles only pebbles — nothing more. When I strained to focus, all of it was suddenly fraught with terror and blurred in my sight. As I turned away in disgust, Hereschell made as if to grab my arm. He quickly dropped his hand, but moved instead to block my way, saying in a thundering voice, "Tazzi, you will not shut your head and walk away! You will stay here and learn this map!"

All eyes turned on me. I drew myself up with sudden anger. No man had ever spoken to me in that way, not even my own father. I looked to Pell and Jhemar for some support, but they were both nodding in agreement with him. In spite of that, I was about to step past him haughtily when Hereschell put out his hand again, not trying to touch me this time. "Please, Tazzi," he said softly, speaking so low only I could have heard him. His tone of entreaty stopped me as nothing else could have. I gave him a nod and turned back.

Yet stare as I might, those lines were still only lines, in no way shaping themselves into the city I so feared. I could make no sense of it at all. Even as I struggled with this I could hear Irdris and Ashai in back of me arguing in rapid Shokarn. I could understand a little of this from time to time. Apparently Irdris was intent on going back to Eezore with us and Ashai was begging her not to, listing all the dangers. Suddenly Sural sided with Ashai, saying Irdris was too well known there. Irdris said loudly, "Jemalia," as if that settled everything. Then she walked away abruptly. It was the first time I had ever seen her angry. All this talk of danger did nothing, of course, to lift my spirits.

I was still staring dully at the map after the others had moved away, when Hereschell stepped up next to me. As I turned toward him he took my hand in his, first looking me in the eye for permission. "Forgive me my rudeness, Tazzi. It is not the Wanderer's way to compel another's will, but I was afraid for you. I feared for your safety if you went on in your head-blind way. There is no need to go into that city in ignorance. You may lose your life on this mission to Eezore. If so, that is the way of things. Life is a risky gift at best. But I would not have it be from stupidity alone when a little knowledge could have saved you." He hesitated, coughed a little, and seemed unable to go on.

Suddenly he was the father I had never had, a man who was afraid for me instead of me. I felt like a small child with an impulse to throw myself into his arms and cry on his shoulder. Instead, I held myself tight together and pressed his hand in return before releasing it. He looked at me with a wry smile. "It is also not the Wanderer's way to care too much. Who knows where the next bend in the road will take us?"

I glanced back at the map. It all swam before my eyes. "Oh, Hereschell, if my life depends on it, I may well die there, for I can make no sense of it at all." I was shocked at the wail of despair in my voice.

"Well, at least that is something that can be easily mended." Squatting down, he drew me down beside him. "If you think of streets as paths grown wider and more numerous, then you can begin to see them. They are only cow paths paved over and given names, even the fanciest of them. Look, here is the central fountain and a circle around it. Streets run out from it in all directions like this. Here is Bird Street and Carriage Square and Long Street that runs across the whole city at a long diagonal." He went on in this way, talking and pointing, naming places and streets till the sticks, stones, and lines in the dirt began to come alive for me, turning into a city. I knew I must be seeing it through his eyes. I could even picture myself slipping safely from street to street. Finally, I was the one pointing and naming. Hereschell was sitting back on his heels with a wide grin on his face, nodding his encouragement. "I told you some things are easily mended. You see, you will not even need me there."

With those words, my heart leapt up into my mouth again. "Hereschell, if you cannot come with us, will you at least light candles to the Goddess for our safety?"

He shook his head, very serious now. "No, Tazzi, you must light your candles to Her yourself. The Goddess is yours, not mine. That is not how the Sacred Spirit speaks to me, the One who is Many, the Many who are One."

"Is that what you Wanderers believe in, the Sacred Spirit?"

"Believe?" he shrugged. "I do not understand this 'believe.' It is what I feel, what I know in that inner place. How the Sacred Spirit speaks to each of us, that is our life's gift, our life's message. It is not for another to question or criticize or even understand. It is for each one of us alone to open our hearts to, not something that can be written or turned into law or held captive in a building. And one person's 'knowing' — that must never, never be forced upon another. That would be the deepest breach of 'the Code.'"

"What is this 'Wanderer Code' I hear spoken of?" He was so serious and turned inward, I was almost afraid to speak to him. I was not at all sure he would answer.

After a moment of silence he nodded, "Ah yes, the Wanderer Code, something not easy for the Ganjarin to understand. It is not written anywhere, only in our hearts, yet we all live by it, each in our own way. It is the Cerroi, the circle of fate that binds us all together. My own words for it would be, 'Wander wherever your heart takes you, harm none, and put your love out into the world.'"

We sat for a while in silence then, my own bitter, angry heart chewing on those words. When Hereschell began to speak again it was so low I had to strain to hear him. "When I leave you I will go into the Cave of the Spring to ask. There I will set my little pile of pebbles on the moss and look into the water for some peace. I will wish for this thing to be safely done with as little harm as possible, hoping no deaths will come of it and of my part in it. Though I am no foreteller, yet even I can see much blood and fire in this time to come. The Ganjarin do not seem to mind killing, but for the Wanderers, unnatural death is always a deep distress. The shedding of another's blood is a tear in the fabric that holds us all." He fell silent again, looking as distant as if he were already seated before his spring. I sat studying his face. This man who had just spoken was as different from the proud and bitter man I had known as that one was from the fool I had first met. There seemed to be no bottom to this well.

17

I have a great dread of writing this part and wish I could leave it out of my account altogether. I find myself making excuses, delaying and delaying, fearing to be thrown back into that state of terror. Besides, so much happened there, so much so fast. How am I to piece it all together? But now it is blocking the rest of the story. I have no choice but to try.

Eezore! The feelings I remember from that day are terror followed by an icy calm. The terror was not like any ordinary fear, not like the fear of being killed or of encountering the guard. It was more like the terror of being thrown headlong from a precipice and finding myself whirling helpless through the air toward the rocks below. It was the city itself that terrified me, a place so alien to my very being. I can thank Hereschell for forcing me to learn the map, saying over and over, "The streets are only paths and trails paved over. Watch for signs, observe everything, remember to smell and feel and listen as well as look." And in truth, as soon as I began doing what was needed, the terror abated and that icy calm came over me. But I am ahead of myself now. Let me go back and try to tell the story as it happened.

★

My group had stopped, uncertain how to find the others who had gone before us. The night was dark. Out of it the towering heap of the Bargguell loomed even darker before us. Its stench filled the air, making it hard to breathe. Beyond the Bargguell, I could see the walls of the city topped by watchlights. Rishka leaned toward me and muttered, "We could have found our way here by smell alone."

Just then an owl called three times and then three more. I answered with three hoots. Without a word, we moved almost soundlessly in that direction. Soon I saw the dark, huddled shapes of the others. From close by I heard Pell say softly, "That is all of us now, all together and accounted for." A shiver went up my back. The last players in this game were in place. Eezore was waiting there for us.

It had taken us all three days to reach Hamiuri's shelter with little sleep on the road. We had come in after dark and been on our way again well before dawn, slipping out in small groups, no more than six or seven at a time. With a day of hard riding we had reached the edge of the city shortly after dark. Expecting the roads to be well guarded at such a time and not wanting to give any sort of alarm, we had kept our groups separate from one another on the way, putting on dark cloaks for concealment when night fell, and even muffling the sound of our horses' hooves with rags as we drew near the city. But the ride, at least my part of it, proved uneventful. Pell had gone first, along with Askarth, Hereschell, and Kazouri. Rishka and I had been in the last group to leave. I had stayed to the end to make sure all went smoothly. Those few guards we passed had been easy to evade. Sometimes we had only to draw aside. It seemed Eezore had not only shut its gates, it had shut in on itself, thinking perhaps that all its troubles were inside already. A few farm boys on the road were of no concern to a city at war with itself.

Gathered together now we were more than sixty, six double hands, enough for three or four to enter each Great-House, while others watched from outside, waiting there and ready to help those within. Some were to roam the city streets, stopping trouble or making it as was needed at the moment. Still others were to stay outside the walls of the city, guarding our backs as we went in. Some, Jhemar, Zenoria, and Zari among them, were to be ready to bring our horses as soon as they were needed. How wrong I had been that evening by the fire when Jhemar had first spoken to me of Eezore and I had answered her with such certainty. In the end, I was the one going into Eezore and Jhemar was to stay outside the city gates. In fact, our places had already been assigned. I was being sent with Rishka and Askarth to the Great-House of Starmos. At least I was to have a guide in the city. I felt a rush of relief at that.

Pell had been giving last-minute directions when our group rode up. Hastily I dismounted. Zenoria and Zari came instantly to take our horses.

It was hard for me to let Marshlegs go out of my hands so quickly. I hugged her for a moment, arms around her neck, pressing my face into her sweet-smelling hide. Then I quickly put the reins in Zari's hand. When I turned around so as not to see her being led away, I found Pell at my side. She grabbed my arm, saying urgently, "Rope, Tazzi, we need more rope. If you have some, take it instantly to Kazouri and help her there."

The tunnel entrance had already been cleared of brush. Kazouri and several others were there trying to fasten ropes around a huge rock that blocked the way. This was no easy task, since the boulder was pressed against the tunnel sides as well as the rocks behind it, leaving little room to pass. Candles kept blowing out and tempers were short. Kazouri, who was much too large for the job, paced about beating her fist in her palm as if ready to tear the thing out with her bare hands. "If this rock delays us much longer," she muttered, "we will be doing this foolishness by the light of morning with an audience of interested guards. We may as well blow a horn to announce our presence here."

At last Cruzia, a tiny woman, smaller even than Zenoria, succeeded in wedging her agile little body into a crevice and worming a length of rope underneath the bolder. There was a hushed cheer. Instantly many hands were reaching out to fasten it to a net of ropes already in place around that monstrous rock. Then, while Kazouri got herself off to the side with a pole the thickness of a small tree, ready to pry, the rest of us added our lengths to the rope and took our places along it. At Pell's whispered count of three we all threw ourselves against the rope. Nothing moved. The rope might as well have been tied to a mountain. Four times we tried, panting and struggling and at the same time trying to keep our silence.

As we were catching our breath for another try, Pell began to talk of bringing back some of the horses. "We could fashion a rope harness for them. They are certainly far stronger than we are."

"No," Kazouri said instantly, "too dangerous, too exposed. There is no way of vanishing into the night with our horses tied to a boulder."

Without a word, Hereschell went to stand opposite Kazouri with another pry-pole. This time when Pell counted I heard Kazouri growl with effort deep in her throat. While she and Hereschell pried, the rest of us pulled with a will. There was a strange, tearing, grinding sound. Suddenly those of us hauling on the rope fell forward in all directions, rolling out of the way of the boulder as it broke free from the tunnel walls.

The way was still blocked with large rocks, but now we all rushed forward to help each other pry them loose and roll them away. Megyair and Josleen seemed to be everywhere at once, working together like a four-handed person. Pell kept warning us for quiet. Suddenly, in the midst of our efforts, there came a single owl hoot, repeated three times more. Instantly we flattened ourselves to the ground. Almost at the same moment I felt a clawing, dizzying pain and heard a high-pitched screaming. "Guards!" came the whispered signal passed from one to the next.

A clump of guards, carrying something or someone, quickly disappeared out of sight around the other side of the Bargguell. I held my breath, certain that they would swing around to our side, stumble over the boulder, and catch us all crouched there in hiding. Then they would raise the alarm before we had even breached the city.

The guards, however, appeared very intent on their own errand and unaware of our presence. In haste they heaved what they were carrying on the Bargguell, then quickly turned and rode back for the city gates as if pursued by demons. The screaming went on. I was doubled over, fighting with pain, unable to move from there till Irdris came and grabbed my hand to pull me up. "Come quickly, Tazzi, we need your help."

I stumbled after her as best I could. When we got to the far side, several of the others, Maireth among them, were already there, crowding around whatever was on the Bargguell. Silently they moved aside to let us pass. The stench of fastfire and burning flesh filled the air. There were three dark forms lying there, two of them groaning and the other screaming. Trapped in the pain, I gripped Irdris's arm, nails biting into flesh, trying to breathe, trying to remember what Alyeeta had taught me of shielding.

Alyeeta herself was holding up a light sheltered by her hand. In a voice rough and hoarse with feeling, she turned and said to me, "These two might be saved as Maireth was saved. The other is beyond all hope in this world. Only mercy can help her now."

The screaming went on. Pell pushed up next to me. "Do something, Tazzi! For the love of the Mother, do something to stop this, give her something." Maireth, on the other side of me, was saying much the same thing.

So I was being made into a murderer again. A sudden coldness came over me, and with it a strange clarity. The pain left me. "Hold this," I said, handing my pouch to Pell. "Alyeeta, turn your light here." In that flickering light I fished around in the pouch for what I needed. "I have some ghero-paste here. That is the best I can do, as we have no way to heat water for a strong brew of diraithia and orinth. Maireth, pour me a cup of water and hold it steady."

With the tip of my knife I mixed the paste in the water. That cold seemed to encase me, filling my ears. I could barely hear the woman's cries now. When I finished mixing, I said urgently, "Maireth, Pell, help me hold her. Alyeeta, bring the light close." I squatted down at her side. Even with three of us trying, much of the brew spilled out the corners of her mouth. Afterward her screams were even louder. I stared down helplessly. Then, out of that same cold and calm, I reached out my hands and pressed them firmly over her nose and mouth. The silence was loud and sudden. I could feel her struggling under my hands, but it did not touch me. If others came to help I did not know it. I stayed squatting there in that way even after the thrashing had ceased and her body had stilled under my hold.

I think I had left with her, gone away to some far place, till Alyeeta shook my shoulder. "Enough, child, it is over. Come away from here now. Others will take her wherever she needs to go."

I picked up my pouch and stood up slowly. My teeth were clenched. Grief was like a rock in my throat, but I wiped my hand on my pants as if from any ordinary dirty job. When I turned away dry-eyed, I found Irdris was staring at me with tears running down her face. Maireth was standing next to her, her scars livid and raw-looking in the light of Alyeeta's flare. I thrust my pouch into her hands. "Here, take this and see to the others with whatever help you can find there. It is you they need now, not me. I cannot be a killer and a healer with the same hands." Still without a tear, I went to join the others at the tunnel. Killing the second time is not like killing the first.

All the rocks had been cleared from the tunnel entrance now. Women were crowding around it. The air from there had a damp, fetid smell. Pell was already back at her post. The light she held up did not reach very far. It looked to be a narrow way. I had no great eagerness to go plunging into that dark trap, but at least it would take me away from the scene at the Bargguell.

When Pell saw me she said quickly, "Good, you are here now. I will go first with the light and Askarth will follow. The rest of you save your flares. There will be little enough air in there as it is. Tazzi, go gather the others quickly. Then enter last to guard the rear and make sure all is well."

As I turned to go back, Rishka reached out and gave me a sudden, hard hug. "May the fates shelter you this night, Terrazen, and bring you safely through." I had no idea what that strange word meant, but understood from her tone that it was not one of her usual insults. Later I learned that in Muinyairin it meant 'comrade to the death,' a word not said lightly among those desert people.

With the help of some of the others, Maireth had already taken away the two burned ones. Jhemar and Zenoria had vanished into the night with the horses. After gathering up the stragglers, I found my place at the end of the line. At the very last moment, as we were already moving, Irdris slipped into line just in front of me. Shuffling and whispering, we wound ourselves into that darker darkness with Pell so far ahead I could barely catch a glimmer of her light. The smell of burning clung to me in that airless space. We each went following the back ahead of us, guided by whispered warnings and commands passed down the line. When I heard Irdris muttering, "Goddess guide us through. I do not want to die trapped in this cursed place," I wondered again what had driven her to come back to Eezore. At that moment I was very glad for the watchers left outside who guarded our backs.

As we went on, the passage grew even narrower. Several times I bruised an arm or knee or bumped my head. How they could have brought condemned men that way, I could not imagine. In places rocks had fallen and we had to squeeze through, sometimes going at a crouch or even having to crawl on our bellies past dislodged boulders. Each time I felt a clutch of dread, as if the tunnel were closing in on us. Suddenly there was a muffled cry from in front of me and I ran blindly into Irdris's back, throwing us both against Kazouri. She was just in front of Irdris and had evidently gotten wedged between some fallen rocks and the tunnel wall. I could hear her whispering desperately, "Wait! Wait! Wait!" The whisper passed forward in the tunnel like a strange echo. "Wait! Wait! Wait!"

Flares were lit ahead of us. I pressed up next to Irdris to help push Kazouri from our side while those on the other pulled. Kazouri was groaning and cursing, begging the Mother to let her go. For once her great size was a hindrance rather than a help. Here she could not even use her own strength. We could only move her inches at a time to the sound of tearing fabric and Kazouri's gasping breath. Irdris kept whispering encouragements to her. After what seemed like a long, hopeless struggle, she suddenly slipped away from my hands. There was a groan and a cry, and then muffled cheers from the other side.

Not till I, too, had squeezed through the opening did I realize how wet my tunic was, whether from dripping water or from sweat I could not tell. Now it clung to me. I was chilled through, shivering in that damp, cool air. In misery I crept along after Irdris, dreading the next impasse. What if we could not go forward or go back? At least the way was fairly straight there, and except for falling rocks, it seemed to be level underfoot.

Just as I began to think the tunnel was endless and this misery would go on forever, flares lit up in front of us. By their light I could see that the tunnel had widened. Here the walls were of stacked and mortared stones, no longer cut from the living rock. Now there was space enough for two or even three abreast.The whispered word came back, "We are under the city now." My fears returned fullfold. Eezore was above our heads, waiting for me.

I slipped up next to Kazouri and put an arm around her waist. She hugged me roughly to her, muttering, "Thank you, Tazzi. I must say, that would have been an ugly way to die. I had a bad time for a moment there." I hugged her back, but I think I was seeking comfort as much as giving it. Irdris came on the other side of me and laid her arm across my shoulder. "We do good work together," she whispered in my ear.

After that there were several twists and turns. Then we all stopped again and I heard the words "first gate" pass back along the line. Kazouri pushed up to the front. There were some muttered consultations. Then came a grating and grinding of metal, a sound so loud it seemed that surely we were alerting the whole city to make ready for us. Those around me were silent. All our thoughts were focused on Kazouri's hands. Suddenly we were moving again. I knew that Pell and half the others had left us at that first gate, for that had been the plan. It seemed as if the city and the night had taken a huge bite and swallowed them whole. I wondered if we would ever see each other again, Pell and I. By the time I reached that twisted, rusted gate they were gone. There was only silence from the other side.

Then, just as I was about to pass, Pell's flare lit in front of me and her hand reached out to touch me. "May the Mother bring you safely through this night, Tazzi," she whispered hoarsely. "Remember to wait for the signal." Then she was truly gone before I could think to answer.

"Mother's Luck go with you, too, Pell," I whispered to the darkness. The rest of us moved on, following Askarth now. This time when we halted, I knew it was to be our turn. I could hear another gate opening with a jangle of keys and then the screech of metal on stone. We went forward once more till one by one we squeezed through a small gate and out into a wider chamber. From there we turned to go up a stairway with steps deep-worn by years of passings. The way was so tight and narrow that my shoulders brushed against the stones on either side. I pictured Kazouri up ahead of me having to turn sideways to pass. A faint, dim light shone down from somewhere above us. Suddenly, with my last step, I found myself out in the clear. I was standing in a courtyard under the night sky. A warm, soft breeze was blowing in my face.

We had come out at the back of a huge block of stone, all deeply carved with signs and symbols. Most of these were unfamiliar to me, but among them I saw some that were like the pendant I wore or like the other signs we used among ourselves. This stone must once have served as an altar. Probably it had helped to conceal that little staircase, keeping secret the tunnel beyond it. As I glanced around me at the ruins, I thought that this must be the deserted holy place Askarth had spoken of.

Everywhere great stones had been tumbled down and scattered about in confusion, as if by violent hands. Clearly, that was far in the past. Now ivy grew over it all. There was a strange silence there that even muffled our shuffling steps. It was as if we had emerged in some forgotten Goddess shrine deep in the country instead of in the middle of a great city. I stood there breathing the fresher air deep into my lungs. Relief and terror were mixed in me. I was overjoyed to be free of the tunnel, yet very fearful of what lay ahead. Given the choice, I could easily have sunk down on those ancient, ivy-covered stones and stayed there among them. Even in that jumble there was a kind of peacefulness. It was like an invitation that called to me, or like a blessing, some faint memory, perhaps, of what once had been. Then I heard Rishka calling to me impatiently, "Tazzi, Tazzi!"

Hastily I went to do my duty as second-in-command. "Into your groups!" I whispered urgently, moving women forward. "Quickly, hurry, we need to start leaving at once!" As soon as we found our groups, we speedily gathered around Askarth for her final directions.

"We will come out into the Alley of the Pebbles," she told us. "Follow it to the left till it turns into Long Street, the street that traverses the whole of Eezore at an angle. From there we go our different ways. I must warn you that Long Street is likely to be full of folk even at this late hour, but in this part of the city it is mostly thieves and whores and those who deal with them, or others on their own nocturnal business, none of them likely to ask questions or take much notice of some cloaked and hooded figures hurrying by."

Group after group, we began slipping out into the night, pieces of moving darkness in our dark cloaks. Our group was the last to go. No matter how well I had memorized the streets with Hereschell's help, I was glad that Askarth was going with us. And in spite of our private troubles, I was also very glad for the toss of the pebbles that had put Rishka at my side. Irdris, Josleen, and Megyair, as well as Renaise's friend Tzaneel, had been assigned as our street watch. Irdris, I knew to be familiar with that part of the city that lay around the Great-House of Starmos, so that was some comfort as well.

We followed Askarth, going from the ruins down a little alley so narrow and twisting it was more like a path. This suddenly opened into Long Street. It was there that the city hit me with its full force: lights, horses, carts, carriages, and wagons, people and more people and still more, all rush and confusion and under it a hum and rumble that made my head ache and throb so that I wanted to cry out in pain. The terror of it all swept in on me. My eyes glazed over and my feet refused to walk.

"Move," Askarth said impatiently, giving me a hard push. "Try to blend in. No use to stand gaping about. We are not here to view the city. It will bring us more notice than we need."

"She is spelled," Irdris said quickly. "Take her arms."

Unable to move on my own, I found myself being propelled forward rapidly between Askarth and Rishka. We were rushing down the street through a crowd of others. I was lost in some space of my own, dizzy and nauseous, feeling as if I were spinning and falling through space, not even sure if my feet touched the ground. I shut my eyes against the sight of the street swinging and tilting before me. Then, in that sudden darkness, I saw the symbol I wore glowing in gold against the blackness of my eyelids, the circle inside the triangle inside the circle. With that I felt a sudden steadying. I pulled hard enough against Askarth's grip to place one hand over my pendant. As its warmth flooded up from between my breasts, I opened my eyes cautiously. The street gave a last heart-clenching lurch, then settled before my sight: a busy, crowded, dirty, ill-lit street that stayed in its place while we rushed by.

I could breathe again. In a few minutes I got my bearings and was ready to collect my feet under me. I tried to shake loose of the others, saying, "I can move on my own now. This is too dangerous." It was also too hard on my pride.

"Easy, Tazzi," Rishka whispered to me, "you can be our drunken comrade being helped home, not a bad disguise in these streets."

I gave a slight nod and dashed on between them at a lurching stagger while at the same time trying to watch and pay attention to the way. Now that my head had cleared, Hereschell's lessons started coming back. Even at that pace the city began to fall into place around me. With only a few signs to go by, I knew the names of most of the streets we passed and how and where they connected to others.

In several places I saw our symbols painted. They were marking a doorway, a wall, the corner of the street: the circle and triangle, or the double triangle, or the six-pointed star. I wondered if Askarth knew who had painted them and for what purpose, whether as a sign for us or for the Zarn's men. There was, of course, no time to ask in that rush. At one of those symbols two dark-cloaked figures that had been moving along swiftly before us disappeared, one through a doorway and the other into a narrow alley.

Keeping our faces covered, we stayed close to the walls and doorways and away from the light. At a fast pace we went from Long Street into another alley and from there out onto a broad avenue. Suddenly, straddling the avenue before us, the walls of a Great-House rose dark and solid as if everything stopped there, even the street itself. It towered over the buildings around it. In front of it I glimpsed a whole company of guards marching back and forth. Behind them its gates, lit by flares, arched higher than the roofs of most of the houses. The Great-House of Starmos, our goal for that night — I felt my knees go soft.

"And how are we to get in there?" Rishka hissed angrily, looking up at those walls. "This is work for fools."

"Not that way, surely," Askarth whispered back. "We go elsewhere. That gate only leads into a formal courtyard. There are other walls and gates behind it. Besides, it would not do to march up the main avenue to the front gate and demand entry."

Askarth was still rushing us on. Soon we had turned into a whole maze of little alleys that seemed to be leading us away from the Great-House until at last we turned back on one of them. "Fish Seller's Alley," Askarth whispered. "This is the way ordinary folk come when the gates are open. Even here it will be well guarded."

Soon we came within sight of another wall. The gate there was much smaller, with a low stone door set into it. There were guards there, too, many of them. I noticed that they were keeping some distance from the walls, staying far enough back so that nothing could shower down on them from above.

"That gate opens into the kitchen entry hall," Askarth whispered. "If the birds have flown as they should, it is there they will be watching for us." She signaled us to follow her behind a refuse heap that blocked the corner. "This way, this way, quickly. From here we can watch both the guards and the gate."

Moving fast, we were soon squatting down together behind that pile of foul stuff. It had come, no doubt, from the kitchen of the Great-House when the gates were still open. Nowhere near the size of the Bargguell, it was still large enough to conceal us and the smell was almost as rank.

"And how are we to get past all those guards?" Rishka growled after a while of watching. "What are the ways in?"

Askarth shook her head. "If I knew that I would have had them out of there myself. I would not have had to come begging your help. I have gotten you safely here. Now it is up to you."

"What do we know of Great-Houses? That one was born in a dirt-village, and I have lived all my life in the country of blowing sands."

Irdris put her hand on Rishka's arm. "Watch for a while and see where their weakness lies. They are only men, after all." Our other three shadows had already disappeared into the night. Irdris had been so quiet I had all but forgotten her. With a growl Rishka shook off her hand and hunched into herself to watch.

The guards seemed restless and disorganized. Some were pacing, some lounging about, and a few playing a noisy game of cards. One of the guards kept spitting and muttering, looking up at the walls. Another called out loudly, "Hey, Yanoff, where is your Leesha tonight? Whose arms does she sleep in, eh? Not yours, surely, while you are trapped behind those walls!"

There was a thud and a cry of rage from inside. Another of the guards growled, "Shut your mouth, Arn, this is bad enough! Why make it worse?"

"Why not," the other grumbled. "Who knows but that something interesting might happen. How many nights are we expected to stand here? Why not make a great fire and cook them all out? I hear that is the only way to kill those star-brats anyhow." Just then a fight broke out at the card game that had to be quelled by the others.

"Well, it is easy to see they are bored and restless and badly organized, though they are still far too many for us," I said, shaking my head.

Irdris nodded. "Bored, more than anything. Bored men are easily entertained. The guards at the front gate look to be trained troops too well disciplined to be bored, but I think these fellows are mostly raw recruits from the country."

Askarth grunted, "This little siege along with all his other girl hunts must be straining the Zarn's larder. These fellows look to be green as cabbage."

At that moment another guard rode around the corner and gave a whistle. Several of the others came to crowd around and make comments on his horse, which clearly he had come to show them.

"This is what I earned for my part in tonight's business. Not bad, eh?" he bragged as he spun the horse about in front of them.

Suddenly there was a hiss. The guard on his horse disappeared into the shadows. The cards and dice vanished. The men all tried to scramble for their places, but the guard commander was already in their midst. He rode up and down, looking at them with contempt.

"You are no better than scum straight off the farm. There is not a decent soldier here. What if an attack were to come while you were lounging about in that way, then where would you be? Dead, most likely! Garbage is what they are sending me now. You cannot make fine goods out of garbage." He turned and rode off the way he had come. As soon as he was out of hearing there was a volley of rude remarks about the captain's ancestry.

"Attack, eh? Not likely. I, for one, would welcome it. At least it would be something to do."

"Who is going to attack, tell me that? A pack of star-brats? Well, hopefully we will not see that fool of a captain again for another hour. Perhaps next time we will be better warned."

The cards and the dice were out again. The young man had come back with his horse. Everything was as before.

"Well, what do you think?" Rishka whispered. "Have we seen enough of their weaknesses? Cards and dice are interesting games, but for me I prefer horses."

"You have an idea?"

She nodded. "Something that might be worth a try. Now, when we go to play this horse game, we had best all be drunk and not very bright."

"Stay here and watch for us," I told Irdris.

She nodded. "Mother's Luck go with you all."

When we staggered out of hiding there were shouts from the guards warning us to stay back if we wanted to keep a whole skin on our backs.

"This house is sealed by order of the Zarn! Keep away! No one may pass in or out through the gates!"

Rishka wavered on her feet. "I want nothing to do with your Great-House. You may have it all, for all I care, every worthless stone of it. It is your horse I want to see," she called out as she gestured wildly. "Yes, that one. I used to have one much like it before I bargained him away for some bottles of drink, fool that I am."

Some arguments broke out between them, and I heard one say, "What harm? He is only some drunken idiot here to amuse us. It passes the time."

I followed after Rishka, calling plaintively in my poor Shokarn, "Ricko, wait, do not leave your friends. Wait, Ricko, come back. What have you done with the quillof?" Askarth came staggering after me, her face well hidden by her hood.

Rishka pretended to ignore me. She walked forward with a bold, drunken unsteadiness, going right between the guards and up to the horse. When she put out her hand to make contact, the pull and snap of it was so strong I felt it in my own head.

"Why, I believe this is my old Lightfoot. Hello, fellow, you never thought to see me again, eh? You and I, we could show them a trick or two, eh, things they would never dream of."

There were many shouting to drive 'him' off, but there were also some who were curious to see. The young man himself who owned the horse was clearly angry now. He was trying unsuccessfully to back his horse away from Rishka's touch, but the horse was fretting and tossing its head, unwilling to move.

"Leave be, you drunken clod. This is my horse, given to me in payment for this night's work." I caught the smell of smoke and fastfire even over the stench of the rubbish heap.

"Oh come on now, soldier, what are you afraid of? Do you think I will best you in front of these men? Are you afraid to let me try?" With those words she lurched forward so that she stumbled against the horse and stood leaning there. "If I fall off you may run me through with your sword in great style and say you caught me trying to climb the walls. How is that for a bargain?"

"Come on, Thorgan, let us see what he can do. Who knows if he can even stay on. It will pass the time. The captain will not be back around for another hour. If he falls off you heard what he said. We could all have the chance of a little blood."

Thorgan shrugged. He dismounted with evident reluctance. "Well, fool, you have your few minutes. Show us what you are bragging on, but do not frighten my horse with your foolishness. And if you fall off, remember what you said. That part of the bargain I accept with pleasure."

Rishka rubbed the horse's nose. "Well, Lightfoot, are you ready?" The horse seemed to nod, rubbing back against her hand. Rishka tossed me her cloak and said with drunken boldness, "Hold that, will you, while I show these green guards how to ride a good horse. Then we go to water our thirst."

With this she leapt on the horse and almost fell off the other side, to the loud guffaws of the men. All their eyes were now on Rishka as she rocked in the saddle, teetering back and forth as if trying to regain her balance. She finally righted herself. There was some lively betting going on with the odds heavily against her.

She waved her hands for attention. "Watch, watch carefully. Are you really watching now?" Suddenly, with no apparent signal, the horse spun about and stood straight up on his hind legs with Rishka clinging to his back. As soon as he was down, she swung him the other way and he reared again. Then she had him bow first one way and then the other. By now the guards were cheering. After that she began to do a series of high, fancy steps, weaving back and forth, but always moving a little farther from the gate. After each step she would call out to the young 'owner,' "Can you do that near as well? I wager not."

With a sudden growl of anger he grabbed for the bridle, shouting, "Enough, give me back my horse!"

"*Your* horse?!" Rishka shouted back. "This horse is mine! Mine! You will never see him again, you fool!" With that she spun the horse around and plunged away at a run through the surprised guard, shouting back at us in Kourmairi, "Run for the gate!"

I grabbed Askarth by the arm and ran toward the gate, almost carrying her. Most of the guards had raced after Rishka, shouting, "Horse thief! Stop that horse thief!" But a few had more sense or were lazier. I heard one of them shout, "Block their way to the gate! It was all a trick!"

There was a scramble in back of us, then a thud and a groan. Dragging Askarth along, I kept running with my eyes fastened on the door in the gate. That door stayed stubbornly shut.

Askarth was screaming, "Open, open, open up, you fools!"

I could hear a horse galloping in back of us and could only hope it was Rishka and not the commander of these men. At the very last moment, with the fateful sound of stone scraping on metal, the door swung open just wide enough for us to squeeze through. Then, seconds later, Rishka catapulted through the opening after us, landing on the floor in the midst of the startled guards. There was a roar of rage from outside and the sound of many feet running as the door scraped shut again and a huge metal bar dropped into place.

Panting for breath, Rishka struggled to her feet. "Well, the getting in was not so hard," she said to us with a grin. "I hope the rest goes as easily." Though her words were brave enough, she was shaking and gasping for breath.

I looked around. We were surrounded by the same guards who, under another's master's orders, would have been trying to burn us alive. One of them, the one in charge, had his sword raised for a blow.

18

"**W**here is Askarth? What have you done with her?" the man shouted, taking a threatening step toward Rishka.

Askarth struggled free of my grip and threw back her cloak. "Here! Here! Right in front of your face, Merrik. Did you not hear me shouting to open the door? Drop your sword. It makes it hard to talk."

He lowered his sword, sheathed it, and made a slight bow. "Greetings, Askarth. I was not sure in these strange times if we would ever meet again. So you have really come back." I was surprised at his tone of respect, almost deference, and at the manner of the other men as well.

Askarth seemed to bristle at his words. "Of course I have come back. When I left I said I would and that you were to watch for me. Did you expect any less of me than my word?" She looked at each one in turn, as if to make sure they understood.

Meanwhile, from outside a pounding began on the door that shook the whole gate, as if those we had tricked meant to break it down. One of the men near me leapt to the door to peer out an eyehole. There was much noise from above, then the whistle of arrows, the rush and splash of something being poured, shouts and cries of pain, much running, more shouts, and finally loud cheers from above, no doubt from the defenders at the top of the walls. After that there was a strange silence.

The one who had been watching turned away with a laugh. "That should hold them off for a while. Do those fools think we are undefended, that they can just come up to our gates as they please?" He turned to Rishka then. "Well, girl, that was a good show with the horse, very good. You had that pack of clowns running in circles after you out there. I saw you hiding by the midden and wondered how you were going to get past them. The Zarn's guards think they are so clever, eh?" He began to laugh and shake his head. "And the way you came flying in here, flying by me so fast I even felt the wind on my face. And the look of surprise on their faces," he gave a nod of his head in the direction of the other men, "when you landed right in the middle of them. Now *there* was a sight to see." He was laughing even harder now, and slapping his leg. Soon he had the others laughing with him. He apparently took great personal relish in the besting of the Zarn's guards, but to me the guards inside seemed not much different from the ones outside, all of a cloth. I felt no great friendliness for any of them.

Askarth interrupted their laughter impatiently, "Where are they, then, my girls? Where are Lhiriasha and Nunyairee? Are they all prepared? Are they ready to leave? Why are they not standing here? There is little time. We have to be out of here at a moment's notice." To my surprise she was now speaking to the leader of these men in Kourmairi.

I was even more surprised when he answered her in the same, "They cannot go with you, Aunt. The Lord Starmos has said that you may take the rest of them if you can get them out safely. If not, they go anyway. He will not harbor them any longer. He wants the other star-cursed out from under his roof, says he is tired of sheltering Witches in his house. But his daughter, my Lady Nunyairee, and her slave Lhiriasha, those two he will not allow to leave. He says he has heard many stories of the star-women, that they are an immoral, nasty lot and much more, begging your pardon." This last was said with a bow in our direction. "And that he would not let his child go with them, that he can protect her better here and needs Lhiriasha to stay and care for her." All this Merrik said while looking off to the side, as if ashamed to meet Askarth's gaze.

She burst out angrily, "Then the lord of this house is a great fool. This is their one chance of escape. Did you tell him that I would care for them, that they would be in my hands again?"

"Pardon, Askarth, but he said if you were the Goddess Herself he would not put them in your hands."

"Then I will go speak with him myself. He must be made to understand."

She took a step and instantly Merrik moved to block her way. "He has expressly forbidden it. I have orders to turn you back if you should get this far."

"Surely he will hear me. There is an old debt between us."

"No, Aunt, he has made that very plain. He will not see you at all."

Askarth put a hand on his arm and drew him aside. With heads bent together, they talked intently. I could only catch a few words here and there until I heard Askarth say passionately, "...if you have ever loved her..." Later Merrik raised his voice and I heard him say, "...cost my life."

Meanwhile, Rishka and I stood there surrounded by guards and some of the kitchen drudges as well, who had crept out to stare at us. None of us spoke to each other. All ears seemed to be intent on that secret and almost soundless conversation where our fates were being decided by the words of others. I could feel the weight of that house around me and the weight of Eezore pressing in around that house and wished myself anywhere else at that moment. What if the master of the house, roused by the commotion, came to see for himself? Would he order us thrust out of his gates into the waiting jaws of the Zarn's guard, as he was so willing to do with the others?

Before I had time to work myself into a state, Askarth and Merrik came back. In his commander's voice Merrik ordered six of his men to stand guard by that gate, sent another to fetch the Star-Born who were to go with us, and dismissed the rest to other duties. Then he beckoned us to follow him.

We went down a barely lit corridor and from there turned into a narrow hall. A short way down this hall he stopped and told us to turn our backs. There was a sliding, grating sound. When we were allowed to turn back, I could see that a door had opened in what had appeared to be a flat wall. Merrik's flare lit a narrow stairwell. We followed him up and up until the stairs ended in an even narrower passage with many turns. We all four went with the utmost quiet. I could hear the sounds of the house around us, people walking, a dog barking, and at one moment the sound of voices so close that if there had been no wall I believe I could have reached out and touched the speakers.

Finally, after another short set of stairs, we stopped again. Merrik slid open another door and we were in a small room, clearly used as a closet. "You go first, and I will stay out of sight," he said to Askarth. "They will be less afraid that way." He tapped lightly on the door. When there was no answer he tapped again, opened the door slightly, and thrust Askarth into the room. Rishka followed right on her heels, and I was just behind Rishka.

Even in the midst of all this danger, the sight of the room overwhelmed me. I had never imagined such luxury. Everything seemed decked in rich, red fabric that covered the walls as well. The candle holders were hung with bits of bright glass that flashed in the candlelight and filled the room with dancing colors.

A young woman, no darker than Rishka, had rushed up, grabbed Askarth's arms, and put a finger up to her lips to sign for silence. "Askarth, how did you get in there?" she whispered, pointing at the closet. "Be very quiet. There are guards posted right outside our door. I had not thought to see you here this night."

"Oh, Lhiriasha!" Askarth whispered in return, throwing her arms around the young woman, "still safe, still alive. I was not sure..."

Another young woman, very white-skinned, who had been lying on the bed, sat up quickly and stared at me with a startled look. "But you are so dark!" she said in surprise. "Dark as any Kourmairi. I had not thought..."

Rishka pushed past me and in two strides was at the bedside. "What had you expected, 'Lady'? Were you thinking that some handsome young Shokarn lord, white as swan feathers, would ride in to save you from your own? If our color is so offensive to you we can leave you here for those of your own color to deal with. You can easily see how kind they are!"

"No, please, I meant no offense. I was only surprised ... I had not expected..."

"No offense!" Rishka's voice was rising. "You had a look on your face as if a toad had pissed in your hand. No offense, eh?"

The other one, Lhiriasha, turned and hissed at Rishka, "Quiet, I beg of you! Do you want all those guards rushing in here at us and alerting the whole house?"

Rishka was about to answer when I pulled at her arm. "Leave be. It is all those years of training and habit. She will soon learn."

Rishka pulled free of my hand and turned away, muttering, "She had better be quick at the learning. I have not much patience with this Shokarn ignorance." But after that she held her peace.

Askarth was rushing about the room, saying, "Are you ready? Do you have dark cloaks, men's clothing, money, jewelry, whatever of value you can bring? Quickly, quickly, we must soon be gone from here!"

"We *were* all ready," the young woman on the bed answered, "and then my father said we were not to go."

"And I suppose you always do what you are told, Nunyairee, even when it will no doubt cost your life. On your feet! Be quick! The Zarn's guard left three young women on the Bargguell to die this night, all horribly burned, one so badly we had to help her out of this world. If they can, they will do the same with you. Now move! We are leaving as soon as the signal comes. This is your one chance. After tonight we are gone from here. All who remain in Eezore are abandoned to their fate!"

Nunyair jumped up and threw her arms around Askarth. "Save us, Askarth. I will do whatever you say."

Lhiri was already gathering up their things, piling clothes on the bed. As they both dressed in haste there was a knocking on the door. One of the guards called out, "Lady, I hear voices in there. Are you alone? Are you safe?"

There was a moment of fearful silence. Then Askarth shook her, and Nunyair said clearly, "Thank you, but all is well. I had a bad dream that made me call out and Lhiriasha has been comforting me." Merrik had come into the room and was beckoning to us frantically to hurry.

The instant Nunyair was dressed, Askarth drew her over to a table all covered with jars and bottles. She took up a pot of dark stuff and a rag and with some quick smears darkened Nunyair's face and hands. Then she pulled the cape and hood around her. Just that quickly the Shokarn 'Lady' had become one of us, one of that immoral, nasty lot.

The guards were pounding again, calling loudly, "Lady, you must open the door so we can see that all is well with you, and you are not being compelled!"

"Please, Yargon, give me a moment to dress. It would not be proper for you to see me this way. Then Lhiriasha will unlock the door for you, and you will see that all is well."

Merrik went to the window and opened it on what appeared to be a courtyard or an inner garden. He set a chair below it and scattered some clothes there, whispering, "Let them think they have gone out that way." Then he signaled to Rishka and to me. Together, we three pushed a heavy bureau in front of the door as Nunyair called out, "I am almost ready."

At Merrik's signal we all melted into the closet. Merrik shut that door, opened the other one, and we were back in the passageway. He gave a quick look up and down the hall, then touched something. The door shut and all signs of the doorway vanished. We went at a run after Merrik's flickering light, more worried now about speed than silence. Soon we could hear the guards banging and shouting in back of us.

When we reached the downstairs hall, Merrik turned to Askarth and said angrily, "You can have no doubt that I will hang for this night's work!"

"Not while I have breath in my body," she answered quickly.

We were met in the passageway by other guards so that I froze with fear, but they merely said to Askarth, "The others who are to go with you are ready and waiting." We were joined by several dark-robed, silent figures. Then we all went together, this strange crew of guards and fugitives, to stand near the door in the kitchen gate.

Merrik turned to me and said, "Now, Lady, I must ask you what we are to do next since you seem to have some sort of plan here?"

"Keep a watch at the eyehole and listen for the cry of the Oolanth hill-cat. That is the signal. The moment you hear it, slide the bolt. As soon as you see that the Zarn's guards are occupied elsewhere, open that door and get us out of here. I can only hope those on the wall will cover for us. That is as much plan as we have." Then, to those other women who seemed more like dark shadows or ghosts, I said, "Be ready to move instantly when the signal comes. Try to follow us, but if we become separated, head for the West Gate by whatever way you can. Somehow it will be held open." Even as I said those words with such seeming assurance, I wondered how it would really be. I saw a few of them nodding back and was reassured that there was some life there in that silence.

Then I went to the guard who watched at the eyehole and signaled that he should move aside. Looking out, I saw that the street was quiet again. A much more dignified and organized guard was marching back and forth before the gate at a safe distance from the walls. They seemed to dominate the street, but beyond them I could see shadows moving at the edge of the refuse pile.

When I turned away from the eyehole, Askarth drew me aside and said, "There is a thing I must set right. If I am not back when the signal comes, go without me. I will find my own way clear of here."

I grabbed her hand with a terrible rush of foreboding. "Askarth, stay with us. This house does not wish you well. It will be far worse after we leave." Already I could hear the sounds of commotion from above us growing louder.

She pulled away and said firmly, "I do what I must, just as you do." Then she was gone.

I went to stand again by the guard at the eyehole, tense with listening. Out there the night seemed quiet, as quiet as I could imagine a city would ever be. It must have been close to night's-turn. I could hear the sound of the guards' boots on the cobbles and a dog barking far off.

At any moment I expected the guards from upstairs to come rushing down on us. Suddenly there were shouts and thumping and the sounds of a loud argument from somewhere above us in the Great-House. Almost at the same instant I heard the cry of the Oolanth hill-cats seeming to come from everywhere at once, and then the great roar of a fire close by.

"Draw the latch, get ready to open," I shouted to the guards as I pushed aside the watcher. When I looked out again it was on a scene of utter chaos. Flames were shooting skyward from the garbage heap. There was flaming debris lying scattered about everywhere in the streets. The guards who moments before had marched smartly in step were running every which way, either in flight or in pursuit.

"Now!" I yelled. "Now!"

The stone door creaked open again and we all flung ourselves out into the night. It looked as if the whole city were running about in the streets at that moment, townfolk, guards, horses, dogs. The quivering red light of fires rose over the rooftops, and the terrifying cry of the hill-cats echoed from all directions.

"Which way?" Rishka yelled to me as we poured out into this madness. I glanced up and down the street trying to set some course.

Instantly a shadow came forward to fasten on my arm. "This way," Irdris said next to my ears. "Follow me." She turned left, going swiftly away from the fire.

"You lead, you know how to go," I told her. "I need to go back and make sure the others are all coming." Some of those young women from the Great-House seemed as bewildered in the streets as I had been. It was not an easy task to get them all moving fast in the same direction.

"Come on, come on, go quickly! They will all be on us in a moment. Do not stand about. Keep your feet moving. There, follow that one, go where she goes. She knows the way," I urged, sounding much as Askarth had sounded with me.

That is how I know what happened. I know because I went back for the others and so was the last to turn down the alley. There was a bone-chilling cry from high in back of me. I turned and looked up to see a woman topple from the corner of the Great-House wall with flaming arrows in her back. She fell outward with a long, terrible scream.

"Askarth!" I cried out, then clapped my hands over my mouth and ran after the others. Better if they did not know, at least for now.

As I caught up, I heard Irdris saying, "From here we can start angling toward the West Gate." I kept my mouth tightly shut on what I had just seen.

Hereschell's lessons stood me in good stead. As we ran I knew the streets before we came to them. We had to dodge the fires that had sprung up everywhere around us. In places people were looting houses and fighting with each other. Some streets were almost blocked with overturned furniture and debris. Often we had to choose another course, zigzagging our way across the city.

Now a new cry arose to add to the cry of the hill-cats. "STAR-BORN TO THE WEST GATE!" began resounding through the streets. When I had breath enough I added my own voice to one cry or the other. "STAR-BORN TO THE WEST GATE! STAR-BORN TO THE WEST GATE! STAR-BORN TO THE WEST GATE!" rang in my head while the cry of the Oolanth cat tore along my nerves.

It seemed as if all of Eezore were rushing toward the West Gate in a great flood. I began running next to Nunyair, for she was tiring. Lhiri kept close to her other side. Soon Nunyair grew so winded I had to call a halt in an alley. She sank down against a wall, panting as if she would break apart, while Lhiri squatted beside her, talking softly in her ear. Those who were left with us crowded around. We had already lost half our company. Sanna and Eshrell had taken some of the newly freed ones and gone on, but Rishka was still with me and so was Irdris, as well as three or four others from the Great-House. Rishka was leaning against the wall beside me, watching Nunyair with a look of annoyance on her face, or perhaps disgust would be a better word.

Irdris came up to me on the other side. "Do you know the way now, Tazzi? Can you get safely out of here? I need to go and see to someone if I can."

"Well enough, and Lhiri probably knows it, too. Besides, Shalamith will pull us all to the West Gate like fish on a line." Even as I was speaking Irdris vanished into the night. When I turned to look for her she was nowhere in sight. With a jolt I realized I had let her go without asking anything of where she went or what she went to do.

"Are you sure you know?" Rishka asked sharply. I was surprised to see such fear in her face. "I thought Askarth would see us out of here as well as bringing us in. I had not thought she would desert us in this way."

"She must have had her own good reasons," I answered quickly, biting my lip to keep back the tears.

I averted my face, hoping Rishka would not think to read my thoughts, but she seemed too preoccupied with her own. She was shaking her head and looking frantically in all directions. "Well, I am as lost as if someone had spun me around in a bottle. I can find my way through the trackless drylands, but here in this rat maze..." She shrugged, then said with sudden passion, "Tazzi, I have no wish to die trapped behind these walls. This is no place for a Muinyairin."

"Rishka, I know where we are and where the West Gate lies, believe me. I will see you safely out of here."

"Good, then what are we waiting for? The sooner we are clear of the city the better."

"I cannot go on," Nunyair said with a groan.

"Oh, Goddess," Rishka growled, "I am willing to save their worthless lives if I must, but not for all the gold in Eezore will I play nursemaid to one of these Shokarn brats." Her eye fell on Lhiri as she said this and her tone was full of insult.

I turned to Lhiri. "Is there a stable near here with an outside pen?"

"Very near, on the Street of the Doves. The stable of Orwin One-Eye has a large outdoor holding pen."

"Can you go that far?" I asked Nunyair.

"I will try," she answered weakly.

Rishka was shaking her head. "We cannot ride through that madness. We would be worse off on horseback than on foot. And these new ones probably cannot even ride."

"Not we — you. You are the only one who has the skill. We cannot leave her here and we cannot carry her out. The gate will only be open for a short while."

"You want me to ride out with *her!?*" Rishka let out a string of words that must have been Muinyairin curses.

When Rishka was finished I simply said, "Yes." I knew I must try to get Nunyair to safety. It was the only thing I could do for Askarth now. I motioned for Lhiri to help me pull her to her feet. Then we were in the street again and running. The alley had been only a momentary respite. If anything, the madness in the streets was worse than before. I took Nunyair's arm on one side, and with Lhiri on the other, we went as fast as we could, half dragging and half carrying her along. The others stayed as close to us as they could, and I was aware of Rishka running right at my elbow.

There was a fire close to the pen. In the light of it we could see the horses rearing and snorting in terror. "The rest of you get those gates open while I get the horse," Rishka called out as she ran past me, pulling a length of rope from her pouch. Then she vaulted the fence and disappeared from sight in the melee.

As I struggled with the gate, Nunyair tugged on my arm. "I cannot ride one of these," she said, her eyes wide with terror.

"Let loose of me so I can do this," I growled at her. "You will hold on behind Rishka and ride for your life. Since you cannot run, this horse is your one way out of here." I struggled with the gate while Lhiri worked frantically beside me. On the far side I thought I glimpsed hooded figures at the other gate. The rearing horses were like great black shadows against the leaping flames. I feared for Rishka's life in that tumult.

Then, suddenly, I heard her voice over the uproar shouting, "I have the horse. Open that fool gate and let me out of here!"

Just at that moment a man with a patch over one eye ran out of the stable, roaring with rage and waving his stick. Others came running out of the tavern. From the opposite side I saw guards running straight at us, shouting, "Stop them! Stop them!"

I pulled the last bolt on the gate, pushed Nunyair behind me, warned Lhiri back, and swung the gate wide. From somewhere came the cry of the cat. Horses poured out in a wild flood, snorting and whinnying. I pressed myself to the fence to keep clear of their hooves as they rushed by. Soon I could hear the guards screaming in panic as they scattered before the crush.

Out of the dust and smoke Rishka suddenly appeared before me, laughing wildly and clinging to the same horse she had ridden earlier. She swung him around so that she was beside us. "Fate or the will of the Goddess. It was the only horse that would come to me in there. Get my baggage on so we can be off."

With Lhiri's help I pushed Nunyair up in back and wrapped her arms around Rishka's waist. "Shut your eyes and hold tight for your life!" I told her.

Rishka was off at a run. Some of the loose horses that were milling around gathered themselves up to follow in her wake. It looked as if she were riding off in their midst, the wild Queen of the Horses.

"Now for us," Lhiri said. We were the only Star-Born left at that spot. The men from the stable and the men from the tavern and the Zarn's guards were all converging on us. They had been momentarily distracted by Rishka, but now she was gone with no chance of capture, and they saw us trapped between them.

"They are star-cursed who have escaped from a Great-House," called out one of the guardsmen. "Close in and keep them surrounded."

The other men were shouting their agreement. I think we looked to be good sport for the night. I pulled Lhiri close to me. "See that man from the tavern in a red tunic? He is very drunk and unsteady on his feet. Likely he will not be able to hold his place. When I give the signal we will both run straight at him and keep on going. Hopefully those fools will end up running into each other. For now stand back-to-back with me so they have no chance of surprising us."

I waited, watching carefully for our chance. They did not rush us. For all their loud talk, those men were not too certain of how to deal with the Star-Born, though there were only two of us to their more than twenty. Then I saw our man in red waver slightly on his feet and look uncertainly at the others.

"Now!" I yelled to Lhiri. She spun around next to me and we both set out at a run, heading straight toward our chosen drunk. For good measure I let out the cry of the cat. As he saw us almost upon him, his eyes flew wide in fear. With a cry of alarm he leapt hastily out of our path. The others were shouting at him, cursing him for a fool. We ran past him and kept running till their voices faded behind us.

When I finally stopped and dropped to the ground gasping and heaving to catch my breath, Lhiri threw herself down beside me. We had run for as long as we could and had come to some quieter place. There were few fires nearby and not such a crush of people.

After a while Lhiri sat up and looked about. I saw a look of amazement on her face, and then of fear. "I am lost! For all the years I have lived in Eezore I have never been here before."

I took several deep breaths to quell the panic that instantly threatened to take hold of me, then I shut my eyes, cupped my pendant in my hand, and waited till I could see Hereschell's map as clearly as if it had been printed in red on my eyelids.

"Never mind," I said to Lhiri with a grin. "I think we are at the crossing of Stone Cutter's Way and Viyaire Street. If so, we are not very far from the Avenue of the West Gate."

We set out again, but more slowly now. No one in that vast chaos seemed intent on pursuing us any more. Besides, I could not run another step. They would simply have to hold the gates open for us. As we approached Merzia Street I could feel a strange vibration, a rumbling underfoot. It felt as if the city itself rocked and shook on its foundation. As we turned into the Avenue of the West Gate, the rumbling became words, thundering out over our heads and yet coming with such sweetness it made one want to cry.

"OPEN THE GATES, OPEN THE GATES, OPEN THE GATES OF THE CITY." Over and over and over those words resounded. They rang out like the tolling of a great bell, louder than the death bell itself, or like my heart beating outside of me as well as inside, or really like nothing I have ever heard in this life with the terrible compulsion they laid on me. It had to be Shalamith. She had said she would open the gates for us one way or the other. If I had ever imagined the Goddess speaking, that would have been Her voice. "OPEN THE GATES! OPEN THE GATES! OPEN THE GATES!"

All of Eezore seemed to be rushing down the avenue. Before us I saw Kazouri turn out of a side street. She was running, hauling along a woman under each arm. Beyond her I thought I glimpsed Rishka riding in a mass of horses. "OPEN THE GATES, OPEN THE GATES!" I felt a sense of urgency and began to run again, suddenly finding new strength. Lhiri caught hold of my hand and held it tight. The ground shook underfoot as we went. Before us the gates rose higher than most buildings and the gates were closed. "OPEN THE GATES! OPEN THE GATES! OPEN THE GATES OF EEZORE!"

Just when it seemed as if that giant tide of humanity would crush itself against their solid metal bulk, the great gates that had been closed and sealed by orders of the Zarn swung wide. Abruptly the voice stopped. There was a roar from those running. It looked like a living river pouring out of the city: Highborn, tradesmen and slaves, Shokarn and Kourmairi, guard and townsman, Star-Born and thieves, as well as horses and donkeys, cows, cats, and dogs. All, all poured out of the city as if the dam had broken and we were the fish in the flood or perhaps the floodwaters themselves. I saw several dark-cloaked figures in the crowd, one of whom I thought to be Pell, before I myself was carried out on the human tide.

I had lost all my companions, even Lhiri, and could barely keep my feet under me. Before me I saw what looked like a shining, golden figure riding away. I followed as if on a leash. The voice had begun again, changing its message but not its power. Now it was calling, "The

Star-Born come forward, all else go back, the Star-Born come forward, come forward, come forward!" That terrible, compelling voice was pulling, pulling, pulling at me, making my teeth ache and my head throb. I had no choice but to follow. If both my legs had been broken I would have crawled after that shining being on my hands and knees. "THE STAR-BORN COME FORWARD, THE STAR-BORN COME FORWARD, ALL ELSE GO BACK."

19

Eezore was burning below us and I was caught by the sight as if by a great rapture. But it was hate, not love or joy that flared up in my heart. Those who had chased us and harried us from place to place, seeking our deaths, were now the ones scurrying about down there, trying to save their own homes and hides. A demon of satisfaction burned in me at the sight.

It had taken all of Pell's abilities as leader to gather us together out of the chaos and confusion at the gates. She had done it mostly with Hereschell's help. Her captains were too spelled by Shalamith's voice to be of much use. Instead of leaving by any of the valley roads, we had followed Hereschell up a short, steep way into the hills. Our horses were quickly winded by the climb. Near the top we had all stopped to rest them and look back at the burning city. The others had soon seen enough. They were ready to move on, especially the new ones, who were in a frenzy to put as much distance as possible between them and Eezore. I knew I should go with them, yet I could not tear myself away.

I had crept out to the edge of a bluff for a better view and was watching greedily, my terrors finally appeased. One after the other they had all urged me to go, Jhemar, Kazouri, Zenoria. Even Hereschell tried. I did not turn my head to look at him. I was too rapt by the sight of the fires below me. Finally Rishka crawled out on the ledge by me. I could feel her tugging at my arm. She kept saying, "Come, Terrazen, this is no place to die. We have too much else to do."

I shook my head. I could not move from there. "I will come soon," I told her. "I only need to watch a little longer."

Pell even tried to command me by saying, "As your leader I order you to leave at once!" But what good are commands for those who cannot be compelled?

One by one they began to leave, saying it was too dangerous to stay, warning me that soon we would be hunted there. I hardly noticed their departure. Alyeeta was the last of them to go. I was so rapt that I neither heard nor sensed her as she stepped up beside me till she gripped my arm and shook me. "Tazzia, Daughter, you are fire-spelled. Four times I have spoken to you with no reply. Come away from here. This sight is sickening your soul. Your anger rides uneasy with your power this night." Her voice was full of love and concern for me. I had no wish to feel it.

Without looking at her I answered, "No, I cannot. I must stay and watch the evil that is Eezore burn itself out."

Alyeeta gave a short, explosive laugh. "The what that is what do what?!" she exclaimed. Then she added, with all of her usual mockery, "Indeed, child, now that would be a long wait. You might be windblown bones before that time. It will not happen this night, not with little thief-set trash fires. Eezore will not go under in this generation nor even in the next. I, for one, will not live to see it. You star-brats have many miles to ride and much living to do before you can meet Eezore's power with your own. Come with me now, Tazzi. There are far more roads still ahead of us."

"Soon," I said, "soon I will come to meet you. Soon. Leave me for now. This is a thing I must see. I am no child, Alyeeta, I can take care of myself."

"No one who is caught in the spell of a compulsion can take care of themselves. Tazzi, you are not sane at this moment. If you have ever loved me, girl, come away with me this instant, for this is a very dangerous place to be. Even now they may be riding up these roads in search of us."

"Enough, Witch! Go! Leave me be! I will meet you at Hamiuri's shelter."

There was a silence then that made my hair go up. This time I turned. Alyeeta stood with her hand raised as if to strike me. Then she dropped her hand, shrugged, and turned away. I heard her call softly to her pony and felt her mind-reach for him. When she had gone I was so glad to be alone that I did not have the sense to be afraid. I did not even see at that moment how she had laid out all her love before me to be trampled.

How long did I lie there watching with bitter pleasure, mindlessly gorging myself, feasting on the sight? By the time I heard them it was already too late. The light of a torch flashed across me. There were shouts. Lying flat that way had been willfully stupid. I struggled up, stiff from the cold rock, and went stumbling through the dark, running in a half crouch to leap on Marshlegs's back. The light of the torch caught me again just as I reached her and managed to scramble up. I heard one of them shout, "The horse, shoot the horse! For the sake of your lives do not shoot at the Witch! Shoot the horse!"

Their torches were raised all around me. I heard the whistle of arrows and the terrible dull thuds as those arrows hit living flesh. With a frightful scream Marshlegs reared up, shuddered, and sank beneath me. I had only an instant to jump clear or I would have been crushed under her falling body. As I leapt back, I felt her hot blood splatter on my hands and face. In that instant, Marshlegs was gone and I was surrounded.

With no time for thought, I plunged headlong into the thickest underbrush, where horses could not follow, passing so close I felt the breath of one of their horses on my cheek. Behind me I could hear the men cursing and stumbling. Their searching lights made bewildering flashes through the trees. Now that they were unhorsed I had to trust to my better night sight and my knowledge of woods to see me through. It was all I had. They were many to my one, and I was already exhausted from the night.

My only thought was to keep moving. Several times I scrambled dangerously close to the curving bluff edge. Once I heard a man scream as he went over. The chase seemed endless. I tripped over roots and ran headlong into rocks. I felt branches whip across my face. Keep moving! Keep moving! the voice in my head shouted. I could still hear them in back of me. Whenever some of them tired and fell back, there always seemed to be more of them to take up my pursuit. Finally I lost them in the night, though I think my own fear drove me on long afterward.

It took three or more days of stumbling about in the forest to find Hamiuri's hut, much of the time probably spent floundering in circles. At that, I did not really find it. I was the one who was found. A young woman had come in search of me. I had sensed her presence and was crouched in hiding, huddled behind some rocks near the path. She came directly toward me as if she could see right through those rocks. I would have run from her also, but I could not run any more, could not summon the will for it.

"Come, come, do not be so frightened," she said softly, reaching out her hand. "I will take you to Hamiuri. She will be pleased. We have been looking for you everywhere." Beyond fear now, I took her hand and went with her like a small child.

Hamiuri did not look pleased at all. She was standing in her doorway, staring at me with fire in her eyes. As the young woman helped me in, Hamiuri stepped aside, shaking her head.

"I told you I could feel her nearby," the young one said. "Let me get her in a chair while she still has legs under her." With a groan I sank into the cushions like a sack of grain.

Hamiuri moved to stand in front of me with her hands on her hips. "Fool! Fool! Fool! Have you had enough of gazing on the fires of victory? Look at you, all covered with mud and blood and filth. You should be left outside for the rains to clean off. Understand, young woman, it is not your life alone you risk by such folly, it is all of ours, all of ours. You could have led that pack of slavering hounds right to my door. Goddess knows, they may yet come."

I held up my shaking hands to ward off her words. "Please, Hamiuri, please, not now. I have had more than enough for the moment."

"Have you, now? Well, what a shame, for I am only just beginning."

To my surprise the young woman stepped between us, faced Hamiuri, and said with authority, "Enough, Hamiuri, enough for now. We can talk about it all later."

I was even more surprised when Hamiuri shrugged and said, "You are right, Olna. Enough said for now." Then to me she added gruffly, "There is a pot of hot water there for washing. Leave those filthy clothes in a pile by the door. When you are finished there is some soup heating in that other pot. It will help you sleep." She turned her back on me and walked away, saying, "Some heads are hard, some lessons are hard learned."

I tried to do as she told me, but the clothes clung to me, wet and muddy or stiff with blood. My hands shook on the fastenings. "Wait," the young woman said, "let me help you." I was amazed at the gentleness of her hands as she peeled off that ruin of clothes, and the healing force in them as she carefully sponged away the mud, dirt, blood, and weariness with warm, sweet-scented water. "I am Olna the Witch," she told me as she worked. With that, I understood that she was probably not the dovelike young woman she appeared to be.

When she finished, she slipped a soft robe around me and said, "Sit there," pointing to a little stool by the fire. With the warmth of a soup bowl in my hands, I probably would have fallen asleep staring into the steam if she had not reminded me again and again to eat while she ran a comb through my leaf-tangled hair. When I lay down on a mat by the wall, I was gone into sleep before she could step away.

Later, when I woke aching all over, I saw my clothes washed and hung to dry on a rack of branches, the worst of the tears neatly mended. Olna was on her feet in an instant and called out to Hamiuri. Hamiuri came to stare down at me with no kindness at all in her face. "Good that you are awake," she said harshly. "I hope you are also in some shape to take care of yourself. Useless as you are, still we must get you back to your own. I think they will soon be moving on. You need to go with them. That will take some horses if we can find them. Hamiuri the Witch certainly has no intention of being your caretaker for long.

"While we are gone, stay out of trouble, if that is possible. We have had enough trouble already because of you. Do not play the fool again, understand?" I had lowered my eyes and was nodding silently to everything she said.

Olna came and put salve on my cuts and bruises. I saw her wincing with the pain it cost me to be touched. Gently she stroked my hair and back and said some soothing words in my ear. My heart contracted. Tears filled my eyes. In some ways Olna's kindness hurt even more than Hamiuri's angry reproaches. I knew only too well that I did not deserve such kindness. Nothing Hamiuri said could be bad enough to touch my own self-loathing. This talk of horses brought back Marshlegs's death and my own part in it.

★

While Hamiuri had been scolding me I had vowed silently to myself that I would not set foot outside her hut when she was gone, not even for the call of necessity, as I had seen a pot for that purpose under the bed. As soon as they left, however, a demon of restlessness took hold of me. I found myself pacing around in the small confines of that space, back and forth, back and forth. Now that I was alone, Marshlegs's death and the manner of it preyed on me. "Shoot the horse! Shoot the horse!" echoed in my head. Over and over I heard the sound of arrows and her final scream. Your fault, the air around me hissed, your fault, your fault, your fault.

Hamiuri's hut had not much room for pacing. It was different from Alyeeta's in every way, all stark, plain, and bare. There were no dark, hidden corners or secret places. Everything in it could be seen at a glance. A small, six-sided building, almost circular in shape, it was made of rough, whitewashed stone and crude timbers.

The furnishings were as humble as the hut, except for the wall opposite the door. There a tall wardrobe of dark wood loomed over the room, looking strangely out of place. I had seen something like it once when I had gone to do a healing at the headman's house in another village. Next to it was a bureau of the same dark wood. This was evidently used for an altar, as the surface was covered with ritual objects. These two together nearly filled that portion of the wall. Both were of fine make with deeply carved corners, clearly salvaged from some other time in Hamiuri's life.

My eyes were caught by a peculiar darkened glass standing on the bureau that reflected things as the surface of a pond reflects. It held a double of everything in the room. Several times I had been startled by my own movement flashing across its face. When my grief began to weary itself, I found myself drawn to that strange glass. Finally I came to sit on the bench before it. As I had never had much chance to look at myself, I stared with interest at this person that others saw. Leaning forward, I looked deep into her eyes, made faces, turned as far as I could one way and then the other, gestured with my hands. She, of course, copied everything I did.

I must have passed some time occupied in this way when I began to sense another's presence in the room, yet each time I turned there was nothing. There was nothing in the corners of the glass, either, however deeply I peered. Still, I could feel it, stronger and stronger, that insistent tapping on my consciousness, the pull and energy of life, of another's existence. At last my attention was drawn to a big, lidded basket on the floor next to the bureau.

It was a very ordinary basket, a basket such as market women use to carry their wares. There was a slight sound from it like fabric moving against fabric. Very cautiously I unlatched and opened the lid to peer inside. Instantly there was a hiss and a large snake raised its head out of the darkness, then a second, and a third. No chance of shutting the lid again, that was clear. I stepped back quickly and with some alarm. With all that had happened to me, I had lost the fearless innocence of my childhood. Besides, these were by far the largest snakes I had ever seen. Snakes and human, we regarded each other for a while with mutual wariness. Then the first of them bent forward and poured herself out of her basket, coming straight for me. I sat back down on the bench. There was nowhere in that hut to run even if I had chosen to do so.

The snake did not hesitate. Now that she had made her decision, she seemed to have lost all fear of me. All in one motion she slithered onto the floor, moved up my leg, slid into my lap, and crawled up to drape herself across my shoulders. I sat very still, trying to breathe normally while she settled herself there in what seemed to be her accustomed place. She was cool and heavy, smooth as water and beautifully marked in bands of bright colors. After my first rush of fear passed, I quickly grew accustomed to her weight. The snakes appeared quite old and perhaps even fangless. Still, I was very glad to see the other two choose their places on the altar.

Now I had company and a diversion of sorts. My reflection in the glass had become far more interesting. "You are very grand and fearsome," I said to my companion. "You could scare away a whole company of guards." She arched her neck and wove her head from side to side as if bowing to the snake in the glass.

As I was occupied in this way, I noticed a small painted carving on the bureau in front of me. It was of a Goddess or priestess or Witch in a long, richly patterned robe. She had two snakes wound around her arms. Another one was wound around her neck. Its head rose arched and hooded over hers in a sort of headdress, much like the snake I myself wore at that moment. With excitement, I leaned forward to examine her robe more closely. It was a thing of splendor, like nothing I had ever seen before. Having already trespassed this far, I now began to wonder if there was anything in that dark wardrobe as fine as what that little statue wore? Or did it hold nothing but more of Hamiuri's dull brown clothes behind the temptation of its closed doors? When it seemed safe to do so I unwound my friend from my shoulders and lowered her carefully, coil by coil, to join her companions on the altar. Then I went to stand before those forbidding doors. I could sense nothing living there, yet I hesitated. I almost sat down again. Then, in one quick gesture, I turned the handle to fling them open.

I sucked in my breath. Robe after robe hung there; bright colors, heavy fabric, rich embroidery, and the flash of metal. These were even finer than what the little statue wore. Above them on a shelf were headdresses, sashes, breastplates, necklaces, and much else. I stood transfixed, staring at it all. Of course, after a while of staring, nothing would do but that I must try something on. Only one, I promised myself, only one. What harm could there be in that? Then I would replace it carefully, shut the doors, and be done with my prying, for Hamiuri might be back at any moment now. Perhaps I could even coil the snakes back into their basket and be seated at the hearth, drinking tea, or dozing in a chair when Olna and Hamiuri returned.

Soon I had the bed littered with robes and was turning myself about this way and that in front of the glass. I tried on headdresses, a necklace, a breastplate. I even darkened my eyes and reddened my lips from some of the paint pots on the altar. Dancing about with my reflection as I suppose a young lady from one of the Great-Houses might have done, I forgot everything I should have been remembering.

Just as it turned dusk, my reflection began to fade. With that, some sense returned to my head. I was about to light a lamp and turn to quickly repairing the damage I had done, when suddenly a chill of fear ran up my spine. Hamiuri! I thought frantically, readying myself to rush about and make order. Then, instantly, I knew it was not Hamiuri. It was not trouble. It was danger, danger advancing, danger all around. Quickly I ran to peer out the windows. I could see nothing but trees in the deepening gloom. Still, the sense of danger thickened with each moment. The snakes that had been dozing, coiled around each other, now raised their heads. Turning from side to side, they spread their hoods and hissed as if at an intruder. At that moment I smelled smoke and then I knew — men and fire — they had come for me. They had been moving in to trap me while I played at being a lady, trap me as Maireth and Shaleethia had been trapped in that barn.

As I could still see nothing in the outer world, I cupped my hands over my pendant, shut my eyes, and stood very still, staring into the inner dark. Doing that, I felt them rather than saw them, felt a large number of men advancing stealthily to surround the hut. No doubt they wanted to burn me alive if they could, or rather to burn *us* alive, for it was likely they thought to catch many of us there. They would hardly have moved so carefully or mounted so large a force against one star-brat. They were coming slowly, probably struggling against the force of their fears as well as the powers of the house. Sooner or later, however, I knew they would close that circle of fire if I could not find a way to stop them.

I lit a lamp. As the flame flared up, my eye was caught by the statue of the Goddess with her raised snakes. Blazing in the shimmer of the light, she looked huge, with her great shadow looming behind her. Suddenly I had my plan.

I had seen some blocks of wood by Hamiuri's hearth, piled there for carving or for burning. Finding two of near the same size, I hastily tied them my feet with a cord I cut in half. These added at least two hands to my height. Tottering on my wooden feet, I went to the wardrobe and quickly pulled out the longest robe I could find there, one stiff with metal threads that would flash in the torchlight. I slipped this down to my waist like a skirt and bound it on with a sash. It covered my block feet and gave me a dizzying height. Next, I drew on a sleeveless tunic of some shimmering silvery stuff and over that fastened a set of brass breast-cups that would also shine and flash in the light. After that I wound some wide gold bracelets over my bare arms above my elbows and added Hamiuri's heaviest necklace, all hung with red stones. Over my short hair I pulled on a wig of tiny coiling braids. In the midst of this I set the most fearsome of her headdresses, the one that rose high over the head with a great central gleaming eye.

Thus altered, I leaned forward to peer at the apparition in the glass. "Almost," I said to her, "almost." I took up a paint pot and made a row of red slashes diagonally across each cheek. I took up another and painted the six-pointed star on my forehead and huge black rings under my eyes. "All right," I said, nodding to my twin in the glass. "Good enough." The face that stared back at me was no longer human. Something else had entered there, something of power. If I had gone on looking any longer I could even have frightened myself. "Now with the help of the Goddess we go to meet with them," I told her with a nod as she nodded back at me.

Carefully I gathered up the snakes, winding one around each arm like those on the statue and one around my neck so she could raise her head over mine. I could tell from how easily they settled themselves that they had done this work many times before, though likely at a very different sort of ritual. Just as I turned away from the glass I saw reflected there the first of their flares, flickering through the trees. "Mother, help me now," I said aloud to the little figure on the altar.

I took the lamp with me and set it on a low table in front of the door. Then, hidden at the edge of the window, I watched their approach, trying to breathe evenly and keep my calm. I needed them near enough to see me clearly when I chose to appear, but not so near as to close their circle and start their fire. It was clear they did not have fastfire or they would already have set it. That was some comfort, at least. They were moving so slowly now it made my nerves crawl. They seemed to be pushing against an invisible barrier. Suddenly I realized that I myself must be shielding. There was also the force of the place and of everything I wore, Hamiuri's force added to my own. By a conscious act of will I lifted my shield.

Instantly one young man rushed forward with a cry, waving his torch wildly. It was as if an unseen gate had been flung open. I could see him clearly, see the fear and confusion on his face. He looked to be a farm boy pressed into the Zarn's service, a farm boy much like those I had grown up with. Something in his face brought to mind my brother. "Witches," he shouted, very frightened and full of rage, trying to sound bold, "Witches, come out or we will burn you alive with our circle of fire!"

That was my signal. Here was my chance, the crack in their circle. For just that moment the others were in disarray, shouting angrily at him to move back. He was looking about in bewilderment, as if unsure how he had gotten himself there. It was time. I lifted the latch. With a roar or a howl, some terrible loud sound that rushed up from my belly, I kicked open the door. There were gasps of surprise and cries of fear from that line of men when I stepped through the doorway with my arms raised. The light from my lamp cast a huge, leaping shadow out among them. The flare of their torches flashed on my breastplate, and likely from the eye of the headdress as well.

With a shout of fright, that poor young fool rushed forward and flung his torch at me. All in an instant he himself was in flames. Howling in a madness of pain, he dashed away and threw himself down to roll on the ground. Others rushed to help him. Those from the back of the hut came running around to the front to see what had happened. Their circle was broken now, their discipline undone. They did not look to be seasoned soldiers. Many of them seemed to be raw recruits, dragged from their farm villages to hunt down the star-brats. They were all milling about in confusion, some shouting to make the fire then, others to flee. I knew this might be my only moment. Raising my arms high and shaking the snakes so that they hissed and wove their heads about, I made my voice into a fearsome roar. "Stop where you are! Take care with your fire! If any of you are careless with your torches and set fire to this sacred ground, you will end like that one." With a snake head rising above my fingers, I swung my arm and pointed to his crumpled form. I was very afraid they would drop their flares and make their fire by accident in the dry summer grass.

"If you come any closer," I roared again, "the magic serpents of the Great Mother will strike you dead with their venomed fangs." I shook my shoulders and the snakes did their part, hissing and striking out fiercely in all directions. Those men answered with groans and cries. I was almost sure I had them now. The ones who had been urging speedy action were no longer so eager.

I took a step forward, sweeping them all with my pointing fingers, and was glad to see them take a step back. I wanted to keep my back close to the shelter and so had no wish to go any farther. Besides, I could feel the fastening on one of my blocks loosening itself. A lame and hobbling Goddess would not keep her powers long. Most likely she would be speedily unmasked.

Casting about hastily for something of use, I noticed a large flat rock, a little off to the side. It lay between me and those men. Swinging my pointing finger at it, I said with all the authority I could summon, "Now, one by one, go place those torches on that altar. There they can burn out and do no harm. Take care. Your presence here is displeasing to the Great Mother and could bring down all Her wrath on your heads. As it is, it will take weeks to purify this sacred ground again."

No one moved. They all stared fixedly at me, frozen in place. Clearly, this was the moment when I might lose it all. Choosing the youngest and most frightened-looking of them, likely another green boy right off the farm, I swung those terrible fingers at him and shouted, "You! Now! Or do I have to come with my snakes to help you?!"

He was shaking visibly, clearly caught between his fear of me and his fear of the other men. "Now!" I shouted again, putting all my force into that one word. With a whimper he slouched forward to lay down his torch, never taking his eyes off me. As no one else moved, I turned and pointed to another. "Now you!" I thundered. When he moved to do as I said, I pointed to another and then another. Suddenly they were all rushing forward on their own, one after the other, faster and faster, as if eager to be rid of that dangerous fire, all the while watching me as rabbits watch a snake.

I never took my eyes from them or dropped my pose, not for an instant. The snakes kept up their part of it, too, continuing to writhe and hiss and strike. Soon there was a fair-sized blaze on that flat rock. The men were shuffling about uneasily. They needed one last push. I raised my arms to the sky and drew myself up to my greatest height. Trying to make my voice even more terrible than before, though by now I was growing hoarse, I bellowed, "The Goddess is very angry at your intrusion into Her sacred space. Do not return or send any others. From now on the snakes will be watching. If any of you come here to do evil again it will cost your life. Be grateful you are being spared by Her mercy. NOW GO! BE GONE!"

They were staring at me in silence, eyes bulging, mouths open. I could see it would take something more to dislodge them. I had nothing more. My voice was going fast and would likely crack the next time I tried to use it in that way. One block had come loose and I could scarcely keep my balance. My arms were aching, bending down under the weight of the snakes. Sweat was pouring down my face and running like a little river between my breasts. I saw the end coming soon. Help me, Mother! I called out silently. Suddenly, with a cry, one man broke and ran. At that signal all the others followed, running pell-mell, dashing out of the clearing, stumbling and crashing through the woods.

Sucking in big gulps of air, I stood there till there were no more sounds of men. When I heard the first night bird call I took two careful steps backward into the house, shut the door, and slammed the bolt in place. One block fell off and I kicked free of the other. With aching arms I went to slip the snakes back into their basket, where they quickly coiled about each other while I replaced the lid.

As fast as I was able I undid the breast-cups, slipped off the wig, the headdress, and the necklace, laid the bracelets back on the altar, and undid the sash so I could step out of my gilded skirt. Soon I had stripped down to my own skin. I stood naked and unbound in the center of that space.

On sudden impulse I flung my arms wide and shouted with relief. The house, the snakes, myself — all were safe. Outside, only a remnant of the fire remained, burning like an offering on an altar stone. Other night birds were now answering the first, a good sign that the woods had cleared and were safe again. It was time to set to repairing quickly the damage I had done and have it all in place before Hamiuri returned.

I turned and caught sight of my face in the glass, myself and not myself with the face paint running in the sweat. Suddenly I saw the scene again, saw myself propped up on two blocks playing Goddess, and all those men crashing off headlong into the darkness. I began to laugh, and slapped my leg. I laughed and laughed till I was bent over with it and my ribs hurt, but I could not stop. I fell to my knees laughing, and at last crumpled to the floor. I was rolling back and forth in an agony of mirth. I was choking with it and could hardly catch my breath. My belly ached with the pain of it and still I could not stop laughing. I might have gone to my death that way if Hamiuri had not come in at that moment and slapped me smartly on both sets of cheeks. "So this is how you stay out of trouble," she said, as she pulled me to my feet. "Olna had to climb in the window to unlatch the door."

With tears running down my face, I sobered enough to sit down and tell them both all that had happened in their absence. While I spoke, Olna gently cleaned the paint from my face with a damp cloth. As soon as that was done, she went out to look for the man who had been burned, saying she would call us for help if she found him. Hamiuri, meanwhile, went on with her relentless questioning while I struggled to answer her as best I could. When Olna came back she was shaking her head. "I found the burned place, but the man was gone, probably taken away by his companions."

"What did you want with him?" I asked her suspiciously.

"To see if he was alive and in need of healing."

I felt a sudden flush of anger. "Do you understand that he was the man who just tried to kill me? What does he need with your healing?"

She looked at me with pity in her eyes and seemed about to speak. Instead, she shook her head and turned away.

20

If I needed more punishment for my part in Marsh-legs's death, I certainly found it in full measure on the ride back to camp. I think the horse they gave me must have been designed for that very purpose. My time on his back was a misery every step of the way. I kept my mouth shut on it. Hamiuri had already made it clear to me that it had been no easy task to find three horses so quickly. Most likely they had been borrowed in Pell's style of borrowing. I knew better than to ask. The Witches had brought back with them two sturdy cart-ponies and a huge, lumbering beast who took an instant dislike to me but, nonetheless, was mine to ride.

To go back a little in this tale, as soon as Hamiuri had pulled all my story from me, she jumped to her feet, saying, "Done, finished, over, we must be quickly gone from here."

"You think they will be back?" Olna asked.

"Yes, I am sure of it, as sure as we are standing here. I am sure they will be back, and I think it likely they will try to burn down the hut. That is the way of men. They cannot stand to be made fools of. For a little while their fear will keep them away, but soon enough they will realize they have been tricked. Then they must have their revenge, if not on our bodies then on my shelter. Since it will not burn easily, they will probably have to throw down the rocks themselves to be satisfied." She had been pacing around as she spoke. Now she stopped and said abruptly, "Here, both of you now, help me with this guard-rock."

Together, with me pulling and Hamiuri and Olna pushing, we shoved aside a huge, flat stone that had kept secret a large, rock-lined pit in the floor. I stared into it with surprise. "Quickly," Hamiuri said, giving me a poke, "quickly, everything must go in."

Everything from the wardrobe and the bureau — armloads of robes, bedding, pots and pans, even the window glass — all vanished into the pit. Hamiuri had carefully unhooked the little wooden window frames, and we laid the glass carefully and lovingly between layers of cloth.

"They will not have the pleasure of breaking my windows. That glass was too dearly gotten." That dark glass for looking into was also gently packed away.

At some moment I straightened and said, "Why abandon all this, Hamiuri? Why not stay here and guard the house? Surely I can find my own way back to the others."

"No, I want to have the pleasure of delivering you safe to Alyeeta myself. I have seen enough of her grief. Besides, how could we guard it? We, ourselves, would be done in with it. For all our powers, we Witches are much easier to kill than the star-brats. And what is there to guard, anyhow? Some poles, some rocks, some thatch. How many sleepless nights do I wish to spend on that? They must do what they must. We cannot stop them. A snake trick will not work a second time. Besides, how can I trust you to stay out of trouble after what you have already shown me?"

Now guilt was at my throat. "Oh, Hamiuri, I am so sorry. You are being driven out of your home, and all because of my willfulness."

She gave a loud, sudden laugh, and her whole manner suddenly seemed to change. She even stopped her work to look at me. "You? All by yourself? You are responsible for this? No, child. Life moves, life changes. Things go as they go at the hand of One greater than ourselves. Perhaps I was done here. Perhaps it was time to leave anyway. So be it. They may have tracked you, they may have tracked the others. Or perhaps some clever guard captain in the town of Morthaine thought this a likely hiding place for star-brats and sent out some of his men, or maybe he only wanted a good excuse for burning out an old Witch. I left myself open to this by meddling in the affairs of humans again. The fault is more mine than yours. After all, it was not you that came to fetch me." Then she clapped her hands for action. "Quickly! Quickly! They will soon be back."

Mostly we worked in silence with only a few short, brusque commands from Hamiuri, but every once in a while she would pause and say to me, "Tell me again how you held the snakes," or "Show me how their faces looked when you stepped out that door." Then she would begin to shake all over with mirth. "Hee-hee-hee-hee, a hundred men scattered like leaves by my old toothless snakes, hee-hee-hee." I had never thought to see Hamiuri attacked by a fit of giggles.

As soon as we were finished and had replaced the rock, Hamiuri took up her broom and with the handle of it began knocking bundles of thatch from the roof and scattering it around. Then, with the broom itself she swept the ashes out of her neat hearth so that everything was soon covered with a coat of gray dust. As we walked out, she had Olna help her lift the door. They left it hanging from one hinge at a crazy angle in the door frame. She dusted off her hands on her brown skirt, took one last look at her work, and nodded with satisfaction. "Gone thirty years at least. If they get up the courage to come and look, then perhaps they will not think it worth the trouble." Outside she turned back, raised her hands, said some strange words, and made what I took to be warding signs.

Olna, meanwhile, had packed us trail bread, fruit, and water. I went quickly to help her with the horses. My huge brute seemed unaccustomed to saddle and bridle. He kept trying to step sideways out of my reach until Olna put a gentling hand on his neck and whispered some words in his left ear.

"They could at least have left me a horse," I grumbled ungratefully to myself as I hauled my battered body onto his back.

"Oh, indeed," Hamiuri said sharply, catching my words. "And how could I have cared for a horse in these woods? What would I have fed it on? Nuts and berries and betel leaves, perhaps. Besides, how were they to know your horse would be killed, or that you were even coming back? As it was, they waited and waited for you far longer than they should have, filling up my little space with their noise and clutter."

The last thing Hamiuri did was strap on the snake basket, handling it with care and crooning softly to them. Before that she stood staring at it, her face full of indecision. "If I let them loose they are so old they will likely starve or they will come back here and be killed. If I take them with me, who knows if they will survive the journey." She seemed close to tears. Then, with a sudden nod of her head, she said, " We are too old to be separated now."

There was a little earth glow and a quarter of a waxing moon to ride by that night. The Witches seemed well content with their ponies. They went at a brisk clip and moved with agility through the trees. My big, clumsy beast I secretly named Bone-Crusher. He seemed afraid of the woods and went sideways at a nervous half trot, bumping me into rocks, tree trunks, and branches, or running up against the rear of whichever pony was in front of us so that sometimes that little creature would lash out in annoyance with its heels. Then Hamiuri would turn, flash me an angry look, and say scathingly, "I thought star-brats had a way with horses."

Never in my life had I had so little communion with any creature. When I tried to reach out for that familiar mind-touch that I always had with horses, I was met by a strange, dead tone of absence that made my head hurt. The riding was no better when we came to flat, open land. While the ponies ran on ahead, the fastest I could get my brute to move was at a hard, bone-jarring half trot that left me gasping for breath. In spite of this, I was so glad to be alive and free of the guard and to have Eezore safely behind me that at moments my heart would leap up and I would feel like singing. Then I would think of what lay ahead of me at camp and my likely reception there and my heart would sink back to the pit of my stomach.

We were four hard days on the road. Just before dusk on the fourth, we were met by our sentries and escorted through the familiar circle of great trees into the clearing. I heard my name being shouted ahead of us and felt a sudden rush of dread.

Sure enough, my reception was just as bad as I had feared. Pell would not speak to me, not a single word. She stood waiting in the middle of the clearing with Maireth next to her, arms crossed, dark brows drawn together in a single line, staring past me angrily. When I was off the horse and walking toward her, the force of her anger was so great that I had a sudden impulse to drop to my knees and crawl the rest of the way. Women were quickly gathering around, but none dared greet me or speak to me at that moment. There was a terrible silence. Then Pell said loudly to Maireth, still without looking at me, "Tell 'that one' I will waste no words on her. She is no longer second-in-command here. She has broken my trust and endangered all our lives. She can go make the cookfire for Renaise."

I saw some of the new ones nudging each other, whispering and giggling behind their hands. I remembered how the dogs in Nemanthi would slink away with their tails between their legs when the village boys threw rocks at them. That was how I felt at the moment, though I tried to stand still under the lash of her tongue. Every word she said was deserved.

She said much more, all of it to Maireth and all of it Maireth repeated to me, so that I had the doubtful pleasure of hearing it not once but twice over. Poor Maireth, she seemed quite uncomfortable in this role, too embarrassed to meet my eye.

When there was a long enough silence so that I felt sure Pell had nothing more to say, I bowed my head slightly. Keeping my eyes to the ground, I said to Maireth, "Tell my Captain that I hear her and I understand. Tell her that I regret my folly and the danger it put us in more than I can say. Tell her I will do whatever she commands."

Maireth began to repeat my words to Pell, but Pell spun on her heel and strode away, saying loudly to those she passed, "Ha, who could believe anything she says? She can only see what is right before her face, and even that is not clear to her. What good is she? I was a fool to put my trust there."

While the others began to drift away, I stood staring at the dirt till I felt Alyeeta shaking me. She must have been watching from her doorway, waiting till Pell was finished. Telakeet must have been in the shelter, too. She spit in front of me as she walked by, but Alyeeta opened her arms, pulled me against her, and hugged me tight. "Oh, child, I never thought to see you alive in this world again," she said with her lips against my hair. "You are an uncommon lot of trouble, I must say, but you have taught this old heart to love again, a thing I thought could never happen, so you must be worth something after all."

"Oh, Alyeeta, I am so sorry for those dreadful words I spoke to you that night. It was like a madness ... What can I say? What can I do? How can I make it right again? Will you ever...?"

"You can begin by being quiet about it. After that we will think of some other suitable punishment."

"Alyeeta, I will never, never speak to you that way again."

"Take care what you say, child. There is a lot of living to be done between us before we are finished with each other. Let us not make any rash promises, eh? Besides, my tongue is not always so kind."

"Alyeeta, I promise you."

"Peace! The promise is in the living, not the words." Alyeeta drew me into her shelter and soon had me out of my clothes and lying on her bed while she rubbed some healing salve on my cuts and bruises and caressed me tenderly. At some point she leaned forward and said fiercely in my ear, "No matter what that one may say, I am very glad to have you back. Now I can sleep the night through again."

Very slowly at first, and very gently, she began loving me with her hands as she rubbed me with oil. Soon my aching body forgot its pains and melted open under her touch till I moaned and shuddered with pleasure. I slept in her embrace that night. Later I woke in the dark to hear myself sobbing loudly like a child and felt her arms fold around me.

When I went out the next morning into the confusion of the camp, I was dreading the encounter with the others. With luck, the first person my eyes lit on was Kazouri. Somehow her great bulk seemed reassuring, almost comforting. She was examining my long-legged, clumsy horse, walking round and round, patting his thick neck and heavy rump. Much to my surprise he was rubbing his head against her arm with what appeared to be affection. I was relieved when she turned to give me her big open grin.

"Tell me, Tazzi, how did you come by this fine beast?" she shouted at me in her friendly way. "Surely you did not earn him with all your wickedness." That was exactly what I thought, but I believe she meant it quite differently.

When I came close that brute lowered his ears and snaked his head around. I stepped back in haste. Kazouri laughed and gave him a cuff on the neck. Keeping my distance, I described my ride back on the creature.

"So, you are less than pleased with him. Do I have your leave then to try him out?" she asked eagerly.

"Try him out if you want and do whatever else you please with him. You can leave him on the Bargguell for all I care."

She swung herself up with no effort. Suddenly the stubborn plod of yesterday turned into a new creature. Arching his neck and tail, he trotted off at a nice pace while Kazouri sat very tall and upright on him. In a few minutes she came back with her eyes glowing and her face flushed with pleasure. The horse's neck was damp with sweat. He was tossing his head as if impatient to keep going. She was smiling down at me from her high place on his back.

"What a fine fellow," she said, petting his neck. "A horse built to carry me. That is rare enough. Besides that, we have such good mind-touch. What can I trade you for him? From what you say you will not miss him much. I know you have lost Marshlegs. I also lost my horse in Eezore and was given a nervous little thing in her place. She is too light for me but perhaps you would accept her in trade."

"Anything would be better for me than this bone-crusher."

"Crusher, eh, not a bad name." She leapt from his back and tossed me the reins while she went off to fetch the other one. Crusher snorted, pulling and tugging to follow after her.

When Kazouri came back my heart leaped at the sight of the sleek little black mare who tossed her head and danced sideways at the end of the reins. This was no farm pony, this was a high-bred horse, probably raised for some rich Shokarn lady. I reached out to touch her. As she lipped my hand and blew through her nostrils, I could feel my mind slip comfortably into hers.

"I am afraid she is not worth much," Kazouri said apologetically, "too nervous and high-strung for our use."

"No matter, 'Crusher' is yours. Clearly he was meant to be. I will have this one or some other, it matters little." Even as I said these words my heart was pounding. My hands trembled with eagerness to be on her back. The minute I was mounted, I was hooked like a fish on a line. This little horse fit between my legs as if we had come together into the world that way. She slipped in behind my heart and notched herself into my spirit like my double-self. Marshlegs had been loving and loyal and steady, but this horse was like my twin, our spirits matching each other and meshing together. Eager to go, she shifted about under me, tugging at the rein in Kazouri's hand.

Kazouri shook her head and looked at the horse with disapproval, saying, "She should be called Nervous Dancer. She has not the wits to stay still. I am afraid this is not much of a trade, Tazzi."

"Stop muttering, Kazouri, and give me the reins," I said impatiently.

As we started off I leaned forward to lay my cheek for a moment against the warm silk of her arched neck. "Dancer," I whispered to her, "my Dancer." When I looked up again I saw Rishka watching me with admiration on her face.

I could not give the horse her head in that crowded clearing, but I danced twice around Alyeeta's shelter, conscious of her smiling at her entryway. I was soaring with pleasure as from a good loving until I caught Pell's angry and reproachful eye. Quickly I rode back to Kazouri. "Take her back. I do not deserve her," I mumbled with my eyes cast down and my voice full of pain.

"Nonsense," Kazouri said in her rough, kind way. "You may be a fool, but you still need a horse to ride. Better for all of us if it is one that suits you. Anyhow, someone must ride this nervous fool. It surely will not be me, not if I can help it. Besides, I have already decided you cannot have

Crusher back. You do not deserve him." So, in that way, the horse question was settled.

I spent the rest of the day by the cookfire, trying to keep out of sight and out of the way, helping Thalyisi there and following her commands. This freed Renaise to go about that disaster of a camp making order. As we worked, Thalyisi told me the gossip of the camp, what the new ones were like and who had found new lovers and who was quarrelling with whom. I had been surprised to see Maireth there, thinking she would be at Pell's shelter instead. Thalyisi told me she had come in for supplies and been appointed a reluctant second-in-command in my absence.

While we chopped food and hauled wood and stirred pots, I occasionally heard Renaise's voice over the general uproar. "Is this how you live in your fancy houses? You are worse than pigs in spite of your finery! Or do you think one of us will be your maid and pick up after you? Not likely! Clear all that garbage away or I will add it to the cookfire! Now! Fast! Move!"

Thalyisi laughed and said with some malice in her voice, "The fancy ones of Eezore are not used to this sort of living. They have much to learn."

"And Renaise is out there teaching them," I said with a companionable laugh. Perhaps it soothed my pain to hear someone else being scolded.

While I was scrubbing some potatoes, daydreaming of running Dancer through a field of spring grass with her mane whipping in the wind, a sudden loud commotion broke out near Alyeeta's shelter and caught my attention. A dark, skinny woman was yelling at Pell, her arms flailing like sticks in front of Pell's face.

"What took you so long to get your fancy ass into the city? We had been living in sewers like rats, starving there, waiting and waiting for some help or some hope while you were camping here at your ease under the trees."

"Who is that?" I asked Thalyisi in shocked amazement.

"Murghanth," she hissed back, her voice full of loathing, "one of the Sheezerti, the sewer-rats they brought back from Eezore. I think they should have left her there to rot. Her mouth is as filthy as the sewer she crawled out of, nothing but trouble, that one. She has made an uproar in the camp ever since she came. The one in back of her is Teko, another one of that worthless scum." With a lurch, I remembered saying the same thing of Rishka, "Nothing but trouble, that one."

Pell must have been answering quietly, for soon Murghanth burst out again, "Did you forget you had sisters in the city? Did you think the Star-Born were only birthed in stables in the country? What did you imagine would happen to us all behind those sealed gates? Were you waiting for us to die in their fires?"

From behind her, the woman named Teko said in a loud, strong voice, "Enough, Murghanth, they risked their lives to get us out. We are free. Let that be an end to it." She put a hand on Murghanth's arm, but that one shook her off, shouting again, "Lies, lies, it is not us, the sewer-rats, they came for. They came to free the fine ladies from the Great-Houses. Us they would have left to die."

With no thought I found myself running up from the fire. "Stop that!" I shouted at Murghanth, jumping between her and Pell. "You have no right to speak that way of Pell. She is the one who dragged us all to Eezore to free you. Yell at the rest of us for our reluctance, if you want, but not at Pell. She has given her whole life to saving the Star-Born, gives it again and again. She had been plotting and planning night and day to get into the city, but could not find a way past the gates till Askarth came to show us the tunnel."

"Askarth, yes, she wanted to rescue her pampered babies. And why do you speak up for Pell when she treats you no better than a dog?"

"It is no worse than I deserve," I shouted back. "You know nothing of what happened and it is no business of yours."

"And this is no business of yours, Tazzi," Pell said firmly, putting a hand on my shoulder and pushing me aside. "Leave be, girl, I can speak for myself. Maybe she needs to say these things and have them heard so she can have room for something else in her head. It is for me to defend myself. Go look to the cookfire before it goes out. Renaise is busy elsewhere." These were the first words Pell had spoken to me since I came back, and though they were rough and careless, still they made my heart leap with hope.

As I stepped back I saw Kazouri come striding in, looking like a fire mountain about to explode. She walked straight up to Murghanth as if she planned to pick her up and shake her. Instead, she stopped right in front, looming over her and bellowing, "Pell is chosen leader here. If that does not sit well with you, woman, go find your safety elsewhere. If you are to stay here you must keep the peace of this camp." By now many women were gathering around to watch. The dozen or so ranged behind Murghanth and Teko I thought to be more of these sewer-rats, these Sheezerti.

Not at all intimidated by Kazouri, Murghanth snarled at her, "If you are such a power here, then why are you not the leader instead of that one?" Those last words were said with a contemptuous toss of her head in Pell's direction.

More quietly Kazouri said, "I have my own kind of power, Murghanth, but Pell has the brains here. She has been weaving this network for years, weaving it since long before the Zarn's edict, long before the rest of us saw what was coming. If you cannot accept that, then you do not need to be here."

In spite of her usual good nature, no one in camp would have thought of antagonizing Kazouri. Not even Rishka was so foolhardy, but Murghanth shouted back right into her face, "So now Pell has brought in her bully boy to defend her and do her dirty work. I say she left us to rot until the fine ladies of Eezore needed her."

Kazouri gave a roar of rage and lunged forward as if to kill. At the same moment I saw Alyeeta step out of her doorway with a look on her face that froze my blood. She shouted, "Silence!" so loud the whole camp must surely have heard her. Then she raised her terrible pointing finger. I wanted to call out, no, Alyeeta, no, please, but the words would not come. Swinging her hand so that she pointed in turn to each of us in that circle around Pell and Murghanth, she said some strange words that made me shudder and made some ritual gestures. Then in a loud, clear, angry voice she added, "I have listened long enough to this dog pack, snapping and snarling outside my home. If I had the power, I would silence you all for a day, longer even. But I must save my strength for Shalamith, who lies ill and wasting because of what she did for your sakes. Soon you will be able to speak again. Be careful how you use that gift when it comes back to you." With those words she spun around and vanished into her shelter.

We all stood staring at each other, open-mouthed and speechless. Kazouri was frozen with her hands raised as if ready to bring them down around Murghanth's throat. There was a circle of absolute silence at the very center, though at the far edges of the clearing I could still hear the murmur of voices.

As soon as our own voices came back and we could speak again, Pell said quietly to Murghanth, "I think there are some things we need to talk about and settle between us, but not here. Teko should come, too. Perhaps she can help us find a way to hear each other."

I was trembling inside, my teeth clenched with fear, but Pell sounded as calm as if some small annoyance had just past.

Murghanth's face had changed. There were beads of sweat on her forehead and across her upper lip. Her eyes were wide and her voice shook as she tried to control her fear. "Then let Kazouri come, too," she said in a hoarse whisper.

There was a general movement in that circle of women who had gathered to watch, as if they planned to follow. Pell said quickly, "The rest of you go back to your duties. Thank you all, but we do not need your help." I stood and watched as the four of them went off together through the camp in the direction of the stream. The other women were also staring after them.

After that I went back to the fire to sit by Renaise, who had returned and was finishing my work with the potatoes. She looked up at me with a grin. "Well, you certainly rushed off at top speed to mix into that mess. You would have been better off sitting here with these potatoes. They cause much less trouble than those city women. I wonder if your friend Alyeeta could silence guards that well with her little spell."

Shaking my head, I sat down beside her and let out a great sigh. "If I live to be as old as Hamiuri I will never understand her."

"Who?" Renaise asked me. "Alyeeta?"

"No," I said, "Pell."

"Oh, Pell," she said with a shrug. "Alyeeta I will never understand, not if I live to be twice Hamiuri's age. But Pell, with Pell it is easy enough. She may be proud and bristly and all the rest of that, but in the end she will do whatever she thinks best for the Star-Born, no matter what the cost to herself. In that she has no pride at all. It is that easy to understand." She sat staring into the fire for a while, then added suddenly, "And no matter the cost to any single one of us either, as we both know."

Later, while I was helping serve out the evening meal, Alyeeta came looking for me. "Shalamith is asking for you, Tazzi. She is in much need of healing and calls your name. Will you come back with me?"

"I am needed here," I said quickly, looking down so as not to meet her eye. I could feel myself shrinking away from those loved hands that just the night before had brought me so much pleasure.

"Go," Renaise said quickly. "It is for Shalamith, who has risked so much for us. Surely she deserves whatever we can give her. I can easily enough find someone else to dish out potatoes." I got up reluctantly. As I walked away with Alyeeta, I could already hear Renaise calling out for someone to come and take my place.

Though it ate at me, I did not ask Alyeeta what ailed Shalamith. We walked in silence. I was locked in the confusion of my feelings for Alyeeta, fear and wariness so at war in me with love and trust that I could not speak at all until Alyeeta said, "I did them no harm, Tazzi. After all, I am a Witch. It is hard never to use my powers, especially when the temptation is so great. And look, there has been peace here for a little while. They can band together now that they have me to be afraid of."

I looked around me. What she said was true enough, at least for that moment. I could see Pell conversing earnestly with Murghanth, Teko, and two or three of the other 'sewer-rats' on the far side of the fire pit. None of them were even raising their voices. Kazouri had Crusher out by the edge of the clearing. She was humming loudly and brushing him with long, vigorous strokes while he tried to rub his head against her. A new shelter was being set up under the trees with several of the Star-Born working together. Women were beginning to line up for the evening meal. Far off, someone was playing a ferl. Someone else played a flute in a way that made my heart ache with memory. I nodded and looked up to meet Alyeeta's eyes. I was not prepared for the hurt I saw there. "Please take me to Shalamith," I said softly. Then with a sudden quick gesture I took her hand and kissed it.

We went to a stump chamber at the far end of the shelter. The light there was dim. When Alyeeta lit a small lamp I had to cover my mouth to keep myself from crying out. Who was this old woman, lying there with gray hair and skin so white it looked transparent? It was not white like Shokarn skin, but white as bleached cloth, white as if all her blood had been sucked away. Her eyes were deeply sunk into their sockets, with a circle of dark purple shadows around them. At first it seemed as if she gazed into some immeasurable inner distance and was lost to us there. Then she turned her gaze on me and I knew she saw me very clearly. I had never looked into her eyes before. It had not been possible when she shimmered with glamour even to look full into her face. What I saw in her eyes frightened me. I covered her old, frail hand with mine. "Oh, Shalamith, what have you done to yourself for our sakes?"

"Emptied the well, girl," she said hoarsely, but still with some of the old, sweet music in her voice. "Will you help me fill it up again? It may take a while. I need the touch of your healing hands."

Something moved in the dark corner. I heard Telakeet say with malice, "They are not worth one hair on your head, Sweet One, none of them, especially this one. I warned you it was dangerous to throw all your force that way against a sealed gate." Telakeet came over to glower at me as if I were the one at fault in this.

"So you did," Shalamith said, and for just a moment I thought I heard her musical laugh and saw the slightest tinge of color on her cheek. Telakeet picked up her toad and went out, brushing against me roughly as she passed.

"Shalamith," I said, bending close so she could hear me with no strain, "I will do whatever I can for you, whatever you want or need, but I have killed twice with these hands. I do not know if you want them on you. I am not sure there is any healing left in them."

"Here, come sit by me." She put one pale hand on my arm and the cold of it bit right through to my bones. "I have probably killed also by opening those gates, or at least made death possible that night. None of us is innocent. I welcome your hands on me. I have no fear of them. Put one here on my forehead and the other on my heart."

I sat with my hands on her for a long while, sat with no sense of time and no thought but the sending out of warmth and life, or actually no thought at all. Finally Alyeeta pressed her hand on my shoulder, startling me back to myself. "Enough, girl. Any more and you will drain yourself too much. Then you will be of no use to anyone. Telakeet will sit with her now." I stood up obediently, but it was very hard for me to leave her.

Alyeeta and I walked back to the stump that was her bedchamber through a shelter already crowded with sleepers. As we were sitting on her bed undressing, I remembered my reluctance to come with her that day. "Oh, Alyeeta, when will I understand that I will love you no matter what you do?"

"Not so, Tazzi," she spoke quickly, almost with anger, or perhaps with fear. "There are things one should not be loved past, things that are not forgivable. I have seen enough of them in this life. Goddess grant that I have done no such things and never will, but if I do, then I do not deserve your love or any other. You must not go on loving me then, remember that, and you yourself must be the judge of that moment."

I was so startled by her reply, I felt as if I had lost my balance and was falling. It took me a moment or so to steady myself. Then I grinned at her suddenly. "Do I never, ever say the right thing, Alyeeta?"

"Yes, of course, you often say the right thing. It is only that each time I have to add my own one more thing to it. My bad habit, no fault of yours. Now get under the covers and I will bring you some tea to help restore your strength and give you a good night's rest."

When she came back, I sat with the cup nestled in my hands. "How is it that Shalamith is ill and you are not, when you both opened the gate?" I asked her.

Alyeeta shook her head. "I did not open the gate, child. It is Shalamith who did the work. I was the anchor, the holder, the safe steady place, the rock. She was the one who went out and out and out into the realm of risk. It is not the rock that wearies itself but the bird that flies against the storm."

After that, no matter what else my duties were, I went to sit with Shalamith for a part of every day. Often Telakeet was there. She would try to drive me off with some insulting, bitter words. I knew she was jealous of my closeness with Alyeeta, and now there was another for her to be jealous of. But if Shalamith wanted me there I would not let myself be dislodged.

It was the most peaceful part of my day. I poured out into her whatever I had left of healing, since she seemed so willing to accept it. When I went away I was drained, but also strangely filled. Little by little, some of her golden color began to come back. Her hair was no longer gray but a pale shade of yellow, so that I began to wonder if that gray had been real or only some trick of the light. The golden glow was even returning to her skin. Her hands were warmer now. She looked younger. There was music in her voice again and a tinge of pink in her cheeks. One day when I came in, she drew me forward and kissed me lightly on the lips, saying, "Little Tazzi, you see, you are a better healer than you thought. Just look how well you have done with me." She looked almost like her old self again.

I blushed to the roots of my hair. The heat of that kiss rushed down through my body and lodged between my legs. That night I asked Alyeeta, "Are you never jealous of Shalamith?"

"Jealous?" She sounded puzzled. "Child, she is my comrade, the sister of my heart. We have been through things together you could not even begin to imagine. I wish her whatever happiness she can find in this life. I can no more be jealous of Shalamith than my right hand can be jealous of my left." As she said those words, I myself felt some jealousy. I saw that under the banter the Witches had with each other, there lay a depth of feeling I could not share and did not begin to understand.

★

21

I need to make some accounting of the raid and this, I suppose, is as good a time as any, an accounting of what we lost and what we gained on that one wild night in Eezore. First off, in terms of loss, Irdris did not come back. Even now it is very hard for me to write that down and see those words before me on the paper. She was missing, as were four or five others I scarcely knew. I was likely the last of us to have seen her. Also there was Askarth's death sitting so heavy on me that I had not yet spoken of it, could not bring myself to speak of it, though I knew I must do so soon. These were small losses for a raid of such size against such odds. A trained fighting man, a commander of the guards, hardened to death, would no doubt have been very proud to have come away with so little lost, weighed against so much risked. How easily we could all have been lost in that city, swallowed up by Eezore like so many minnows sucked into the maw of a gramorghi fish. We should think ourselves lucky to have gotten off so lightly. But I kept hearing Irdris's last words in my head, seeing her slipping away into the night, remembering again how I had wanted to warn her not to go, when, in fact, she was already gone.

For the first day or so — before I knew — I thought I saw her with each new blond head that appeared. I would be about to call out her name eagerly when that woman would turn toward me or come closer and I would see a Shokarn stranger in her place.

On my second night back, while we were all eating together, I leaned toward Maireth. Speaking low, almost in a whisper, I asked, "Where is Irdris? Why is she not here among us?" After Pell's public rebuke, I was very shy of bringing any notice on myself.

Maireth turned and looked at me with pity in her eyes. "You did not know? You were not told?" She shook her head. "No one has seen her since the raid. None of the watchers saw her come out through the gates. She has not been reported in any of the other camps. We think she may have died in Eezore, though one can still hope..."

Maireth also spoke very low, but Ashai on the other side of her must have heard her words, for instantly she began wailing in her strangely accented Kourmairi, "Gone, gone, gone. You took her back into the city to die. I told her not to go. I told her ... I told her ... I told her..."

Maireth turned to her to say, "Ashai, no one forced her. She herself asked to go back, she even insisted on it, saying there was something she must do there."

Ashai was not listening. She had jumped up, knocking over her bowl. With a cry she ran off into the darkness, her words, "Gone, gone, gone," echoing back at us.

I did not cry or shout. I sat there with a terrible, cold weight on my chest. How was I to believe this? *Gone! Irdris gone!* Irdris no longer in this world? Kind, loving, gentle Irdris. I sometimes thought she was the very best of us. So Eezore had gotten her after all. I sat there remembering again how I had wanted to warn her not to go. But would it have mattered anyhow? Would she have listened to me? I had begged Askarth to stay with us and now I could not even speak of the manner of her death.

As to Askarth, every time I saw Nunyair it was a torture to me. I would do my best to shield while she asked me persistently, "But where is Askarth? Tazzi, what do you think delays her so? She promised she would be here with us." It was true that camp life was hard for Nunyair, harder perhaps than for the rest of us, but I could give her no comfort. All I could give her was my silence or my terrible truth. Sometimes, sleeping with Alyeeta, I would wake with a sudden cry and she would reach to comfort me. I did not tell her what woke me, but surely she must have seen it in my mind.

Enough of losses now. Better to speak of our gains, much better. No matter how much I mourned Irdris and Askarth, and grieved for those others who had not returned, I knew that on any reasonable scale our gains by far outweighed our losses. By springing open the gates of Eezore, we had freed more than two hundred Star-Born that we knew of. And who knows how many more were still out there wandering in search of us. Every day we sent out patrols to look for them. The stragglers were still coming in.

Of those we could account for, we had gathered thirty or more 'sewer-rats,' or Sheezerti, as they called themselves, those who were not slaves, but had no caste or class and lived by their wits, mostly on the streets. Over fifty of 'the Circle' had been freed, young women who wore pendants like the one Maireth had given me. They were mostly daughters of the middle castes, artisans and tradespeople, Star-Born who had long been aware of their powers and had worked together training them in secret, waiting for this time to come. Also, at least eighty or more had escaped from the Great-Houses, Star-Born of all castes and classes from very white-skinned Shokarn Uppercaste like Nunyair to Kourmairi slaves and servants as dark or darker than myself. Added to that, we had a scattering of those who had been saved and hidden from the guard by their families, as well as a few Wanderers, some Potters, and several Muin-yairin who had been trapped in the city by the sealing of the gates. We even had eight or ten young women from the Thieves Guild who seemed to know Pell, or at least knew her name and regarded her as their bandit chief. And six or seven new burned ones were being cared for in Pell's shelter by Arnella and other healers, which, of course, was where Maireth wanted to be rather than in camp, playing at being second-in-command. All in all, as I said, more than two hundred, perhaps as many as three, safely out of Eezore though they were not all there with us. Many had gone on already to other gatherings north or south of us or to Yaniri's, the new camp to the west.

In addition to all this, I should speak of the horses. Though we had lost eight or nine of our own, each horse some woman's loved companion, as Marshlegs had been mine, yet we had gained a far greater number from Eezore that night. Zenoria said we had near doubled our number. Rishka alone had ridden out with at least thirty. Many more had poured out of the city that night and followed us up into the hills. We were still gathering in some that had been wandering loose. Zenoria and her horsewomen had all they could do caring for them and finding pastureland. Besides that, we had gathered jewels, gold, and other valuables — such things as each woman had been able to come away with. "Not bad for one night's work," as Pell kept saying, rubbing her hands together. The master thief was in her glory.

Balanced on the other side was the pressing need for food, for clothing, for bedding, for dishes and pots and pans, for pastureland and food for the horses, for space, for time, for silence, for everything! Goddess knows, I should have been thankful it was done and over with and we were safely back, most of us, that is, but it surely left a great swirl of confusion, especially for those who had the running of the camp to deal with.

And the stories! The stories and stories and stories that I heard at that time, more stories than I could possibly remember. Each of us had our own story of that night. Each new woman was a story in herself, how she had survived in the city and how she had escaped, all as worthy of setting down on paper as anything I am writing here. And there were many terrible, heart-crushing stories, too, of burnings and of women traps — ingenious and inventive ways to take our lives in spite of our powers.

I heard several times how Pell had gone over the Great-House wall on a wildly swinging rope ladder to rescue Dorcaneesi and the rest of the women from that house, while others made a commotion in the street to distract the guard. I had to tell many times of Rishka's wild ride, and it became wilder with each telling. I even heard my own story, the tale of my encounter with the soldiers at Hamiuri's shelter, told first by Hamiuri and then by others. Often Hamiuri would be so overcome with laughter she could not finish. Though she said scathing things to me directly, she bragged of me to others, saying that there must have been near a hundred men in her clearing and that I had driven them off single-handed with the use of her three aged snakes. "Those poor, old creatures that have not a tooth left to bite with among the lot of them," she would say, holding up the snakes for show. Soon it was two hundred men or more. She particularly liked telling this when Pell was among the listeners.

As to Eezore itself, a few days after my return Hereschell rode in to bring us news of the city. This time he came announced and escorted by a sentry. I could sense Soneeshi in the woods. Occasionally, I caught a glimpse of gray through the trees, but she did not venture into the clearing with so many.

When Hereschell sat down to eat with us that night, some of the new women were gaping openly at him and whispering behind their hands. In spite of this, he did not play dumb or play the fool that night. Rather, he talked freely and seemed in a rare jovial mood, carrying on a lively banter with Alyeeta, who sat opposite him. At some point, he raised his mug in salute to Pell. "Well, friend of thieves and chief of the star-brats, who would have believed it! You really did it! You went with sixty women and cracked open the Zarn's city like a nutshell. Eezore is still picking itself up. It was all in chaos after you left. Whatever Shalamith did to those gates, it took three days to close them again. People poured out like water. Many will not go back, slaves, guards, even some Highborn. There were many new Wanderers made that night. If the Zarn presses too hard, there will be many more. And as to the Thieves Guild, the thieves had themselves a fine holiday while all of Eezore was running about the streets. Now the Zarn and the Great-Houses are struggling to make peace, as neither feels strong enough to conquer the other. Besides, I hear that what they each sought to hold has slipped through their fingers like water. But take care, if they make their bargains — and I think they will — then they may well come after you with redoubled fury. You still have a while of safety, but do not wait too long."

I was just wondering if Merrik had been killed or spared or maybe praised for his work that night, when Hereschell turned to me. "And no, Tazzi, Eezore did not burn down that night, not even close to it, though it took a while for all the fires to be put out. It is the thatched huts of the poor folk that catch on fire easily, not the great stone houses of the rich and powerful. It will take a lot more than that to bring Eezore down. You were a fool to stay and watch."

I blushed and ducked my head. "Please, Hereschell," I mumbled, "I already know that, and so do all the rest of us."

"Ah, well, we are all fools when we are young. How else would we make the mistakes we need to learn from to get wise when we are older? Better to be a young fool than an old fool any day." Then he turned back to the rest of the table and raised his mug again. "To Shalamith, the Shining Lady, who opened the sealed gate of Eezore." We all raised our mugs with shouts and cheers.

Then Lhiri said, "To Askarth, who guided you there." We all raised our mugs again with another shout. I had to force myself to keep my hand steady.

"Where is Askarth?" Hereschell asked, looking around. "Did she not come back with you?"

"No, she has deserted us," Nunyair said in her aggrieved way. "When we were escaping she stayed in my father's house. Surely there was time enough to get through the gate. You said it took three days to close it. Why did she abandon us this way? Why did she leave me like this when she made a promise. She is no better than..."

Her unfair accusation made me so angry I burst out, "She did not keep her promise to you for the only reason she, Askarth, would not keep a promise. She is no longer here to keep it." The words had sprung out before I could stop myself.

"What?!" Nunyair shouted, turning on me. "What are you saying?"

"Askarth is dead," I said in a hard, flat tone. The words had finally been spoken.

"What do you mean?" she screamed. "What do you know? You were with us when we left. How could you possibly know that? I do not believe you. I think you hate me. You are lying for your own spiteful reasons."

I held out my hands, palms up. "Please, Nunyair, this is hard enough. Do not make it worse. It is true I do not like you much, but I have no reason to lie to you, least of all about this. Besides, I could not lie to you even if I wished to, for you could read me easily enough. I went back to help the others from the Great-House, that is how I know."

"How was she killed? Tell me that. Then I may believe you."

"No," I shouted desperately, but not before the sight of Askarth's flaming fall leapt into my mind unshielded.

With a cry, Nunyair slumped forward. Lhiri howled in pain and put her arms up over her head. At Pell's insistence, I told in words all I had seen. "From her own house," Pell said bitterly when I finished. "She was shot from her own house."

We were all too shaken to go on eating. I put my arms on the table and my head down in my arms to cry. Suddenly I felt hands on my shoulders. I looked up through my tears to see Pell behind me. She bent forward and said softly in my ear, "I cannot forgive you for what you did that night after the raid, Tazzi. Some things are not forgivable, but perhaps we can put all that behind us now. Life is too short, our lives are too much at risk..." She left the rest unsaid. At least she would be speaking to me now.

A few days later Shalamith herself joined us at dinner, stepping slowly and carefully out of Alyeeta's shelter. A cheer went up. Someone ran to get her a chair and cushion from the shelter, as the rest of us were sitting on logs or stumps or on the ground. Someone else brought her a plate of food, bread, cheese, quillof. She did not eat much. She did not stay among us long. But much of her golden glow had come back. The sound of her voice was music in my blood.

★

Alyeeta tells me to write and keep writing, to tell it all. Easy enough for her to say. She is not the one struggling with this. How am I to tell of life in the camp for that next two weeks or so. With the best of wills, I can only write one thing at a time. But that is not how it happened. Everything there was happening all at once, everything everywhere and all the time. It was as if someone had set a giant pot on to boil and stuffed the fire under it with logs. And, of course, no matter what else was going on, women still had to be taught to ride, bodies still had to be trained and hardened with exercise, especially all those new ones from the city, the sick still had to be cared for, and all of us had to be fed.

As could have been expected, the peace of Alyeeta's silencing did not last long in all that. At least Murghanth was not the one who broke it, I will say that for her. A few days after her quarrel with Pell, I had gone to the far edge of the clearing, heartsore over Irdris and wanting to be alone. I had taken Jhemar's long, sharp-bladed troga with me to start clearing and cutting brush for some new shelters, grateful for the hot, heavy work that left me sweating and panting and mindless for the moment. When I felt a presence at my shoulder I turned, in no mood for talk. To my surprise Murghanth was standing there. From the closed and clouded look on her face I expected some angry words leftover from that quarrel. Instead, she said quickly, "If you want, I will pull the brush away while you cut. It may go easier that way." I also heard her say, /I have never been out of the city, never in my life. These things they do so easily I have never done before. Will I ever be able to learn? Is it safe to offer my help here? Will she laugh in my face? Will she think me a useless fool?/ Her lips were not moving, but with disturbing clarity I was hearing her thoughts.

I nodded and quickly gave her a reassuring smile, the best I could manage. "Thank you, Murghanth. This work was growing wearisome." I could feel her rush of relief all through my body. We worked for a long while in companionable silence, broken only by a few brief questions or an occasional instruction. By the time the meal bell rang, the shelter was already beginning to take shape.

Would that all the differences among us were so easily settled. Not so! Before, we Star-Born had been mostly Kourmairi and more often than not, born of farm-folk. Now we were all jumbled in together, Kourmairi and Shokarn and Muinyairin, Wanderer and Potter and thief, Uppercaste and Sheezerti and slave, child of city and town and dirt-farm and dry-lands. Often we were not even able to share words with each other. We found ourselves suspicious of the differences. It seemed as if we had brought all the men's old wars with us to fight out on each other. The pot on the fire boiled over many, many times, though never again right in front of Alyeeta's doorway. That much at least we had learned. There was not a woman in the camp who had missed that lesson.

One morning, wearied by all the wrangling and confusion, I retreated to Alyeeta's shelter in search of some peace, only to meet Alyeeta herself glowering just inside the doorway. "Star-brats," she was muttering to herself, "they seem more like star-trash to me, not one clear space anywhere, not one moment of silence..."

I had often wondered if Alyeeta regretted sheltering us there. Stung by her tone, I was foolish enough to ask, "Alyeeta, why did you choose to take up with us if you think us so worthless?"

She whirled on me as if she had just noticed my presence there. "Choose?!" she burst out. "Do you think it was my choice?" She rushed on, with her voice rising and getting louder with each word, "You think if I had my way I would have chosen to play wet nurse to this mis-matched litter of quarrelsome puppies? It might be easier to teach the spider to unspin her web or the eagle to come to earth and burrow in the ground like a mole than to bring this lot of rubbish through to woman-hood and freedom. Sometimes the Goddess decides for us and that is all the choice we have." I backed out quickly. The camp did not seem so bad after all.

To add to all this, Maireth had no wish to be second-in-command there. Her heart was elsewhere. She wanted to be in Pell's old shelter caring for her 'burned ones,' or if that was not possible, then doing her healing there among us. Every day in the camp was a torture for her. She was not good at solving quarrels or passing on commands. Her skills lay elsewhere. After a while, without our even speaking of it, we worked out our own little ruse. Pell would give Maireth a command, and she would pass it on to me. Or if a disturbance broke out, she would 'order' me to go and deal with it. In this way she went back to doing her chosen work while I resumed being second-in-command, in fact if not in name. Pell surely must have noticed this arrangement, though if she did she kept her silence on it.

Soon I became so busy I had little time for myself. By not returning from Eezore with the others, I had lost my place in a shelter. Now I had no time to bother re-establishing one. It was easier to sleep in Alyeeta's shelter. After a few days of that, Rishka came to claim me for some nights of passion. Then I drifted back to Alyeeta's space until Rishka came to look for me again. In this way I went back and forth between them as I had between Alyeeta and Pell. I had no fixed place of my own, but the days were so harried and crowded, it mattered little to me where I dropped my body down at night.

As Pell was often away, either on the road or at one of the other gatherings, it was actually Renaise and myself who saw to the daily running of the camp. Sometimes we joked with each other as to which of us had the hardest job of it. We both, in our own way, kept order there. Each, at moments, must have thought the other had the easier task. It was hard to remember Renaise as she had once been, the timid serving-girl looking up to Pell with dog-eyes of devotion. Though she still shared Pell's bed, I had seen her stand up to Pell in arguments and even win. Barrenaise the serving-girl had turned into Renaise, a commander in her own right, and sometimes she chose interesting ways to do her work.

I was down by the stream one morning when I heard such an uproar I thought surely the camp must have been raided. I ran up breathlessly, to find Renaise and Kazouri in the center of a circle of angry women. There were stacks of belongings piled up in the clearing. Kazouri appeared to be standing guard over them. Renaise was up on the stump from which Pell had made her speech. With Kazouri translating into Shokarn, she was shouting, "Next time I am going to confiscate everything that does not fit in a woman's pack or sack and is not being kept there, everything but her bedroll. We are going to have a clean camp and be ready to ride out of here at a moment's notice. What if the Zarn's guards came riding down on us and you had to leave fast, how would you do it? You would all be running around like fools, tripping on your own litter. If you have so many belongings or so little use for them that they are left lying about, perhaps they should belong to another. Listen closely now, you have a choice: pack it up, give it away, burn it, or bury it. Do not leave it out! Tomorrow morning I am going to inspect with Kazouri's help. Goddess save you if I find anything of yours. We will make a bonfire with it and you will be peeling potatoes for the next four days!"

There were roars of protest, especially from the Shokarn, but Kazouri bellowed even louder, "We are not arguing today! Today we are cleaning up this pigsty of a camp! Nothing left out, is that understood? NOTHING!"

"Now pick up your things," Renaise called out. She clapped her hands, Kazouri stepped out of the way, and there was a mad scramble. As clothes went flying, I saw my second tunic on the pile, the one I had left by the cookfire that day. I found myself having to dive in hastily with the others. Pell had been standing off to the side watching the scene with a grin. Now she was clapping wildly. "Good work!" she shouted to Renaise. "A much better speech than mine, Sister. Look how you inspired them all to instant action." After that, in fear of Renaise's morning raids, the camp had some order to it.

It had been an interesting show, but there was little of use for me in it. Much as I might want to, I could not very well put women's ill will and hurt feelings in piles and demand that they stuff them all back into their packs and sacks or go and bury them. Day after day, I had to talk and listen and try to sort out their troubles one more time. In the long run, most of them would pay heed to my words and do what I said, all but Rishka, of course. Rishka was the only one who would not listen to me. We were too close, our own quarrel was too deep, too much of pride and pain and anger was still tangled there. And she, of course, quarreled with almost everyone, but most especially with the Shokarn. From some perversity, however, she favored Nunyair with her friendship, perhaps because they had escaped from Eezore together, or perhaps because they had such a similarity of character. For the rest of the Shokarn, she made life more difficult in whatever way she could. In particular she singled out Dorcaneesi, who seemed the most sensitive and frightened of them.

I once came on Dorca right after one of Rishka's attacks. She was alone, looking bewildered and close to tears. When she saw me she almost threw herself in my arms.

"Oh, Tazzi, she hates me so. What am I to do?"

I put an arm over her shoulder to guide her to some more private place under the trees. "Nothing, there is nothing to do. It will pass," I assured her. "It is not just you, Dorca. Believe me, she hates all the Shokarn."

"But it is not my fault. I did not make the world as it is, with Shokarn and Muinyairin and Kourmairi set apart as enemies. Nor would I have chosen to. This rift is not of my doing."

I knew that was all true, yet seeing her fine clothes, I myself felt a sudden sting of envy for the comfortable life she had led up till now, the fine house, the food, the safety. Then I thought, what did it all matter now? The edict made no distinction between us. Her fine clothes would soon be tattered, not being as practical for this life as our rough wear. She would have to trade them for something better suited to the road. As for her soft life, her hands and feet would soon be blistered. Camp life was harder for her than it could ever be for me. "Listen, Dorca, it is not anyone's doing," I said as kindly as I could, "but men's old wars have left some bitterness among us that is not yet settled. If you can stay strong at the center and not care so much what she says or thinks, the game will stop giving her pleasure. Then most likely it will end altogether."

"But why would anyone get pleasure from another's pain?"

"Because she has had more pain of her own than she knows how to carry," I answered with sudden sharpness.

"I see," Dorca said, abruptly pulling away from me and drawing herself up very straight. "I will not bother you with this again."

"Dorca," I said helplessly, "please, I am doing the best I can. If all the pain contained in this clearing were water, we would surely drown." I wished she could have used some of that famous Shokarn arrogance on Rishka. It would certainly have worked better than any plea for mercy.

How much I missed Irdris, her calm and her gentleness, her kindness and her clarity. As another Shokarn from Eezore, she might have been able to help Dorca. They might even have formed a bond between them. But Irdris was lost somewhere, swallowed up by the city and likely dead. There was no help to be had there.

Now the most gentling influence in the camp was Olna. Where she passed, women would turn and smile. Some would even reach out their hands to each other. Each time I saw that happen, it gave me a little chill — a shiver that ran up my spine. I liked Olna. How could one not like her? I suppose in some ways I even loved her. And yet she frightened me in a way none of the other Witches did. It was not her powers that frightened me. It was something else. It was as if she could see right into my soul. I suppose at that time that I did not think mine wanted much looking into. I wondered that she did not frighten other women in that way. They all warmed to Olna's charm. It was not a bright, flashing charm like Shalamith's. It came from a different place, dark and peaceful instead of all gold and shimmering.

Even Rishka responded to that charm. When Olna stopped by her, I could see Rishka bend her head toward Olna. Her face would grow thoughtful when they talked, or soften with pleasure if Olna smiled. I thought in some way she was changing Rishka, reaching through to some part of her that lay under all the bitterness and pain. Then something in my own heart — something very ugly — would tighten and harden. I could feel myself closing down when I should have felt grateful instead. Her presence there helped me in my work. She moved through the camp like healing waters. If there had been a dozen Olnas, there would have been no quarrels. Why, then, did she make me so uneasy?

I felt a different kind of uneasiness when I watched Rishka and Nunyair together. Of all the Shokarn to have befriended, she certainly seemed to me like the very worst of them. Yes, Nunyair was right, I did not like her. I had no patience for her incessant complaints about the dirt, the flies, the bad smell, the heat, the crowding, as if none of the rest of us suffered from such things. No doubt everything was new and frightening to her, unaccustomed as she was to rough ways and rough living. She had perhaps been as much a prisoner of the Great-House as its heir and had been suddenly thrust from her home and everything she knew, just as I had. Even so, I felt little sympathy for her. Her ways put me off. She thought herself too grand for the rest of us. She had brought with her all of her Shokarn baggage of arrogance and contempt for others. Perhaps it was because they matched each other so well this way that Rishka had taken such a strange liking to her.

At least I had the sense to keep my silence on it. Rishka was even teaching Nunyair to ride, something I should have been very glad for. I certainly could not have found the patience for it myself. And Nunyair responded to Rishka differently than she did to the rest of us. She treated Rishka as an equal. The rest of us she treated as servants. Perhaps Rishka had told her that she herself was really a Muinyairin princess fallen on bad times among us.

When Pell came to say to me, "Now is the time for your gold coins, Tazzi. We are fast running out of everything and have far more needs than my big coat can furnish," Nunyair's treasure instantly came to mind. I told Pell how she and Lhiri had brought valuables out of the city.

Pell waited while I went to fetch the stash of coins I had guarded for so long. She took them from me with a grin. "How nice of the Commissioner to finance our venture here. It warms my heart to think of it," she said, shaking them till they gave off a lively little tune before she dropped them into her pouch. Then, to my surprise, she said, "Come with me while I pay Nunyair a visit."

Nunyair, when we finally found her, was in no mind to surrender her valuables to us. She stood there with her arms crossed and her head held high, glaring at Pell. "Those are mine, my inheritance from my father's house," she said angrily. Then she turned and snarled at me, "You had no right to tell her. What business was it of yours?"

I looked at Nunyair against the background of this rude camp. With her still uncut blond hair snarled and tangled as if it had not been brushed for days, her fair skin streaked with soot and dirt, and her fine clothes all torn and ragged, her Shokarn arrogance might have been amusing or even pathetic, had it not been so infuriating. I flushed with anger to the roots of my hair. And this is the one I risked my life for, I thought. It was in the saving of this piece of goods that Askarth died.

Pell shrugged, looking more amused than angry. "Well, 'Lady,' the rules of your father's house make no matter to us here. Here we are not Shokarn and Kourmairi, mistress and slave, here we are all fugitives from the Zarn. Understand, Nunyair, there is a price on your Highborn head from one end of this land to the other. If you want to take shelter here with us, then you will share what you have, as we have shared with you. Otherwise, you are quite free to take your jewels and your gold and go out into the Zarn's world on your own to seek your safety there. If that is what you choose, then you must do it now, before you eat one more meal from our precious store of food that you refuse to contribute to."

Pell seemed to be enjoying this. Crossing her arms and leaning back against a tree with her eyes narrowed, she went on, speaking loudly for the benefit of the other women who were gathering around, "I venture you will not go very far. You can barely ride a horse, and besides, none of the horses are yours. You know nothing of the land. The first time you try to use your valuables in the market, you will likely be fingered by an informer. He may well end up with your gold and jewels as well as a reward. Even I cannot go buy potatoes in the Hamishair market with Shokarn gold without having the market spotters on me in a second. We need the Wanderers and the Thieves Guild as go-betweens. You, of course, know nothing of all that. But if you want to try it on your own, be welcome to it." Pell made a mock bow. "Let me know your will in an hour, 'Lady.' We can have a sentry take you out blindfolded and leave you near a road to town. Understand that you cannot come back to us no matter what. You are too inexperienced. You would bring the guards riding down on our necks."

Pell turned as if to leave. By now there was a fair-sized circle around us listening to her every word. Lhiri had come up beside us looking quite agitated. "Wait, Pell, please," she said, pulling insistently on Pell's arm. Then she whirled around to Nunyair. "Nunyairee, have some sense. Everything she says is true. It is too dangerous for you out there."

Nunyair ignored her. She was glaring at Pell and actually stamped her foot. "You are the leader here?! You are no better than a common thief. You are telling me I must give over my jewels and gold or lose my life, is that it?"

At that Pell chuckled, looking openly amused. "Exactly right, very observant. I am indeed a common thief, as you say, and have been for some time, though what I steal goes into the 'common' pot and not my own pocket. And yes, you are right again: it is your valuables or your life, that simple." She nodded to us all and once more seemed ready to walk away. Lhiri was looking back and forth between them frantically. "Do not be a fool," she shouted to Nunyair, grabbing her arm. "You would not make it through one day on the road alone. Do you think Starmos Great-House prepared you for any of this?"

Nunyair shook off Lhiri's hand and drew herself up to an even haughtier pose. "You think to speak to me that way, you who less than two weeks ago was my slave in my father's house!?"

"Oh come, Nunyair, what nonsense. I was no more your slave than you were mine. What use is a slave who cannot be compelled? That is no slave at all, but someone to be feared. I sheltered in your father's house because Askarth made a place for me there."

"Fool's talk! All lies!" Nunyair shouted, all her anger turning now on Lhiri. "You know as well as I do that you were my slave since we were children together. My father bought you for me."

"Only because Askarth persuaded him to," Lhiri answered instantly. They were facing each other now, old anger flashing and flaring between them, the rest of us forgotten. "You," Lhiri was pointing at Nunyair, stabbing the air with her finger as she spoke, "you are the one who was a slave to the Great-House of Starmos. Being a 'Lady,' you were like a prisoner there and could not leave unguarded, while I had free run of the city."

Nunyair knocked her hand away and began to shout something back in bad-tempered Shokarn, too fast for me to follow. Lhiri was shouting in return. Both their faces were ugly and distorted with anger. Other women were backing away in haste. With shame I thought, that is how Rishka and I must look to others when we fight.

Pell bowed again. "Excuse me, 'Ladies,' but this *thief* has business elsewhere. I think you can carry this on without my help. Only let me know soon what you decide."

This time Pell went striding off decisively. I had to struggle to keep pace. Behind us I could hear Lhiri and Nunyair, their voices rising higher and higher in anger. "Pell," I said anxiously, "what will you do if she refuses? Will you really put her out on the road?"

Pell slowed her steps a little and gave me a funny, sideways look out of the corner of her eye. "Now, Tazzi, do you think me such a fool as all that? We will just have to find some other way to persuade her. After all, she would be as much danger to us out there as to herself. Most of my little talk was for the benefit of other ears. Besides, I could not do that to Askarth, we owe her too much. Rest easy, though, she will settle up. Lhiri will bring her around soon enough, after they are done with their shouting. Nunyair has her fears as well as her prides." Then, much to my surprise, she threw an arm over my shoulder, saying, "Well, Tazzi, my foolish friend, after that little exchange with a real fool, you do not seem so foolish after all. I can even see your value shining through." She was shaking her head. "So, having said all that, now I suppose I must forgive you." At these words she stopped suddenly and turned me around so that we were facing each other.

I began to protest, "But you were right, Pell, what I did was unforgivable..."

She cut me off. "Hush, hush, enough said. If I am going to forgive you, then you must forgive yourself, else you make a fool out of me."

We went on, more slowly now, with her arm over my shoulder again, the weight and warmth of it resting there like a badge of honor. I saw other women watching us curiously. Most of them were new ones, women who had witnessed my abject re-entry into camp and only knew Pell as a leader. /My Pell! Mine!/ My thoughts broke through as clear as spoken words. /Mine before any of you saw her./

Pell threw back her head and laughed, while I blushed and looked away. "Well, would you fight for me, then, Tazzi?" she asked, grinning with amusement.

"I would try to," I answered, serious in spite of her mockery. "Oh, Pell, I hate it when they call you names or lie about you as Murghanth did. It is so unfair!"

She shrugged and answered, still with a look of amusement on her face, "Believe me, Tazzi, I will be called worse things than 'thief' before this is all over. It matters little. In fact, it matters not at all. I have none of Rishka's bristly pride. How glad I am not to have to carry that heavy burden everywhere I go. What am I, after all, but a Kourmairi thief and also the child of dirt-farmers just as you are? They can call me whatever they please, as long as they end by doing what is needed." Then she said, more seriously, "But thank you for your loyalty, Tazzi. It is not that I am mocking. In fact, I am quite touched by it. I have not treated you very well, have I? But then, I suppose I have not treated any of us very well. It is these times. These are the Zarn's times. I do the best I can. Later, when we are free of his power, I will be a very different person, the one who for now is locked away inside. Know that I love you, Tazzi, maybe not in the way you might wish, but I love you nonetheless."

I was crying and grinning at her at the same time. "My Pell," I said, speaking aloud this time, "my comrade, my captain, my chief."

She kissed me on the cheek. "Well, you may as well take back your second-in-command, since I know you already have it in all but name."

Soon after that Lhiri caught up with us. She held up a little red pouch encrusted with embroidery in front of Pell. "You see?" Pell said to me with a wink as she took it. When she opened the pouch I saw her eyes go wide in surprise. "Well, well, well, it may not be such a skinny winter after all," she said, pulling the strings tight to close it again. "Good thing I am not greedy. Now let us get packs or hats and take up the collection."

The three of us walked through camp and valuables poured into our hands, sometimes from the most unexpected sources. Women seemed almost in a rush to be rid of them. In the end we amassed quite a sizable stash. Some of this we turned over to Hereschell. He was leaving that day and would pass it on to the Thieves Guild in return for spendable currency. This he would use to arrange for food at our final gathering place. The rest of it we hid in a crock on Alyeeta's shelves, where she could watch over it and it would be instantly available.

After that the three of us went arm in arm down to the stream to bathe. I hoped all the camp was watching Pell walking next to me. Afterward we lay out on the bank together. Lhiri had a strange, pained look on her face. Pell watched her for a while before she said, "Nunyair gave you a bad time of it today, eh?"

"There is another side of her, loving and kind, that she does not show among you. We have been together so long, I know her so well, I cannot help loving her. I know she loves me, too, and always has. But she is also a child of her house, trained by them in the uses and abuses of power. In some ways it is a blow to her Shokarn pride to have her heart held captive by a slave.

"Sometimes her love for me is like an open flower we can both take pleasure in. Sometimes it is like a bleeding wound for pains we both have suffered. Then she tries to find ways to remind me that she is the mistress and I am the slave."

Pell nodded, saying thoughtfully, "You said yourself a slave who cannot be compelled is no slave at all, but a thing to be feared."

Lhiri burst out, almost in tears, "Why does she have to talk that way? Even slaves and servants are people with feelings and some will of their own. Look at Askarth — she was only the servant to a Great-House, yet there was no finer woman, no one braver or stronger or more loving."

Pell sat up and drew something from her pouch which she handed to Lhiri. It was the pendant Askarth had pressed into my hands for trust. I heard a gasp of surprise from Lhiri. "Is it yours?" Pell asked, looking at her intently.

"Oh yes, yes," she said, snatching it from Pell and pressing it against her heart. "Where did you get it? I gave it to Askarth for a safesign when she left us to go in search of you."

"Lhiri," Pell said softly, "Askarth was your mother."

"What are you saying? What do you mean? My mother died when I was born."

Pell was shaking her head. "When Askarth gave that to Tazzi to gain our trust, she said it belonged to her daughter. I did not think to give it back to her while I had the chance. Now I give it back to you."

"Is it possible? Is it possible? All that time I never knew. I thought she was my mother's friend." She was turning the pendant over and over in her hands. "Why did she never tell me? All those years ... all those years ... why did she never tell me?" The tears were running down her face unheeded now.

"I think she was under a pledge of silence," Pell said gently. "Perhaps under threat, perhaps for honor's sake."

"All those years," Lhiri said again, shaking her head. "All those years lost." Suddenly her expression changed. She turned to face Pell. "Then who was my father, tell me that?"

Pell shook her head. "That I do not know."

I turned away and bit my tongue to not blurt out "The Lord of Starmos," so strongly did I feel it to be so. I was not sure if this was the time to say it or even if it was mine to say, and so shielded my thoughts from her as best I could.

Soon after that Pell got up to leave. Lhiri reached out to take hold of my hand. "Please stay a while, Tazzi, and tell me everything you knew of Askarth. Of my mother, I mean."

I stayed and did as she asked, telling her how I had first seen Askarth selling apples by the road, and how calm she had been when the soldiers came, and how she would go with no one but Hamiuri. I told her how she had prodded and pleaded and insisted that we go to Eezore to free Lhiri and the others. I described our terrifying trip through the tunnel with Askarth leading and told her of our wild entrance into the Great-House itself, telling her everything up till the very moment we were in their closet. Then I told her what I knew of Askarth's death and how she had likely gone back to try to save Merrik's life after his part in their escape.

We cried and laughed and cried together many times over. Some parts she made me tell again and yet again. At moments she gripped my hand so hard I felt as if my bones were cracking. After a while, we talked of other things. I was even able to speak of my own mother and cry for her with Lhiri's arms around me. While we sat close together, sharing so many things, I kept remembering Lhiri's hand pressed in mine as I was fleeing Eezore, the last person to be at my side when I escaped. That afternoon by the stream was when we began our friendship. How strange to think that I was becoming Lhiri's friend as Rishka had become Nunyair's. One might have thought that would have brought us all together, but it was not to be.

That night at dinner, after Pell had given me back my command in front of everyone, there was another sharp exchange between Nunyair and Lhiri, with Lhiri saying again fiercely, "I was never your slave there, never. Get over that notion. I always had more freedom in Eezore than you did."

I saw Rishka lean forward suddenly as if for an attack. Her eyes had a strange gleam in them. "Then why did you stay?" she asked in her nastiest tone. "Why did you stay under that roof and in that city if you were free to go? Tell us that, eh?" There was a look of triumphant malice on her face.

Lhiri whirled on Rishka, all her anger shifting to this new target. "And what did I see out there that looked half so free as being a slave in a Great-House? You tell me that! What should I have been instead, a serving wench in a tavern? Some peasant's wife to be used like his beasts? I thought I had the best of it where I was. This is the first time I have ever felt a wind of freedom blowing through the Zarn's lands, the first time I have ever seen something worth risking my life for. Before that, show me where I would have been any bit more free than where I was standing, what you call a slave?" With those words she leapt to her feet, shouting into Rishka's surprised face, "Show me! Show me that! Show me!" Several of the other women who had themselves been slaves were shouting in sympathy with her and banging on the table. "And you, Muinyairin," she went on stabbing her finger at Rishka, "why did you stay among people who beat you, people whose marks you still bear across your back? Was it because you were a coward, afraid to leave? Or was it because you could not imagine being somewhere else, could not picture another life? Because, in fact, there was none for us until now, not for any of us. No place ... no place in the world..." Suddenly her voice cracked, as grief broke through the anger. More gently she said, "We are all slaves to our lives, are we not? Sometimes the only choice left is to die or to be a slave."

The other women who sided with Lhiri, former slaves themselves, all with the brand of Eezore on their foreheads, were gathering around her now, shouting, "Tell her! Tell her! Tell her, Lhiri!" They were banging louder and louder with their cups and bowls. "Tell her, tell that arrogant sand-eater! What does she know about us? Tell that Muinyairin bitch how it really is."

Other Muinyairin had come and were quickly gathering in back of Rishka, glowering at Lhiri and the women around her and muttering loudly about "those branded cows." Rishka herself was looking quite uneasy, frightened even, having likely found far more trouble than she had planned on. Her eyes were darting about, but with no will to mischief in them now. Pell and I signaled to each other across the table, both ready to jump to some quick action, and neither of us certain what to do. This was by far the worst scene I had witnessed in the camp and seemed to be worsening by the minute. I was aware that Renaise had come up from the cookfire and was also standing ready. At any moment I was expecting one of Alyeeta's silencings to fall on us, and might even have welcomed it.

One of the women who had been a slave, Yargir, I think her name was, leaned across the table shaking her fist and shouting at Rishka, "You started all this trouble, you devil-woman, and now you call in your Muinyairin bullies to protect you." Another said, in the most insulting way possible, "Are those really the Muinyairin? They look more like piles of horse dung to me." And a third said contemptuously, "What do they know? They are all horse-fuckers!"

With that, Daijar gave a roar of anger. I was sure she was getting ready to vault over the table when there was a sharp clap of cymbals from the far end of it followed by a loud shout of, "Make way! Make way! Make way for the Penny Street Players!" I turned to see Murghanth dressed in bright, gauzy scarves. She was not wearing much else but a wristlet and anklet of bells. With her arms raised, she struck the cymbals loudly twice more, shouting, "Back, back, leave us some room. Clear away all those things. Quickly! Quickly!"

To my surprise women set themselves to doing as she said, clearing away their eating utensils and then leaning back out of the way. All eyes were now on Murghanth. She tossed her cymbals to Teko, who was standing there waiting. With no more warning than that she gave a high, melodious cry and threw herself into a series of flips down the length of the planks that served us as a table. All her little bells were ringing wildly. As soon as she came to the end, she gave that same high-pitched cry and made her flips back the other way, landing on the ground with her arms raised. There was a moment of stunned silence, then a few women began clapping, then a few more. Soon there was a thunder of clapping and stamping and whistling. Many voices were shouting, "More! More! More!" Murghanth leapt back up on the table, calling out, "Give me three cups and three plates." She took them from eager hands and began juggling and dancing, her hands flashing and her bright scarves swirling around her like flames. Teko, all dressed in black, jumped up beside her. The plates and cups flew back and forth between them. Other Sheezerti in bright clothes had gathered and began playing drums and tambourines and snapping their fingers. The women at the table were soon clapping and stamping in rhythm with them.

I looked across at Pell again. She winked, nodded, and made the sign of the circle with her fingers. I signed the same back to her. Now I could breathe again. Much relieved, I retreated up to Alyeeta's shelter. She had evidently been watching it all from her entryway and grinned at me, eyes flashing with amusement.

"Thank you, Alyeeta," I said, "for not blessing us with one of your silencings, though there was a moment or two there when I might almost have welcomed it."

"That little scene was much too interesting to interrupt. I wanted to see how it would end without Witches' meddling."

"Alyeeta, sometimes I think you are a monster."

"A monster, eh? Is it not bad enough then to be a Witch?" She pinched me on the tender inner part of my arm just above the elbow. "Come in with me and I will show you what monsters can do."

With no hesitation, I followed her inside. After all that had happened that day, Alyeeta's shelter seemed an island of safety. Soon we were loving each other to the rhythm of drums, cymbals, and tambourines. Long after we were done I lay awake listening to that wild music.

22

Early the next morning Maireth came to look for me, dressed for the road. Though the scars on her face were still quite visible, she was healing much faster than I would have expected. Clearly, she had some urgent business with me. "It pleases me to see you back in Pell's favor," she said quickly. "It pleases me even more that your command has been returned to you. Now we have no reason to go on playing out our little subterfuge. If you do not need me any more, if you can manage well enough without me, I am going back to Pell's shelter and care for the burned ones."

I laughed ruefully. "After last night I am not sure I can manage anything at all. I thought we were all about to make war on each other right then and finish up the Zarn's work for him." Then, seeing how very serious she looked, I added, "Go, go, Maireth, it is due to my own foolishness that you were kept here for so long against your will. Of course I can manage. If I have any trouble I will call for the Sheezerti. Go, with my love." We hugged, and as she started to turn away I remembered her pendant. "Wait, Maireth, do you need this back?"

"No, that is yours. I have my own. That used to belong to my lover. Where she is now she has no need of it. It is not a thing to hide away in a box. It needs to be worn by the living."

"I think it saved me in Eezore." With my hand pressed against its warmth, I told her briefly what had happened to me with it in the city.

While I spoke, she watched me intently. She looked as if she were peering into my soul and searching there for something. But in the end, all she said was, "Yes, it is good for centering, for keeping hold of oneself." It felt as if there was much she was not saying.

"Is it of 'the Circle'? Are you one of them?" I asked, full of curiosity.

"Not yet time," she said quickly. "Not yet time to speak of such things."

"Not even here?"

"Not yet time," she repeated. "Wear it down inside your shirt. Do not flaunt it about so. The time will come when we can gather all that up again, but not in the midst of this chaos." She gestured around the camp. "Not here and not now." After she gave me another quick hug, she held me away to look in my face. "There was a time, Tazzi, when I could have cursed you for saving my life. Now I am grateful. The pendant is a gift of life for a gift of life." With those words she shouldered her pack and ran across the clearing. Kazouri was waiting for her there with two horses. She was planning to ride with Maireth and help her take supplies. Then she was to report back to Pell on how things were progressing at the shelter and what was needed there.

As they rode off, Alyeeta stepped up beside me. "Now that is the one I should have taught my healing to," she said sharply. "Why did I waste that time on you?"

"Not waste, Alyeeta, it will all be used. Now is not the time for me to be a healer."

"You healed Shalamith."

"No, Shalamith healed herself. I helped her with my energy. It was my energy she needed, not my healing." As I saw she was ready to continue in this vein, I said quickly, "Do not chide me at this moment, Alyeeta. Let me come back into your shelter. Too much has happened too fast. I need a quiet place. I am not ready yet to meet the morning." Silently she nodded and stepped aside. I slipped past her and went in to sit alone in a far corner behind a stump.

I believe Alyeeta was teaching some reading that morning, but I scarcely noticed the voices. After a while I thought I heard the sound of rustling from a shelf above me, or maybe I only felt a presence. I looked up into the gold-flecked, hooded eyes of Telakeet's toad. For a moment the two of us regarded each other. Then I reached out my hand, palm up. With no hesitation she hopped into my hand. I brought her down so that we were looking at each other eye to eye. Slowly her warmth spread out in my palm. She shut her eyes. I cupped her between my breasts and began to rock slowly back and forth in the chair.

I must have gone away to some far place. It was very startling to suddenly come back to myself and find Telakeet standing in front of me, radiating hate. She reached out her hand as if she wanted to snatch her toad away.

"Ah, so you want to steal *her* from me, also," she said in a venomous tone.

I looked up at her in bewilderment, not able to respond to her anger with anger of my own as I had before. "She was only keeping me company for a moment," I said softly. Then I went on in a rush of words, "Please, Telakeet, I have no wish to take anything at all away from you. Why can you not let me have a little place in Alyeeta's life? What have I ever done to you that you should hate me so? You are so angry at me for helping Shalamith, yet she was the one who sent for me."

I saw the rage in her face suddenly turn to grief. "There are things you would never understand," she said. "Never! Not if I talked to you for a whole year. But I must thank you for helping to heal Shalamith, saving her, perhaps. I am not sure we could have done it without you. Something was needed that was beyond the power of Witches. Yes, for that I am grateful."

Though she said it in such a grudging way and such a grudging voice, these were certainly the kindest words she had ever spoken to me.

"Thank you for that, Telakeet," I said, holding out the toad to her, all warm and soft in my hand.

"Keep her a while longer if you want," she said as she turned to go.

★

Most of the conflicts in the camp began to settle themselves after a while. Even the Muinyairin of the Drylands and the former slaves of Eezore made some sort of peace. Even Rishka and I stopped warring so loudly with each other, at least for that time. I think that scene around the table had frightened us both and sobered us considerably. Not so with Lhiri and Nunyair. Their quarrel grew deeper and more explosive with each passing day. It also grew more disturbing to the rest of us. It was as if all their years of silence were being given voice. They loved each other, and they hated each other, and they could not seem to stay out of one another's way. Whatever one said the other had to answer. Then, in an instant, all the rage and frustration of a lifetime would boil up. We all took our turn at trying to make peace between them. After a while we all gave up. Even Rishka and I tried to talk to them as their friends. Even Olna could not reach the sore that festered there. Even Pell's threats had scant effect. They would promise and hold to their promise for a while and then begin again. One moment they would be holding hands and leaning toward each other in the manner of lovers as if the rest of us did not exist. The next moment they were screaming curses and accusations till the whole camp was in turmoil.

After a particularly ugly scene between them, Hamiuri called all of us together, Hamiuri, who so seldom tampered with our affairs. When we had assembled she beckoned to the culprits. "Come, Lhiri, Nunyair. Come stand before us so we all can see you. We have heard you often enough."

They came forward reluctantly, looking embarrassed and defiant and under that, afraid. I could only be glad that it was not myself and Rishka standing there in their place, as it might well have been. Hamiuri kept her silence for a while. She let them stand in front of everyone while others stared and whispered and giggled and finally began making louder and louder comments on the disturbances they had caused us all. I was in an agony of embarrassment and relief, thinking how easily I could have been the one up there shifting from foot to foot under the scrutiny of all those eyes.

When she thought them sufficiently well cooked, Hamiuri clapped her hands for silence. An instant hush fell. Pointing at them, she said clearly, "You two are waging your own small private war here in the midst of this larger one. I think the rest of us have had enough of it." Hamiuri spoke loud enough so that all of us could hear, and in a tone of power that made me tremble inside. "What you are doing weakens and endangers us all. You must cease until we are in a place of safety. If you cannot or will not do that, then you must leave and never shelter among Star-Born or Witches again, neither here with us nor in any other gatherings, for very soon we shall all be together in one great gathering. Is that clear enough for you both, or do I have to repeat myself?"

Lhiri was nodding and looking at the ground, but Nunyair burst out indignantly, "Would you call a banishment on us, then?" She sounded incredulous.

"A banishment? Is that what the Shokarn would call this?" I saw a slight flicker of amusement cross Hamiuri's face. "Well then, yes, a banishment it is. Yes, if there is no other way." There was a long pause while Hamiuri seemed to be gathering herself up to her full power. No one moved or said a word. When she finally spoke I felt as if the ground were shaking under my feet. "Hear me now and remember well what I say. This is your choice. If you are to stay here among us, you are to separate. You are not to sleep together or be lovers in any way. Do not speak to each with words or eyes or gestures or with your minds. Do not make any contact whatsoever of body or spirit. You must be as dead to one another. If you cannot keep to those terms, if this talk is not sufficient to free us of this uproar, then yes, in your words, I call for a banishment on you both, a banishment from all the gatherings of the Star-Born. Does this seem unfair to you? If so, let us hear what you have to say on the matter."

Though Hamiuri had not asked Pell, or any of the rest of us, for that matter, I saw Pell nodding, and many other women as well. I could not speak, caught as I was between my caring for Lhiri and my knowledge that we could not go on in this way. There was another long silence. Lhiri was still looking at the ground. Slowly she raised her eyes till she was looking straight at Hamiuri. "I accept," she said with resignation. "I accept because I can see no other way." Though she spoke in a clear, steady voice, her hands were shaking.

"And you?" Hamiuri said to Nunyair.

"I accept also," Nunyair muttered, almost in a whisper.

"Well, good, then let us have some peace here." Hamiuri made a wide sweep of her arm as if dismissing us all. The circle broke, with Lhiri and Nunyair going off in opposite directions.

★

"Yaiee! Yaiee! Yaiee!" The cry rang through the camp as blood-chilling as the cry of the Oolanth hill-cats. "Yaiee! Yaiee!" A troop of riders, clearly Muinyairin from the look of them, came charging into camp with some of our sentries riding full after them. The first of them stopped so short that her horse reared up on its hind legs. "Where is Rishkazeel, the Muinyairin?" she called loudly. "Tell her Hayika is here. She is the only one I will speak with." As she spoke she was casting suspicious glances in all directions.

The other women of the camp had all stopped what they were doing. They quickly stepped aside for me as I rushed forward to meet with the intruders. I was wishing Pell or Kazouri or even Rishka herself were there to deal with this rude entrance so reminiscent of Rishka's first appearance. The other wild ones meanwhile had all reined in and were in a line in back of their leader with our sentries shouting futilely at them.

I was reaching for the leader's reins, wondering what I was going to say to this invasion, when I heard Rishka shout from in back of me, "Off your horses, all of you! Hayika, what do you mean by riding in this way!? Have you no respect?"

One of the women in the line flung herself off her horse shouting, "Rishkazeel! Rishkazeel! You are really here!" This was followed by some rapid Muinyairin I could not comprehend.

Rishka herself dashed forward into that woman's arms, shouting, "Kilghari!" while I hastily backed away. Drawn by the commotion, Alyeeta stepped up beside me to watch. She bent her head and said in my ear, "Humility must be a much-prized trait among the Muinyairin, it is so rare. Here they are, the most hunted beggars in the world, yet they ride into my clearing as if they were Shokarn lords demanding taxes from a village of cowed dirt-farmers. Perhaps I should..." She began to raise her hand, fingers outstretched.

"Please, Alyeeta, no!"

"Ah well..." she said with a shrug, "perhaps later."

By now all the new Muinyairin had dismounted and were hugging Rishka in turn. Daijar and Noshir came running in, and shortly afterward Zari appeared with some of the Muinyairin that had been freed from Eezore. Soon they were all hugging and clasping hands and shouting greetings in rapid Muinyairin while the rest of us watched in a loose circle.

"I wonder if all the Muinyairin of the Drylands know each other?" Renaise muttered to me.

"It would seem so," I answered with a laugh. Then I called out to the sentries to go back to their places.

★

Later Rishka came to look for me, calling, "Tazzi, Tazzi, come meet my cousin." She was walking, arms linked, with the Muinyairin who had first leapt off her horse to greet her. "Tazzi, this is my cousin Kilghari," Rishka said with evident pride, speaking of the young woman standing at her side.

I turned to look into eyes that gazed back at me from a clear, quiet center, a gaze much like Olna's. This was not what I would have expected from a Muinyairin. She looked like Rishka and yet not like Rishka. There was some vital difference at the core.

"So this is Tazzi," she said in a serious, almost formal voice. Then she smiled suddenly so that her whole face lit up, and my heart melted. I reached out to clasp the hand she offered me.

"Kilghari wants to know why we have not yet done a naming circle here and a circle-of-peace, Muinyairin style."

The words "circle-of-peace" on Rishka's lips made me want to howl with laughter. I struggled to keep a good face on it while Kilghari said in her strange, soft-sounding Kourmairi, "We have been looking for you everywhere. The star-cursed are certainly not easy to find. We had to leave not long after Rishka and have been riding hard all this time, asking questions and trying to stay clear of the guards."

As Kilghari was speaking, the one Rishka had named as Hayika walked up in back of her. She stood glowering over Kilghari's shoulder, looking angry enough to make trouble, but keeping her silence for the moment.

"And what is this 'circle-of-peace'?" I said, trying not to smile at the words and ignoring as best I could Hayika's hostile glare.

Kilghari burst into a flood of rapid Muinyairin I could not follow. Rishka said, more slowly, "To start with, each of us needs to bring a knife tied to a staff or stick, or a sword, or something that is strongly personal to that woman. The Muinyairin usually use swords, but most women here do not have one, so something else will be needed. After that it is easier to show than to tell."

I heard Hayika thinking, /What use is a circle-of-peace when all we need is to get Rishka and the others and leave. The less time I spend with these chaka the better./

"When do you think we should do this?" I went on, as if I had not so clearly heard Hayika's thoughts.

"As soon as you can, tonight if possible. Rishka told me what has been happening here. There is no time to be lost if more conflict is to be avoided. And first you must have a naming circle or the circle-of-peace will be weakened."

Well, I thought with amusement, even the gentlest of these Muinyairin had some touch of that Muinyairin pride. Here was this stranger who had been among us less than four hours telling us how to conduct our camp. I wondered if my thoughts were as loud as Hayika's. Then I shrugged. After all, what harm could there be in such a circle? Goddess knows, we needed some way to bring a measure of peace and harmony between us. All we had now was a brittle, fragile truce. Pell was away. It was up to me to call for a decision. "Good enough," I said, nodding, "let me see what the will is here."

I called over Renaise, Kazouri, Zenoria, and Teko, as well as Alyeeta and Hamiuri. Those two had been watching from the shelter entrance, perhaps expecting another outbreak among us. The rest of the Muinyairin had already gathered. Kilghari spoke earnestly while the others listened and I watched, nodding and trying to hide all traces of a smile. At the end Hamiuri echoed my thoughts, saying, "Why not? What harm can there be in it. Something is needed here that will tie this quarrelsome rabble together." The others nodded. It must have been the shortest conference ever held in that camp. Off to the side I could see Hayika arguing with Rishka.

Kilghari had said we could not use the cookfires, that there was too much troubled energy attached to them, so that night we made our circle fire in a new place. While Kazouri beat on a great pot that sounded like a gong, we gathered ourselves in a spiral that wound several times around the fire.

The Muinyairin had all dressed for this occasion, decking themselves with scarves and sashes and strings of multicolored beads over their brightest tunics. Their hair was braided with ribbons or twists of wool and hung with all manner of decorations, shells, feathers, and shiny ornaments. Some had painted patterns on their faces and some were bare-breasted and had painted their nipples and breasts. They had all brought with them some fancy sword or blade that flashed and sparkled in the firelight. Most of the Sheezerti wore the costumes of their performing troops, as bright and colorful in their own way as the Muinyairin.

I felt strangely shorn and naked in the midst of all that rough finery. For the first time, I regretted the cutting of my long wavy hair and vowed to grow it back when this was over. Kilghari told me she would have done it up Muinyairin style with braids, beads, and feathers, but, of course, that was not to be. I had hardly given a thought to what I was going to bring for my part in the circle. Then, at the last possible moment, the knife Kerris made for me fell out of my belt. It landed standing in the dirt, blade first, a sure sign if ever I have seen one. I bound it to a stick and went to take my place in the spiral.

Seeing us all gathered there, looking from face to face, I felt a shiver of excitement. Let the Zarn issue his edict. We would shape our own lives in spite of him. With no hesitation Rishka took charge that night. Though Pell had returned, I saw her staying well back, keeping her distance, letting things happen as they would.

It was Rishka who jumped up on the stump and shouted to us all, her speech leaping from Muinyairin to Kourmairi to Shokarn and back again.

"We need a name under which we can gather together, a name in which we can speak our new powers. We all have different pasts. That cannot be changed. But now we share a future. For that we must have a name that speaks for us all."

I was staring at Rishka in amazement, finding it hard to believe. Was this the same woman who such a short time back had baited Lhiri into a rage? There was a kind of passion in her as she said, "As long as we are Muinyairin and Shokarn and Kourmairi, then all we have for names are the curses on men's lips: star-brats or star-cursed or star-crossed. Sisters, what name do we have to call ourselves? That is what we choose tonight."

There were many shouts of agreement. Several possible names were being called out. Rishka raised her hands for silence. "Some of us have given much thought to this. The word 'Terrazen' in Muinyairin means 'comrades to the death,' and that is what we are, so perhaps that is what we should call ourselves."

There was a loud cheer from the Muinyairin, but Kazouri called out in her booming voice, "I am a Kourmairi. What need do I have for a Muinyairin label? Star-Born is good enough for me."

Next, Nunyair was shouting angrily, "Why would a Shokarn want a Kourmairi name to pass on to her daughters' daughters?"

Other voices quickly took up the argument, each speaking against another's name or for some name they favored in their own language. The gathering had just begun and already it was threatening to dissolve in conflict. I began looking around anxiously for Pell when I heard Alyeeta call out, "Enough! Enough! You will all be at war with each other before your circle-of-peace can even be made. How easily you forget that you are all hunted by men who only want you dead. They care nothing for what language you speak or the color of your skin or whether you are country or city bred." She came striding over to the stump and signaled Rishka down. I saw a look of fear cross Rishka's face as she stepped down and backed away.

"Enough squabbling, all of you," Alyeeta said as she swung her finger around the circle, seeming somehow to point at each one of us in turn. "It is plain the name cannot come from any of your own languages. You are still too attached to your fathers and your fathers' fathers and to their words, so we must seek elsewhere for a name. Now if you can all be silent for a moment, Telakeet has something to share with you, but only if you have it in your hearts to listen."

Alyeeta stepped down and Telakeet climbed up in her place. It was not her usual angry visage scowling down at us. She looked transformed. Hard to believe, but she even had some of Shalamith's golden glow about her. Perhaps that stump had a magic of its own.

When Telakeet spoke it was very slowly and in no language that I knew, but somehow I understood every word. Beyond the sounds of the words, I felt the enormous pull and power of them. I heard in my head: /This land has been fought over and struggled over by Shokarn and Kourmairi and Muinyairin since long before there were written words, but you are not the first people here. Long long before any of you came, the Ashara lived here in peace, following their own ways. Your wars have driven them back into the hills to the furthest fringes of the settled world. Who knows if there are even any Asharan left alive today. But their language, or at least some remnants of it, remains with the Witches. Asharan is our ritual language and our private language as well. It is the Asharan words that are our holy words when we make our spells or call on the Mother. With us they still live. Let them live with you also and make peace among you, you who are the Daughters of the Great Star, the Khal Hadera Lossien./

There was absolute silence when she finished. The silence continued as Telakeet resumed her own sour countenance and stepped down. The silence went on and on, seeming to stretch out into the night, far past the boundaries of the clearing. Just when I thought my head would crack with waiting, Rishka's raised sword flashed in the firelight as she shouted, "To the Khal Hadera Lossien!" Instantly, as if freed from a spell, we all took up the cry and began shouting, "Khal Hadera Lossien! Khal Hadera Lossien!" till our throats were hoarse. I could hear Kazouri's roar carry over the rest of us, "To the Khal Hadera Lossien!"

So the naming was over, that part was done. Now we must become the thing we had named, likely a more difficult piece of work. Kilghari was next on the magic stump, her face flushed and glowing and her eyes bright. "I greet you, Khal Hadera Lossien, a new name for a new people," she called out to us in her softly accented Kourmairi. "We cannot blood each other with these weapons. Our powers will not allow it. So let us shape a peace with them instead." Soon she shifted to Muinyairin with Rishka translating, "Among my people, if any are seeking peace, they draw in the sand a small circle around the fire with their knife tip and outside that a much larger circle. Then they lay their weapons down, points toward the fire and just touching, hilts out and more than the width of a foot apart. If any lay down their blade across another's blade there will be no peace. But if the circle is closed with tip lying next to tip, that is an end to bloodshed among them. Then they are as kin."

When she finished speaking, we all gathered closer to the fire. Its light was flashing on our very different faces. Kilghari was the first to do this thing. She stepped forward holding up a beautiful, ornate sword. Raising it high in both hands, she called out in a clear, ringing voice, "To the new peace, to a new people, no longer Muinyairin and Shokarn and Kourmairi, but Khal Hadera Lossien together." There were wild shouts and cheers. The circle-of-peace had begun.

Lhiri came next with a small jeweled dagger bound to a branch. "No more slaves and masters!" she shouted, waving it over her head. "Free women together! Khal Hadera Lossien!" As she bent to place her dagger with care next to Kilghari's, women were shouting and stamping, "Yes! Yes! Yes!"

I stepped up next and suddenly found I could not speak. Then Rishka caught my eye and raised a fist for me. "May we always be Terrazen," I said, choking out the words and trying to hold back the tears. Around me I heard the Muinyairin echoing, "Terrazen, Terrazen." Bowing my head, I laid down my little knife carefully next to Lhiri's.

Rishka laid her long sword next to my knife, saying, "We have shaped a name, now let us shape a future."

When I saw Dorca step forward to place her blade next to Rishka's, point touching point, blades not crossing, a shiver went up my spine.

The circle was beginning to fill, blade against blade or stick or staff. When it was half filled, Nunyair stepped up and laid her Shokarn dagger directly opposite Lhiri's. Looking at her across the fire, Nunyair echoed her words, "No more slaves and masters. Free women together." Then she looked directly across the fire into Lhiri's eyes.

Lhiri stepped forward from her side. Their eyes locked and Lhiri said, clear and loud, "No matter what they make me say I love you now and I always will." There were gasps of shock from around the circle and then muttered comments.

Pell stepped up quickly and the muttering stopped. She looked at me across the circle, a look so full of pride it made my heart ache. She had no sword, nothing but her clever little thief knife bound to a staff. She did not raise it but leaned on the staff while she looked at us all. Along with the pride shining in her eyes there was a glitter of tears. She spoke slowly, as if drawing up each word from a deep well. "Since I was a girl of eleven

I have dreamed of this day. May our blades always touch and never cross. May we be Terrazen all our years. May the Khal Hadera Lossien find a safe home in this world." When she finished there was an uproar of clapping, shouting, cheering, and whistling that went on and on while Pell grinned and ducked her head and slipped to the back.

Once the first circle was filled, a second, larger one was drawn. That too filled rapidly, blade lying next to blade like a great sun flashing in the firelight. All the other blades went down until only Hayika's was left. She had been prowling about in back of us, muttering to herself under her breath, never truly one of the circle.

"It is your turn, Hayika," Zari said softly. "Your blade will close the circle."

Hayika came to a sudden stop and burst out at Zari, "Of what use is all this sham and mockery? Words, words, and more words, all empty show. Sister, how have they fooled you with this? Do you think this little gesture will make the Shokarn and Kourmairi love us? Do you think they will ever accept the Muinyairin?" She whirled around, looking for the others. There was desperation in her voice. "You fool yourselves, my sisters. They will always see us as wild things of the desert. We will still catch in their teeth like the blowing sand. Are you fool enough to think there is any love for us here, Kilghari? And you, Rishka, what have they done to you? They have tamed you and hobbled you and forced a bit between your teeth. I only came looking for you so we could ride together as far from all these draiga as possible. Guards, Shokarn, Kourmairi, it is all the same. And now you are trying to trap me in this circle of foolishness. I told you I wanted no part in it. I should have stayed away while you did this, I should have left, but I did not want to ride alone forever through the world."

Pell turned toward her and said sharply, "Hayika, I am chosen leader here. Do you wish to cross our blades? Is that what you are saying?" There was a challenge in her voice.

"No!" Rishka shouted. "No, Hayika, it is over now, the old ways are gone. Though we will always be Muinyairin, we can never go back to being Muinyairin again the way we were. The Muinyairin have no more use for us than the Shokarn guards and mean our death just as surely. We have no people any more. These are our people now." With that, she pulled off her shirt and turned her back to the fire. The lash marks showed livid and seemed to move in the quiver of the firelight. Women gasped and cried out. Rishka went on, "Look, Hayika, that was done to me by Muinyairin hands. They would gladly do it again and worse if they could."

Hayika was shaking her head, looking from one to the other of the Muinyairin. "I had not thought when I came here to throw my lot in with draiga," she said stubbornly.

"It could be worse than camping with a bunch of draiga," Pell called out to her. "It could be much worse. You could be roast meat for the Zarn's guards, think on that, Sister. I have seen it, it is not a pretty sight."

"Please, Hayika," Zari said, close to tears, "this is our one best chance, the only tribe left to us. All else means our death."

"Kilghari...?" Hayika looked at her as if making one last appeal.

Kilghari nodded. "Yes, I am staying with them. I do not want to live all my life like a hunted animal. Hayika, put down your sword. There is no place left to run."

Very slowly Hayika laid down her sword, filling the last place in the circle with that blade. "Peace, then," she said through her teeth. There was a burst of wild cheering from among the women.

The circle was complete. The blades on the dark ground flashed in the firelight like the Great Star itself shining in the night sky. For that moment all the women in that circle seemed to me filled with beauty, even those I had quarrels with. The sword circles with the fire at the center quivered and shimmered in my tears. I heard Rishka say, "Now we must do a Muinyairin sword dance." When I looked up it was Shalamith who shimmered in my tears, all golden again, the Goddess Herself. She had come out of the shelter and was standing with her ferl in her hands.

"Back," Hayika shouted in a suddenly changed mood. "Back out of the way, all of you. Now you will see the fastest feet to dance in freedom." We all drew back to watch. Some of the Sheezerti took out small drums. Two of them had flutes. Shalamith went to sit by them. Music poured out as if the night itself had come alive.

To cheers and shouts, Zari stripped off her shirt and boots. She flung her arms high. "To the Goddess who shines in all of us," she called out. "To the Mother who guides all our lives." Then she leapt into the circle of swords, dancing with incredible grace and speed between the hilts so that no blade moved, while the other Muinyairin clapped in time to her feet. She went four times around the circle alone. Then with a shout, Rishka joined her. After her, Kilghari and several other Muinyairin jumped into the dance. Finally Hayika herself threw back her head and gave a loud cry before she leapt in.

All shirtless, their bodies flashing bronze and copper in the firelight, they wove round and round between the swords, meeting each other in steps so quick and intricate that it was hard for the eye to follow. A strange, wailing cry rose from the dancers, to be echoed back by some of the watchers. Beads, braids, and flashing breasts caught the light as the drummers quickened their tempo and the flutes wailed in a sad and joyful echo of human voices. Over it all rose the sound of Shalamith's ferl. Her voice was like the voice of the Goddess Herself. It seemed that the dance went faster and faster with wild leaps, claps, turns, and the thunder of stamping feet from those watching. After a while it all began to blur: color, light, sound, motion, all flowing together till I grew too dizzy to watch any more. They may have danced all night. I finally sank down right where I was standing and fell asleep there on the hard ground.

★

That next morning there was a sort of wild gaiety around the camp. In those few hours I heard more laughter and singing than I had in all the time we had been together. Women who had never exchanged a word before and had given each other nothing but hostile and suspicious glances were talking eagerly together. I heard Rishka's laughter ring out across the clearing as she taught one of the new Shokarn to ride. I had never heard her laugh that way before, sounding so free and young. Always before her laughter had an edge of bitterness in it, and some pain as well. Someone had laid out a loose circle of swords, and Zari, who was usually so shy, was glowing with pleasure and exertion as she leapt agilely between them. She was teaching Murghanth and some of the other Sheezerti the steps of the sword dance while the rest of them watched and clapped along with some of the Muinyairin who were shouting encouragement.

It looked like a giant festival that morning, not a camp of fugitives. Thalyisi had even put dried fruit in the porridge so that it tasted like pudding. All of us cheered for her, but under all the gaiety I felt the tension, the threat, the ominous waiting for the inevitable. I wondered that the others did not feel it, too.

Walking back up from the stream, I noticed Hamiuri and Telakeet standing by the cookfire, heads bent together, talking intently. When Hamiuri looked up and swept the clearing with her eyes, clearly looking for someone, a shiver went up my spine. Lhiri was just coming out of the trees with a huge bundle of wood for the fire. I wanted to shout a warning to her. When she dropped it on the stack, Hamiuri silently beckoned her over. Unashamedly I moved forward to hear what was to be said, as did several other women. Now I saw that I was not the only one who had been waiting that morning.

Lhiri went with slow, reluctant steps, eyes to the ground, but when she reached Hamiuri she suddenly threw back her head and said defiantly, "Do what you want with me, Witch. It is hopeless. I cannot stop myself from loving her even if it means my banishment."

Before either of the Witches could answer, Nunyair ran up, appearing as if out of nowhere to throw her arm protectively over Lhiri's shoulder. "It was my fault, not hers. I could not stop myself from looking. Send me away, but not her."

"No, no, Nunyair, you would die out there. Send me if you want to, Hamiuri. I broke the pledge, I was the first to speak."

"Oh, Lhiri, the fault is mine. If not for my Shokarn pride that does not want to let you be my equal there would be no quarrel. Neither one of us would have to be standing here, begging in front of Witches for each other's lives."

"And that must be very hard on that same Shokarn pride," Telakeet said quickly with a grin of malicious amusement.

Hamiuri was shaking her head. "There is no question that you love each other and no need to prove it. It is only that the rest of us cannot afford the uproar of your loving. There is also no question but that you both broke your pledge. We all could see the looks of longing you gave each other across the fire circle long before the first words were spoken." She turned and said something rapidly to Telakeet in words I did not understand. Then, with a nod, she said to her in Kourmairi, "Yours now. Do what you can." With another nod to the rest of us, she turned and walked away.

"Well," Telakeet said, looking at each of them intently, "you have been left to my mercy and that is something I have little of, as I am sure you both know." Lhiri and Nunyair had clasped each other's hands and were standing as close as possible, looking much like two frightened children facing a monster together.

Telakeet intoned some words in that other language and made some signs in the air with the glowing end of a stick she took from the fire. My eyes were caught by that bright line of red. With a sudden twist of her wrist she flung the stick back in. When it burst into flames she silently signaled them both to separate, took each of them by an arm, and walked them toward the fire. She stopped just before it, saying, "Lhiri, Nunyair, each of you hold out a hand just above the flame, as close as you can bear it." They did as she said, seeming to move without will, as if they could not help themselves. When the heat grew too intense and they tried to draw back in pain, she gripped them tightly just below the elbow. "More, more, that is not enough. If we do not do it well this time it will all be to no purpose and must be done again." Though they cried out and struggled against her hold, something in her words appeared to bind them. "Hotter! Hotter!" Telakeet hissed. "It must be hotter for burning out the fires of anger, for burning out the fires of pride, the fires of conflict."

None of the rest of us seemed able to make a move to stop this or even to speak. When they were both screaming, Telakeet withdrew their hands, saying, "Perhaps that will be enough to remember by." Then she crushed their tortured palms together, rubbing them against each other so that they screamed again. "A bond of pain to replace the bond of anger," she said loudly, as she bound their hands together with a scarf. With some ritual words she passed her fingers back and forth across the knots. "You will not be able to untie this till I tell you to. Meanwhile, you will feel each other's pain as if it were your own, as indeed it will be. Bound together in this way you cannot move without the other's consent. You will go everywhere together, to eat and sleep and even do your most personal business. Hopefully, by the time you are freed, you will have found a way to talk without insults, perhaps even some better way to show your love than by fighting with each other. Now go and work out your lives." Awkwardly and hastily they backed away from Telakeet's fierce glare. I heard myself screaming as I fell face forward on the ground.

When I came to I was lying under the trees and Pell was holding a damp cloth to my head. "Well, Tazzi, for all Alyeeta's training you are still too much of an empath."

I reached up and took her hand. "Pell, how can you let this happen? Do something! Talk to Telakeet! This is too cruel. It has to stop. She will listen to you."

Pell shook her head. "In the first place Telakeet listens to no one but herself, certainly to none of us and seldom even to the other Witches. Besides, I think she had Hamiuri's consent and perhaps even her direction in this. In the second place I have done all I can for those two, all I can think of. So have you, and so have many others. Let it run its course now. Let Telakeet do her worst or her best, however that might be and Hamiuri, too. They are welcome to it."

"But Lhiri only spoke of love," I pleaded.

"And how long would that take to turn to hate again. No, no, let it go, Tazzi. Let it go, I tell you, and do not turn to me. It is out of my hands now and I am glad of it. I think all this playing at being a leader is a fool's game, good only for making trouble for oneself. When this is over I plan to lie about in the sun getting fat and lazy. If women want something done they will have to ask me, maybe even twice or perhaps three times."

"Who will be leader then, Pell? Who will keep us all together?"

"You, Tazzi," she answered instantly, as if the answer had been waiting there. "You, but not yet, remember that, not yet. It is still my curse to carry for a little while longer. Now if you are feeling well enough I will go back to what I was doing." With no more words she stood up and strode away, leaving me shivering in the shade of the great trees.

Later I went with Lhiri and Nunyair to ask Olna for some healing salve, as nothing of mine seemed to ease the pain. She shook her head, saying to them, "This is not my healing to do, nor is it Tazzi's. It is your own. Put all your healing energy into each other's hands. When you have learned to do that, you will have learned much else as well."

It was hard to believe that Olna would be so unfeeling. At last I ran to Shalamith in tears, saying that the Witches were as cruel as the Zarn's guards. She looked at me with a look that seemed full of pity and much else besides. With a gentle hand she reached out to stroke my hair. "It is far less painful than a banishment, Tazzi. What other choices did we have? This hurts only the hand and that only for a short while. A banishment would likely cost their lives, and what a waste that would be. Sometimes, when all else fails, a new pain is the best cure for an old pain." This last part she said with great seriousness, then suddenly flashed me her shining smile. I shook my head, thinking this a harsh wisdom and did not speak to her for several days. Telakeet and Hamiuri I avoided altogether.

But, of course, Shalamith was more right than I was. Lhiri and Nunyair spoke softly to each other as they moved with care around the camp like bound twins. They slept wrapped together for comfort. When their hands healed they turned again to being lovers, but this time it was safe. The rage did not return. Later Lhiri confessed to me that if ever she felt some hint of her old anger coming back her hand would start to burn. That would be enough to quickly cool the fire.

Meanwhile my own affairs did not run so well. Rishka and I had fallen to quarreling again, though with some caution this time. At last it grew so apparent that Olna finally sought me out to ask, "Tazzi, how is it you can mend the quarrels of others when your own heart is so bitter you cannot even mend your quarrel with your lover?"

Her tone was gentle enough, but I felt reproach in the words and bristled with offense. "Why ask me," I snapped. "How would I know of such things? I am only a simple farm girl. Ask the Goddess. It is She who distributes gifts. You no doubt speak to Her with ease."

Olna raised her eyebrows at that and gave me a strange look. It was not hurt, it was something else, though feeling rebuked I had no doubt meant to be hurtful. She said thoughtfully, "Well, Tazzi, a time may come when you will need an answer to that question. Asking the Goddess may be the best way to find it."

I stared after her when she left, in an agony of confusion. Now, added to all my other feelings about Olna, there was my shame and embarrassment. I had spoken spitefully to someone who never treated me with anything but kindness, even when it was least deserved. Her question was fair enough. It was the same question I asked myself so many times. Still, every time I saw her talking to Rishka, I bristled again and felt a rush of unreasoning anger. They talked together more and more now. When I asked Rishka what they spoke of, she shrugged and would not answer. This, of course, only added to my anger.

★

There was a sense of expectancy all through the camp. It would soon be time to go. It was in the air, in every word we exchanged, in every piece of work we did — time to leave, time to leave, time to be moving on. I was restless and discontented, eager for the change. The clearing, with so many of us crowded together there, had become almost untenable. Being on the move again meant being that much closer to some place where we could finally make a home, wherever that was, whatever that might mean.

Renaise, with the help of the Sheezerti, kept us all in readiness. Kazouri and Zenoria were constantly urging Pell to leave, saying it was only a matter of time before the Zarn moved against us. I saw Pell caught in between, wanting to be on the road as much as any of us, more perhaps, yet knowing that leaving meant an end to waiting for Irdris and the others, meant abandoning hope for them. She was also waiting for the last stragglers to be found, not wanting to leave anyone. And indeed, new ones kept coming in, but never Irdris.

We doubled our sentries, set watchers at all the roads, but in the end it was not our own vigilance that kept us safe. It was Hereschell riding back with word. With an air of urgency he rode straight up to Pell while the rest of us crowded around.

"Tov from the Thieves Guild said you would remember him. He says that he owes you a life-debt. He sought me out to tell me that the guards know where you are and are massing in the hundreds. They hope to catch you all together in a great circle of fastfire and be done with star-brats and Witches all at once, or to scatter you and hunt you down one last time. You must leave as soon as you can make ready."

Before he had even finished I saw Zenoria dash for her horse. She leapt on and rode past Hereschell at a run. "How long?" she shouted as she passed.

"Not long, they are already on the road in back of me," he shouted back. "They are riding fast and gathering more as they come."

Zenoria gave the loud, wailing cry that was their signal. Jhemar, Rishka, Zari, and Daijar were all running for their horses. They galloped out of the clearing after Zenoria while the rest of us rushed to break camp with Pell and Renaise shouting orders.

23

Leaving! We were leaving! We were going at last! We were going west, west to the sea, west away from Eezore, west out of reach of the Zarn's guards, going away from burning death, away from posted edicts that turned us into hunted animals, away from the hatred of men. West!

Everyone was scrambling to pack. The clearing was in an uproar, a fast-turning wheel with Renaise at the hub, shouting commands. Pell had beckoned me over for some last-minute directions when I heard Alyeeta call out, "My books! The books must be saved!"

Pell began shaking her head. "No time for books," she was muttering. "No time for that now."

"Pell, we cannot leave her books. There is a world in them we will need. Besides, we cannot do that to Alyeeta, not after all her help to us."

"There is no time for that now," Pell said, louder. "Remember your promise to obey me, Tazzi."

I drew back from her. "No, Pell, not in this, no matter what I promised. This I must do even if you never speak to me again, even if afterward you drive me out of the gathering."

She threw up her hands in disgust. "Goddess save me from such stubbornness! What use is it to be leader when no one listens? Go then, and be quick about it!"

Ashai was already there before me, as well as the other Witches, all of them packing Alyeeta's shelter in a frenzy. "The books first," Alyeeta kept saying, "only the books, nothing else matters."

I crouched beside Ashai, stuffing books into oiled sacks that could be strapped across a horse's back. We worked together, mostly in speed and silence, until Ashai burst out in a voice thick with grief, "If Irdris were here she would be doing this with me instead of you."

"Well, Irdris is not, so we must do it ourselves," I snapped savagely, anger covering my own grief. Ashai turned back to her packing, looking as if I had slapped her. After that she said nothing to me that was not needed for our work together.

In less than two hours the horses came pouring into camp with Zenoria in the lead. Women came running quickly to find their horses. Those with no horse to ride were hastily paired with one. The rest of the horses we began to load with everything from camp. All that Alyeeta was taking was already stacked by the entrance to her shelter. Ashai and I saw to it that the books found horse-space before we went on to other loading.

Well before nightfall we had cleared the camp. We even scattered our temporary shelters, but there could be no question that a great number had gathered there. The clearing was deeply trampled with the hooves of many horses. As Alyeeta mounted Gandolair I saw her looking back one last time. When she turned back and caught me watching, she said with a shrug, "Who knows what will be left when I see this next."

There were far too many of us now to ride quietly or secretly any more. The noise of all those horses on the move was like a steady rolling thunder in my head. We went by the straightest way, going northwest till we reached the Zarn's highroad that ran true west from Eezore to the sea. Pell had already sent Kazouri and Jhemar riding north and south to warn the other gatherings that the time had finally come. We would likely meet with them again on the next day's ride. Josleen and Megyair had ridden ahead of us to warn Yaniri we were coming. Tzaneel and several others had gone back to Pell's shelter to help organize the burned ones for departure. They would be coming by a slower and more secret route. Hereschell had promised that he would send back some Wanderer wagons to help with their moving.

We rode most of that night, only stopping for quick rests, and were on the road again shortly after dawn. Always before, I had ridden in fear of discovery. Now it was very different. The way cleared in front of us as if by magic. Riders, farm wagons, even some fancy carriages pulled off to the side to let us pass. When we rode through villages people shouted and poured out to see us, but kept a careful distance. Each time, after the first rock or so returned to the sender, nothing more was thrown.

Often people watched in silence. "Khal Hadera Lossien!" Rishka would shout like a greeting, waving to them as we rode past. She had raised some sort of bright banner on a pole attached to Lightfoot's saddle. I noticed that most of the other Muinyairin had returned to their own style of dressing. Many had banners or streamers decking themselves or their horses — brave, bold colors flapping in the wind. I had grown used to dressing in drab browns for concealment and for trying to pass as a farm boy. Sporting bright colors and drawing attention to oneself in the Muinyairin manner seemed an act of outrageous daring.

By midmorning we even encountered a small company of guards, no more than ten or so. Pell, riding at the front, called out to them, "Quickly now, clear the road to let us pass and we will leave you unharmed. But do not try to block our way!" There was a frightened shout from their captain and some quick orders given. I must confess, it gave me delicious pleasure to see them spin about and scramble up the bank to make way for us.

"Khal Hadera Lossien!" I shouted into their startled faces. Others took up the cry, "Khal Hadera Lossien!" The sound rose and rose until the words lost all shape and meaning, like wind howling through the trees when a storm is rising. Khal Hadera Lossien! Khal Hadera Lossien! Khal Hadera Lossien!

Shortly after midday I heard shouts in front of me and saw Kazouri's great bulk at the head of another gathering, riding in from the right to join us at a crossroad. We flowed together, merging like the water of two rivers. Later that afternoon Jhemar joined us from the south. As far as I could see, looking forward and back, the road was filled with horses and with women riding. The Khal Hadera Lossien were on the move.

Cruzia, riding near me, began to sing in a high, clear voice, "The river is rising, gathering more. We are the waters, we are the shore." It was a simple Kourmairi farm song, sung in the fall for the return of rain after the summer drought, but it brought sudden tears to my eyes. Thalyisi joined her and then Renaise and then Zenoria. Other women all around me took up the song, some voices sweet and high, others deep and rich. "...We are the waters, we are the shore..." I could even hear Pell singing, and a deep booming that must have been Kazouri. The sound rose and fell, sweeping forward in waves like a summer breeze through a field of grain. Ahead I could hear Shalamith singing with that heart-searing sweetness and power, "...river is rising, gathering more..." I added my own voice, "The river is rising..." The song itself was like a river. It seemed to gather us up and carry us forward. "The river is rising, gathering more. We are the waters, we are the shore..."

In some places there were people all along the road. Word must have gone out that the Star-Born were riding. They stayed safely back, sometimes staring at us silently as we passed, simple Kourmairi farm folk who themselves must have sung that song many times at Fall Festival. Khal Hadera Lossien, I said to myself over and over in my heart. We are the river, the river is rising...

★

The next morning Alyeeta rode up next to me. I was surprised to see her, as the Witches had been keeping mostly to themselves. She was on a different horse, no doubt to give Gandolair a rest. She looked quite uncomfortable and out of sorts. I sensed immediately that her sudden appearance at my side was no accident, that in fact something was wanted of me, though at first I had no notion of what it might be. She complained about the ride, the road, this fool of a horse she was stuck on, the guards, "May their guts rot out and their members drop off," this stable-food she was expected to eat, and worst of all those Khal Hadera Lossien that she had been foolish enough to join up with and for whose sake she had lost her home. The way she spit out those words, as if they had a bad taste, she made our proud new name sound like so much trash. Still, she said not one word of what she really wanted.

"Alyeeta," I finally shouted in exasperation when I could not listen to any more, "what in the name of the Goddess is this all about!? What do you want of me?"

"I was about to tell you, when you interrupted me," she snapped. With that, she fell provokingly silent, chewing on her lip.

"Alyeeta, please..."

She looked at me for a while with her eyes narrowed. Things were clearly working in her head, but well shielded from me. At last she said slowly, hesitating as if thinking aloud, "How do we know ... How will we ever know ... Maybe, after all, they did not ... Maybe Hereschell was wrong or Tov from the Thieves Guild was wrong ... Maybe..." She fell silent again.

"Alyeeta, what is this all about? Say it so I can understand. *What do you want?*"

"To go back to see my hut and my clearing. To go back to see if they really came there, if everything is really burnt and gone."

"And you want me to go with you," I burst out, finally understanding. She nodded. "Only if you want to."

"Oh, Mother," I groaned. I turned away and found myself face-to-face with Pell, who had ridden up on the other side of me and was looking at me intently. "And what do *you* want?" I snapped at her.

"I need to know what it is that follows us, how many and how fast. I could send another back, but I would rather see for myself."

"You want to go back and you want me to go with you, is that it?"

"Yes, but only if you want to. Otherwise Alyeeta and I will ride back together."

"Madness! A fool's plan!" I growled at her. "Only a madwoman would go back there."

Pell nodded. "Only a madwoman, no doubt you are right. Find yourself a different horse and give Dancer a rest."

That is how I found myself going back into danger, riding east on a strange horse in the company off two madwomen, when I wanted with all my heart to be riding west on Dancer's back in a great river of women flowing to the sea. In the end, of course, I had no choice. I went back with them because I could not imagine going on without them. I would have had no peace with it and no sleep either. What if they did not return? What if, like Irdris ... No, it was better to go with them than not to know. Besides, I owed Pell a great debt. My debt to Alyeeta I could not begin to count. And I could not even grumble too much. What if they decided to leave me after all? Well, it was not the first time Pell and Alyeeta between them had decided my fate. I wondered as I rode if they had planned this together.

With Pell swearing to our swift return, we left the rest of them on their way west to Yaniri's under Kazouri's leadership. This time we did not go on the open road. We went stealthy and silent, following where Pell led. Or perhaps where Torvir led. Though she had told me to let Dancer rest, she had taken her own horse. He was snaking his way through the woods on paths and trails I could not even see. Not for the first time, I wondered if it was really the horse who knew the way instead of Pell. Alyeeta did not once complain of her horse or lack of food and sleep or the hard road or of anything at all, for that matter. In fact, she took Pell's guidance in everything, with no mockery and no question. I had never seen Alyeeta so subdued.

When we drew close we used the utmost caution, stopping often to 'sense' the way ahead as well as to listen and watch for signs. By the time we were on the last stretch of the path from Hamishair, the sun was going down. Long before we reached the clearing I heard Alyeeta's silent, inner cry, /Gone! All gone! All gone!/ Soon we could smell smoke and a sharp, acrid odor that burned the nose and throat and made the eyes water.

"Fastfire," Pell hissed.

Before we went around the final bend we dismounted, leaving the horses to guard our path. From there we crept forward cautiously on foot, but could sense no human presence nearby. As we came within sight of the clearing, our way was blocked by a chaos of crisscrossed branches whose leaves were already wilting. Some of the giant trees that had ringed the clearing had been cut and toppled. Their huge trunks lay across our path. Beyond them we could see the charred ruin of Alyeeta's shelter, still smoldering and burnt to the ground. We had to fight our way through the tangled barrier of branches to reach it.

Alyeeta's face, as she stared at it, was all twisted with anguish. She looked suddenly old and bent and incredibly weary. "Humans," she spit out with contempt. "They are so good at destroying. It is in their blood. Even the trees were made to suffer. Nothing left, nothing of all those years..."

"If not for Hereschell's warning...," Pell said in a grim voice, leaving the rest unsaid.

With one of those sudden changes of hers, Alyeeta pulled herself up straight. "Well, I said I wanted to know and now I know. Now I will not have to wonder. It is finished, all gone and done with, nothing to come back for — ever. At least it was only a hut in the woods, not a whole convent full of books and paintings and treasures, only a little hut, not years of pride and glory and learning all pulled down in ruins..." She shook her head. "Not a whole convent full of young lives..." Then, abruptly, she turned her back on what had been her shelter. "At least I have my books," she said in a flat, hard voice with a terrible tone of finality.

I was circling the shelter to see what, if anything, remained, when I saw it — a hand as charred as the wood around it. I had to cover my mouth not to cry out. It was hard to see in that fading light. Until I was right beside it I had thought it to be only a burnt branch, a part of the ruin.

Pell and Alyeeta were instantly at my side. This nameless one was buried in the debris. Mindlessly, we all three began trying to free her, pulling away charred wood with our bare hands. Some of it was still hot and smoldering. Soon we were coughing and choking from the fastfire. Then Alyeeta gave a cry, "A second one! They must have died together."

Abruptly Pell straightened and grabbed my arm. "Leave off! This is madness! We are no use to them now. Dead is dead. They do not care where they lie." She wiped her hands off on her pants and shook her head. "They must have come here looking for us and been trapped by the guard. We should have left a watch."

I knew she was accusing herself now. "We left signs," I said quickly.

"Not enough, as you can see. It is as if I had done this myself. What good is a leader if she cannot think ahead."

"Pell..." I reached out a hand to comfort her.

She looked away as if she had not noticed. Then suddenly she bent down, picked up something from the rubble, and wiped it on her pants. There was a flash of metal. A bracelet, blackened, twisted, and partly melted by the heat, lay in her hand. With a grimace of effort she bent it back into shape and slipped it on her wrist. "To remind me to do everything that needs doing," she said fiercely. "To remind me that forgetting may mean someone's death." With that she turned away from the smoking ruin and said harshly, "Time to leave. We have seen what we came to see. Now we must think of the living." She was touching that twisted bracelet, turning it on her wrist, a gesture I was to see many times. A look came across her face of such naked rage that I stepped back in fear. "Those guardsmen," she hissed through her teeth, "at this moment I would like to have a sword through their guts, or better yet see them struggling helpless in a fire, looking at their own deaths."

"You sound almost like Rishka," I whispered. I may only have thought it. I may not even have said it aloud, but she answered instantly, "Rishka is not always wrong, though she is often mistaken."

As we remounted, Pell said in a calmer voice, "Now we go to find the guard. Since we cannot use swords or fire, we will have to think of some other way to reward them for this ugly work." She sounded like herself again, but under that mocking tone I felt her terrifying rage.

Finding the guard was easily enough done. They, of course, felt no need for concealment. They were openly camped on either side of the Great Road. It had just turned true dark when we found ourselves sitting on our horses at the top of a small hill. We were looking down at their camp, watching the last of the flares being lit.

"Well, Alyeeta," Pell said at last, "you are far better with numbers than I am. What do you think?"

"Less than a thousand and more than five hundred, seven, eight, something like that. You are more than twice their number and with still more waiting at Yaniri's."

"I think they have no idea of our numbers. Perhaps we should simply stop and face them. I, for one, am tired of running."

"No!" Alyeeta said sharply, "you are not yet ready. Soon, but not now. You need this coming winter together."

I was shaking my head, remembering Marshlegs's death. "Pell, they would shoot our horses out from under us. They would continue to harry us and increase their numbers till they more than matched ours. We can face them down once, perhaps twice, but it will not buy us peace or time."

"Yes, yes, all true enough," Pell said impatiently. "But someday, someday we shall find a place to stand, a line of safety from which we will not have to run. Someday soon, I hope. I want to see it in my lifetime. I have lived as a fugitive long enough. I want the luxury of living as a free person." She dismounted and went forward to look over the edge. From there she beckoned to us. "Look how they have their horses penned. A neat enclosure as if made by the hand of the Goddess Herself."

Most of the horses were being held in a natural enclosure between high rock walls, of which our little bluff formed one side. The front of it was closed off by some posts and what looked to be rope strung between them, a fragile gate, but well guarded as I could see.

Pell was nodding as if to herself, muttering, "Good, good, very good." Then she said speculatively, "There is but a little rope between those horses and freedom. That is easily taken care of. It would surely foul their plans if their horses were all loose and running about the countryside."

"No, Pell," I said quickly, putting my hand on her arm. "No, please, we are three to some eight hundred men. I have no stomach for this, not after Eezore."

She shook off my hand and said with a kind of fierce pleasure, "But I have the stomach for it, and, more than that, the heart for it. Since this is the only kind of revenge we are allowed, let us do it well. Besides, I can already see the way. You will only have to stand watch and make sure I get safely out."

"Please, Pell," I begged. My stomach was in knots. I could see her body mangled and battered on the floor of the horse pen, or even worse, falling in flames as Askarth had.

"Enough, Tazzi," she said impatiently. "Do I stop you from doing what you must do? I need you now. I need your willing help, not your well-meant cowardice. Besides, I believe you owe me this one."

I nodded, mutely remembering all my wrongs.

"Alyeeta, what do you say?"

"A clever plan as long as it is you, not me, climbing down that bluff wall."

We drew back and tied our horses in the woods, well away from the edge. "Fasten them securely," Pell said. "They may be frightened by the noise. It would not do to lose our own horses in this little game."

With the utmost care we crept to the edge of the bluff to peer down into the horse pit below. At one point the rock face curved in sharply. The area of the fence was the narrowest part of the enclosure. In that curve was a crack or crevice partly hidden from the guard. It appeared to run almost to the ground.

Pell pulled a coil of rope from her pouch. "Here is a good stout tree to tie to. Not for nothing was I a thief all those years. It is about to serve us well." Though I could not see her face, I could hear in her voice how much she was enjoying this. "It will delay the guards for a while if they have to walk about like common folk. They think themselves so well protected, but all their numbers will not save them from one spider in the night."

After Pell had the rope securely tied, she judged the distance and made a foot loop in the other end of it. "Now, keep a wrap around the tree and let me down smoothly but swiftly," she cautioned. "This is much easier and faster than trying to climb the rope, though I could do that too, if I had to. Be ready when I signal to pull me up fast. That will be the hard part. I will tug on the rope to let you know. No matter what else is happening, always keep a hand on it. Here, wrap some rags around your hands, or the rope will burn your palms going through." Saying that, she took her knife, made a little cut near the hem of her tunic, and tore a wide strip from it. After giving us each a piece of cloth, she slid her knife back into a sheath in her boot. I saw her pull it out and put it back several more times, as if to assure herself it would come easily to hand.

While we wrapped our hands, Pell crept to the edge again. She watched intently for a few moments and then came back to say, "There are many guards before the gate, but only one who really patrols there, walking back and forth." She rubbed her hands together briskly as if to get them ready. Then she drew a pair of gloves from her pouch and pulled them on, fitting them snugly and with care over each finger. This was the first time I had ever seen Pell wear gloves. That done, she took off the bracelet, slipped it in her pouch, and handed the pouch to me. "Strap that on to keep for me. I need nothing to encumber me now."

Beckoning us forward, Pell asked sharply, "Are you ready? Get a tight grip on the rope and stand firm. Good, now he has turned his back." Saying this, she slipped her foot into the loop and wriggled to the edge. "Hold tight," she warned us as she vanished into the darkness. Alyeeta and I braced ourselves. Suddenly I felt Pell's weight fall against my hands. The rope seemed to whistle through my palms. I was afraid we would drop her. Then I heard Pell hiss in the dark, "Faster, faster, give me more rope."

My arms felt stretched to the breaking point when abruptly the rope went slack. After that I could hear nothing of Pell over the noise of the encampment. I kept my eyes glued to the guard who had turned and was coming back our way. When he turned back again he had an extra shadow. My heart was in my mouth, but even as I watched, I kept my hand securely on the rope. I saw Pell slip forward. Just for an instant her knife flashed. Once, twice, three times, four times. The ropes of the fence went slack and the shadow melted back again into a pit of shadows.

The guard was halfway back when he gave the cry, "The ropes! The gate! 'Ware thief!"

The savage cry of the Oolanth cat ripped the air, twice and then twice more. With wild cries and snorts of terror, the horses dashed about in panic, then turned as if at a signal and rushed for the opening. Guards ran forward, shouting, "Stop them! Catch them!" while at the same moment other guards leapt out of the way of the galloping horses, colliding with each other in the confusion. There were screams and shouts and the thunder of horses running. I felt a tug on the rope.

"Now," I hissed to Alyeeta. We both threw our weight against the rope, groaning with effort, hauling it up hand over hand with Pell dangling somewhere in the darkness below. More and more flares were being lit. Pell was only partway up when the wall was caught in the light of the flares. Someone shouted, "There he is! The horse thief! Up there climbing a rope." There was a series of loud commands followed by a shower of flaming arrows that went far wide of us. I could feel the swing of Pell's weight. There was another command and a second volley of arrows, much closer this time. Alyeeta and I were struggling to pull hard and keep low at the same time when from below I heard one of the guards shouting, "The rope! The rope is burning! We have him now!"

"Hurry, Alyeeta!" I shouted frantically. "Faster! Hurry!" Almost immediately the rope went slack. In the next instant we staggered back, followed by the burning rope end that landed at our feet. I was tensed for the cry and the sickening thud when I heard Pell's voice coming from close by.

"Give me a hand here. Bring the end of the rope."

The deepest part of the crevice itself was still in shadow. Crawling quickly to the edge and leaning far out, I could just make out her dark form below me there.

"Make another loop and snake it down to me," she whispered hoarsely. "I cannot let go of my handholds to do that." Her words were scarcely audible over the uproar rising from the guard camp. Trying to control my shaking hands, I rushed to do as she said, lowering the rope into the darkness. In a moment I felt a slight tug on it.

"Now, very slowly, haul me straight up in this corner. I do not wish to swing out in the light of their flares and have to test my powers by being a target for a hundred flaming arrows." My arms aching with effort, we hauled on the rope again. "Slowly, slowly now, easy, very good, just so, keep steady." Pell kept up a constant stream of encouragements and cautionings. From behind me I could hear Alyeeta's ragged, panting breath, and now I could see Pell rising out of the shadows under my feet. She swung her arms over the top. With a groan I reached out and grabbed her shoulder. With Alyeeta helping on the other side, we hauled her up over the edge and pulled her to her feet. Her hair and clothes smelled singed. She shook her foot free. The rope swung out in front of the bluff face. There was a loud shout from below, followed by another round of arrows. Most of them fell short, but some lodged in the trees around us, lighting up the woods. "Keep low and run for the horses," Pell hissed at us.

In my one quick glance below, I saw that most of the horses had poured out of the horse pen. The guard camp looked like an overturned anthill, with men and horses rushing in all directions. Whoever had ordered those shots at Pell had done well to keep his head in that tumult.

When we reached our horses they were snorting and throwing their heads, pulling nervously against their reins. At that moment I was very glad I had not ridden Dancer into this madness. Pell was laughing and panting, both at the same time. "Not a bad job of work, eh?" she managed to gasp out. "Not bad at all. We are all alive, our horses are here waiting for us. I have no bruises that will not heal in a day or so. And best of all, the guard will be too busy chasing horses for the next few days to think of chasing star-brats. I even got to use my knife for vengeance." She quickly turned her attention to our horses, speaking softly, petting and soothing them. Torvir calmed instantly, rubbing his bony head against her arm.

I was breathing too hard to answer her. Alyeeta, when she could catch her breath, said sourly, "You are gloating now, but you could have had us all killed with your tricks. If I had known what kind of games you planned I would not have come along with you."

"So the Witch is too good to ride out with the horse thief? Well, you were not the one at risk, dangling there on the end of a rope. It was my hide that would have been full of burning holes, not yours. Besides, do you think it was safe and sensible to go back to your clearing right after a guard raid? What if they had left watchers for us? We might have been trapped like..." Her words stopped abruptly. She reached out to me for her pouch, groped about inside for the bracelet, and slipped that twisted metal on her wrist. "Let us be gone from here before they find the way up."

I had to help Alyeeta onto her horse. "I am much older than I look. This is not a healthy way for me to live. Now I suppose we are to ride night and day again," she grumbled.

"Is there any other way to go?" Pell asked jauntily.

This time I had no wish to stay and watch. We rode as hard as horse and rider were able to go. Even so, when we finally reached Yaniri's, the others had already gone on. Even Yaniri herself had left. Her shelter and clearing looked as abandoned and trampled as Alyeeta's had when we departed. The sight of it made my heart ache.

Two women Pell knew from the northern gathering were waiting for us with fresh horses and news of the others. I unsaddled and freed my poor, weary beast and went to greet Dancer, but she was not there. They had taken her with them and left me another in her place.

We slept that night in the abandoned shelter, slept hard and heavy, and were up again by dawn. By late afternoon of the next day we caught up with the rear guard of the Khal Hadera Lossien to loud cheers of welcome. Pell soon wove her way up to the front. Not long after that a halt was called, to rest and make plans.

We were fast approaching the Drylands, that difficult and dangerous crescent of rolling sands that runs up and down the length of Garmishair and is home to most of the Muinyairin. Rishka kept assuring us that the part we were about to cross was under the domain of a particularly wild and ruthless band of tribes. Whether she spoke in truth or for mischief I could not tell. Even without that added worry, the drylands were too dangerous to travel through in the heat of the day, nor were there many places where it was safe to camp. One possible place, Kilghari told us, was the Drugha-Malia. This deep canyon had grass, shade, and a stream at the bottom of it, she said. There we could feed our horses and claim a night's shelter, if it was not already in use.

It was finally decided that a group of Muinyairin, Hayika, Kilghari, Daijar, Noshir, Zari, and two or three others I did not know, would go on ahead so that we could be assured of the place, if possible. If it was already occupied, they would ride back with word. Rishka planned to stay with the line of march and be our guide.

With a touch of envy I watched them get ready. At the last moment Kilghari turned to me. "Why not come with us, Tazzi? Your Dancer is as fast as any of our horses. It grows wearisome after a while plodding along in a line with this vast number."

I was about to shake my head. I had not, after all, spent much time plodding along being bored. I might even have gotten some sleep that way. Instead, much to my surprise I found myself saying, "Why not," as if this were the most natural thing to do. I was wearied beyond all sense and reason, but something in me was restless. Besides, truth be told, I was enormously flattered to think I was good enough to ride with the Muinyairin. I went to find Dancer among the extra horses. For her part, she was overjoyed to see me again and ready to be off.

Pell shook her head and shrugged when I told her. "Well, I have dragged you backward. I suppose I cannot begrudge you rushing forward, though it seems a piece of utter foolishness. Go, go then. Have your fun with the 'Wild Ones.' I do not need you here for now." It was clear she did not want me to go and would not order me to stay.

The Muinyairin teased and raced and sang their wild songs the whole way. They even traded horses at a run. Once Daijar reached out too far doing this and rolled off her horse. We had to stop and swing back for her. She got up laughing and dusted herself off, seeming none the worse for it. I could not begin to match their reckless games. The most I could do was try to keep up with them. I understood little of what was said, but I was glad enough to be riding with them. My heart felt lighter than it had in weeks.

For a while the vegetation had been growing sparser and more bristly. We reached the edge of the drylands toward late afternoon, just as the shadows were beginning to lengthen. Of one accord, the Muinyairin stopped their horses to gaze out at that vast stretch of rolling sands.

"Ochabi Briathi, the Drylands Crescent, the Sea of Sand," Kilghari said, after a moment's silence. "Home to Muinyairin tribes since time remembers."

"Mother's curse to the lot of them," Hayika muttered. She suddenly urged her horse forward, and the rest of us followed.

Soon after we crossed into the drylands I started to be uneasy. After a while my skin began to crawl. It felt as if we were being watched or followed. Yet, when I turned to look I could see nothing. Besides, where was there to hide in that 'sea of sand'? But the feeling persisted. Finally I rode over next to Kilghari. "Something...," I said with a shiver, "something — I cannot explain what..."

"Yes, I feel it, too. It makes the back of my neck prickle." She called Hayika over and spoke in her ear. Hayika nodded as she listened and then gave a sharp cry, Muinyairin style, to gather the others. As if that had been the signal, a horse whinnied from somewhere ahead of us and a cry rang out from the empty space. Horses and riders sprang up out of the sand to charge straight in our direction. Apparently they had been lying in wait, hiding in a pit behind a hump of sand. Flashing their curved swords, they rode at us with frightful screams and cries. At the last minute they swerved and began to circle us at a run, shouting threats to our lives as well as taunts and insults to our 'manhood.' Some of this was in Kourmairi, no doubt for my benefit. All of it was interspersed with high, shrill yells intended to terrify. There were ten or twelve in all, no more than that, but at that speed it seemed like thirty. From what I could gather, they were saying that we had no 'rods' and peed squatting down, true enough though clearly they thought us to be men and meant it as insult, not as fact. It might all have been funny if they had not looked so threatening.

I heard Hayika saying, "Have no fear for the horses. It is the horses that they want. They will be very careful of them. Just be glad for the powers we have to protect our own skins."

As she spoke, the one who was leading the circle and seemed to be even more daring than the others, turned and charged right at Hayika, shouting, "So you are the leader, eh? I will pick you off first. With you gone the rest of these draiga will soon fall to their knees."

"Well, you are welcome to try," Hayika said, as she urged her horse forward so that she was directly in his path. She did not even flinch when he raised his sword and swung at her with a terrible yell.

In an instant he was slumped over his horse. His yell had turned to a cry of pain. As the horse dashed past Hayika, the rider toppled off and flopped on his back in the sand, blood spurting from his neck. Hayika grabbed the horse's reins as it ran and pulled it to a stop, shouting, "Ours!" With loud yells of rage the other men were turning to charge at her. As she spun to face them, she raised her hand, much as I had seen Alyeeta do. Pointing at the first of them, she called out, "You are next. Are you ready?"

"Witch!" he spit out with a cry of fear. Suddenly he veered away. The others slowed and drew back to consult with each other. It seemed we were not going to be such easy prey after all.

While those men circled together, Hayika took off her shirt and laid it over her horse's neck. Her breasts shone copper red in the setting sun. When the men turned back they began pointing and yelling in surprise, "A woman! A woman!"

"We are all women," Hayika called out over the uproar.

"Then we shall have your bodies as well as your horses."

"You think so? Ask your friend there. First pull him into the shade of your hideaway and stuff that hole with a clean rag before his life's blood leaks away in the sand. Then we can better talk of who will have whose horses or whose bodies or whose lives."

Both sides waited in silence while four of the men dealt with their fallen leader. When they returned and remounted, a big hulking man whom the others called Zarnak seemed ready to take his place. He rode right up to Hayika, looking straight at her breasts and saying in an insolent way, "Well, Witch, what have you to say?"

"There is no use to all this bloodshed. I call a challenge instead." She threw her shirt down in front of them with a flourish. "I challenge the best of you to single combat, mounted, no weapons, no saddles. The first to be unhorsed is the loser. If you win you can have our horses, our bodies, and our goods. If we win we want four horses, those four," she said, choosing and pointing, "as well as the one that is already mine by right of contest. In addition to that, four tents, some food, and a promise of no further obstruction by any Muinyairin from here to the end of the drylands. Now you must talk among yourselves. If you accept, you need to choose your man. Meanwhile, I must ask my women if this plan is suitable to them."

Zarnak gave a signal. With some contemptuous words for shameless, naked women, the men spun their horses about and rode off a short way.

Hayika gathered us together. "It is growing late. We need to be gone from here. This is the fastest way I could think of to be done with these fools. Do you accept me as your 'champion,' or do you have some different plan in mind? Whatever we do, it needs to be something quick."

"Do you ride as well as Rishka?" I asked her.

"Better," she said instantly, not bragging, only stating it as a fact.

"What if you lose?" Kilghari asked. "Do you intend to honor this pledge of our goods, horses, and bodies?"

"Do I look like some kind of a fool? No, I do not intend to turn over anyone's horse or body to those men. But how can I lose? And if I do, then we are only where we were before and no worse off. They will keep attacking us and end up killed or wounded. I, for one, have no wish to go to the Drugha-Malia over a pile of bloody bodies."

"There is not much honor in all this," Daijar said with a strange, one-sided grin on her face. It seemed that she was joking and not joking with the same words.

Hayika gave a snort of laughter. "Honor indeed! Honor me this and honor me that. I may be a Muinyairin, but I am also too much of a star-brat for that. Having a price on your head changes your ideas of honor. I owe honor to those who honor me, not those who think to kill me at every turn. Why should we keep to their rules? We are not the ones who blocked their way and threatened their lives."

"Will they keep to their part of it?" I asked.

"Oh, yes, yes of course," Daijar and Kilghari answered together.

Hayika added, "They would feel it a deep disgrace not to. It would be an offense to their precious manhood." She looked around at us all. "Well, what do you say?"

"I say do it and get on with it and Mother's Luck to you," Daijar answered. "We have a place to ride to, we have work to do, and time is rapidly passing." The rest of us nodded.

Hayika turned and called out loudly to the men, "Are you ready?"

They came riding toward us. "We are ready and I, Zarnak, accept your challenge." This Zarnak was the largest and most imposing of the men. I saw that his eyes were on Hayika's breasts rather than on her face as he spoke.

Hayika did not seem to mind. In fact, she seemed to be displaying herself. She sat very straight on her horse and answered with mocking insolence, "Aha, you have made a mistake. The big ones always fall harder and are not near so agile. You should have chosen that wiry little fellow over there, or that one. But perhaps you chose this great hulk for his loud mouth, or more likely his greedy eyes."

"Argh!" Zarnak growled, taking his eyes from her breasts for the first time. "Take off your saddle, woman, and let us see what you can do. The rest of you, down from your horses and clear the space. Get back in two lines to give us room."

Zarnak and Hayika jumped down to strip their horses, keeping close watch on each other as they did so. "Throw down your shirt, man, if you really mean to do this," Hayika called to him.

Zarnak threw his shirt over hers, shouting, "Done!" The rest of us stepped back in two lines while one man carried the shirts and saddles out of the way.

As if at a signal they both leapt onto their horses. Zarnak swung his horse about, making it rear up while the other men hooted and cheered and clapped. "Well, woman, I am glad to see you half undressed. It will save me the trouble. I have some good uses for the body you are about to forfeit."

"Good uses, eh?" Hayika laughed. "You are not man enough." She danced her horse quite close to him, prancing just out of reach. "First you must get your hands on me, but I think you are secretly afraid." As he lunged toward her she swerved to pass in back of him. "Surely you can see I am the better rider. Too bad you men made such a poor choice. It will be a shabby show, hardly worth the bother. He thinks his strength will win him something, but here it will be of no use. What do you say, women? Should I ask for a better challenger? That one, or perhaps that one?" All this time she kept her horse just clear of him so he could not close with her. "Where is your honor?" she called out as she swerved again. "We risk all in this while you risk so little." By now the men were shouting and stamping, calling her a coward and a cheat.

"Who is a coward?" she shouted as if suddenly angry. "Not Hayika, the Muinyairin. I am afraid of nothing! Nothing!" With that she rode straight at Zarnak. I could see the eagerness on his face, the hunger to get his hands on her body. At the last possible moment she swerved away again before there was contact. If Zarnak had not been so excellent a rider he might easily have lurched forward to a fall.

The men were jumping about wildly now, shouting in a frenzy, "Get her down! Throw her off! Tear her apart! Let us at her!"

Twice more Hayika rode by him in that way. Zarnak was finally in a rage of frustration, turning and turning to keep her in sight. "Come closer so I can get at you, you bitch. You are the one who is afraid. You know it will all be over the moment we close in combat."

"Lies, all lies, as you will see," Hayika taunted back. She rode in again and this time her horse seemed to stumble, bringing her within range. I gave a gasp of fear and the men roared. Zarnak, seeing his chance, lunged hard at her, twisting his shoulder so that the impact would dislodge her without unseating him. In the next instant he was lying on the ground gasping for breath, with his horse galloping off. Hayika was grinning down at him from her horse's back. "Be glad, fool, that it is not your body at forfeit as well as your horse." Without turning, she called out to us, "Catch that horse. It is one of ours now." Daijar leapt on her horse and went speeding after the fleeing animal.

The other men were running forward, shouting in surprise. Hayika was shaking her head. "Just as I said, the heavy ones fall hard. I told you to chose someone more agile." With those words she swung off her horse and went striding over to pick up her shirt. Slinging it over her shoulder, she strolled back to the cluster of men who were helping up their fallen comrade. He was still gasping for breath, shaking his head as if to clear it from a blow. They were teasing him cruelly for falling before a woman, though I noticed that none of them looked at her breasts any more. They all occupied their eyes elsewhere. Now I could breathe normally again. The whole contest had taken less time than the talking on it had.

Hayika sauntered right in among them, saying, "Now we have some business to discuss." Several of them reached out to clap her on the back. I could hear them saying, "Well done!"

"Is that safe?" I whispered anxiously to Kilghari. "Is she safe among them?"

"Perfectly safe," she whispered back. "A short while ago it would have been deadly, but yes, now it is safe. They will honor their pledge."

Soon they were all sitting down and bargaining together with good-natured banter, Hayika and a circle of men who minutes before would have robbed, raped, and murdered us.

24

The Drugha-Malia — in the setting sun the walls of the canyon glowed red, orange, and yellow in bands of color, the deep shadows lay purple at the edges, and a stream flowed through, almost black with the reflection of the coming night. Trees, grasses, flowers — all seemed to flourish there in abundance, and clouds of small birds rose before us in a rush of feathered singing.

"What does that mean, Drugha-Malia?" I asked Zari, who was riding next to me. She blushed and would not answer, but from behind us Hayika gave a snort of rude laughter, and Kilghari said, with amusement, "It means 'Cunt-of-the-Great-Mother' or 'Great-Cunt-of-the-Mother,' depending on which way you weight the words, but it is not nearly so rude in Muinyairin as in Kourmairi." It was easy to see how it had gotten its name, this deep crevice in the earth that was lush and moist and welcoming, opening so suddenly out of the rolling sands.

As we rode down into the purple shadows, cool air rushed up to greet us, a blessed relief after the heat of the drylands. Some of the Muinyairin men had insisted on riding with us so that no "bad men" — their own words, truly — should bother us on the way. Hayika and Daijar had ridden along beside them, chatting like old friends till suddenly Zarnak had said, "Aha! So that is it. That is how you bested me so easily. You are one of those, one of the star-cursed, are you not?"

Hayika drew herself up very straight. "Yes, we are Star-Born, all of us. We are the Khal Hadera Lossien, but I did not use the advantage of my powers. There was no need for that. You gave it all away yourself in your eagerness to get your hands on this woman's body. I only gave you a little help."

The others roared with laughter. Zarnak himself appeared to be quite pleased with this turn of things. "Well, well, think of that, the star-cursed. That will make good telling sometime around a night's fire."

Hayika explained to them that we were expecting about several hundred more, flashing her hands many times to give them some notion of the number. They seemed amazed at this and may not have believed her, but in the end they took away their own gear as well as several horses they had staked there, for they had been camping in the canyon. They even left us their cookfires and wished us well. By the time they left, these Muinyairin men were swearing their friendship to us, even asking if we would give them another challenge sometime, but only for horses and blankets, they said, not for our bodies or our lives this time. Much impressed with our abilities, they promised to practice hard in the meanwhile, if we would honorably pledge not to use our secret powers.

Hayika laughed about it afterward, saying, "I wager that every Muinyairin tribe in the Drylands Crescent will hear this story sooner or later, not such a bad thing for us, really. We will probably become a legend."

Personally, I did not feel near so friendly and was only too glad to see them leave. I had been afraid they would want to settle themselves down for the night to 'protect' us. Though it was already dark by the time they rode away, I instantly stripped off my clothes and waded out into the stream. Shivering in the chill, I scrubbed away, with soapstone and fine sand, the crust of sweat and road-grime that coated my body from all those days of hard riding. Whatever the others may have done toward preparing camp, I knew nothing of it and did nothing for it. Exhausted by my double travels, I spread my sleep roll out on a grassy bank by the stream and, lulled by its music, fell instantly asleep.

When I woke next, it was bright and clear. From the slant of the sun it was already late in the morning, though my sleep place was still in shadow. Rishka was sitting by me, gazing into my face. She smiled when she saw my eyes open. "You are very lovely when you sleep, Tazzi. I have been watching you for some time now. My Muinyairin sisters must have given you a hard ride yesterday." She pulled up a blade of grass and began slowly stroking my face and neck and the inside of my arms with it till I shivered with pleasure. "I hear all of you had a little encounter on the way with some Muinyairin men."

"Little encounter indeed!" I exclaimed, struggling to sit up. "What they wanted was to rape us, rob us, and leave us for dead, all with some peculiar code of honor. But Hayika bested them and then made friends with them. I think she is even wilder than you are. Is it true she is a better rider?"

"Yes, it is true and there is no one else of whom I would say that. There is much else she does as well as or better than I do. She would be a fine woman, but for the bitterness that eats at her heart and sometimes blinds her vision. Hayika was even more ill-treated than I was, but that is hers to tell and not a story for such a fair morning."

I bit my tongue to not reply to this. Rishka in such a fine mood was a rare thing, and I had no wish to spoil it. "You seem very happy today."

She nodded, with a dreamy look on her face. "My happiest times of childhood were here. I love this Drugha-Malia. There is something in this place ... It even seemed to soften my father's hard hand, and perhaps his hard heart as well. The men would all meet together and talk for hours, telling stories and trading horses. The women would gather to play games of padjic or toss-the-pebbles. We children would be forgotten, free to play and explore and go our own ways. Yes, there surely is some magic here. Look at our captain."

I turned where she pointed. Pell and Tamara were strolling arm in arm further down the stream, Tama leaning against Pell and Pell bending to say something in her ear. So they had found each other again. I felt a sudden rush of happiness for them both.

"Come," Rishka said, tugging on my hand. "There is something I have been waiting to show you."

"But I have not yet eaten," I said plaintively. With all my riding back and forth, I felt as if I had not eaten for days. The smell of porridge was wafting up from the cookfires, rich and enticing.

"It will wait," she said, impetuously pulling me to my feet. "We should climb up there before it gets any hotter. I have some trail bread for you here in my pouch." She bent, and all in one motion twisted my bedding and draped it around her shoulders. "Here, I will take your bedroll for you. Leave your pack. We will come back for it later."

Leaning on Rishka's arm for support, I struggled into my boots. I did not even bother with my pants but left them by my pack. Wearing only my boots and tunic and munching on stale trail bread, I followed where she led. We walked rapidly downstream, going away from camp till we came to a crevice in the rock face. Stopping in front of it, Rishka made an upward gesture with her hands. "This is my own secret place that we are going to. I have never shown it to anyone before."

"We are going up that?" My heart sank, and blood began pounding in my ears. I looked up and up that shear rock face. It was like Pell's climb all over again, only now I would be the one doing it, and with no rope.

"It is easy. Just slip inside the crevice. There are deep hand and foot holes carved there. I think others used this place before the Muinyairin — the Ashara, perhaps. Perhaps it was the 'First People' who cut those steps." Saying that, she wedged herself into the crevice and began scrambling up in front of me with little effort till she vanished in the shadows above. She was right. Once I squirmed in after her, I had no trouble following. As if made for much smaller people, there was a little secret stair cleverly concealed there. Much sooner than I expected, we came out on a wide ledge that went along the bluff face for a ways and was almost as flat underfoot as a floor.

I looked out and gave a gasp of surprise. The view from there made me dizzy. I could see the stream below flashing blue and silver in the sun, with our whole busy camp laid out along it. Opposite me, the bluff rose steep and shear with its bands of warm sunset colors. Above the bluff stretched the wide expanse of drylands we had crossed, lying soft and golden in the sun. Way beyond, on the edge of the horizon, lay a dark line that must have been the beginnings of the hills and woods we had ridden through.

"This is where I used to come when I wanted to escape notice and still be able to watch everything." She shrugged off my bedroll and reached out her hand. "Come..." she said, beckoning me.

Together we crawled to the very edge and lay on our bellies, looking straight down. The whole camp was visible from that vantage, even the part that lay past the far bend of the stream where the canyon widened out into a grassy bowl and the horses were grazing.

It was easy to see the Drugha-Malia was having its effect. Not only were Pell and Tama strolling together, I could also see Lhiri and Nunyair lying in each other's arms by the stream, and directly below us I glimpsed Murghanth and Teko tangled in a passionate embrace, no doubt thinking themselves private behind some willow shrubs. I started to pull back, embarrassed, but Rishka pressed a restraining hand in the middle of my back to hold me down and whispered in my ear, "It does not matter. In the Eyes of the Mother all things are sacred." Then she began running her fingers up and down my bare legs, and I forgot about the others. "I used to come up here to play with myself," she breathed softly in my ears. "But it is so much more pleasurable to play with another."

Now she was caressing the back of my neck, now her hand was creeping down my back, sliding ever so slowly to lodge between my legs, spreading me out gradually in the sun. Soon I found myself pressing back insistently against that hand that was turning its bony hardness against my soft flesh, grinding with torturous pleasure. Suddenly she pulled away, saying, "Wait, now. Do not leave."

Leave? I had no thought of leaving. I could not even move. I heard Rishka rustling behind me. "Now," she said in a commanding way and reached down to turn me over onto my sleep roll, shifting me safely away from the edge and spreading me out faceup in the sun. She stood for a moment looking down, then knelt beside me, pulled a feather from her hair, and began to stroke me with it. A little line of chill followed each stroke, and then sweat broke out all along that line. I wanted to watch her, but had to shut my eyes against the sun. The darkness under my eyelids bloomed red and orange. "We should cover your eyes," she said in a voice full of concern. I sensed something else under her words that made me shiver. "Here, help me, stretch up your arms." I did as she said. She slipped my tunic up till it was over my face, then she did something with it so that my arms were imprisoned in the sleeves and my face covered.

"Rishka, please, help free me of this," I mumbled from the confines of the fabric.

"No, no, that does very well for now. It shades your eyes and keeps your hands out of my way. Just do as I tell you. You have only to lie still. You look very fine spread out there in the sun, a gift from the Drugha-Malia herself, just what I dreamed of when I was young and came here alone."

I tried to move my arms, but somehow she had me helpless. Softened by the heat, I lay back under her hands. She spread my legs wider, raised my knees slightly, and opened my cunt to the sun. The heat flowed into my body. Sweat ran from me in lines of cold. She stroked her feather across my nipples that rose to meet her touch, then down my belly, up the inside of my legs, and finally across my cunt. With a groan I tried to close my legs around that teasing feather, but she forced me open again with the pressure of her hands.

"Slowly, slowly, not so soon. Let the sun do its work."

Sweat was pouring off my body now and trickling down between my legs. The sun was blazing like fire and at the same time a light breeze ran its chill across my skin. "Please, Rishka," I found myself begging, "Please," but my voice was muffled by the tunic across my face.

Suddenly Rishka's whole body slid over mine, her leg between my legs, giving relief. "Is this what you want, Tazzi?" she asked, pressing hard with her knee. She was as wet with sweat as I was. It was as if we were melting together. The whole world had turned red and orange. She pushed back the tunic so that her mouth found mine, biting all along the edge of my lips till my mouth was burning. Then she turned the other way and slid her face between my legs, her mouth on me cool and hot and soft and violent by turns. Then she opened me to the sun again, peeling me open with her fingers. Then her mouth was on me again, wet and soft, then the sun again with all its heat till I could not tell if it was Rishka who made love to me there or the great Drugha-Malia herself. When I started to cry out she slipped her hand under the tunic to cover my mouth, and I thrashed against her hold. When I had finally stilled she slipped the tunic up over my head to free my arms. "Sorry to still your cry, but I could not let you give away my secret place." She held up her palm in front of me so I could see the teeth marks there. I reached for her. "No," she said quickly, jumping to her feet. "The sun has grown too hot now."

We pulled my sleep roll back into the shade of the overhang and sat for a moment side by side, breathing hard, our bodies wet and glistening. Suddenly Rishka said with a glint of mischief, "Well, Tazzi, do you think you can do better?"

Without a word I turned to her, put a hand on each breast, and pushed her down, covering her body with mine and covering her mouth. I made love to her there in the cool shadows, then we dozed till the sun found us, then we made love to each other again, rolling in and out of sun and shadow, then we dozed again until we were wakened much later by someone beating the pot.

We had just scrambled down from our secret aerie. I had put on my pants and picked up my pack. Arm in arm we were strolling toward the cookfires and the savory smell of food when Ashai rushed up to us, saying breathlessly, "Tazzi, Tazzi, I am so glad to see you. I have been searching for you everywhere. Pell sent me to fetch you for a meeting of the chiefs. Where have you been? What have you been doing all this time?"

I gave Rishka a wicked grin. With no hesitancy at all she said, "Feasting on each other's bodies all day in my secret place."

Poor Ashai. She blushed to the roots of her hair, her very white skin taking on a lovely sunset glow. Clearly, she had not found anyone to enjoy the day with.

Rishka bent and gave me a quick nip on the neck, saying, "Till later, Tazzi." Then she went striding off in the direction of dinner, whistling through her teeth, while I followed Ashai along a narrow pathway at the base of the bluff. Ashai walked ahead, not looking back at me and barely answering my questions with a mumble. It occurred to me that I should have given Rishka my bowl and told her to save me some dinner. Ah, well, I was now missing my third meal, but as Rishka said, we had been feasting all day.

After my first few attempts at speech were rebuffed, I went in silence, enjoying the glorious sensations in my body, the sounds of the water, the colors of the flowers and their sweet pervasive scent. Some women had already gone to eat or were walking in that direction, but many were still lying on the grassy banks of the river, resting or talking or caressing each other, half-dressed or altogether naked. I think I had never seen the star-cursed look so at ease. It was almost as if we had a place in the world after all, as if, for that moment at least, we were not every man's lawful prey.

Ashai and I were walking rapidly upstream, and soon the camp began to thin. Ahead I could see the place where a spring gushed out of the rock face, clearly the spring that fed our stream. Mounds of moss and ferns clung to the rock below the water and surrounded the little pool that formed at its base. A semicircle of women sat there in silence, their fingers barely touching. Among them I saw Lhiri and Maireth and Tamara. Women of 'the Circle,' I thought, as I touched my own pendant. *Source.* The word came to me and filled me with a joyous wonder, yet I was sure I had not heard it spoken aloud. *Source.* I stopped for a moment, drinking in the peace of that place. Not hearing me behind her, Ashai turned back. "Come quickly," she snapped impatiently. "I have already been too long in search of you." I think her embarrassment made her sharp with me. One of the women of the circle, a stranger to me, looked up at this disturbance and I moved on hurriedly.

The meeting was being held away from the tumult of the camp, in a little hollow in the bluff overhang, a small natural room carved in the living stone by years of waters. Ashai silently pointed the way, then quickly left. I went up the few steps to the entrance and they all turned to look at me. Clearly, the meeting was already finished. Everyone was sitting back smoking jol so that the little chamber was blue with smoke and thick with its heavy aroma.

Pell grinned at me and said jovially, "Well, here is Tazzi, my second-in-command, who has been somewhere mysterious all day, and from the look of her has clearly been minding something besides camp business." This was met by howls of laughter all round. "Glad you could join us." She made a little bow of her head. "Though, as you can see, our meeting is already done."

One of those women, a Muinyairin by the look of her, said to Pell with a wink, "Well, we must not be too hard on her. The Drugha-Malia has powerful magic, as you yourself should know." She gave Pell another broad wink, and the other women laughed again. Then she turned to me. "I only want to know how you hid from us so well. I thought I knew all the little secret places here." This was followed by more laughter.

Now it was my turn to blush. I could feel the heat rushing up from my toes to my scalp. If they said one more word in that direction I thought I would catch fire on the spot. I could not look any of them in the eye. To my relief, Pell beckoned me over. "Come, Tazzi, you are not the only one. None of us is immune to her charms. Have you had any food yet?"

I shook my head. They gathered up what was left in their bowls. When all their leavings were put together, I had at least a semblance of a meal, enough to keep my stomach from leaning on my backbone. With a bowl in hand I was able to recover some composure and look around me. From among us, Kazouri was there and Zenoria and Renaise. I was told that the thin, dark, somber woman to my left was Permeeth, the leader of the northern gathering. Mouraine, the startling-looking woman with dark skin and fair hair as gold as grain, was the southern leader, and Shartell, the Muinyairin who had first spoken to me, had been captain of Yaniri's encampment.

As I ate my little dinner, they told me their plan between puffs of jol. That plan was simple enough, though it had probably taken much heated talk to arrive at. It was to move on and keep moving, to push forward as long as we were on the Zarn's highroad, hoping to outrun the guards and vanish altogether. This past night had been our last camp, our last full night of sleep for a while. From now on we would only stop as we had to, to rest the horses. I nodded silently to everything they said. It seemed a good enough plan. I could find no fault with it, but my bones already ached with weariness at the thought of what lay ahead.

A few days' ride from there we were to find a cutoff and head northwest, following a winding road through the hills to a sheltered secret valley. This valley was sometimes used as a Wanderer encampment and would be large enough, they told me, to feed all our horses, at least for a while. That was to be our final gathering place before heading straight west to the sea and the hot-spring caves that were to be our winter home.

At the head of the line of march, they went on to inform me, there was always to be the leader of one group and at least the second of another. Clearly, it was important that we know one another. As soon as I finished eating, I set down my bowl and went around the circle, touching each woman's hand, looking into her face and saying her name so that this time I would remember. When I passed Kazouri she gave me a huge grin and wink so that I blushed all over again. Finished, I sat back down next to Pell. The jol smoke and the murmur of talk made me drowsy. Suddenly the pot was banging again, and Pell was shaking my shoulder. "Time to break camp," Kazouri shouted, jumping to her feet.

"Nice to know we are so entertaining," Pell muttered in my ear as we scrambled out of the rock chamber.

I was glad to see Rishka coming to meet me with my pack and bedroll, but when she pulled me into an embrace and began kissing the back of my neck, I freed myself, pushing her gently away. "I think I had better go and make myself useful. I am already the cause of enough talk."

"I promise I could show you a far better time," she said with a mischievous laugh. When I shook my head she ran off to join Zari and Zenoria and the others who were just then bringing in the horses for loading.

Feeling guilty for my day's absence, I went to help Renaise pack our part of the camp, and found the Sheezerti already hard at work there. Murghanth stepped aside to make room for me, saying in a knowing, teasing tone, "Well, how was your day, Tazzi? Did the Great Malia treat you well?"

"No better than she treated you," I said, looking her right in the eye with meaning. For a moment she looked flustered and her eyes went wide. Then she quickly recovered herself and nodded. "Well, you must have been sharing the nest of a hawk if you saw that," she said with a grin as she reached for a sack of grain. I helped her on the other side, and together we settled the sack into a basket pack.

"Not far from the truth," I mumbled. "Not far from the truth."

★

The sun was casting long shadows behind us when our many-legged snake gathered itself up and wound its way out of the canyon. We rode into a sunset of spectacular beauty with more than half the drylands yet to cross. Even that late in the day, the sands were hot underfoot.

Not long after night's fall we were back at the Zarn's great paved road that stretched straight as a tight-drawn string across the drylands. We followed it for guidance, but kept to the side to spare our horses' hooves while we could. I placed myself in the middle of the press and rode asleep on my horse for most of the night, hoping that someone somewhere kept watch. Early next morning Pell rode back and tapped me on the shoulder. "My turn to sleep and yours to watch," she told me.

I worked my way up to the front of the line and found Permeeth there, hunched over her horse, staring glumly across the vast expanse of sand that stretched endlessly before us. My first few tries at speech were met with one-word answers, so I was glad when Murghanth rode up next to me to keep me company, Murghanth who herself had been a stranger such a short while ago. I saw how awkwardly she sat her horse and thought how painful this endless riding must be for her. She must have caught my glance or my thought, for she asked quickly, "Do you think I will ever learn, Tazzi? I find myself being clumsy at those many things you do so easily, not a feeling I am used to. In Eezore I was always the agile, clever one. Now I so often feel I am the fool. It is hard not to hate myself." She said this last with such vehemence it startled me.

I turned to see her glowering furiously. "Soon enough," I told her, "soon enough. You have just begun. Give yourself time. You will learn as you have learned other things. In Eezore I was the one who was the fool."

"And it is not the riding that is the worst of it. Even that I suppose I could get used to. It is the endless empty space we ride through with nothing to mark the way, not one solid building on the horizon. I have a terror of that emptiness, a fear that we shall ride to the edge and stumble over it into a great dark pit. All the vastness could swallow up one's soul or stretch it thin as mist. It makes me feel like a speck of dust that might blow away, as forgotten as if it had never been."

I shook my head. "How different we are. For me it is the city that terrifies, that is the pit that will swallow me up. All the roar and motion, the flood of people, the maze of streets, the hard stuff underfoot, the press of life. Yes, I could drown in the city."

"And for me it is all these minds at once, all clamoring, clamoring, clamoring, with their pains and their fears and their wantings. I can find no rest and no mind-peace anywhere." Jhemar had ridden up on the other side of Murghanth.

"And for me," Permeeth said suddenly, "it is the constant planning and worrying, being always responsible for others, most of whom I do not even know, being accountable for their very lives, as if I cannot make a mistake as easily as the next one. I will be glad for a good night's rest again, where I do not sleep with my boots by my hand and start awake at every sound."

I turned to her, no longer made shy by her dour countenance. "Permeeth, at the end, when all this is over, what do you want?"

"Oh my, what a question! Well, my answer is simple enough. My garden, my shelter, my lover, and myself, all together in some safe place. Oh, Goddess, would that it might be! Great Mother, hear me, I would make You a shrine and offer fruit and flowers there and not forget You a single day of my life."

"And you, Murghanth, what would you want?"

A look of pain crossed her face, then she smiled with a sweetness I had never seen on her before. "A beautiful city where I could walk with my sisters, free and proud and unafraid, where the parks and the gardens and the fountains were for the Sheezerti as well as for other folk."

"And you, Jhemar?"

"To follow the road wherever it leads me, whether alone or with companions, and not be afraid we will meet flaming death around each bend. Not much, really, in the sum of things."

"And you, Tazzi?" Murghanth asked me suddenly.

I felt a great ache in my heart. "To stand still, to stop running. To find a home." Even as I said those words I knew this was only part of what I wanted. The rest was still shaping and forming. I could not speak of it yet. I did not even understand it myself, but at that moment it filled me the way the sound of flute music or the sight of a glowing sunset could fill me.

The women in back joined us, saying what was hardest for them in the journey and what they most wanted at the end of it, not a bad way to pass the time and get to know each other. We went on in this way till Shartell came up to relieve me and a woman named Yoshar relieved Permeeth.

I drew off to the side to let the line pass by me till I could find a place beside Rishka. She leaned toward me and said with amusement, "I think we are being followed." After that I began to catch glimpses of a lone rider far off to one side or the other. I passed word back along the line to Pell and up to the front riders, but I felt no fear now of the Muinyairin. Of the Zarn's guard there was no sign at all in that barren landscape.

Rishka and I rode next to each other for the rest of the morning, saying little but sometimes touching hands or exchanging glances, intense with meaning. I went all that day with the warmth of her loving bubbling high in my blood, and the heat of it, too, that being a different thing. The heat of it rushed up in me when sweat dripped down between my breasts, or the saddle pressed in my crotch, or we passed a small outcrop and the smell of hot rocks rushed to my nostrils. Then I could feel the pleasure of her hands and mouth on me again and shivered with delight in spite of the heat. This is what life is for, I thought. This makes living worthwhile. Perhaps we can patch up our little differences after all. Then we could do this again and again. That thought brought a rush of joy with it, but in truth that was the last time we were lovers. At one of our resting places, not too long after that, Rishka and I went off to fetch water together. We had some foolish quarrel. I cannot now remember what it was about or who started it, though likely it was Rishka. Suddenly there were swords of rage and anger flashing between us, cutting and cutting as real swords could not have done with us. How strange not to remember a single word of that quarrel, not a single word, only to remember the rage bubbling up and spending itself almost like passion, and afterward the sense of waste and loss and emptiness, as if the Drugha-Malia and all we had shared there had been a lie or a trick of the place.

★

Before the sun reached its midpoint and the heat turned intolerable, we rode out of the drylands and into woods and fields again. Now we were forced back onto the hard road, and our horses' hooves were a steady thunder ringing in the ear. Rishka and I parted there, though this was well before our quarrel. She went forward to keep company with Shartell, and I rode for a while with strangers.

What can I say of those next few days? We rode on and on and on. Tempers were short. The horses were stumbling. There was never enough water, enough food, enough rest. The relentless riding was wearying us all, wearing us down. I began to lose track of the days. As a child, many times I had seen cattle being driven along the road to market, heads down, reluctant and helpless and harried, lowing their distress. It felt as if we were cattle being driven on and on by an invisible master. For the first day or so we sang. Then we fell silent, plodding, enduring, only wanting it to be over. I so longed to be free of these hounds at our heels that, like Pell, I was almost ready to turn and face them, but I knew the uselessness of that. If we were ever to have any peace, we needed to vanish out of the Zarn's sight as suddenly as if we had all ascended to the Great Star itself.

It began to rain, the first of the fall rains. Perhaps we should not have sung that song, perhaps we had called it to us. It was a gray, relentless, slanting rain that soaked us through and chilled us to the bone so soon after being burned by the dryland sun. There was nothing to do but go on. We could not even stop to make our fires and dry ourselves out. If we had been miserable before, that was now increased a hundredfold. Clothes clung like a second skin; water ran down our backs. The saddles rubbed and chafed. We were each our own island of misery, enduring, huddled inside ourselves, moving along in silence through the grayness. Even the sound of the horses' hooves was muffled.

Toward evening of that day I was in the lead, peering through rain and gathering dark for some sign. Finally, ahead, I saw a tiny glimmer of light and soon, through the trees, the red and yellow and orange of Vanhira's little travel-wagon glowing like a sun of hope through that gloom. I passed the word back along the line, and Pell made her way up next to me. She squeezed my arm. "We are almost home, Tazzi. The Zarn's palace and all the fine houses of Eezore could not look half so pretty as that little wagon looks at this moment." Home, I thought bitterly. To driven fugitives what is home but another temporary stopping place? Luckily I had sense enough to keep my silence.

Permeeth had ridden up on the other side. The three of us dismounted and went to greet Vanhira. "Well, you have quite a crowd there from what I can see in this dusk," she said, grinning widely. "Who would have thought when I sent those poor, speechless girls to shelter with you that you would gather such an army."

Pell reached out her hand in greeting. "You will never know how fair your little light looked shining through the rain."

I saw a flash of gray, then Hereschell himself stepped out of the gloom and somehow I felt closer to 'home,' whatever that might mean. He clapped his hands on my shoulders and looked in my face, nodding and grinning at me. "So, Alyeeta's little book-girl has come through it all, a little thin on the bone but alive enough." Then he turned to Pell. "Well, I am the one left here to guide you this last part of the way, with Johalla's help, that is. Vanhira will cover the traces of your turning as soon as you are all safely off the Great Road."

I was wondering how, by the Mother, Hereschell had gotten there so quickly and who this Johalla was, when a slim young woman who seemed barely out of childhood stepped from Vanhira's doorway. She looked at us all with her wide, dark eyes — one of the silent ones! "Oh, you are so many!" she said with amazement, the first clear run of words I had ever heard her speak.

Hereschell smiled at her as if to give assurance. "Her twin-born, Illyati, is already in the valley encampment. This is a hard road at night, even for me, but they have a strong mind-bond, the strongest I have ever known. She will help draw us there."

"Let us go as quickly as we can," Pell said urgently as she remounted. "It will take some time to get us all off the highroad, and we hope to do it unobserved."

Hereschell swung onto his horse. "I have no doubt this rain has been a misery for all of you, but it will help with secrecy. This rain has kept the curious off the road. Also, this is a very isolated spot, not near to any farm or holding. We may yet manage to have you vanish off the earth."

Vanhira drew Johalla to her in a great hug. "Mother's Luck go with you, child, and keep you safe until we meet again." Then she kissed her on both cheeks and pressed a pouch into her hands.

"Time to go," Johalla said with a nod to Hereschell as she swung up on a little mountain pony. It looked so much like Marshlegs that for a moment my heart leapt up in my chest. Johalla on horseback seemed taller, older, stronger, as if she had gained years in that one step. In the light of Vanhira's wagon, I could see her draw herself up straight, her hesitancy giving way to a look of pride. She glanced back at us all with something unfathomable in her eyes, then turned and rode up next to Hereschell. So, I thought, this child who had been robbed of everything, even her voice, was going to lead an army of some two thousand women through the night to safety. Alyeeta was right. The Zarns should be trembling in their beds.

Pell and Permeeth went back along the line to make sure everything went swiftly and smoothly, while I fell into line somewhere nearer to the front. As soon as we entered the woods the darkness closed in around us. We went single file, with hardly room enough for our horses to pass between close-growing trees. Branches hung low, wet, and heavy, with their leaves slapping in our faces. The way quickly turned steep and winding, making the damp saddle chafe between my legs. In spite of these new miseries, I was so relieved at no longer being pursued by those phantom guards on the Zarn's road that I dozed off quite easily in the saddle.

I have no notion of how long I slept, but I think it must have been several hours. I was wakened by the woman in front of me calling back, "Wake and beware. Steep way ahead, danger on the right. Pass the word on." Wide awake now, I passed the word on and heard it echoing down the line. I thought the way already steep enough, but soon I was clinging to my saddle with one hand and the horse's mane with the other. The path there seemed even narrower. Off to the right there was nothing but a dark void. Far below I could hear the sound of rushing water. I hugged the left-hand rock face. One glance to the right had been enough. Once Dancer stumbled, and I felt myself lurching in that direction. I gripped the horse's mane in terror till my fingers ached from my hold. Then I thought of those women among us who had hardly ever sat on a horse before and what this ride must mean for them.

At least the rain had stopped. Once the worst of the danger had passed and it felt safe to look around, I could even see stars, some looking so low they seemed caught in the branches of the trees. The air had a sharp chill in it, a warning of fall. Unable to sleep again, I watched the stars fade and the ghostly shapes of trees emerge out of the misty dark. We had cut away from the bluff edge. Soon we were moving through such a confusing maze of trails and paths that we could only creep forward. Often we had to stop altogether while Hereschell and Johalla consulted with each other and I suppose with Illyati somewhere ahead of us. Finally, much to my relief, the road flattened and widened. Filled with a sudden excitement, I rode up next to our two guides.

When the sun rose, the light of it glistened and sparkled in tiny rainbows of iridescent colors from every leaf and branch. As soon as its warmth reached our wet clothes and wet horses, steam began rising from all along the line. Though the day above was bright and blue, we rode in our own swirling clouds of mist. For a short way the road grew steep again, then we topped a small rise and saw stretching below us the bowl of a wide green valley with hills rising in the far distance and mountains blue beyond them. I found myself shouting and crying, both at once. The women all around me were shouting, a great, wild, deafening roar.

There were people already camped in the valley. They were rushing toward us, greeting us with their own cries and shouts of welcome. Tired as they were, our horses quickened their pace at the sight of all that grass. We poured over the hill in a huge mass, singing and shouting for joy. Over all those other voices I heard one calling, "Johalla, Johalla, Johalla." Johalla put her pony in motion and went dashing down the slope ahead of us.

25

"But why have they done all this for us?" I asked, gesturing at the scene below in the valley.

Hereschell shook his head. "Not for you. Make no mistake about it, Tazzi, it is not for you, not for the Khal Hadera Lossien that the Wanderers have set up this camp within their camp. It is for the sake of their own daughters."

Hereschell and I were standing together at the top of a small rise. From there we could look down at the Wanderers' brightly painted travel-wagons gathered in circles and watch the bustle of activity around them. This was the Wanderers' Great-Gather, so much like the Essu, the fall festival of the Kourmairi that I remembered from childhood. In the midst of all this they had somehow made our huge numbers welcome, setting aside camp space a little ways past their own circles, stocking it with grains, vegetables, and dried fruit, and offering us whatever help we needed.

"The Wanderers have done this for their own daughters," Hereschell repeated, "those daughters whom we must give over into your hands. Having no way to protect our girl-children, we cannot keep them with the band. If we did so, the Wanderers could no longer travel freely, but would have to live always in fear and hiding. We have become a danger to each other. Yet it is not easy for Wanderers to abandon their own. After all, what do we have? We own nothing. We have our children, our horses, the clothes on our backs. We have only each other in this world. And among us, daughters are just as welcome as sons. We do not sell or trade away our girl-children as the Ganjarin do." There was a raw edge of pain in his voice, this man who had no children of his own and no other person in his life, only a gray wolf.

Sounds of laughter and music floated up to us. The bright colors of clothes and bedding, hung up to dry after the rain, made the scene look festively decked. It reminded me again of the Essu. I felt a sudden, aching longing for home and for the familiar things of home. With a stab of grief, I wondered if my mother and sister still lived and if, at this moment, they themselves were on their way to the Essu. I even gave a passing thought to my father and my brother, but when my mind touched on Kara, I snapped that door shut.

Shouts interrupted my thoughts. At the far edge of the valley I saw Muinyairin racing their horses with banners flying. Rishka was no doubt among them, probably in the lead. At the thought of her, my heart filled with pain and a bitter anger rose in my throat. Rishka! Rishka, whom I had loved and protected and defended when no one else wanted to be near her. And what did she care for me now, now that she was among her precious Muinyairin? Perhaps she had never really cared for me at all. Perhaps all that had passed between us at the Drugha-Malia had been a trick of that place. It was clear to see that she preferred even Olna's company to mine.

Suddenly I was conscious of Hereschell speaking to me again. "Besides, it was the coin Pell gathered that paid for the goods, and some extra for us as well. It will be a well-stocked winter this year for Wanderers, better than most." He turned to look at me with amusement. "Khal Hadera Lossien, that is a fine, fancy name. It sounds Asharan to me. Did Alyeeta choose that for you?"

"No, Telakeet did," I answered sharply.

"Ah, yes, no doubt in memory of old glories when there were Witch convents in every city and Witches still had some power there. Alyeeta used to tell me of those times. It is a name well suited for that glorious past, but it will not last long here in this world. It will soon be shortened. You will end up being Hadera Lossi, or perhaps even Hadra. Yes, Hadra, that would suit you better and it is far easier to say, though not near so grand. What does it mean, this 'Khal Hadera Lossien'?"

"'Daughters of the Great Star' in the Asharan tongue," I told him curtly, annoyed at his mocking tone.

"Ah, yes, very accurate, no doubt, but still too much of a mouthful." With a sudden shift in mood, he clapped his hand on my shoulder and turned me so he could stare straight into my face. "You seem troubled,

Tazzi. I feel some sickness in your soul. Life does not sit well on you at this moment. Look to some healing for yourself, girl, while the Khal Hadera Lossien stay still in one place for this little time." With that, he turned and was gone in that quick way he had, striding back down into the valley and over to a cluster of tents, where people soon gathered around him.

"Hadra," I said aloud, staring down into the camp. A shiver ran through me. The scene below me wavered and shifted, changing to something I had never seen before, another camp altogether. For that moment I seemed to be in a different place, in a different time, though whether in past or future I could not tell. Then the grass rustled. Startled, I turned to see Zari near me. "Greetings," I said softly.

She looked around in surprise, not having seen me. I thought that perhaps she had come there to be alone, yet she did not turn to leave immediately. Zari had hardly spoken to me since the day she had come to plead for Rishka. After a little while of awkward silence, I said, "It looks like a Kourmairi Essu, a fall festival, down there." I was embarrassed at the sound of naked longing in my voice.

"You seem sad, Tazzi. Are you not happy to be here in safety?"

"Happy enough, I suppose, but now that we are safe for the moment, I am missing my home and my mother and sister."

She shook her head. "I never had a home as you did. It is my grandmother I miss. She may have died helping me escape, but now I will never know. Hayika and Kilghari left too soon after me to have any word of her. Now I can never go back. I think of her every day, though. I was her Lea-Linya, her heart's own, and she was my Lea-Malia, my mother-of-choice. She would have done anything for me and I for her and now who knows..." Her words fell away. I had no comfort to offer, only my own painful thoughts. Just when it seemed there would be silence between us again, she said in a different tone, "This Great-Gather of the Wanderers is like a Muinyairin 'Riding-In.' That is when all the tribes assemble at summer's end to trade horses and stories. Girls are promised in marriage then. I had to leave before..." She shuddered and once more left her words unfinished. Looking as if about to cry, she suddenly turned and went running down the hill calling back, "I must find Rishka." Something in her manner made me wonder if she and Rishka had gone back to being lovers.

Now I was left alone again with my sad mood. Perhaps that was for the best. I had no wish to go on trading words with Zari at that moment.

I should be happy, I told myself, overjoyed, in fact, that we were all safely here and had met with such welcome in this fair place. Instead, I felt this strange, flat grief and under it a gnawing anger. Everyone else seemed to have found someone from home. Who was there to care for me? There was no one there from my village, and Kara was dead. Slowly I walked back down. I felt very separate in the midst of this throng of people who all seemed to have found their heart's circle.

That night it was even more like an Essu. Flares were lit. There was drumming and singing and dancing. The air was thick with jol. Barrels of quillof were emptied into outstretched cups. To the sounds of bells and rhythmic clapping, Murghanth and Teko and the other Sheezerti danced, juggled, and did their acrobatic stunts, much as they must have done in the streets of Eezore before the edict. Many of the Wanderers came to watch. When the Sheezerti wearied, six Wanderers did a knife dance, their blades flashing fast as lightning. Afterward, Hayika and Rishka challenged all those gathered to a riding contest.

This was the first time I had ever seen Hereschell among his own people. He had thrown away his proud reserve, along with his idiot disguise. With abandon he laughed and danced and sang songs and told stories. He even graciously and gracefully made a fool of himself, playing the clown for the children. They jumped up and down, begging him over and over to "do it again, do it again."

As the evening went on I saw couples slipping away into the dark. Some came back rumpled and disheveled with grass and twigs caught in their clothes and hair. Then their friends would set to joking and teasing. When it grew late, so late we should all have been thinking of sleep, a strange silence suddenly fell on the camp. Every head turned as one. There was Shalamith, riding toward us, mounted on Crusher's back, all golden in the light of the flares. She threw back her head and began to sing. The power of her voice filled the night and echoed up and down the valley. All other occupations ceased for that time. When she grew weary and slipped from the horse's back, Hereschell quickly pulled off his shirt and flung it down on a mound of grass near the fire. "Sit here, Lady, this is a soft place," he said with a deep bow.

★

There we were, the Khal Hadera Lossien, waiting again, waiting and gathering one last time. When we left this place we were headed for the coast. I was eager to be on our way, riding toward the end of our journey.

The others did not share my impatience. They all seemed to be finding some enjoyment at the Gather. In spite of the festivities, the life of our camp soon settled into a routine, a routine that left me feeling excluded and unnecessary. Renaise ran the camp well and efficiently with the help of the Sheezerti. Pell was keeping company with Tamara and appeared to have no need of me. Rishka and Zari always seemed to be together. I took my sour mood and camped apart from the others by a small rock outcrop that thrust up from the valley floor. At Alyeeta's urging I wrote every day. It was the only useful thing I did at that time. This spot offered me privacy, and the ledges made a sort of crude table and seat.

The Witches had formed their own small gathering within the Great-Gather, separate from us. That is where they mostly stayed, all but Hamiuri, that is. Hamiuri often sat at the Wanderers' campfires, where they made much of her and fussed over her, covering her with shawls and bringing bowls of broth, calling her "Beloved Grandmother," "Blessed One," and "the Old Wise One." There she would sit with her snakes wound around her, telling stories while the little ones leaned against her or sat by her feet. Though I felt neither particularly welcome nor wanted in the Witches' circle, I sometimes went to sit with them for the sake of Alyeeta's touch, especially in the evening. Nothing else could soothe my aching spirit. Alyeeta, who was so often mocking and clever and could be so cruel with her tongue, was very gentle with me for that time. And Shalamith was kindness itself, always touching me when she passed, the kind of caress that seemed to ease the rawness. Even Telakeet forbore from her usual insults. But there were many new Witches who had come in with other gatherings of Star-Born or with the Wanderers. These ignored my presence and spoke among themselves, often in words I could not understand.

One of these new ones, Nhenoma by name, seemed to be a very formidable Witch even among the Witches. She had just finished a passionate speech, most of which must have been in Asharan, when suddenly Alyeeta said to her in Kourmairi, "But you are right, Nhenoma, I think the next generation of Witches will be the Star-Born." Then she turned to fix me with her eye, looking at me with that disturbing mixture of love and anger, pride and envy that made such confusion in my heart. "I think Witchcraft will end with you. It will die out. You will swallow it up. You, the Khal Hadera Lossien, you will be the last of the Witches and the first of a new breed. You are not like us, with skills and talents that can be sharpened with training and focused by the aid of spells. What use have you for spells? You were born with powers and need only some training in the wielding of them. And who knows their limits? Not us, surely. We, who think to be your teachers, may yet live to find ourselves your students. It is hard on Witches' pride."

"At least they must be easily taught, seeing as they have so much talent," Nhenoma said with a wolfish grin, turning to stare as if she had never noticed me before.

"Not at all," Alyeeta retorted. "I think obstinacy must have been among the gifts of the Great Star. Before, when I had apprentices, they bent themselves willingly to my will. They wished to please me and learn well. These Star-Born have to resist and argue and do a thing their own way though it must be done twice over. They have little respect for Witches, I can tell you that." I slipped out from under Alyeeta's hand. It no longer felt comforting. I wondered what else they had been saying that I was not able to understand. Now Nhenoma began telling in Kourmairi a terrible story of persecution in some village at the hands of 'humans,' a story not unlike my own, though each time she spit out the word 'human' in that spiteful way, I somehow felt accused. Then Telakeet took up the refrain, saying, "All true, all true. I swear I would rather come back next time in the shape of a toad or a snake. It is far too difficult and painful trying to inhabit this human form. Sometimes the talk of flies and spiders has more charm."

Alyeeta laughed, her eyes gleaming with spite and malice. "Well, if the Goddess had consulted me I certainly would not have chosen to be born in human form, and certainly not a woman, as women are treated here on earth. But a Witch — yes. Being a Witch has some power to sweeten this bitter bargain. Clearly, I have no great love for people and no reason to have any. I much prefer the company of Witches, though I think even bats and toads would be better than humans." This last was said looking at the toad nestling in Telakeet's hands.

Whether or not this was all meant for me, as it seemed to be, I had heard enough. "Then you must hate us, too, for we are also here in 'human form,'" I said, flinging the words at Alyeeta as I made ready to jump to my feet.

Before I could move, she fastened her hand on my wrist and pulled me close beside her. "No, no, I love you well enough, all of you, whatever form you are in. You have given me cause to live that I did not have these past few years. It is not the love that one should question. There is more of that than I had ever thought to find in this life, though I may not always know how to show it. It is whether you are truly human. I think not. I think you are something other."

"Well, the Zarns must think the same," I said bitterly. "They hate us and fear us and pursue us as if we were monsters."

"It is more fear than hate," Olna said from the darkness where she had been sitting quietly. "Sooner or later, Tazzi, your very existence must mean an end to Zarns, not in my lifetime, surely, perhaps not even in yours. But if the Khal Hadera Lossien continue to survive, the power of the Zarns as we know it now will fall. They know this, if not in their minds, then in their hearts. They are desperate. That is what makes them so dangerous and so cruel. That is why they try so hard to kill all of you now before it is too late. They will not succeed, of course. It is already too late. They do not begin to comprehend your powers, but they see in you an end to everything they have. Those who cannot be controlled are a great threat to those who must control."

I had sat through all this Witch-talk with my feelings pulled this way and that. Suddenly, with no forethought, I jumped up and whirled on them, shouting, "Too much! Too much! You are all so full of envy and spite. We did not ask for this burden, this curse of powers. I would give it to you in a minute if I could, if everything would go back to being as it was, if I could go home and the Zarns would call off their guards and the edict could be unwritten."

Alyeeta was shaking her head, a sadness almost like pity on her face. "Your powers are not something that can be snipped off or wished away, Tazzia. They are a part of you, embedded at the very core of being."

"What do I care!" I spat back at her. "I would cut them out if I could! I would be glad to."

"Tazzi, Tazzi..." Olna stood up and reached out for me, but I evaded her hands and dashed off into the darkness, running blindly, tripping over tent lines and cook pots, running as if I could leave it all behind me.

"Tazzi, come back, come back, come back," I could hear Alyeeta's call echoing down the long valley.

Was it true? Would I have gone back? Could I have gone back? Who would I have been without the powers? A very ordinary and ignorant girl growing up in my little village, not even a healer, not a speaker with creatures, not myself, in fact. Perhaps one of those who threw rocks at Tolgath, who tried to throw rocks at the child Tazzia, one of those who longed to kill the wolf — in other words, a thoroughly contemptible 'human.' Oh, but it cost so much not to be 'human.' At that moment I felt unwilling to pay the price and wanted to lash out in a fury at fate. And, in truth, it was not the edict that had driven me out of my village, it was my powers. Even without the edict I could not have gone home. Besides, who would I have been and where would I have gone without Pell and the rest of them?

For the next few days my thoughts went round and round in a torment of questions. I hid out from the others, staying by myself among my rock ledges and writing to close out the thoughts. When the uproar in my head grew too loud to bear, I rode off on Dancer, going along the far edges of the valley. I did not return to the Witches' circle. There was no comfort to be had there, only more confusion. I felt like an outlaw among outlaws. One good thing, however, came of that pain. I discovered that I could ride Dancer as I had ridden Marshlegs, with no bridle, with mind-touch only. I resolved never to put metal between her teeth again.

The questions, of course, did not get answered. The Goddess did not appear before me, nor did She speak in my heart. But I could not stay away forever. After a while I began following Olna and Maireth on their rounds among the burned ones. There were many in the camp, and it was one place at least where I could be useful.

It was amazing to watch Olna's composure as she moved from one to the next, always with a kind word. She never looked away in horror or disgust. Even at the worst of sights her hands did not shake, nor did I ever hear from her the rage that ate at me constantly for what had been done. It felt as if her spirit was seated deep within her in a well of calm and love and pity. Even from my hard, angry place I recognized this as a kind of wisdom. When I spoke to Alyeeta of this she turned away. After a while of silence she said without turning back, "Wisdom, eh? Well, let me tell you, girl, that wisdom was hard won and dearly paid for in the time of the Witch-kills."

"Tell me," I said quickly, hoping to find some answer in her words.

"No, no, that is hers to tell, not mine. You may ask, though I doubt she will speak of it even now."

The next afternoon, when a young woman died in our arms, I began raging against the guards, saying wildly, "I could burn them alive for this and listen with pleasure to their screams."

"Then you will become one of them," Olna said quietly as she pulled a cover over the woman's face. "No different. All to be done again."

"You do not hate them? How is that possible?"

"No, I do not hate them, but I pity them, and perhaps that is worse."

"Pity!? How can you pity them when you see what they do?"

"All the more reason for pity."

"Olna, do you really have no hatred and no anger? What are you made of?"

"The same stuff you are made of, Tazzi. I had enough rage and hate in me once to have burned down the city of Eezore like a torch. It left me." She looked me straight in the eye. "Do you really want to know?" I nodded, meeting her eyes with mine. Suddenly I felt pulled into her gaze. I was falling into a great swirling depth of pain and could barely stand. From the bottom of that depth I heard Olna say, "Let me tell you, Tazzi, there came a time during the Witch-kills, a time that was so terrible, so full of death and horror it seemed that the living could not go on living, that life itself would die. Finally, there were only two places left to stand, two choices left in the world — at least for me. Hate or Love, nothing else, nothing I could see. And I had to make the choice. I think I went mad at the time, down, down, down into a pit of madness. Believe me, I understand your rage and hatred better than you think, better than you can imagine.

"If I chose Hate, then I knew I had to hate everything, even the sun that came up in the morning, even my lover's gentle face, even myself right to the very core. If it was Love, then I had to love everything, yes everything, even 'the enemy,' even those who hated us and tried to kill us at every turn, yes, even them. I had to love them and understand them and grieve for them, and yes, even pity them, poor driven souls. Love or Hate. One or the other. I had to turn myself into an instrument of one or the other, fully and completely, with no turning back. I chose Love, but it was close, very close. It seemed easier to choose Hate. It was very tempting until I really saw where it led. They would have won after all, and everything, everything would have gone down. That is what you call my wisdom. It is the choice called Love. All else followed from that. It has not always been an easy road, but at least it has allowed me to live. Now you know."

I kept looking into her eyes, wanting to cry, wanting to scream with what I saw there. Finally I asked in a sort of choked whisper, "And what about me?"

"You are very different. You began with love and have had to learn hate, which is very dangerous to you. But in the end you will stretch out around all of it, hold it all in one person, and then you will understand. That is as much as I can tell you now, and as much as I can speak of this."

Whenever I was with Olna her words touched some deep, clear spring of life inside me, but as soon as she was out of sight the bitterness returned, sometimes with redoubled strength. To my surprise, I began to notice that Rishka was spending more and more time with her. At that the demon of jealousy bit into me with a fury, though it would have been hard to say which of them I was most jealous of. Rishka had continued to ignore me, though I often contrived to be near her. We barely passed a civil word. Even so, I kept watch on her, always aware of where she was, sometimes aware even when I could not see her. The memory of the Drugha-Malia still boiled in my blood, burning now like an angry fire. Pride kept me silent till one day it was too much. When she went to walk by me without a word, I stepped into her path, blocking the way. "Am I a ghost or a rock that you pass me without speaking? We were lovers and that is still between us. How can you pretend not to know me?"

She stopped, and I saw a look of indecision cross her face. Then suddenly she burst out, "Oh, Tazzi, Tazzi! Yes, I love you, and yes, it is still between us, even now. But it is like poison for us both. No good comes of it, only more pain, and so I pass in silence though it cuts my heart. Every time we come together in a place of love, afterward we come together in a place of rage. It pushes me back again to where I have been. I am trying so hard to heal from all that. I have had enough in my life of blows and lashes and red rage. I need to be done with it, to live, to go on. When it seems hopeless, when the darkness begins closing over me, then Olna shows me a way. She is the only one. She has been there herself and gives me hope. None of the other Witches and none of the Khal Hadera Lossien, either, know how to help. Tazzi, your anger and your bitterness are too much for me. I am afraid of you, afraid you will drag me back into despair."

Such a wave of fury rushed up in me at those words that it almost threw me off my feet. The taste of it filled my mouth and for a moment even blinded my eyes. "I am too much for you, am I?!" I screamed at her. "It is *you* who have poisoned my soul and my heart with your rages. Alyeeta told me to beware of you, that you would suck my blood and leave me dry."

Alyeeta, of course, had said no such thing. Alyeeta seemed to be softening to this new Rishka and had even said some good things of her. But at that moment what did I care what Alyeeta had said? I was being left again, left by a lover one more time, left by this Muinyairin I had taken pity on, this woman who had torn open my heart. She was standing there telling me it was my fault, my fault, MY FAULT! Suddenly I was spitting and snarling like an Oolanth cat, fangs showing, claws out, cutting and slashing, wanting to hurt, to do damage, to draw blood, wanting not to care, though of course the pain of my attack came back at me in full force. I talked wildly, going on and on, throwing out words like weapons, throwing out obscenities that amazed me even as they flew from my mouth. She was leaving me for my anger? Well, I would show her something of anger! Let her see it unsheathed!

Rishka for once was silent. When I stopped for a moment to catch my breath before charging on, she put up her hands before her and said, "Peace, Tazzi. That is enough." Then she turned and walked away, leaving me alone with my seething, boiling rage, leaving me to be consumed by it.

Lucky for both of us that we could not harm each other bodily, or in my pain and despair I might have rushed at her departing back with a knife or a stone. Instead, I shouted after her, "You are just one more to leave me, no different from the others. Go! Go! What do I need you for?"

Never again, never again to win that incredible sweetness out of the fire, to feel flesh and spirit melted, consumed and reborn. For a while everything looked like ashes after the blaze. Later, though I burned for her in a torment of longing and ripped at my body with my nails at night, I did not try to mend the rift between us. Let her go to her healing if she needed that more than she needed me. What did I care, anyhow?

A day or so later Alyeeta caught up with me and said sternly, "You are not to lie about the things I say. Rishka has as much right to the truth as you do." So now even Alyeeta was defending Rishka. I felt angry again and betrayed as well, though I did not lash out at Alyeeta as I had at Rishka. There was something about Rishka saying she was trying to heal herself that had put me in a towering rage. It was as if she were trying to be better than I was, as if she were trying to heal herself of me, as if I were the sickness in her life and Olna the health.

It was Olna that I lashed out at next, saying angrily, "I see you are trying to steal away my lover."

She looked at me for a long time, not laughing or mocking me as Alyeeta might have done or saying cruel and insulting things like Telakeet. The pity in her eyes was worse than any insult. She seemed to be truly trying to understand, for she finally said, "Do you really believe that, Tazzi?"

Much as I tried to, I could not break free of her gaze. I wanted to give back a bitter, clever answer, but those eyes demanded truth. I found myself saying, "No, that is not what I believe."

Oh yes, I heard that next question coming and did not want to answer it. "Then why did you say that to me?" she asked in that seemingly simple and direct manner. Behind that question was the power of her eyes.

Against my will I heard myself answering, "Because it was a hurtful thing to say and I was hurt and angry and afraid, and wanted to lash back." I was flushing with shame as I heard my own words.

"Oh," she said softly, and I saw that look of pity deepen. "When we pass on the hurt in that way then there is more hurt in the world that needs healing. There are other ways..." She shook her head, breaking the contact of our eyes, and went on in a different tone, "Well, Tazzi, I am glad you do not really believe I would do such a thing. If you did, then we could not be friends. It is a terrible thing to steal away someone's affections, but that is not what I am doing. There is something that Rishka needs that you can neither give her nor help her with. Your anger and your pain are too much like hers. They feed on each other. She has been deeply hurt and needs to mend."

My heart clenched with fear at her words. "You see, it is true," I said with more bitterness. "With all your talk of healing and mending you will steal her away just as I said, though you may not mean to in that way. But what does it matter. It will all come to the same in the end. She and I will not be lovers again, and it will be because of you."

"Oh, Tazzi, your spirit has grown sick from all you have seen. Let me help. I understand. I have been there."

"No, I want none of your tampering," I shouted at her, backing away. "No! Ask me no more questions, I will tell you nothing else." Her pity and her kindness weakened me. It was like having my heart pried open with a hay hook. I turned and ran for the edge of the woods, not looking back. I knew she would not follow.

In some part of my heart I longed for Olna's touch and her kindness. I wanted to cry out, I need something from you, too, as much as Rishka does, but pride and pain thickened my tongue and cut off the words. It was my silence that spoke instead. I was still nursing too much anger. That anger was the first thing I would have to give up if I were to ask for Olna's help. I knew that and was not ready. I was still too raw.

Oh, I loved Olna and I hated her. I was in a rage of jealousy at her caring for Rishka, yet I would not let her near me. She frightened me in a way none of the other Witches did. It was not her Witch powers I was afraid of, it was something else, something for which I had no name that went straight to the core of life. It felt as if she could see right through me, as if I were glass or water. I was not so pleased with what lay in my heart that I wanted it clearly seen by anyone.

★

In spite of all this I wrote whenever I was able to, with Alyeeta always driving me on, saying, "Do it now. Who knows when there will be another chance?" It gave me some satisfaction to see the pages piling up and know what had already been recorded.

Other things went on in that camp besides my own private war with madness. Vanhira finally came with her travel-wagon, though by a very different road from the one we had used. She was in a great good humor, very pleased with herself. "Well, I sold the soldiers plumcakes, read their fortunes, and fattened my purse. They still think you are ahead of them and are rushing on, planning to chase you right into the sea. I told them that this enormous mass of women like a great snake had passed me on the way, crowding me and my little wagon right off the road. They, in turn, told me some wild stories of this thief who had scaled a wall to cut their horses loose and vanished in a hail of flaming arrows, delaying them by at least three days." Pell laughed and slapped her leg as if this were the best joke of her life, but I shuddered, seeing her again swinging on that rope, a target for all those arrows.

Somehow Hereschell had obtained a small quantity of fastfire, probably through a connection with the Thieves Guild. No matter what else was happening, Pell and Jhemar worked with it every day on a little sandbar island in the middle of the river, trying to find some way to control it. Sometimes there were strange explosions and huge gouts of fire rushing skyward. Then the children would crowd the shore to watch. Often one or both of them came back with singed hair or clothing. Always they carried with them the smell of flaming death, but they were so sure they were close to an answer that nothing could be said to discourage them from their dangerous sport.

The Muinyairin set up games every day that many Wanderers joined in, riding or wrestling or throwing the short spear. Murghanth and Teko taught juggling to the children. The Wanderers, men and women alike, sewed patches of colored cloth together to make winter covers while they sat around their fires, for it was growing cooler every day. There was always music and song, which seemed as much a part of Wanderer life as breathing or eating. Watching him now among his own people, I wondered what Hereschell's long periods of silence cost him. He seemed to be one of their best singers, and his storytelling always brought him a crowd. I watched him from a distance, but when I saw him turn worried eyes on me, I looked away quickly.

I avoided everyone who loved me except Soneeshi. Dancer, after her first panic, had grown used to the wolf. Soneeshi often went on long runs with us. Sometimes I climbed back up to the top of the little knoll to watch and be alone. Soneeshi, who was not comfortable either in the turmoil of the camp, would come and sit by me. Sometimes she lay with her head in my lap.

The hardest thing for me in the Wanderers' camp was seeing every day the flash of red hair — 'Potter red.' The Wanderers who so far had kept most of their own daughters out of the Zarns' hands had also sheltered many of the Potters' daughters among them. Their people had an old history of comradeship on the road. Many times I would think I saw Kara among, them only to dash forward and stare dumbly into a stranger's face. After a few days I stopped chasing. I watched from a distance with my heart aching. It was like having her die over and over. It was like watching for Irdris again, only worse.

26

Someone was playing the flute. The notes floated up to me where I was sitting with Soneeshi on the little knoll. Suddenly I was on my feet and running, running down into the valley with my heart pounding in my throat. The notes had formed themselves into a tune, a tune I knew by heart, knew at the very core of my being. It was one of the tunes Kara had fashioned when we were still children, a tune made just for me. "Tazzia's Song," she had called it. Trying out different patterns of notes and different rhythms, she had grown more confident till suddenly the music had taken on its own sweet, clear form, as if it could only be that way and no other. I had heard it played over and over, though never so well or so boldly. Who else could it be? I ran headlong into camp, dashing past startled faces. Then abruptly I slowed to a walk. What if she had taught that tune to some other Potter girl when her family traveled to the fairs?

That familiar music tore at my heart and drew me on. I kept walking forward as if under a spell, though now every step was torture. The sound came from a group of women in dark, hooded cloaks. They were still mounted on their horses. At first I could not tell who played that fateful flute. Then, by the sway of her body, I knew which one made the music. Still, I could not see her face, for she was shrouded in her dark hood. I advanced toward her, forgetting to breathe, pulled in spite of myself, terrified of that moment when the stranger would turn and in her unknown face Kara would die for me one more time. It was too cruel that out of all the possible combinations of notes in the world she was playing that one tune.

Suddenly the music stopped. I stopped, too, praying for it to continue. Just one more time, please play it one more time, I wanted to call out to that stranger. I was fixing my eyes on the back of her head, willing her to continue, when with a laugh and a quick, impatient toss of her head, she threw back her hood. Her red hair tumbled to her shoulders, and I saw her face. "Kara!" I shouted, "Kara!" as I ran, stumbling and panting. "Kara! Kara! Kara!" In an instant she was off her horse and in my arms. As we hugged I could feel our hearts pounding together and the hard wood of her flute pressing into my back.

"Oh, Tazzia, Tazzia, they told me you were alive and here in the camp, but no one seemed to know how to find you. I thought if I played that tune you would come."

"Kara, beloved, all this time I thought you were dead, yet I have searched for your face again and again with every flash of red hair. When I heard those notes I dared to hope ... Is it really you? Are you really here?" With shaking hands I reached out to touch her face, to caress the soft waves of her bright hair, to run my hands down her arms. Suddenly I was sobbing and laughing and shaking all over at the same time. When I could speak again, I said, "Come sit with me and tell me all that has happened and how you came away alive from that mob." As I spoke I noticed another red-haired young woman who was watching me over Kara's shoulder, eyes as intent as a hawk's, and with as little friendliness in them.

Kara threw her cloak on the ground, drew me down beside her, and put an arm around my shoulder to hold me close. Others quickly gathered around. "Tazzia! My Tazzia! Thank the Goddess I have finally found you after all those months of grieving. Hard to believe you are really sitting here beside me. So much has happened since I saw you last. So much! How can I tell it all?" She was shaking her head. "Well, to start with, you will be amazed to hear that it was your father who saved me, though I think it was not for my sake nor even for yours, but for his village.

"You saw how those men lost all their fear and threw themselves on me, ready to kill me with whatever they could find, even their bare hands. I was crushed to the ground by their bodies, my face pressed into the dirt. I could hardly breathe and was sure I was about to die. At that moment I was far more afraid of being smothered under their weight than I was of any harm from their hands.

"Then I heard your father's voice, louder even than the shouts of those angry men. 'Get off her, you fools! Do you want to bring the Potters' curse down on this village? A curse to blight your fields and sicken your cattle and your children? Get off, I tell you! Do not kill the girl! Up! Up!' He must have been using a stick as well as words, for I could hear thuds and curses and cries of pain. 'Get up! Get up! Her blood marks our ruin. If you shed Potter's blood it will bring us seven years of misery!' He went on in this way until finally I could feel the terrible weight on me easing. Even when he had pulled the last of them off I could not move. I could hardly suck in a breath of air. It felt as if all my bones had been broken, but, in truth, I think it was my will to live that had been broken. Your father had to haul me to my feet. Even so I could not stand. If he had not had a grip on my arm I would have fallen to the ground again. I had never been afraid before, and now my whole being was flooded with fear. My body was shaking uncontrollably.

"My attackers, meanwhile, had backed into a circle around us, still shouting and threatening me, calling me Witch and Puntyar and 'bloody murderer' as if I had stabbed Jortho with my own hands. In spite of them your mother came up, threw a shawl over my shoulders, and put her arms around me. 'I will not let them hurt you again,' she whispered to me. Seeing that, the villagers began cursing and shouting at her too, calling her Puntyar as well and whatever other foul things came to mind. At that, your father jumped in front of us to protect your mother. He shook his stick at them and they shouted back at him. I feared they might all tangle soon in some terrible, bloody fight.

"Just at that moment my father galloped into the yard, his face red with rage. He began bellowing at the men to back away from me quickly or he would ride them down. My father in a rage is a formidable sight, as I am sure you remember. Muttering and grumbling, the men stepped aside to give him room to pass. 'What is happening here?' he roared at your father, as if he were the one at fault.

"'Get her away from here, and quickly. She can tell you the story herself.' Your father handed the stick to your mother and helped me up on the horse. As we rode out of the yard I heard him shout at those men, 'Go home now! Out of my yard! Tomorrow you will be very glad you have not shed any blood this night.'

"We rode home in silence. When we got there my father tried to question me, but my mother intervened. She took me to my bed, stumbling and staggering and exhausted beyond reason. For three days afterward I lay in a fever. As soon as I was out of danger they shipped me south in a Wanderer's wagon, hidden among the pottery. By then the edict had already been posted and there was no going back." She shook herself, as if shaking off the memories. "That is the end of that part. I will tell you the rest later."

When she finished speaking, the watcher who now stood in front of us coughed for attention. I looked up to see her frowning down at me. Kara turned and smiled up at her. "Tazzia, this is Vestri, my Zenda. We are..." There was a roaring in my ears so loud I could not hear the rest of her words. I knew well enough what Zenda meant, for Kara had called me that more than once. It meant beloved bond-partner in the Potters' tongue. Pain slashed through me. All my joy poured out from that wound. It was as if I had found her and lost her again in less than a heartbeat. When I could regain some composure, this stranger and I nodded stiffly to each other, but if thoughts could grow fists she would have been lying flat on the ground. I am sure she could read my thoughts and that hers were not so different.

Kara jumped to her feet, pulling me up. She took my arm in hers as if suddenly eager to have me away from that crowd. "I am stiff from riding. Come walk with me and tell me everything."

I was compliant for that moment and steered our steps toward my little knoll, but as soon as we were free of the others I pulled away from her hold and turned to face her. "Oh, Kara, how could you forget me so quickly in this way?"

She was shaking her head. "I could never forget you, Tazzia. You are my sister of the heart. I trust we will be friends and sisters the rest of our lives. Far from forgetting you, I looked for you in each new face and asked for news of you everywhere we went. But I had to go where I was led. I would not have survived those first months alone. The Wanderers kept me alive. As you heard me say, those I was sent with traveled south. Not till we turned north again for the Great-Gathering did I hear word of this Pell and that you might be her second-in-command. Then I tried to hurry our steps in your direction as best I could, though Wanderers, of course, are not easily hurried. They travel at their own pace."

"I do not need your sistering," I burst out angrily. "I have enough sisters here to last me a lifetime. It is your love I want, Kara, and your passion again."

"You have my love, Tazzia. You will always have my love as long as we both shall live, that I can promise you, but not my passion. That part is over. It died under that heap of men who meant my death. I think that kind of innocent loving died in my heart that day when you rode off."

"I did not ride off!" I shouted at her in desperation. "My mother hit the horse to make her run. She did it to save my life because I could not move to leave you. After that I wandered lost in the woods for days, lost even to myself. If Pell had not found me I might well have died. I thought I had seen you killed before my eyes and so cared little for my own life after that. Oh, Kara, if I had known you still lived I would have tried to find my way back to you no matter what."

"Just so, Tazzia, the Goddess did not mean for us to be together in that way. Even if you had come back I would already have been gone. You could not have tracked us. Wanderers are not easily found when they wish to hide.

"Listen to me, Sister, Vestri is my Zenda. That is done. We have pledged to each other, and I honor that pledge. That one day changed everything. I am not who I was, the child you remember, and I doubt you are either. Your father saved my life, but not my spirit. I was like a shadow, a walking ghost, and might have remained so all my life. It was Vestri who reached out to me and taught me to love again. She struggled with patience and kindness to reawaken the heart that I thought dead. Now you tell me to shut my heart to her, to cast her off like broken pottery. I ask you, what kind of person would I be if I could do such a thing?"

"So you shut your heart to me instead," I said bitterly. "And your precious Vestri hates me, that much is plain to see."

"Well, how could she love you when you glare at her as if you wish her dead? Come, Tazzia, by some miracle we have found each other again. Can we not be at peace? This small war between us is like a victory for the Zarn. Besides, you yourself have other lovers, several I hear."

"None of that matters now. I thought you were dead, gone out of my life forever. I had to find a way to ease the pain, to go on living. Now that you are here I would let that all go in an instant. Then we could be together again as we were meant to be. You are the only one that really matters to me. Oh, Kara, it will be like losing you all over again, like having you die again, if I have to watch you hold another's hand or look into her eyes as you used to look at me."

She stepped back from me with a look of shock on her face. "Tazzia, what a terrible thing to say. Here I am, very much alive, asking for your friendship and your love, and you wish me dead if I cannot be as you want. No, you must take me as I am. Vestri is part of my life now. I cannot throw her away like a cracked vessel." She reached out to put her arm around me, trying to draw me close. "Come, let us stop this quarreling and rejoice that we have finally found each other, alive and well."

I pulled away from her. "Have you forgotten? Does it mean nothing to you now, all that we were to each other?" The pain swelling in my chest was such that I could hardly speak those words. I was ashamed to hear the beggar's whine in my voice.

"Tazzia, Tazzia, do not try to cast a spell over it. We were little village children together, foolish and innocent. What did we know of life or the world? Our love was childhood fumbling ended at men's hands even before the Zarn's edict. Come now and sit beside me and tell me all that has happened since we parted."

"You can read it if you are able to read," I said with cutting bitterness. "I am writing it all down. Alyeeta has set me to that task."

"Well, I can read well enough. You know that Potters' children are taught to read. But I would much rather hear you tell it. Oh, Tazzia, do not make me beg for your friendship."

"Kara, Kara, you ask too much. I cannot sit here next to you, close and warm, wanting so much to touch you in that way. It tears at my heart. I cannot sit here telling stories." I was ready to spring away.

"Please, Tazzia, please, do not take it so hard." There were tears in her eyes. She put her hand on my arm as if to hold me there.

I groaned at her touch. "Oh, Kara, lover, sweet one." On sudden impulse I leaned forward to kiss her, all my passion leaping up at that moment. With a quick motion she turned so that my lips found her cheek instead of her lips. Rebuffed, I straightened instantly and pulled free of her hand. "Kara, you are breaking my heart." It was like a cry. The words burst out before I could stop them. Quickly I turned and walked as fast as I could up the knoll, through tears that blurred the way.

★

Kara! Kara! Kara! I was filled with pain and longing for her. Even sleep did not bring relief, only troubling dreams. It hurt me so to be with her and yet not with her, to hear her laughter and see her loving glances turned elsewhere. I could almost wish her dead again. Then at least the loss was not always with me and constantly before my eyes. When I said this to Alyeeta she gave me one of her long stares, saying at last, "Be careful what you say, girl. Sometimes the future shapes itself to our words."

It should have shocked me that I could think such a thing, that I had fallen so low, was so full of rage and bitterness, yet I could not change that nor did I really try. Instead, I fed on it. Of all the things that had happened in those past months, losing Kara and regaining her only to lose her again was perhaps the last blow, the final push to make me lose what little balance I had left. The gentle, loving child who had been my mother's daughter, the child who had talked to birds and animals and had been the village healer was gone. The little Witch-child had grown up into some kind of monster.

Rage — I was being consumed by a terrible soul-tearing, teeth-gnashing, blind, bitter rage that wanted to torch every living thing. I almost expected the flowers and green leaves to wither and blacken under my feet and the little birds to fall scorched and songless out of the sky. Nothing said or done around me gave me any joy or even any pleasure. Longing to hurt all within range of my voice, I picked quarrels over nothing with everyone who crossed my path. My hands would clench into fists, itching to strike out. From the hurt of it, Kara soon stopped trying to speak to me. After a while she avoided me altogether as Rishka did. As for Vestri, it was fortunate that violence could not pass between us, for I surely would have caused some.

Pell tried to speak to me, as my captain and as my friend. Instead of heeding her words, it gave me a fierce, ugly pleasure to see a look of fear cross her face at some of the things I said. Olna tried in her kind, loving way, but I had no ears for that sort of thing. Even Rishka tried, this new Rishka I hardly knew. I mocked her, calling her soft and girlish.

One morning Hamiuri herself blocked my way. As I tried to dodge past her, she grabbed my wrist. The power of her grip brought me to my knees. "Daughter, I see you running straight for the cliff's edge as fast as you can go. Do not count on us to be able to stop you. You must do that for yourself."

"I want nothing from you Witches!" I spat out savagely. She let me go, stepped back, and made a sign with her fingers. That should have been enough to frighten me, but instead I scrambled to my feet and ran off heedlessly.

Even Telakeet tried to speak to me, gently and with none of her usual mockery. All to no use. I listened to no one, not even Hereschell, not even Lhiri when she came to me with tears in her eyes, saying, "Beware, Tazzi, remember what happened to us."

The monster that had been growing all that time had broken loose. I had been embittered by the terrible cruelty I had witnessed, and now I myself was cruel. A fury burned in me that only more fury could appease, a fastfire of the soul with nothing to put it out. It was madness. I was mad. There is no way around it and no other word for it.

I could sense Alyeeta watching me, but always from a distance, watching and waiting. Then one morning I woke to find her sitting next to me on my ledge, stroking my arm. When she saw I was awake, she leaned forward and said, so softly it was almost a whisper, "Tazzi, all of us live on the bosom of the Mother, but some of us live closer than others to Her great beating heart. Those are Her chosen ones, the ones to whom She gives Her gifts, with whom She shares Her powers. You, child, are one of those..."

I did not let her finish. I sat up, my mouth opened, and a voice I did not know shouted, "A curse on the Mother and all Her gifts! I did not ask for them. I do not want them. Rishka was right, before Olna turned her all soft and girlish. She said all she wanted was a bloodied sword and a skilled arm to wield it, and I would say the same."

There was a moment of shocked silence. Then Alyeeta's fingers bit into my arm, so deep that for many days after I wore a row of dark, purple bruises to mark the place. "Say what you will to me," she hissed low and fierce in my ear, "but when you curse the Mother you have gone too far. Blasphemy, Tazzia, that is blasphemy. You must leave this place or you will bring a curse down on all our heads." I struggled in her grip. She released me suddenly and stood up. Swinging her hand so that her pointing finger aimed at my heart, she said, "Go to the hills. Seek out an asking place to be cured there or to die. That is all that is possible now. You cannot go on living among us like a festering sore. There is nothing left for me to say to you." With that she turned and walked away. At the sight of her retreating back a rush of fear cut through my rage.

★

That evening, for the first in many days, I went to sit at one of the cookfires. Women quickly made space for me, more space than I needed, but there were no friendly smiles, no one would meet my eyes. Kara was telling a story, seemingly unaware of my presence, and Vestri, of course, was sitting beside her. I watched Kara as she spoke, thinking, Kara is mine, my lost love, my childhood sweetheart. We would be together even now if not for that woman.

When we first found each other again I had thought all my searching, my pain, my emptiness was over. I was sure that the shattered pieces of my life would come together in her arms as if by magic. But it was plain to see she loved another. She would not throw her arms around me and make me well again, promising that we would always be together. This stranger, this intruder had come between us. How easily I forgot that already in Nemanthi things had been hard between us.

Suddenly her story was ended and she looked across the circle into my eyes. I got to my feet, wanting to run off and hide, wishing I had stayed away. Before I could make my way out of the crowd she had crossed the circle and was standing in front of me. Taking my hand in a firm grip, she said, "No, I will not let you run off again with me calling and calling after you. This time we will talk. Not even your bitter words can drive me away." With tears brimming in her eyes she stared straight into mine. For a moment my heart was touched and softened.

Then Vestri stepped up next to her and asked me spitefully, "Do you always run away like that from what you do not wish to hear?"

There was a roaring in my head and blood seemed to fill my eyes so that I saw her mocking face through a haze of red. With no thought I threw myself at her, hands reaching for her throat. Such was the force of my attack that I found myself flat on my back with my head ringing. I was in a dark place and barely conscious. "Help me," I heard Pell say to someone. Then I was being carried, laid out on a bedroll, and covered up.

27

I woke the next morning to the sound of bells being rung, or rather to the tolling of bells, a terrible, doleful noise that scraped on my nerves and set my teeth on edge. Since my head still hurt from the night before, I tried my best to shut it out. All to no use. No matter how I wrapped my ears it still came through. It seemed to be rising from the very ground itself, coming up through my body to lodge in my head. As there was no more sleep to be had, I got up reluctantly and went to see who made that dreadful sound and to what purpose.

Others were moving in that direction also, Wanderers as well as Khal Hadera Lossien, though none crowded close. Looking between their backs, I could see a circle of Witches, those I knew and some of the others as well. With Nhenoma leading, they were following each other round and round in slow, heavy steps, tolling black bells with strips of white cloth tied to them that fluttered in the breeze. I found the sound of those bells intolerable. The chant that went with it, all in words I could not understand, raised the hair on the back of my neck. I had never heard Witch bells rung except in the joy or solemnity of ritual. This time they seemed to ring of death over and over.

Suddenly I knew. A belling out! That was what they did. A belling out! I remembered Alyeeta telling me of the Witches once doing such a thing to a Witch named Morgea and that she had died of it rather than change her ways. It was what Witches did when one of their own profaned their practices and could not be persuaded to stop. I shivered and went to stand next to Pell.

"What Witch are they belling out?" I asked her in a whisper.

Startled, she turned and looked at me. A terrible pity came into her eyes. "No Witch," she said, shaking her head.

"But..." Just then I heard my own name sung in the chant. The words leapt at me out of all those meaningless sounds, striking terror into my heart. Now I knew. It was for me they tolled their black bells.

"Tazmirrel of Nemanthi," they chanted three times, then turned and changed the direction of their circle. I saw Alyeeta among them, tolling her bell along with the others. For just a moment I thought she saw me and caught my eye. I shivered again. It felt as if a cold blade pressed itself against my heart.

"Pell, will you let them do this?" I whispered to her in desperation. Now the terror was at my throat.

"Let them!?" she exclaimed. "Have I a choice, Tazzi? Have you left me any choice? I have tried everything I know. We all have. You listen to no one. Perhaps you will listen to this. Besides, I have no power to stop this. Just as with Lhiri and Nunyair, it is out of my hands now."

"It will likely mean my death, Pell, do you understand that?"

She shook her head. "Only if you cannot heal yourself or do not try. You had best forget all your great quarrels with the rest of us and look to your own healing, Tazzi. You had best do it quickly." She put her hands on my shoulders and turned me so she could look into my face. "Speak the truth, Sister, if you were me, what would you do with Tazzi?"

I looked down at my feet, unable to meet her eyes. The bells seemed to be beating in my blood, throbbing and reverberating in my head. "I would send her away," I whispered hoarsely. At that moment I could not even feel angry. Put in those words it all seemed very simple.

"Then go make yourself ready. Take only what is necessary. The Witches will tell you where to go." She released me and gave me a little push back in the direction of the ledges. Just at that moment all the Witches turned in unison and pointed toward the northern hills. Even with that the tolling of the bells did not cease for an instant.

Needing to be away from that sound, I turned and walked quickly back the way I had come. A path parted before me. None of the women would look me in the eye, not even Rishka or Lhiri or Maireth. Back at my ledges I set to tying up my bedroll and began stuffing my pack with trail bread and a change of clothes. I worked in haste. No matter what else might happen, at that moment I wanted nothing more than to be gone from there and away from those bells.

At almost the same moment I became aware that the tolling had ceased and that Alyeeta was standing at my side. "You!" I hissed accusingly as I whirled to face her. "You were there among them, tolling your bell along with the others. Alyeeta, how could you do this? I thought you loved me."

"And so I do, Tazzi. You know I do. I love you more than my own life, whatever that may mean. But I do not love you more than what the Khal Hadera Lossien could become. That is too much to ask."

Such was the tempest raging in me that I wanted to shout, Then what is your love worth? You do not love me much at all. Somehow I had sense enough to bite my tongue on it, though Alyeeta no doubt heard it from my head. Instead, I stared at her with no love at all in my eyes until she herself was forced to look away.

Gazing off at the northern hills, she said in a cold, flat, distant voice, "I have come to tell you the way to the Asking Place, no more than that. That is all I am allowed to say. Go there. Be cured or die. That is the meaning of a belling out." She had set her bell down on a rock ledge, and I could see the strange markings cast in the metal. When the strip of white cloth rippled in the breeze, a chill went up my spine.

"So you want me gone from here?" I said, still with some defiance in my voice and stance.

"There is no other way," she answered, in that same cold voice. "As it is, you are a danger to all of us and to yourself as well. We are sending you to an old Asharan place of healing. Seek out the cave, open your heart, and ask the Mother for healing. She is wiser than we are. We will wait seven sun-turns for you. If, before that, you return to us healed, we will all rejoice. If not, we will consider you dead to us and to the world as well." After that she gave me some directions that I am not free to repeat here.

To my horror, even as I shouldered my pack, she picked up her bell and began to toll again. She might as well have driven me off with a whip. Almost at a run I went toward the horses. Seeing me, the other Witches began tolling again. I saw Nhenoma point at me. Over the tolling I heard her shout, "Not the horse. Alone! Go to the Mother alone!" So I was not even to have Dancer with me for comfort and for company. So be it. What did I care, anyhow?

It was my anger that carried me out of the camp and beyond, mindlessly keeping my feet moving down that long valley toward the northern hills. My head was filled with all my grievances toward others, Kara and Alyeeta especially for what I saw as their betrayals. As I went through the camp, the way parted for me again, faces moved away from me, and backs were turned. All eyes were averted. I might as well have been the walking dead. No one wished me farewell or good journey or safe return. Not one person, Khal Hadera Lossien or Wanderer either spoke a single word of love or luck, save for Murghanth. Out of the corner of her mouth, she said in a hoarse whisper when I passed close to her, "May the Mother guard you, Tazzi." All the others let me go in silence.

In a last rush of defiance I turned and shouted back at them, "I can see I am not wanted here!" No one answered. My own voice echoed back at me from the hills. A curse on you all, I thought as I saw their backs turning. "Cowards," I muttered. "Cowards, every one of you, afraid of the Witches."

It was not till I was out of the camp and alone in the valley with the sound of the bells long faded behind me that my anger abated and the terror of it hit me. It bit so deep into my soul that with a cry I stumbled in the path and went down on my knees. Alone! Oh Mother, what was to become of me? I was doomed. "Alone!" Nhenoma had shouted. I was indeed alone. My family of women, my lovers, my tribe, and all else that mattered to me in the world — all gone with that one word. Alone! It was like being lost in the forest again, only this time fully aware and with no town in front of me. At that moment my sense of despair was so great that in spite of my pride I might have been tempted to crawl back and beg for mercy. No use. I knew it would be of no use. "Be cured or die!" Once that curse was laid there was no mercy to be had from a belling out. And there was no cure for me, none that I could imagine. I did not think to call on the Goddess or to pray to Her. I had cursed Her and cursed the powers She had given me. What was there left to pray to?

Finally it was my anger that got me to my feet again. Aloud I said to myself, "Get up, you fool. Are you going to lie down here in the road to die? At least go to this Asking Place and see what is there." I stood there for a while, unable to move, wrestling with this terror as with a giant snake. Then suddenly I found myself on the road again, going forward, setting one foot before the other in the direction of the northern hills.

It had been cool when I had set out in the morning. By the middle of the day it had grown unseasonably hot. The sun was beating down on me. As the land on either side was open and grassy, there was no shade to be found. The pack straps were rubbing sores on my shoulders. My feet were soon blistered. Sweat was pouring down my body, making my clothes cling to me and stinging my eyes. I had to keep blinking it away in order to see. From the grass around me there came a loud, heavy drone of insects that seemed to be boring into my head, making the day even hotter. It almost felt as if the land itself had turned hostile and was punishing me. The hills shimmered in front of me in the heat, appearing to come no closer no matter how fast or far I walked. For a while I was sure they were floating, backing away as I approached so that I would never reach them.

It was not till late afternoon that I got to the end of the valley and the land began to rise under my feet. At the start of the first hills I went in search of Alyeeta's path, not an easy thing to find. Those are Alyeeta's directions, however, and not to be spoken of here. Once found, it was clear enough to follow, as it was cobbled with river stones unlike any path I had ever followed, stones all smoothed and shaped by the water. I climbed up and up, the noise of the valley dying out behind me. As the climb grew steeper, a dull despair settled over me. Alone, alone, alone — that word seemed to echo back at me from the rocks. At moments I even imagined the sound of bells still ringing in my ears. I had no doubt I would die there, since I saw no possibility of being cured.

Suddenly a shiver went up my spine, and I was instantly alert. Well before I saw it I sensed its presence. Then I heard a deep, menacing growl that rose and rose until it burst into the terrible, spine-chilling cry of the Oolanth cat. Instead of fear, all my anger came rushing back. With a challenging laugh I took two more steps forward. It was above me on the path, its rust-colored mane raised stiffly in warning, its tail lashing, looking down at me as it paced back and forth to block my way. Lucky for me, I thought, that I am not riding Dancer, or she might dash back down the path, killing us both.

I shrugged off my pack and stood staring back at the beast, waiting with my hands on my hips. As a child I had made friends with the great cats. The child Tazzia would have soothed this creature with her thoughts. She would soon have been stroking its stiff, rusty fur with her little fingers, reassuring it that its cubs were safe with her. I had no friendliness in me now. Instead of sending out soothing thoughts I sent out a blast of rage and felt a twisted pleasure when it screamed again.

"Attack me, you fool," I said through my teeth. "Attack me and you will soon be lying broken in your own blood." I took two more steps toward it and did not even flinch when the cat took a great bound in my direction as if to leap at my throat. It stopped only feet away. I could feel the heat of its breath.

"Here I am if you want me," I shouted. "Are you afraid?" Then I squatted down, looking it in the eye. "If you want me you must come for me," I taunted.

The cat had also crouched down. With its ears laid back, it was shaking its huge head back and forth as if in puzzlement, snarling menacingly, lashing its tail like a whip and all the while staring at me with its wide, yellow-green eyes.

Growling deep in my throat, I drew back my lips in a grimace and snarled back at it. Then, on sudden impulse, I threw back my head and howled like one of the great cats myself. With a cry of bewilderment the creature leapt to its feet, whirled about, and fled back up the path, yowling as it went as if in pain. I stood up and laughed a bitter, mirthless laugh at the sight of an Oolanth cat fleeing from a human and howling in fear.

When there was silence around me again, I picked up my pack and went on. Soon my footsteps were faltering. I had gone no more than a short distance from my encounter with the cat when I had to stop altogether. I had a moment of fear when I thought of sleeping so close to a great cat and wondered if my powers would guard me as well asleep as awake. Then I thought, what does it matter, anyhow, if I am bound to die soon one way or the other. Not caring any more, too weary to go on, I unrolled my bedding on the only flat spot I could find, fell out on it, and slept with surprising soundness, utterly exhausted by all that had happened.

When I woke I was chilled and shivering. The weather had turned cool in the night and seemed to grow cooler as I trudged upward, munching my meager breakfast of trail bread. It was cool enough that I soon stopped to pull on whatever extra clothes I carried. The way was so steep that at moments I caught glimpses of deep, green valleys through the foliage. Sometimes I saw the blue flash and rush of a river. Though I had little heart for it, the path I traveled was rich with amazing beauty: vines, ferns, deep moss, lush brilliant flowers, huge leaves, and everywhere a myriad of bright butterflies moving and shifting through the scene. Instead of this bringing me any joy, I felt saddened by it. It was a last gasp of summer before the chill of winter closed in. Soon all that beauty would be dead and gone, withered and blackened in the cold.

Thirst nagged at me as I went. I had neglected to fill my water gourd. Now I emptied it in a few quick gulps. After that I went on with my throat dry and painful until I heard the roar of falling water. Then I hurried my steps, going as fast as I could, struggling and panting up that

FILENE'S
THE MALL ROCKINGHAM PARK
SALEM, N.H.

CASH   033684 091 032   00032 38245
        04/28/93   08:39 AM

PRINTED CREPE 00216481 365/14
 TKT 84.00 25% OFF 1 @   N63.00
                TOTAL   63.00
AUTH - 008188
003605477

                CHECK   -63.00

THANK YOU FOR SHOPPING AT FILENES

steep incline with the noise of the waterfall growing louder and louder in my ears. At the end I had to fight my way through a tight-woven thicket of shrubs to the pool. The pool itself was quivering under the impact of the water, which was falling some hundreds of feet from the cave mouth above. Even the ground under my feet seemed to vibrate with the pounding of it.

For a moment I gazed up at the silver sparkling water. It caught the sun in tiny rainbows as it arched outward like a long silver tongue flashing out of that dark cave mouth. That must surely be my destination if I could ever reach it. With a loud shout, I rushed forward, knelt down, and scooped up water in both hands. I was about to suck it up when I suddenly saw Kara's reflection quivering in the pool and heard her voice in the sound of the water. "Tazzia, let me go, let me go, let me go."

With a cry I spit out the water and jumped back. This spot that had seemed so inviting just a moment ago now seemed haunted and full of menace. Hurriedly I backed away from there and began pressing up the path again. Now the way grew even steeper and my thirst more painful. In my rush to be away from there, I had not filled my water gourd. I could see the path ahead of me winding up almost perpendicular till it reached the cave mouth. The air seemed thinner the higher I went. My lungs ached from struggling for breath. My heart was pounding in my chest and in my ears, mixing with the roar of the water. When I wanted to give up and lie down where I was, right on the stones of the path, it was my thirst that pulled me on. I went the last few yards on my hands and knees, hauling myself over the lip of the cave and crawling to the pool that had formed at the front of it. There I threw myself flat out with my pack still on my back and drank like an animal, sucking up the water in huge, noisy gulps.

When my thirst was finally sated, I pushed myself up to my knees. I stayed there, staring into the dark water. It seemed to hold my gaze with some power of its own. Like Hamiuri's dark glass it reflected what was before it. I was shocked at the mad face that stared back at me, haggard and hollow-eyed, and could hardly recognize it as my own. I looked for a long time at that person, trying to understand who and what I had become.

Then a breath seemed to blow across the water, the reflection shivered, and my face thinned and faded. Kara's appeared in its place, rising out of the darkness. This time I did not leap up and run off. I knelt there gazing at her. At first she appeared much younger, the village girl I had loved.

Then, as I watched her reflection, she changed and changed again till she was the young woman I had left in the valley. She looked at me with pain in her eyes and seemed about to speak. Just then the water quivered again, her image faded, and my mother's face appeared. She was calling out, "Tazzia, where are you? Where have you gone? I cannot find you anywhere." I gave a cry and reached for her, breaking the reflection. When the water calmed again it was my sister, Ghira, looking back at me, then Irdris's gentle, loving face, then Askarth with her forehead bare and the brand clearly marked there, then Shaleethia, the first burned one who died, then more burned ones, one after the other, even the one I had smothered under my hands. Tears were running down my face. I began to cry, rocking back and forth on my knees. Thinking myself to be where no one could hear me, the crying soon turned to howls of grief for all that had happened, howls that filled the cave and were not so different from the cries of the great cat.

Suddenly, sensing another's presence, I shut my mouth on my grief and looked into the pool again. The water was still and black. The face that looked back at me was very old and wrinkled, with deep-set dark eyes and golden yellow skin. It was a face I had never seen before. When the hand fell on my shoulder I wanted to jump up and flee, but though the touch was very light I could not move. With just a slight pressure she turned me around to face her.

"Who are you to come here destroying the peace of this place, wailing and howling in our sacred cave? For two days now I have sensed you coming closer and closer with your uproar. What do you want of us that you make this terrible disturbance? What do you want of the Ashara, Valley-Dweller? And how did you find your way here?"

Very embarrassed, and frightened as well, I bowed low, my forehead almost touching the ground. "Nothing, Mother, I want nothing of you. I was sent here. I had not known this was another's place, or I would not have come. Please forgive me, I thought this shrine empty and the Ashara long gone from here."

"And so, no doubt you would like us to be. We, the Ashara, have gone from everywhere else. We have left all that we made and all that mattered to us. We have watched you fill up our valleys with your noise and your power, your games of war and bloodshed. In despair we have left you the valleys and then the river edges, and finally the hills, going up into the steep, rocky mountains, going as far away as we were able into desolate and infertile places. We ask so little, only some peace and that our sacred places not be defiled. All the rest is yours, all the wealth and plunder of the world. Yet you presume even here. Will you rejoice when we are all gone, when there is no place left on earth for the Ashara, the First People? Will you finally be satisfied then?"

I tried to look up at her, but it made my eyes hurt. She had some of Shalamith's golden glow about her. It had been easier to see her reflection in the dark water of the pool. "Please forgive me," I repeated. "I came here because my soul was sick. The Witches have belled me out. They sent me to the Mother for some healing, saying that if I cannot be cured I will die. My grief was so bitter the Witches themselves could not cure it. It was like a poison among us." I was amazed at this sudden rush of honesty, as if my words had been compelled.

All in one smooth motion she sat down cross-legged in front of me. "So, so," she said, in a very different tone, "poor little Kourmairi, the Witches have belled you out and now this mad old crone is scolding you for coming here. Sometimes life is a hard place. Belled you out, eh? I did not know they still did such things. Sometimes I am just as glad to live on the far fringes of this world. Well, let us look at the nature of these troubles." She reached out her hand to press it to my forehead, then drew back quickly without touching me. Immediately she shook her hands well away from her body as if shaking off some dangerous and invisible liquid. It seemed to me that sparks flew in the darkness of the cave. "What are you, then? I thought you to be Kourmairi, you are dark enough. But you are something other."

"I am indeed a Kourmairi, but I am also..." I stopped, shy of saying the words to her in Asharan.

"Yes, tell me," she insisted.

"Khal Hadera Lossien," I answered, almost in a whisper, with my eyes lowered.

"Khal Hadera Lossien," she said slowly and thoughtfully, speaking in a very different accent from my own, but with no trace of mockery. "Then it has finally happened as it was foretold so long ago. The old prophecy was right after all. The Star's Children have come to take our place. I have heard some talk, sometimes a Wanderer comes through to us, but I never thought to meet one such, certainly not to have one come wailing into the Malia-Humia, the Cavern-of-the-Mother-of-Waters. Was it you that sent the great cat running off howling in distress?"

I nodded, still looking down, flushed with shame now at what I had done and too embarrassed to raise my eyes.

"Not a very good use for so much power," she said dryly. "I trust you will not think to do such a thing again. She is my neighbor and we live in peace here. Now raise both your hands and set them against mine, palm to palm, so we may see the manner of this soul sickness."

I raised my hands and then began trembling. I could not make myself reach them out to her. "I am afraid of your power, Mother. I saw the sparks."

"Not my power, your power, your own power all in disarray. I was unprepared. This time I will shield us both. Give me your hands, shut your eyes, and let your mind open to me."

I gave her a quick glance. This time my eyes did not hurt as much, so I ventured a longer look. She was smiling, though I could not tell if it was for me or only for herself. At that moment she was just a tired-looking old woman, watching me with care and concern in her dark eyes. With a quick nod I shut my eyes and did as she said, abruptly surrendering to her will. The contact did not hurt, though I could feel the power flowing from her hands to mine and running up my arms. How long we stayed that way, hand to hand, I have no way of knowing. After a while all I could feel was heat from her hands and a gentle pressure in my mind, nothing more, until the contact was suddenly withdrawn and my eyes snapped open. The old woman was shaking her hands again in that same way. This time I could clearly see sparks flying from her fingertips, showering into the darkness of the cave.

When she was done, she took a deep breath and shook her head. "Well, child, that is more contact than I have had with your world for many years. I cannot say that I find it very comforting. If that is how things are done there, then I would far rather live in these wind-torn mountains than in your lushest valleys. So they hunt you like wild animals for your powers? I must say, things in the world of men have grown even more terrible and I see no end to it. But you, the Star's Children, you are a new people. You have some of our powers and more of your own. And you are different from us, all sunlight and burning fire, while we are cool like moonlight on water. We have slipped away like shadows out of that world, but you will stay and make your place in it, that much I can see." With those words she stood up suddenly and held out her hand to me. "Come, poor little hunted animal with the angry heart. We must try to make some peace in that heart. Only in that way can we bring peace back to this place."

I looked up at her. "Mother, what is your name, that I may call you something?"

She shook her head. "My name is of no importance now. I am only an old Asharan who will not live much longer, abandoned even by my own people for returning to this place."

"Why are you here when all the others have gone away?"

"I have served Her at this Asking Place since I was not much more than a child, younger than you are now, served Her as keeper. How could I leave and stay away and not know what happened here? Who would keep the cave swept and the altar cleared and make the offerings?"

"But you are all alone."

"You are never alone with Her. Come, come, time is passing. I have not much strength left to do what needs doing. It would be a waste to have you die for lack of a little healing."

I stood up slowly and reached for her hand, a little unsteady on my feet, still dizzy from her probing of my mind. She was shorter by at least a head. The hand that held mine was no bigger than a child's, but there was no mistaking the power in it. She drew me back to a darker part of the cave. There she had me spread out my sleep roll and lie myself down on it. There was no sign of where she herself slept in that place.

When I had stilled myself, she came and sat cross-legged by me, laying one hand on my forehead and the other over her own heart. She spoke softly, and I seemed to hear it in my inner self as well as with my ears. "What you have of power is new and raw, still untried, but it will serve you well. Respect it, learn to live with it, shape it, and be shaped by it. It will grow as you grow. And the symbol that you wear there at your breast, that is an old Asharan sign from way before your time, from before the Witches, even." My hand flew up protectively to cover the pendant I wore concealed under my shirt. "It will serve you well," she went on, "if only you remember to use it for protection in times of peril. Remember also to use it in times of peace, for it will take you to the core of things. Now keep your hands cupped over it, and we will begin. Are you ready?" I nodded wordlessly, glad that she did not ask if I was afraid.

With her body swaying slightly, the old Asharan began intoning words in a steady, repetitive, melodic drone. Almost immediately I was caught in the tide of her voice like a leaf caught in the flow of the river. Utterly at peace, I floated there for what seemed like a long while. Then suddenly I found myself being pulled, drawn, sucked in by a faster and faster current, pulled into what felt like the center of a whirlpool, taken at great speed through many unknown places, split open to the core, peeled back and turned inside out. These are only words to speak of experiences for which there are no words. How long this all took as measured in the ordinary mortal world I have no idea, but when I finally came back to myself the light in the cave had shifted from morning to well past noon. The Asharan had not moved and was watching me with a look of concern on her face.

Of what happened after that, of what I learned there, I am forbidden to speak or to write in this account, though I am free to say that just before the Old One left me, she leaned forward and said in my ear, "If any of those Witches have the wish to speak to an old Asharan and the strength to climb up here, they are welcome to it, for I do not think I will leave this place alive. And you are right, sometimes it does grow lonely, even in Her presence, but tell them to come only one at a time. More than that would be too much for me now. And that one that I see so much in your head, that one especially I would like to share some thoughts with."

"Alyeeta," I said softly. I could picture Alyeeta sitting by the pool in the cavern, 'sharing thoughts' as the Old One had said, speaking or not speaking as was needed.

"Yes, Alyeeta. Be sure to tell that one to come." Those are the last words I remember her speaking. Then she passed her hand across my eyes. I closed them, and almost instantly fell asleep.

I was awakened by the cold and the rising winds. From far off I could hear the thunder rolling, coming closer each time. Then the lightning began to flash, tearing open the darkness. Soon the sound of the wind rose to a screech and then a howl, sometimes blowing fierce gusts right into the mouth of the cavern itself. It almost felt as if there were some malignant presence coming at me there. When the rain began in earnest I went to sit against the cavern wall, pulling my bedroll up around me for protection. The rage and fury of the storm seemed to be rapidly increasing. The lightning was close and frequent now, and the roar of the thunder shook the ground under my feet. Added to that was the pounding of the rain, lashing against rock and earth. I thought that soon the water in the cavern would begin to rise, but I was far too afraid to go and look. Then the wind began tugging at my covers as if to tear them out my hands. It seemed clear now that the storm was coming after me, a malevolent force seeking me out with its violence. Trembling, I hunched myself down even smaller, clutching my covers around me. By accident, my hand touched the pendant and I remembered the Old One's words. Holding tight, I was able to shift the covers to one hand and press the pendant between my breasts with the other.

At first all that happened was that the wind grew even fiercer, pulling first this way and then that. My fingers cramped with pain as I wrestled with it. Then, very gradually, the warmth from the pendant spread through me and with it a measure of calm. After a while the wind and thunder and lightning appeared to draw back and have less force. The storm seemed to be abating somewhat, or I was less afraid.

★

When I woke next, the space around me was lit by a shaft of sunlight breaking through some hole in the cavern roof. I was stiff and cramped, leaning at a strange angle against the cavern wall with my pendant gripped in one hand and my covers in the other. It took some effort to loosen my fingers. Outside the sun was shining brightly. Inside the cavern there were torn leaves and branches strewn about. The pool had risen to cover most of the floor. With a groan I pushed myself upright and found that I was swaying on my feet. I felt light and hollow, like something washed clean and hung out to dry, my anger gone like the storm. Of the old woman I saw no sign. It was as if she had never been there.

Cautiously I went to the edge of the pool to fill my water gourd. The face that met me there was my own — calm, clear, and somehow vacant. Then the face of the old Asharan floated up through mine so that I turned quickly to look for her, but there was no one behind me. When I turned back there was another old woman's face in the water, familiar and not familiar. I leaned forward to look more closely and she leaned forward, too. I opened my mouth to speak and she opened hers as well. Then I understood. It was myself as an old woman who looked back at me. The word 'Hadra' came into my head as if she had spoken it. With that I felt that same twisting and shifting of time inside me that I had felt on the knoll that day. "Enough," I said quickly to the pool, dipping in the gourd and so breaking the reflection.

The slope down was a scene of devastation, the path strewn with torn and broken branches, leaves and flowers and dead butterflies, the bright, scattered remnants of yesterday's beauty. Water was flowing everywhere, not one waterfall but many. The main waterfall from the cave was foamy and brown with mud. Branches and boulders made the scramble down even more difficult and dangerous than the way up. When I reached the valley floor, however, there were few signs of the fury of the storm, only some broken twigs and some puddles already reflecting a blue sky.

Once I was down in the valley, I walked back as quickly as I could, fearing that some unexpected happening might force the others to leave without me. But I moved strange and dazed, as if spellbound, almost absent from myself, seeing nothing of the land around me. I had little thought of the future as I went, or even of what lay ahead for me in the camp. All I knew was that my anger was gone and that I had not died in parting with it, though at times I think I had come very close. There were moments in my encounter with the Old One when it had seemed as if body and spirit might be wrenched apart forever. And perhaps some part of me had indeed died there, leaving me with a strange, aching hollowness. Things had passed in that cave, some of terror and some of wonder that I will never find words to speak of even if I were free to do so.

I dropped by the road when it grew dark and was up and moving again with the first light. Altogether I was in no way prepared for or expecting the welcome that came rushing at me. I must have been spotted by a sentry, for long before I was in the camp, long before I was walking among the tents and wagons, a mass of Khal Hadera Lossien, with some Witches and Wanderers among them, poured out to greet me. The same women who had turned their faces away and shown me their backs were now shouting greetings, eager to reach out and touch me, hugging and kissing me if they could press close enough. At the edge of the crowd I saw Hereschell watching me anxiously, but not trying to force himself a path.

Suddenly, pushing her way through the others, it was Kara who stood before me. For that moment, out of all the crowd, hers was the only face

I saw, the only voice I heard. "Oh, Tazzia, I thought I would die when they sent you away."

I gazed at that familiar pale face with its mass of copper red hair, and everything else stopped. Her green eyes were staring intently into mine. It was almost like that first look between us back when we were children and she had stared into my soul till suddenly I had come alive in her eyes. In the silence I felt her pleading with me, or rather heard her in my head. Finally, not even knowing what I was going to say, I opened my mouth and heard the words rushing out. "Kara, I will love you always. No matter who you share your bed with, you will always be the sister of my heart." I reached out to her. At the same moment a weakness came over me and I began swaying on my feet. Rishka had ridden up next to me leading Dancer. Before my legs could buckle under me she was off her horse and boosting me onto Dancer's back with Kara's help. Hereschell had finally forced his way through and was steadying me on the other side. Rishka quickly tossed her horse's reins to another and leapt on behind me. In this way, clinging to Dancer's mane with both hands and held upright in Rishka's strong arms, I rode into camp with Kara on one side of me and Hereschell on the other, surrounded by a swarm of shouting, cheering women.

While I was trying to eat, women were showering me with questions, questions I was forbidden to answer or not yet ready to put words to. This went on until Pell shouted for silence and Kara raised her flute to play. Then I was free to finish in peace.

Afterward, while I was resting in front of Alyeeta's tent, Vestri came striding in that direction, clearly in search of me. Much surprised, I jumped up instantly, ready to defend myself, but there was no anger in her face. She even took a step or two backward. Looking down at the ground, she said slowly and clearly, as if she had practiced the words, "Tazzi, you may not believe me, but I am very glad to see you safely back. It was I who provoked your anger and in so doing helped drive you away. There may even have been some intention in that. If so, I have paid dearly for it in sleepless nights, tossing and turning, fearful for your safety and ashamed of my part in what happened between us. I hope you may have it in your heart to forgive me." So saying, she held out her hand to me.

I looked away for a moment as if I had not seen her gesture and had to bite the inside of my lip to keep from laughing. I did not want her to think I mocked her, but it felt as if fate had just spun me around in her fingers. Was this the Cerroi at work, that circle of connections that Hereschell had spoken of so often? I remembered all too well my own guilt-ridden, sleepless nights when Renaise was on the road. At that moment I could see again in my mind's eye Pell standing so humble-proud with her hand outstretched, waiting for Hereschell to accept or refuse her. Vestri had much the same look on her. What had it cost her to come and say these words to me? I hesitated for just an instant longer, then quickly reached out to clasp her hand in both of mine. "The Goddess must think us great fools to hate each other for loving the same woman," I said with a sudden grin.

"I think perhaps you are more generous than I could have been," she replied, looking into my face for the first time in that encounter.

I shrugged, still trying to hold back the laughter. "I would not bet any money on Tazzi's generosity," I answered with amusement. "That one has much to learn of such things. It is just that she has been emptied of anger, emptied as a cracked pot is emptied of water. It has all run out; there is nothing left to hold it in."

Vestri was staring at me as if trying to read in my face the meaning of those strange words. Suddenly the laughter rose up in me irresistibly and broke through. Instantly Vestri withdrew her hand, looking at me sharply to see if I mocked her.

"No, no," I told her quickly as soon as I could speak again. "It is not you I laugh at, it is myself. It all comes round, oh Mother, it all comes round." I choked out those last words and began laughing again. It must have been clear to Vestri that I meant no harm, for this time she joined me. That is how Kara found us. We were leaning against each other and laughing together like two fools or like two old friends. When my laughter subsided I took both of their hands in mine. "As Pell would say, what does any of this matter, anyhow? We are alive, we are free, we are all here together. The rest is details." Brave words indeed, and for that moment I meant them, though later there were still times when it was very hard for me to see them together. Of course, now that I was no longer angry with Kara, she spent far more time with me, even seeking me out, but all that is ahead of my story.

For her part Alyeeta welcomed me back. She greeted me as lovingly as if I had never said those dreadful words. I heard them over and over in my own head, but she made no mention of what had passed. Contrite and ashamed, I finally mumbled, "I was not sure you would miss me at all. I thought I had been so troublesome that you would not grieve for me if I died there."

"Daughter, if I lived to be three hundred I would have grieved for you always, grieved for you dying alone in those hills. Thank the Mother there is no need for that grief, though I can tell you I did not sleep well these past few nights. Instead, you have come back to plague us and tug at my heart again."

"Oh, Alyeeta, when I think of all the pain I have caused you..."

"Well, pain lets us know we are alive as much as joy does. I am seldom bored. And at least this time you have the grace not to make grand promises you cannot keep about your future words." I bowed my head and looked at the ground in shame, remembering where my tongue had led me. On my side of it I did not mention Alyeeta's part in the belling-out. It was all over now. Perhaps it had been for the best, after all.

That first night back I slept with Alyeeta, held in her arms, not for passion but for protection, for shelter. I was much like a child again, though far more fragile than the child Tazzia had ever been. And first we talked. With a sly smile Alyeeta said, "It is a shame there are no Ashara left in the Asharan Hills. An Asharan could best have taught you what you needed to know. Tell me, how is it that you came away from there cured?"

I nodded and said nothing, trying hard to shield my thoughts, not sure if I wanted to speak even to Alyeeta of what had passed between me and the old woman in the cave. Then I understood from her smile that she mocked me gently and could see into my head. "There is much I cannot speak of," I said quickly.

"Tell me what you are free to tell and shut the door of your mind on the rest. I will not try to pry my way past that barrier."

I told her all I have written here and no more. She listened sharply to everything I said and asked few questions, though when I told her the message that was for her ears alone her expression changed. I knew without a doubt that she would go. I have told Alyeeta and Kara and these pages what happened in my time away, no one else, neither Star-Child nor Witch, no matter how they begged. When I finished my tale, Alyeeta sat silent for a while, staring off into the dark, a strange look playing across her face in the light of her little oil lamp. Finally, to draw her back, I whispered, "Alyeeta, did you ever meet with the Ashara?"

She turned and looked at me as if surprised to see me there. "Yes, many," she said at last when I had almost given up hope of her answering me at all. "When I was still a child I was sent for a short while to live in one of their villages high in the hills. It was my mother's plan that they should have the teaching of me. She herself had only modest powers, but she knew my talent and had ambitions for me. She wanted me to rank among the great Witches. In spite of my bent toward mischief she thought I had the makings of it, but only if I could be well trained. That was in the old days, in the time before the Witch-kills, a time when a mother could have such hopes for her daughter. And, indeed, I fulfilled her hopes, at least for a while, becoming the head of the Witch convent at a younger age than could have been expected, but that is all part of another story. Now the mother of a Witch-child is glad if her child survives and can pass herself off as a simple healer with the rest of her powers well hidden. Ah well, as it must be. It is all gone now, a whole world gone.

"As to the child Alyeeta, they took me blindfolded on a two-day ride. When they unbound my eyes we were high in the hills. The horses were struggling up a steep, rocky path. Mist was swirling around us, sometimes obscuring everything but the ground a few steps in front of the horses' hooves. In the next moment it would rise, revealing the steep, craggy drop that fell away next to our path. As I was a valley child, I clung for a while with terror to the pony's mane. Also, I was much afraid at being separated in this way from everything and everyone I knew.

"But I was a curious and daring child at the time. Soon I recovered my spirit. Besides, the Ashara were kind and gentle to me. They taught me with never a raised voice or hand, not what I had been accustomed to at home. Yet I, who had no habit of obedience and had been struck often enough by my mother for my willful ways, strove my best to please them and do just as I was bidden, trembling when I failed. For all their kindness I never felt a closeness with them. They took me into their homes, but not into their hearts. I never even knew where their hearts lay. They are not like us, the Ashara — human, yes, but they are different. Though they were always good to me, I never felt included in the core of their lives. It was as if I were an intelligent animal or a pet, something to be well treated. Yet in some ways I am their daughter. I learned much from them. Who else is left to carry on their ways? And you, the Khal Hadera Lossien, you are their granddaughters. Yes, much of what I still practice is what they taught me. And still, with all that, I was very glad to return to my quarrelsome family and my mother's quick hand."

"Where is your family now? You have never spoken to me of a family. Are any still living?"

I saw her stiffen suddenly and a look of pain filled her eyes. "No, no, all gone, all dead. Murdered at the time of the Witch-kills. Even my poor old father, a kind, gentle man with no more powers than a winter's leaf.

All butchered — my mother; my father; my older sister, Cassil, who truly had the makings of a great Witch; my younger brother and sister, who had no talents at all but for living a good, simple life; all their children, even little babies — all slaughtered.

"All that survived were myself, for I was living in Mecktash by then and running a Witch convent there, and Cassil's man Torrin, along with two of their daughters, the two who had gone with him to market in the next town that day. Who knows where they are now or if they are still living. A friend had ridden in haste to tell them to flee for their lives. When the news was brought to me, I thought my time would be next. I was sure that the Zarn of Mecktash would soon do as the Zarn of Eezore had done and set his sword against the Witches of the city. To my great grief I was right. All those who would not listen to my warning perished in those next few months. But that is another tale. Enough of these horrors."

I was staring at her in shock. "All your family? All gone? Were you not bitter, then, and thirsty for vengeance? Did you not long for blood?"

"At first I was running too fast to think of such things, trying to save my own life and the lives of others, trying to salvage something of the convent. Later, yes — yes, I was bitter and I longed to kill. I am not Olna that I can make peace with such things. But in the end I saw enough blood and enough dead bodies on both sides to last me a lifetime or more. And yes, I am still bitter and it still eats at my heart. Surely you can see that."

"And yet I was belled out for my bitterness."

"It was more than bitterness, Tazzi. It was bitterness gone mad. Besides, the Witch and the Star-Child are not the same. Your powers come from a different source and that source must be kept clear and clean. You have been muddying it for too long. A Witch can find ways to live with such bitterness and a Star-Child cannot. Understand this, child, if the Great Star had never passed over, you would still have been born a Witch, and so you have both powers, but at the core you are a Khal Hadera Lossien, though there are times when I wish it were not so."

"Alyeeta, I cannot understand your subtleties. You are too devious for me with your weaving of words."

"Yes, yes, that is part of it. The Khal Hadera Lossien are neither subtle nor devious. They are pure, clear, direct, honest, and need to remain so if their powers are to serve them well. Witches are something else altogether. Now that is enough of this talk. The Goddess has sent you back to us, and it is time for sleep."

"Oh, Alyeeta, you lost everything, and I cursed Her for far less, speaking those dreadful words so full of evil."

"Well, others have cursed Her and She has survived. I have probably cursed Her in my day, though I still follow Her ways. It is by Her will that you are here among us again. Let it be in peace." She blew out the lamp, pulled the cover up around me, and held me close. Next morning when I woke, Alyeeta had already left. She was gone for five days, long enough for me to wonder and to worry. Later, when she came back, she would say nothing to any of us of where she had been.

★

For the next week or so I wrote and wrote, bent over the paper, trying to lose myself, or rather find myself in those pages, trying to fill myself up again. The anger was gone and there was nothing to take its place. I felt only emptiness where that raw, raging pain had been. Also, I felt much shame for all I had said and done, the ugly words I had spoken. That made me reluctant to be with others. Though no one appeared to hold a grudge against me I often found myself making apologies. They all seemed glad enough to see me, even Rishka, even Olna after all I had said to her. As for the Witches, their circle opened for me now as if I had become one of them, though I told them little of my trip to the cave. Sometimes, when my eyes blurred from writing, my head ached, and my hand cramped, I would go and sit among the Witches. Even Nhenoma treated me with a sort of wary respect. Shalamith, if she was there, would come and sit by me, touching me in that way she had, a hand on my arm or a leg against mine, her golden touch so full of healing. If she probed my mind I did not feel it, nor did I try to fight it. If that was what she wanted I let her have her way. For the sake of that touch, she could do as she pleased with me. As always, I was helpless in her presence.

At dusk one evening I came to their circle just in time to hear Hamiuri saying, "I am tired of wandering. I will not hide in a cave in the north, however warm and pleasant it may be. If the Goddess had wanted me to live in a cave She would have made me an Oolanth cat, not a Witch."

"But what will you do, Hamiuri?" I asked, startled by her words.

"Find a village in need of a healer. There is always one somewhere. I am also tired of being alone."

I looked at her in surprise. "But you said you would never do such a thing again."

"So I did, without a doubt. Well, I have said many things in my life, not all of them true. Some of my words I have lived to see turn around against me. If you believe everything an old woman says, you will be fooled more than once."

Alyeeta stood up, the firelight flashing on her dark hair. "But you have lost everything coming with us. Mother, how can we ever repay you?"

"Give me a few coins and a small bag of grain. I will soon gather more of both. Witches may be reviled, but there is always work for us to do. If I cannot have my little house back, if it is truly torn down, then I will find another little hut near a city. Perhaps I will even travel with Vanhira for a while. It is far more comfortable with the horse in front of the cart than between my legs."

"Mother, I had thought we would have the gift of your company and the advantage of your wisdom in these coming months." Alyeeta was shaking her head, looking hurt and puzzled.

"Well, you have more company here than you need. As for wisdom, you will have to use someone else's or your own, perhaps. But I will not live all closed up underground," Hamiuri answered irritably. "After all, I had not bargained to marry you all, only to travel with you for a little while."

After that there was a chorus of pleas and objections, but Hamiuri must have held her ground, for early the next morning I saw her riding out in Vanhira's little travel-wagon. That night the Witches sat in a circle of silence, each with her back turned to the circle and to each other as well, mourning Hamiuri's departure. "I doubt any of us will ever see her alive again," Alyeeta said to me later.

As I could not write all the time, I also went at moments to sit at one of the other fires. There I watched, I listened to women's words and to their stories, I saw all the little games being played out among them and felt separate and set apart from them, not by anger this time, but by that strange emptiness, a hollowness that seemed to fill the very core of my being.

One time when I came to the fire circle it was Murghanth who was talking, gesturing angrily and speaking in her fast, excited way. "I hear told the Zarn is saying he has driven us straight into the sea. I would like to paint the sign of the double triangle in red paint on the very doors of his palace if he thinks he has done away with us so easily."

"Sheezerti recklessness, Murghanth. What does it matter to you if the Zarn thinks he has bested us at his games of death?" Pell answered, standing up to yawn and stretch. "We know what we know. What do we care what he thinks? We need more time to gather and build and learn before we are ready to clash with the Zarn. His ignorance gives us that time. Be glad of it." I did not stay long that night. I had no wish to listen to them argue. Already I could see Murghanth gathering herself up to answer.

The next time I came away from the writing there was only a small gathering at the fire. Jhemar and Pell were there as well as Alyeeta, Olna, and a few others. Jhemar was speaking, evidently answering some question of Alyeeta's, speaking thoughtfully and gazing into the fire. "You are right, Alyeeta. It is true that I am as much a Wanderer as a Star-Child. They are my people also, and the wandering is in my blood. The land calls to me, always beckoning from around the next bend of the road, the next bend of the river, pulling me right to the top of the hill to look out when I am down below, drawing me back down into the valley to drink from the river when I am high on the hillside. Always it keeps me moving. Wandering is as much a part of me as my eyes or my feet."

Alyeeta answered sharply, "Well, if you are ever to win out against the Zarns, I think you will likely have to make a choice in the time to come, a choice to be fully Khal Hadera Lossien and let the Wanderers go."

"Alyeeta, how can you say that? The Wanderers were my first true family, the first people who sheltered me on the road. It is the Wanderers who kept this Star-Child alive."

"And so what does that matter now? That is all in the past. It is the Zarn who threatens now, and the Wanderers are not much of a weapon against him. They drift away like smoke or mist and will never stand up to that power." Alyeeta's eyes were glittering strangely, fixed on Jhemar's face. Her expression chilled me. I thought of our talk of murder and vengeance.

Jhemar's face grew hard and stubborn. "Alyeeta, we are our own free selves," she said angrily. "We are not a Witch's weapon to be used against the Zarns."

"Why not? You are surely the best that has been forged so far. Someone must answer those terrible wrongs. Besides, how do you know why you are here? What do you know of the Goddess's intentions?"

Pell stood up abruptly. "We are not talking now of the Goddess's intentions," she said loudly. "We are talking of Alyeeta's intentions."

From the shadowed spot where she was sitting I heard Olna's calm voice. "Alyeeta, you well know that by the very powers they have, they cannot be used in that way. What is this sudden wish for vengeance?"

Pell sat down again. Alyeeta shrugged and leaned back, her face changing again, losing its wild look. "Ah, well, yes, we Witches have long memories, longer than most, and sometimes what we remember is not pretty." She shrugged again, then laughed in that sudden way she had. "Well, I suppose Jhemar must be who she is and live her own way just like the rest of us, Zarns or no Zarns. Whatever will happen is waiting around the bend of the road for all of us." That night I went back to the rock ledges again instead of sleeping in Alyeeta's tent.

★

It has been growing colder with each passing day. Some mornings the leaves are silvered with frost. The Wanderers' Gathering is over and most of the Wanderers have left, going south for the winter, leaving their daughters with us. Hereschell is still here, for he will accompany us as far as the caves. After that he and Soneeshi will head south to meet with the other Wanderers. Soon it will be our turn to go, for no new stragglers are being brought in any more. We have already begun packing the camp.

★

All day I have worked with the others getting us ready to leave. Now I have been sitting here for hours at the entrance to Alyeeta's tent, writing the last of this by the quivering light of her one small lamp. This is the end to this part of my account, for tomorrow we ride out, going west and north all the way to the coast. Who knows when, if ever, I will write again?

Save for the sentries, I think I am the only one awake of all the camp. Earlier there was a small fire opposite from where I sit, and a circle of Muinyairin, Rishka among them, laughed and talked there, but for a while now there has been silence and darkness in that spot, broken only by the occasional red eye of an ember. Behind me Alyeeta snores gently. Sometimes I hear a horse shift or snuffle in the night. From way beyond our camp, from the hills that ring us, I occasionally hear the hoot of an owl or the cough of an Oolanth cat, those prowlers of the dark. From their watch places I know that Zari and Daijar are our eyes this night, but in our settlement of tents, sleep presses down with a heavy weight of silence all around me.

For me sleep will not come, though my eyes are dry and gritty from the strain of writing in that restless light. My brain turns and turns in my aching skull, tormenting me with questions for which the answers lie before me in the living of them. Who am I now, I wonder? Who is the person who has come back from the hills, changed in ways I cannot yet understand? I have been returned to sanity, but not to my former self. What self is it that beckons from the future? And what of these hot-spring caves and the cold winter of the north? What of the food supply and the horses and all of us closed in together for so long? Questions and more questions that turn round and round in my head with no answers.

In a little while I will rise to wrap these pages carefully in waxed cloth and shelter them in the bottom of my pack. Then I will blow out the lamp and sit here alone, watching the night fade and the morning come.

★

The young women who were the despised fugitives in *Daughters of the Great Star* will reappear in Diana Rivers's next book, *The Hadra*. There, the "star-brats" leave the shelter of their winter caves and travel down the coast. After many adventures, they at last create the settlement that will become the city of Zelindar. In the process, they become the Hadra, a new type of woman, and emerge as a powerful threat to the Zarns who rule Garmishair.

Watch for *The Hadra,* by Diana Rivers, from Lace Publications.

*Alyson Publications publishes a wide variety
of books with gay and lesbian themes.
For a free catalog, or to be placed on our mailing list,
please write to:
Alyson Publications
40 Plympton St.
Boston, Mass. 02118
Indicate whether you are interested in books for
gay men, for lesbians, or both.*